Contents

About the Authors

Susan Bressler, MS, PHR has 15 years of experience in higher education and career development. She now teaches predominantly online courses for Kaplan University in human resource management, conflict resolution, and team dynamics. She lives in Seattle, Washington.

Karen S. Yasgoor, PhD, SPHR, CBT is an organizational psychologist with an extensive background in Human Resources. She owns the Center for Work Life Assessment in La Jolla, California. She is a faculty member of Capella University.

Human Resource Management Overview

Congratulations! You have made an important decision to pursue certification as a human resource professional. The purpose of this book is to prepare you for the certification exam in this field. This text presumes that you are working as a human resource (HR) professional with at least two years of relevant experience in a human resources department. We will lead you through all of the steps you will need to take to successfully pass the Professional in Human Resources (PHR) exam or the Senior Professional in Human Resources (SPHR) exam.

These exams are distributed through the Society for Human Resource Management (SHRM), the industry's leading organization in human resource management (HRM), and its certification affiliate, the Human Resource Certification Institute (HRCI). SHRM and HRCI have partnered with the Professional Examination Service (PES) to process and qualify individual applications and determine eligibility to take the exam. Thompson Prometric, the provider location, is the testing site center where you will take the exam. PES and Thompson Prometric serve as the qualifying testing centers for HRCI, providing the computer-based examination service for the PHR and SPHR examinations. When you are ready to take the exam, you will apply to take it through PES. Once you have been approved, you will be scheduled for the exam at a Thompson Prometric testing site at a location near you.

As the field of human resources has grown, state and federal laws affecting employers and employees and business practices have became more complex. It has become necessary to establish specific levels of competence and experience for individuals working in the field of HRM. Professionals need to demonstrate competency in numerous areas affecting employers and employees. This is referred to as a Body of Knowledge (BOK). A competency-based BOK serves to establish common knowledge for individuals who work in the field of human resources. A key goal is to ensure proper working conditions for employers and employees. SHRM identified the need for best practices in the field and created a certification system through its certification partner, HRCI. HRCI serves the needs of the human resource profession by continually updating best practices in the field through its certification program.

As a result of this need, combined with an expanding global economy, SHRM and HRCI identified four certifying examinations requiring a specific BOK.

Exam Note:

Every three to five years, HRCI publishes revised best practices relevant to the examination process. The last revision was in 2005.

These have been divided into the following specialty domains and specific human resource practice areas:

1. PHR: Professional in Human Resources
2. SPHR: Senior Professional in Human Resources
3. GPHR: Global Professional in Human Resources
4. PHR-CA and SPHR-CA: California-specific state certification for each exam

Please note this **text** addresses only the first *two* levels of professional competence identified above: the PHR and the SPHR. If you are seeking certification for the GPHR or PHR/SPHR-CA, you can go online to SHRM at www.shrm.org or to its certification affiliate, HRCI, at www.hrci.org for specific details.

Or you can contact the following organizations directly:

Society for Human Resource Management (SHRM)
1800 Duke Street
Alexandria, VA 22314 USA
Phone (United States only): 800-283-SHRM
Phone International: +1 (703) 548-3440
TTY/TDD: (703) 548-6999
Fax: (703) 535-6490

Human Resource Certification Institute (HRCI)
1800 Duke Street
Alexandria, VA 22314 USA
Phone: 866-898-HRCI or (703) 548-3440
Fax: (703) 535-6474

SHRM and HRCI testing affiliates:
Professional Examination Service (PES)
475 Riverside Drive, 6th Floor
HRCI Testing Office (470)
New York, NY 10115 USA
Phone: 866-744-HRCI or (212) 367-4200
Fax: (212) 367-4318

Thompson Prometric
HRCI Program
1501 S. Clinton Street
Baltimore, MD 21224 USA
Phone: 800-467-9582

THE BASICS OF PROFESSIONAL HUMAN RESOURCE CERTIFICATION

Why Is It Important to Become Certified in the Field of HRM?

Getting certified as an industry professional means that you have mastered a specific BOK through training, education, and experience. It demonstrates your competence, commitment, and credentials to work in the HR field. Whether it is the PHR or SPHR, you are recognized by industry peers and colleagues as an HRM professional.

What Is Certification?

Certification is a system created by a professional group that recognizes professionals who have demonstrated competence to work in a field; in this case, the field is commonly called *human resources*. It is important to note that certification is a voluntary endeavor and not a requirement to work in HRM. Individuals who work in this field more commonly pursue industry certification to be recognized by peers and colleagues as a trained and competent industry professional. Certification designates a specific level of training, education, and work experience. Certification through SHRM and HRCI recognizes individuals who have successfully passed one of the qualifying exams and have been awarded a qualifying certificate attesting that they have met the standards of the credentialing organization (SHRM). Once earned, individuals are recognized in the public eye and may add the specific credential to their professional title.

The certified credential is usually added after a last name, such as in the examples below (all names are fictitious):

James Campbell, PHR   Leslie Torrez, SPHR

If an individual holds a professional degree and title, the certifying title is usually listed after the degree title, as in the following example:

Louis Foster, MA, PHR   Kathy Youngblood, MBA, SPHR

Similarly, if you are adding a work title, it might read:

Stephanie Ward, MBA, PHR   Donald Martinberg, PhD, SPHR
Staffing Manager   Vice President, Human Resources

What Is the Difference between Certification and a Certificate Program?

Certification requires actual work experience in the field. A *certificate program* designates that a specific BOK has been obtained through independent means by completing course work. Course work can be completed through a variety of resources, which may include colleges, professional associations, employer training programs, or university online programs. In a certificate program, after a specific number of courses have been successfully completed, a certificate is awarded, but this is *not* certification! Certification is earned after all qualifying experience has been documented and after an examination given through SHRM/HRCI has been successfully passed.

What Is the Purpose of Certification if It Isn't Required?

Certification immediately demonstrates to peers, colleagues, and professionals in HRM and outside of the field of HRM, that you have relevant work experience in human resources. You share a common Body of Knowledge (BOK) and have passed a rigorous exam to become certified. Because certification is a *voluntary* effort, it demonstrates your competency in and dedication to the field. Employers frequently request or require that employees and applicants hold certification as a minimum standard to obtain a job in the field. Job specifications and newspaper ads post credentialing requirements as a way to screen qualified applicants. Your credentials may be publicized and used on business cards, letterheads, company email signatures, and other correspondence.

What Steps Do I Need to Take to Prepare for Certification?

1. Experience

You must have two years of documented, exempt-level, professional human resource work experience before you are eligible to apply for the exam. Professional or exempt-level experience is defined as work carried out in a supervisory role or work that is creative and original, requiring advanced human resource knowledge. This is defined under work function (see appendix A). According to HRCI guidelines, it does not need to be current experience or work that is performed sequentially; however, you should be aware that recent HR practices are covered on the exam. The following criteria may be helpful to determine if you are engaged in exempt-level work (work in a supervisory role):

- Fifty-one percent (51%) of your work is engaged in a human resource function (see appendix A).
- Your role or function is found in a typical human resource department (see appendix A).
- You are an educator, professor, or instructor teaching in the field of human resources at an accredited institution of higher learning.
- You are a consultant or serving in a consulting role where the type of work is typically a human resource function.
- You conduct research in the human resource field.
- You serve in an international human resource role or function located outside of the United States, either as an expatriate or as an employee with an international organization. The equivalent work must be at the professional or exempt level.

2. Skills

You must demonstrate mastery of skills and competencies specific to a human resource role defined under work *position* (see appendix A).

3. Education

You must learn about competency areas that will be covered on the exam through course work, a study guide, or a study group (see appendix A).

How Do I Know Which Exam Is Most Appropriate for My Background?

Both the PHR and SPHR are *generalist* exams and test the broadest range of human resource knowledge that a practitioner is expected to know. If you are not a generalist, but a specialist (e.g., benefits, staffing, labor relations, etc.), these exams may not be the appropriate choice for you. If you intend to be a generalist, you will need to learn about a broad range of topics before taking the exam, but you may still pursue examination.

If Both Exams Are Generalist in Nature, Why Are There Separate Exams for the PHR/SPHR?

Both exams are similar in nature and content; the main differences are the level of professional experience and the time in the field. The PHR exam assumes two to four years of experience, while the SPHR exam assumes six to eight years of experience. Questions found on the SPHR exam will require a higher level of expertise and experience.

Which Exam Is Right for Me—the PHR or the SPHR?

Eligibility requirements defined by SHRM/HRCI are outlined below and will assist you in making this important choice:

The following guidelines will help you determine which exam is the best fit for your experience:

- A PHR candidate will have:
  - Experience in program implementation
  - Basic orientation experience in tactical or logistical planning
  - Accountability to an HR professional in the same organization
  - Two to four years of exempt-level experience as a generalist
  - Progressive HR experience that is limited due to short career length in HR
  - Roles and responsibilities found within an HR department (versus organization-wide)

Exam Note:

If you are currently enrolled as a student and have completed courses or a certificate program in human resources, but lack work experience in the field, you may still apply to take the PHR exam *only*. If you take the exam and pass, you are not considered certified until all relevant exempt-level work experience has been documented and approved.

- Knowledge and credibility as an HR professional who knows how to implement policies and guidelines to make HR decisions.
- A SPHR candidate will have:
  - Tactical design and strategic planning responsibility
  - Proposal expertise working with senior management
  - An understanding of the organization's overall strategy and "big picture"
  - The highest level and accountability in the HR department
  - Six to eight years of progressive HR experience
  - HR generalist knowledge and experience demonstrating best practices in breadth and depth
  - Application of knowledge and strategic judgment gained over time
  - A generalist role in the organization
  - Knowledge and understanding of how decisions impact internal and external organizational threats
  - Knowledge of business and how it operates in addition to the HR function
  - Influence in the entire organization and management of those relationships
  - Expertise in negotiation skills throughout the organization
  - Credibility recognized by the organization, community, and field at large

What Are the Eligibility Requirements for Students?

If you are a currently enrolled student and do *not* have documented human resource experience, this section is for you. If you are a student with documented exempt-level human resource experience of at least two years' duration, this section is *not* for you.

Students enrolled in an accredited program for a bachelor's or graduate degree may take the PHR exam prior to obtaining the requisite two years of exempt-level human resource experience. The PHR is the only exam you will be eligible to take. At this stage in your career, you are not eligible to take the SPHR exam. You may apply and register for the exam at any time; however, you may not sit for the exam earlier than 12 months before your graduation date or more than 12 months after your graduation date. If you apply more than 12 months after your documented graduation date, you must apply as a regular candidate (nonstudent). In this case, you must submit documented work experience with the initial application. If you are a student, you must apply and submit documented work experience within five years of the test date on which you passed the exam.

Exam Note:

Students need to complete a specific application called the Student/Recent Graduate Verification Form.

What Is Recertification and Does It Impact Me?

Once you have successfully passed the exam, certification is valid for three years. At the end of this period, recertification is required. You may recertify in one of two ways:

1. Document and submit 60 recertification credit hours of one or a combination of the following: human resource–related continuing education credits, activities, experience, and/or professional development.

2. Retake the exam. If you elect to retake the exam, you must take the exam prior to the original certification date, and you may only recertify at the current certification level. Note that you may not retake the recertification exam 12 months prior to your original certification date.

Once you have determined that you are eligible to apply for recertification for either exam (PHR or SPHR), you are strongly advised to visit the SHRM and/or HRCI websites to review the application process at www. shrm.org and/or www.hrci.org. (The SHRM website has a link to the HRCI website.)

What Should I Know before Applying to Take the PHR or SPHR?

Deadline dates, called testing windows, are postmark dates. Postmark dates for online applicants include system date/time stamps. Postmark dates sent via regular U.S. mail are figured by the date stamp (12 A.M. midnight) and EST (Eastern Standard Time). International applicants are encouraged to apply online, because traditional mail can be unpredictable and slow. Your application will be carefully reviewed and this takes time to complete by the qualifying organization. Once you are notified of eligibility to take the exam, schedule the exam as early as your schedule allows.

The exam will take place in a testing center; therefore, the person to your right or left will also be taking an exam—not necessarily the same exam you will take. Because it is a testing center, you will be competing for a test seat and location with a variety of other test takers. Keep in mind that the PHR and SPHR exams are offered only twice per year, in two-month windows, so you will need to plan ahead.

How Do I Apply for the Examination?

The first step in the process is to apply online with HRCI at www.hrci.org. As of the test year 2007, Professional Examination Service (PES) and Thompson Prometric are the testing affiliates for the PHR and SPHR examinations. Once you have been approved to take the test, you will receive an approval letter from PES advising you to schedule a test date with Thompson Prometric. Thompson Prometric has testing center locations all over the United States so that you can schedule your test date at a convenient location near your home or work.

How Much Does It Cost to Take the Exam?

The examination fees in the table below include the application fee, exam fee, and any late fees incurred. Applications submitted after the regular deadline (but before the late deadline) will be assessed a $50 late fee. For students and recent graduates taking the PHR, the balance of the exam fees will be required upon meeting work experience and graduation requirements.

Table 1.1   PHR Exam Fees (as of 2008)

	Application Fee	Regular Deadline Exam Fee	Total Regular Deadline Fee	Total Late Deadline Fee
SHRM Member	U.S.$75	U.S.$200	U.S.$275	U.S.$325
Nonmember	U.S.$75	U.S.$250	U.S.$325	U.S.$375

Table 1.2   SPHR Exam Fees (as of 2008)

	Application Fee	Regular Deadline Exam Fee	Total Regular Deadline Fee	Total Late Deadline Fee
SHRM Member	U.S.$75	U.S.$300	U.S.$375	U.S.$425
Nonmember	U.S.$75	U.S.$350	U.S.$425	U.S.$475

How Far in Advance Will I Need to Schedule the Exam?

You may only schedule the exam twice per year. Schedule as early as possible so you have the best chance of taking the exam during the time/day/month that you want to take it!

Typically, exams are scheduled in two-month windows. For example, the 2008 test windows are as follows:

May 1–June 30, 2008

December 1, 2008–January 31, 2009

For the most up-to-the-minute information on test dates and fees, be sure to check HRCI's website.

When Will I Take the Exam?

Applicants may apply to take the exam after completing at least two years of exempt-level human resource experience. It is strongly recommended that if you are undecided about which exam to take, you should understand the function and practice areas thoroughly, how many years of human resource experience you have accumulated, and if your job/role/function is operational or organizational. If it is primarily operational in nature and your direct report is in human resources, the PHR exam is recommended. If your job/role/ function is organizational, and your direct report is an officer of the company or a senior-level officer or director, the SPHR exam is recommended.

How Is the Exam Administered?

The PHR and SPHR exams are administered by computer. Your application will be assigned a number and a code prior to the date of scheduling your test. There are different versions for each test that are computer scrambled and randomly assigned. You will not know which version you will take until the day of testing.

When you arrive at the testing center, you will check in and present identification documents to the test center manager (such as a driver's license, Social Security card, or passport), and your photo will be taken along with a written signature. You will be given a locker to store any items brought with you that will not be allowed in the testing area. Even a tissue or your own pencil will not be allowed. You will be given pencil, paper, headphones, and earplugs to use if you need them during the test.

When you enter the test area, you will see cubicles with computers at each desk. Desks are spaced closely together but have dividers between them. You will be assigned a computer and seat where you will take the exam. If you are easily distracted by noise or activity, you may request in advance (with your application) to file an exception so that you will be able to take the exam in a private room. This is considered to be a test accommodation that must be approved in advance of the date of scheduling. The test begins when you sit down at the computer desk and verify your name at the computer station; however, the test time will not begin until after you have read a brief review about the test you will take. This review explains how to take the test and gives you an option to complete an example. Once you have reviewed the testing procedures, your test time begins. **You will have exactly four hours to complete the exam**. If you finish early, you should follow the instructions given to complete and end the exam. If you extend beyond the four-hour time limit, the test will automatically shut down and end.

How Will the Exam Be Scored?

The passing score for the PHR and SPHR exams is based on a scaled score. The passing score is 500, the minimum possible score is 100, and the maximum score is 700. If you do not understand scaled scores, a detailed explanation can be found in the certification handbook that can be downloaded from the HRCI website, www.hrci.org, listed under "Understanding the Score Report" and "How the Passing Score Was Set."

How Do I Know if I Passed the Exam?

The exam will be scored automatically at the time you complete the exam; however, this is an unofficial, preliminary report. You will receive an official report and a letter by mail about two to three weeks following your Test Date. The date and time of year you took the exam, as well as how many others took the exam during this same period, will impact how quickly you are notified. The typical time frame is two to four weeks.

What Happens if I Fail the Exam?

If you do not pass the exam, you may apply to retake the exam during the next *available* testing window, but not during the same testing window in which you took the original exam. You are encouraged to wait six months before retaking the exam. You may take the exam as many times as you wish following HRCI's guidelines for those taking the exam multiple times. Note that each time you retake an exam, the same application procedures must be followed, including exam fees and scheduling, as if you were taking the exam for the first time.

Is There an Appeals Process?

Yes, you may request a review of your exam score within six months of your exam date. PES processes scores electronically through a quality assurance procedure prior to scoring and mailing your exam results. In an extremely rare case, it is possible that an error occurred, but it is unlikely that a test score will change. Still, you have the right to request a review up to six months following your Test Date. After this date, any requests for review will not be honored. If you still wish to dispute a failed exam, you can contact HRCI directly.

After I Pass the Examination, How Do I Remain Certified?

It is important to note that you may only recertify for the following titles: PHR, SPHR, and GPHR (the GPHR is not addressed in this text). If you originally certified for the PHR exam, you should plan how you can prepare for the next level of certification, the SPHR. As you know, the SPHR may open more doors for you once you have gained the required professional experience to be eligible to take this exam.

Successfully passing the exam demonstrates to peers and colleagues that you are a seasoned HR professional and have mastered the requisite BOK in the field. However, the field is always changing and growing, and you are expected to remain current in the field if you wish to remain certified. Recertification is the process that HR professionals complete in order to maintain their title and certification. Recertification is required every three years. The date that you became officially certified will include an expiration date. This is referred to as your recertification cycle. Recertifying can be met in two ways: 1) accumulating 60 contact hours of current HR experience or 2) retesting and passing the exam. If you prefer to retest, you will take a new exam at the same level you originally certified, but you will register as a recertification candidate. For the most current information about recertifying, visit the HRCI website at www.hrci.org/recertification. If you prefer retaking the examination, review "Recertification by Examination" in the HRCI handbook at www.hrci.org.

STRUCTURE OF THE PHR AND SPHR EXAMINATIONS

The PHR and SPHR examinations are based on U.S. federal law, not state law. Except for those residing and working in the state of California, all applicants will take the PHR or SPHR exam. Through SHRM and HRCI, California has its own examinations: the PHR-CA and SPHR-CA. For more information about the California-specific examination, visit the HRCI website at www.hrci.org.

Test questions on both exams are general in nature and include regulations for employers and employees as well as best practices found in a human resource department. Questions assess functional areas in the field of human resources (see appendix A). Functional areas are defined as human resource work functions.

Functional areas addressed on the examinations include human resource generalist questions, employment, recruitment, staffing, benefits, compensation, labor and industrial relations, training and development, organizational development, legal, health and safety, security, employee assistance programs, employee relations, communications, EEO/affirmative action, Human Resource Information Systems (HRIS), research, consultant, administrative, international HRM, and diversity.

Due to the differences in experience level, SPHR questions will differ from the PHR in focus and cognitive reasoning; however, the same basic functional areas will be tested. PHR questions will be more hands-on, operational, and technical. SPHR questions will be more strategic and policy driven. Both exams contain up-to-date information based on the past five years. As noted earlier in the chapter, HRCI publishes revised best practices as they pertain to the exams. You are not expected to know changes in laws or policies beyond this date; however, depending when you schedule the exam and when HRCI updates the most recent changes, you should know roughly when the next revision will take place. The best time to investigate is when you file your application, if not before.

Test questions for both exams are administered at a testing center, by computer. Both tests are comprised of 225 multiple-choice questions. Every question allows four possible choices, and only one choice will be the correct answer. The questions appear in random order and do not build upon other test questions. Of the 225 multiple-choice questions, 200 questions are scored and 25 questions are pretest questions that are *not* scored. You will not know which questions will be scored and which ones will not. You will have a total of four hours to complete the exam, in one sitting and at one testing center.

What Does a Typical Question Look Like?

The following is a typical question you might encounter on the exam:

> A white male is not selected for a position for which he qualifies. Preference is given to a member of a protected group. This is known as
>
> A.   a quota system.
> B.   discrimination.
> C.   reasonable accommodation.
> D.   reverse discrimination.

By looking at the responses given, the answer could be *a*, *b*, or *d*. We know it is not *c* because the response has nothing to do with a member of a protected group in the situation described. It might be *a* except no information is given about a quota in this question. It might be *b* except this response is a bit vague. The answer is *d* because it more accurately describes the situation given in the test question.

CORE KNOWLEDGE REQUIREMENTS FOR THE PHR AND SPHR EXAMS

Here's a breakdown of the types of questions and BOK elements you can expect on the PHR and SPHR exams (as of 2008):

	PHR	SPHR
Strategic Management	12%	29%
Workforce Planning and Employment	26	17
Human Resource Development	17	17
Total Rewards	16	12
Employee and Labor Relations	22	18
Risk Management	7	7

Test questions are constantly reviewed by a panel of certified human resource professionals, who are considered to be subject matter experts. The panel's main function is to ensure that questions are relevant, up-to-date, and in agreement with test specifications. HRCI conducts a practice analysis every three to five years to ensure the quality of the test.

STUDYING FOR THE EXAM

If you are a successful test taker, you will likely be successful on this exam. If test taking produces anxiety for you, brushing up on your test-taking skills in advance is a wise strategy. There are numerous websites about test-taking strategies to assist you with smart study skills to pass the exam. A brief review of test-taking skills is discussed below; however, you should also visit websites that specifically address study skills for *multiple-choice exams*.

The PHR and SPHR exams each contain 225 multiple-choice questions. You will have four hours, or 240 minutes, to complete the entire exam and answer all 225 questions in one sitting. This is roughly one minute per question. For most questions, you will not need one minute; however, you need to build in time for questions that require more thought such as tricky questions, lengthy questions, questions that surprise you, and questions that you do not know the answer to! Recall that 25 questions are random pretest questions that do not count as part of the validated test questions. These questions may unconsciously create stress because there might be words or ideas that do not relate or make sense to you at the time of the test. This can throw off your thought process and upset you. The best strategy in this case is to jot down the number of the test question so you can return to it later. Only answer questions that you know the first time through. Check your watch or a clock on the wall to see that you have answered approximately 30 questions every half hour (be sure to jot down the time you began the test!). If you lag behind, answer every question from this point forward, but mark those questions you are hesitant about. You need to build in time to revisit those questions.

This test may remind you of a marathon. Similar to a marathon, you will experience mental fatigue at different times during the exam and toward the end of the exam when mistakes are most likely to happen. If fatigue occurs at any point during the test, a helpful strategy is to step out of the room to take a short break and stretch. Remember, this break is still part of the four hours allotted to complete the entire exam. Be sure to ask the test monitor how to take a break during the exam so you will not be disqualified or prevented from re-entering the testing room and completing the exam. For the majority of test takers, four hours is more than enough time to complete the exam. For some, it is an endurance test and a stress-producing challenge! Your number one goal before Test Day should be meeting these challenges and learning how to overcome the stress.

Create a Study Program that Fits with Your Schedule

If you juggle multiple responsibilities, such as a full-time job, parenting, or travel for your job, you need to carve out time from your busy schedule to study. Schedule time to study as you would an appointment and post this *study appointment* on your calendar every day, even if you cannot study every single day! As the test date draws near, building in study time and following it is critical to your success. A question to ask yourself during those moments when you don't feel like studying or prefer to do something more enjoyable is: "How many times do I want to take this exam before I successfully pass?" Recall that 64 percent pass the first time. Creating a study program and following it will give you the advantage and the confidence to tackle the exam successfully the *first* time!

Practice, Practice, and More Practice!

This book has practice questions to get you prepared for Test Day. While questions on the Practice Test will not be the same ones you will have on the actual exam, similar content and topics will be covered; consistent practice effort will train you to tackle four hours of practice questions successfully.

Mastering Multiple-Choice Exams

You should build practice time into your schedule. If you have 10, 30, or 60 minutes free, reserve time to study and practice multiple-choice exam questions *every day* that you are preparing to take the exam. Soon, you will begin to memorize questions and the correct answers. As the test date nears, build in longer practice periods. Plan to take four four-hour practice exams once a week prior to the date of the exam.

Tips for Answering Multiple-Choice Questions

- Remember: You will need to answer approximately one question per exam minute. You will need less time for shorter questions and more time for longer questions.

- Answer as many short questions as you are able in a 30-minute time period. Be sure to write down the time you began the test on a scratch pad or paper that the test center provides for your use. The time should also be noted in the bottom right-hand corner of the computer screen. Mark questions that you do not know and return to them later in the test. It is important to quickly answer as many short answer questions where the answer is clear to you and keep moving forward. Do not get trapped by long questions early on in the test, especially if you do not know the answer.

- Be sure to read the question before you look at the possible answers. Think of the answer and then look for it in the responses given. Do not become confused by the answer that adds words only to confuse you. If it doesn't make sense to you, it is most likely the wrong answer. If you are confused by the responses given, mark it and come back to it later.

- If you are prepared, you should be able to eliminate at least two incorrect responses as you read the responses for the first time. By eliminating two choices, it becomes a simple matter of choosing a response between two choices rather than the four that are given.

- If you are uncertain between two choices, mark one over the other and mark the question for review later in the test.

- After 60 minutes, check to see how many questions you have answered and marked. You should have *answered* 60 questions. If you are ahead of this number, keep moving forward. If you are behind this number, you will need to change your strategy at this point in the test.

- If you are behind, continue to answer the short questions that come easily to you. Attempt to answer *every* question you read from this point forward. If you read a long question and don't know the answer, you can mark it for later, but *answer it now*.

- At the end of the test, if you have any time left over, you can return to those questions you did not answer first, then return to those questions you answered but were uncertain about.

- Be reassured that you will more often select the right answer the first time. Sometimes fatigue will cause you to misread a question or convince you that the answer selected must be wrong. This is a challenging moment, so remember that your first selection is probably a better choice.

- Remember that few situations are either "all" or "none."

- Remember that if "all of the above" is given, and two choices are right, then the answer is probably "all of the above."

- Remember that if "none of the above" is given, and one answer is correct, then "none of the above" will be an incorrect choice.

- Remember that if a response provides detailed information, it is more often the correct response.

- Phrases framed as a positive choice are more likely to be true versus phrases framed in a negative form.

Tackling Pretest Stress and Anxiety

Organization is the key to handling stress in most situations. In an exam situation, organization will serve you well if you can manage your time, your life, and all of the multiple roles and tasks you perform as a busy professional, student, or family member.

Here are some practical tips for handling stress:

- *Create a study space*. Where will you study? If it is in an office, think of your office as a safe, uncluttered, structured, and organized room. Be sure to have everything you will need around you to study. Items such as a desk, chair, computer, pencil, paper, and books should be visible and within easy reach during your study time. There should not be other visible distractions that will take you away from your planned study time. Sometimes this is just not possible, especially if other family members are wanting or needing your attention. A practical solution in this case is to visit your local library. If you can find a cubicle to sit at where you can use a laptop computer, the library may become your haven away from the office or home. It will surprise you how much you can accomplish if you visit a library to study.

- *Join a study group*. This is highly recommended because members of a study group take responsibility for outlining chapters, subject material, and content areas. If there is a topic you know little about, a study group is a supportive way to seek help from colleagues who are experts in the field. It is also an excellent way to support each other through this process. If you cannot commit to a study group, don't join one. Everyone in the study group will depend on each member to do his or her share. If you are absent, the group is shortchanged by your absence and you do not benefit from the group's support.

- *Take classes.* If your company or organization is encouraging you to become certified, sign up for a course either online, at a university, or through a professional organization that might be offering one. You could also attend a seminar in your area or at a convenient location. There are numerous benefits when you connect with others by taking a course or joining a professional association. You are not only building bridges toward a better career, but networking simultaneously with others who work in the same field. Take advantage of everyone's expertise!

- *Prioritize, prioritize, prioritize!* In other words, keep revising your action plan and your study schedule. If you are a visual person, draw a road map showing how you will get from here to there. If you prefer the written word, create an outline and follow it. Be sure to build in break periods. Have one day a week when you are not studying. This will give you something to look forward to as a built-in reward for the other six days when you committed to studying.

- *Take breaks.* Taking a five-minute break every hour helps. Get up, stretch, jog around the house, your office, a hallway, or wherever you happen to be; shake out your hands and arms, play with the dog, or listen to a favorite song. Go outside and breathe some fresh air!

- *Be comfortable.* While this seems obvious, wear comfortable clothing when you study.

- *Eat and drink smart.* Drink plenty of fresh water, munch on fruits or vegetables, a protein bar, or a healthy snack. Don't fill up on junk food or alcohol; this only serves to make you feel guilty, bloated, tired, and unhealthy!

Get in the Right Frame of Mind for the Test

While it is important to know content and learn about the most important content areas that will be covered on the test, it is more important to study in the manner of taking the type of test itself. Simply put, study with a multiple-choice mind-set every time you study. Take practice exams. Commit to reviewing 20–50 questions each time you study. If a topic appears as an answer that you know nothing about, research it and jot down notes, enough for your understanding. Keep your notes close to those questions, review them often, and they will become familiar to you. You should also do the following prior to Test Day:

- *Study for the test and to the test.* You need to know content and have a rhythm and flow for taking the test. Remember that multiple-choice tests give you facts and data. Essay exams require broad based knowledge that you are expected to discuss in greater detail. By distinguishing the two types of exams, you can focus on facts and data rather than broad based concepts.

- *Research the test itself*. Become familiar with practice exams and the questions. Analyze how questions are formed. Ask others who have taken the exam what it was like.

- *Visit the testing center where you will take the exam*. This is a huge unknown that clouds the back of your mind until you show up for the exam. Visiting the test center in advance will erase any unknowns, and it won't be a mystery if you check it out in advance. Ask to see the room and where you will be sitting. Ask what kinds of distractions to expect. Ask whatever questions are going through your mind when you visit the center. Having information in advance of the exam will help to reduce your anxiety.

- *Bring an extra sweater or jacket with you*. If the test center is unusually cold, and you get cold easily, dress in layers. Similarly, if you are unusually warm, wear light clothing.

- *Consider staying at a hotel the night before the test*. If you are scheduled for an early morning test, and the test center is located across town where traffic will be heavy, consider staying at a hotel the night before near the test center location. You don't want to be late for the exam nor do you want to arrive stressed out over traffic jams!

- *Request a time slot that works best for you*. If you prefer taking the test early, request an early time slot. If you prefer taking the test after 9 A.M., request a later time slot.

- *Plan ahead*. The evening before the exam, decide what you will need to take with you. Pack a small bag and lay out your clothes and car keys. Check to make sure your car is in working order and the gas tank is filled.

- *Eat a small meal the day of the exam and take snacks with you*. You will be allowed to take a break and eat a small snack during the exam; however, this is still part of the four-hour total you will have to complete the exam.

- *Request necessary accommodations ahead of time*. Remember, if you have a learning disability or require a reasonable accommodation, you must request this on the application and have this accommodation approved in advance, not on Test Day.

How Will You Know When You Are Ready?

As you now realize reading through this chapter, there are many goals to attain before scheduling the exam. The exam measures knowledge and application of principles to ideas and situations. Each exam, the PHR and SPHR, measures a specific BOK in a slightly different way. The PHR exam is more technical and operational; the SPHR exam is more functional and organization driven.

The test itself is a computer-based, multiple-choice examination comprised of 225 test questions. How much practice have you had taking practice exams for a long period of time? Simply put, it is an endurance test. Even if you have the content mastered, if you cannot sit for a four-hour stretch, you will become fatigued, lose your concentration, and miss more questions. Unfortunately, this is a dilemma for individuals who are very bright but who cannot sit for this long. If this is you, do not throw your hands into the air and give up. Speak with a representative at HRCI and ask if there is an alternative way for you to pursue certification by attaining a reasonable accommodation. Work with a test-taking coach, if possible.

Become familiar with HRCI's website and how the exams are described and administered. Make sure that the practice exams you take reflect current knowledge and information from the field. Compare this to the content areas listed on HRCI's website.

HRCI publishes practice exams you can take for a fee. Additionally, it is highly recommended and a good strategy to purchase the PHR and SPHR certification guide found on HRCI's website at www.hrci.org.

Additional Materials to Support Your Study Goals

This text book has been designed to support your test preparation needs, goals, information, and knowledge of the PHR and SPHR exams. However, you are encouraged to review other HRM resources as well. Visit local bookstores, university bookstores, and online bookstores. Be sure to investigate SHRM's website for the latest publications at www.shrm.org.

You may prefer to study alone, find a support group, or take a course—it's up to you! You won't be tested on your study protocol. Find the process that works best for you. Decide how you will study for the exam in advance. For support, you may want to seek a local professional HR group or association. People who have already been in your place can help you make sure that your expectations for the exam match the test itself. If a local association is not available, become familiar with information provided on the SHRM and HRCI websites, and visit them often because they are continuously updated.

When you achieve a 70 percent pass rate on the practice exams, you should feel reasonably comfortable that you are ready to take the exam and pass.

A SUGGESTED STUDY TIMELINE

1. *One year prior to the exam*: Become familiar with the SHRM and HRCI websites to adequately assess if you are a candidate to take the PHR or SPHR exam. Assess if you will be prepared in one year to take the exam.
2. *Nine months before scheduling the exam*: Inquire about local HR associations, university courses, textbooks, and company training programs. Download the application from the HRCI website. Create an action plan on how you will prepare for the exam. Determine which exam your professional experience is best suited for.
3. *Six months before scheduling the exam*: Complete the application in its entirety and send it to HRCI. Once approved, schedule the exam. If the application is returned or rejected, you will need to correct those deficiencies before you can reapply and forward a new application. Do this as soon as possible so you will not miss a test window once approved.

4. *Four months before scheduling the exam*: Assess your HR knowledge (BOK) by taking a practice exam. Determine your knowledge deficiencies, and decide if you should take a course or study independently. Apply and schedule to take the exam.

5. *Three months before taking the exam*: Assess your practice exam skills and results according to the BOK on the exam. If you scored in the 70 percent range, formally apply to take the exam on an exact date and test location. (Note: You may only schedule the exam with the approval letter that you will receive from PES qualifying you for the exam.)

6. *One month before taking the exam*: Schedule a full practice exam at least once a week and take a different practice exam each time. Visit a local test center to become familiar with the location, traffic patterns, test center, room location, and people who work at the center. Make a hotel reservation if you plan to stay in a hotel the night before the exam.

7. *Three weeks prior to the exam*: Review missed practice exam questions and complete one full practice exam during a four-hour sitting.

8. *Two weeks prior to the exam*: Review missed practice exam questions and complete one full practice exam during a four-hour sitting.

9. *One week prior to the exam*: Review missed practice exam questions and complete one full practice exam during a four-hour sitting. Do not take any more practice exams after this date. Continue to review missed questions.

10. *One day prior to the exam*: Gather all of the materials you need to take with you on the day of the exam. Make sure your car has enough gas to get you there.

11. *Exam day*: You may bring snacks, an extra sweater, and your glasses. You are required to bring your driver's license and some other proof of identity and the test letter confirming your appointment date and time. Plan to arrive 30 minutes early; if you are late, the test center may not hold your place for that day.

After the Exam

If you don't pass the exam on your first try, don't lose hope or give up. After all, it is one test, not your entire life and not your entire career. Consider this a learning experience that you can use to prepare for the next time. Don't second-guess yourself or the exam. Allow yourself time, a few weeks or so, to process what happened and why you were not successful. This is a good time to consider seeking a testing coach who can reevaluate where you fell short. Most test takers leave the testing center and return home to take a nap. Before you do, eat a small meal and do something kind for yourself, no matter what.

If you passed the exam, you may want to share the news with family, friends, or colleagues. Celebrate it! (But don't order new business cards until you receive official notification from HRCI.)

Either way, you've taken your first steps on the path to human resource certification. Congrats!

Core Knowledge Requirements

In any industry, having recognized credentials that acknowledge you as an expert in your field is important, not only to gain secure employment, but also to advance in your career. For human resource (HR) professionals, the Professional in Human Resources (PHR) and Senior Professional in Human Resources (SPHR) are the industry-recognized credentials that qualify you as an expert in your field. You obviously already know this, which is why you have made the commitment to study for your PHR or SPHR certification. But you may be asking yourself where to begin, so let's start with the basics—an overview of the core areas and concepts that are important to you as an HR practitioner.

In studying for your PHR or SPHR credentials, it will be essential that you have a very thorough knowledge of all of the components of human resources and competencies associated with it. Some refer to this as the Body of Knowledge (BOK) or core competencies. This chapter will provide a general overview of these components; subsequent chapters will expand on and explain them in greater detail.

THE IMPORTANCE OF HUMAN RESOURCES TO AN ORGANIZATION

In most undergraduate courses on human resource management (HRM), if you ask a group of inexperienced students what comes to mind when you say human resource management, the inevitable answers will always include the following: hiring, firing, interviewing, or, sometimes, benefits or payroll. These inexperienced students would be correct; those things certainly are part of any human resource department. However, as an HR professional with some experience in your field, you know that HR is much more than that. Human resources is responsible for the most critical functions in a company, as well as for implementing the policies, procedures, and mission of the organization. It is also responsible for short-term planning functions critical to an organization's success. The department will undertake job analysis, managing the talent pool, recruitment, and career development. Human resources incorporates the topics of diversity, employment law, training and development, technology, managing records, and much more.

ORGANIZATIONAL GOALS AND NEEDS

At the core of an HR professional's job is the task to clearly align the organization's goals and mission with the HR department's functions.

Needs Assessment and Analysis

The term *needs assessment* is really a fancy educator's term for asking: Where are we now? Where do we need to go? How are we going to get there? The challenge for an HR person is to answer each of these questions in a way that best serves the organization and the individual needs within the company.

It is likely that you might be conducting needs assessment and analysis on multiple levels at the same time. Organizations are constantly changing and evolving. While keeping your eye on the organization's overall mission and goals, you are also going to be managing individual progress and training needs. For instance, at any given point in time, you might be working with the frontline managers deciding what their staffing needs will be over the coming year at the same time you are working with an employee on your own staff to develop his personal training and development program for the next six months.

Organizational Structure

HR professionals are frequently asked to create organization charts for their company to make it easy for executives and managers to assess the organization's structure and how work flow and reporting relationships are structured within the company. All employees, as well as board members and the public, need to understand company strategy and structure and their roles in achieving organizational objectives.

The beauty of the organizational chart, or "org chart" as it is commonly called, is that it gives a quick visual image of large amounts of information.

Organizational charts provide the greatest value when used as a framework for managing change and communicating current organizational structure. When fully utilized, org charts allow managers to make decisions about resources, provide a framework for managing change, and communicate operational information across the organization.

In city government, for instance, an organizational structure could convey a complex structure, where there is a mayor, city council, and multiple divisions and reporting units—all responsible and ultimately accountable to the mayor. See figure 2.1 for a sample org chart for a medium-sized city of approximately 52,000 in the Pacific Northwest.

Figure 2.1 Organizational Structure of the City Government of Renton, Washington

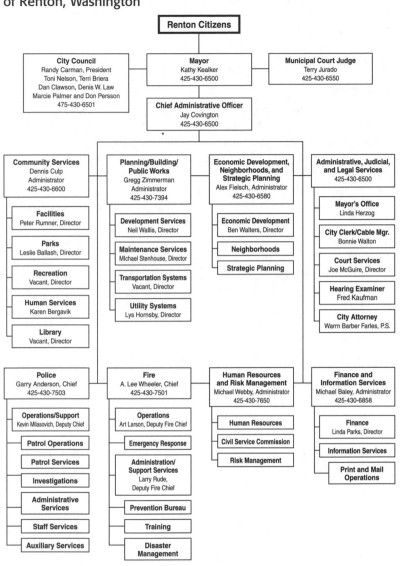

City of Renton Corporate Organization Structure

HUMAN RESOURCES AND STAFFING

Staffing is a critical function for any HR department. An HR manager must be prepared to help her frontline managers develop good job descriptions that accurately describe the skills, knowledge, and tasks for every position that they seek to fill, before any recruitment can even begin. This critical function of job analysis is something many managers are unfamiliar with or inexperienced in doing properly. Too often, it is easier to just fill the job description that is already on file, rather than modify the job to reflect how it has grown and changed.

Job Analysis and Job Descriptions

Job Analysis

Experts in employment and training will tell you that identifying the important skills and tasks for any job is crucial to effective performance. It contributes to bottom-line productivity, sales, retention, and job satisfaction. In fact, in recent years, there has been an ongoing dialogue in workforce education between educators and employers trying to make sure graduating students possess the skills that employers need to be successful in business and industry. Therefore, it is critical to conduct thorough job analyses of key positions on a regular basis. In conducting a job analysis, there are several areas of consideration:

- What are the skill requirements of the job?
- What skill levels do the incumbent workers currently possess? (Note: It could be that the incumbent worker does not possess the skills required of the job.)
- What skills, knowledge, and abilities does a job applicant need to do this job successfully?
- Can you identify the basic skills necessary to do the job, such as reading, writing, mathematics, or listening? Are there other advanced skills that the employee needs, such as applying basic technology skills, locating information, observing, or working in teams?
- What training, support, and education does an applicant or an incumbent worker need to have to perform this job adequately?
- How much time does the incumbent worker spend on critical tasks? How much time is spent on tasks that are not as important to the job?

Job Descriptions

Only after a job analysis has been completed can a true and accurate job description be written. Sadly, this is often not the way things happen. Many times, it is all too easy to go with the current job description on hand, rather than spend time seeing how the position has evolved, or how technology has replaced certain tasks that used to be performed.

The essential components of a job description should include many of the following items:

- *Job title and description.* This includes the title of the position, department, reporting lines, supervisory responsibilities, exempt status, salary range, and sometimes a percentage of duties completed in each functional area of the job.
- *Position summary.* This is a short summary of the position, usually in a few sentences. A position description might look like this:

- *Essential duties and tasks.* It is wise to use action verbs to describe the key functions of the job. As described in the job analyses, the essential duties and tasks should be broken down by the level of complexity and the amount of time spent on tasks. An example of action verbs would be the following: direct, manage, advise, coordinate, control, etc.

- *Equipment/computer skills.* This section lists specific software programs and/or equipment that will be used in this job and the frequency of use. If Microsoft Excel, for instance, is used only occasionally, it should be stated as such.

- *Job qualifications.* These are the minimum qualifications needed for successful job performance. At a minimum, this section should include the following:

  - *Education, licenses, or certification.* These must be listed to comply with the Americans with Disabilities Act (ADA) standards. These requirements must be related to the essential job functions, as in the following examples. College administrator: master's degree required, PhD preferred; editor for a small newspaper: minimum bachelor's degree in journalism, experience using Adobe Photoshop and PageMaker.

  - *Years/level of experience.* The minimum/maximum level of experience preferred to do the job successfully should be noted.

  - *Communication skills.* Does this job require a high level or low level of communication skills? What about experience working with the public? What level of writing skill is appropriate to the position?

  - *Special skills.* Are there special skills necessary for this particular position? Note the editor for the small newspaper listed above. Are there special computer program, design, or copyediting skills necessary for this job?

- *Work environment.* The job description can include a description of the work environment and should mention any kind of hazardous equipment or work in difficult or confined spaces. Any physical requirements of the job (heavy lifting, for example) must be listed, according to the ADA, and directly related to the duties of the job.

Job Satisfaction, Human Relations

The basic premise that satisfied employees are more productive employees has been a tenet of organizational behavior models for many years. The hard part is figuring out how to make employees happy. A basic definition of job satisfaction is the difference between what your employee receives in reward and compensation and what they *think* they should receive. Let's face it, we've all been overworked and underpaid at some point in our lives. We like a fair paycheck, a comfortable and safe environment, a boss who says thank you once in a while. But it is hard to quantify job satisfaction. As an HR professional, your role is to understand that in terms of job satisfaction and human relations, the main objective is to provide employees with jobs that are challenging and rewarding, while reducing turnover and absenteeism. Because job satisfaction is an attitude of an employee, rather than a behavior to correct, it is difficult to measure.

DIVERSITY

There is no topic more relevant to a discussion of human resources and human relations than diversity. The truth of the matter is that the planet is becoming "smaller," and businesses are becoming increasingly more diverse. In major metropolitan areas, it is not uncommon to have more than 100 languages spoken in a school district! This means that the surrounding communities and businesses are going to be representative of and responsive to the families sending their children to these schools. It is crucial to an organization's success to understand not only why diversity is important, but the impact that it will have on productivity and results.

Workforce Diversity

Your workforce should reflect the local community. The operative word in this statement is *should*. Workforce diversity presents a challenge in almost every business today. Even in the most diverse of communities, working and communicating with someone whose language and cultural beliefs are different than your own can be difficult. Anyone who has traveled to another country knows this to be the case. When you add the complexities of the workforce, close personal relationships, organizational deadlines, and long-held personal beliefs about different cultures, it can be a significant organizational challenge.

Overcoming this challenge is worth the effort. When companies increase the diversity within their business, they increase their ability to attract new customers.

Diversity and Creativity

Diversity in your work environment also creates a work space that has the potential to be much more creative. It was not too long ago that men didn't become nurses or chefs, and women didn't become carpenters or builders. You only need to turn on your local cable channel these days to *Emeril Live* or *Extreme Makeover Home Edition* to see that is no longer the case. By increasing diversity in your workforce, you have increased the opportunity for hearing new opinions, channeling creativity, and creating an environment of out-of-the-box thinking.

It is also worth mentioning that as baby boomers age and remain in the workforce longer than previous generations, the typical worker over 65 is an untapped resource of creativity and information.

Recruitment and Diversity

When we challenge our thinking about what the candidate pool *should* look like and open that pool up to a wide variety of applicants—men and women, young and old (whatever old is!), and any ethnic group—we also open up the possibility for a greater selection of applicants. As the baby boomers do retire and there becomes a shortage of candidates qualified for positions, this will become exceedingly important.

HR ETHICS AND PROFESSIONAL STANDARDS

The Society for Human Resource Management (SHRM) and the Human Resource Certification Institute (HRCI) both have standards for professional behavior in the human resource profession. The Code of Ethical and Professional Standards in Human Resource Management provides guidelines for professional responsibility that are developed around several key principles. The full code of ethics is available online at the SHRM website at www.shrm.org/ethics.

The code's standards, which are summarized below, are based on the following principles: professional responsibility, professional development, ethical leadership, fairness and justice, conflicts of interest, and use of information.

Professional Responsibility

- You are expected to hold yourself to the highest degree of ethical and professional behavior, comply with the law, and achieve the highest level of service.
- You are expected to positively influence the workplace and encourage responsible and ethical decision making.
- You will encourage social responsibility.
- You will inform and educate current and future HR professionals about practices that help to achieve the profession's goals.

Professional Development

- You will actively seek continuous learning and skill development and encourage others to do the same.
- As a professional in HR, you must strive to seek the highest standards of competence in your profession and understand how organizations work.

Ethical Leadership

- You will be expected to conduct yourself as a role model for maintaining the highest level of ethical standards and to set an example for others.
- You will be expected to act ethically in every professional interaction.
- You will be expected to seek guidance in questions of fairness, decency, and ethical standards.

Real World Note:

At a new teacher orientation at a school district on the West Coast, it was reported that 175 new teachers were added during the 2007–2008 school year. These teachers would be teaching students who spoke over 70 different languages and dialects, such as Ukrainian, Chinese, and Spanish, to name but a few. With families from so many different countries around the world, you can imagine how diverse the town's workforce was.

Fairness and Justice

- You will be the model for creating an environment of fairness and justice for all employees.
- You will be expected to respect the unique and inherent worth of each individual.
- You will be expected to treat people with dignity and respect.

Conflicts of Interest

- You will conduct yourself with professional integrity and not engage in activities that are actual, apparent, or potential conflicts of interest with the company.
- You will adhere to published policies on conflicts of interest within the company.
- You will refrain from using your position for personal or financial gain of any kind, or the appearance of such.
- You will refrain from giving preferential treatment in any human resource process, including hiring.

Use of Information

- You will protect the rights of individuals in the acquisition and dissemination of any personal and private information.
- You will ensure that all personal and private information is held in confidence.
- You will make certain that only appropriate information is used in making decisions about employment.

EMPLOYEE RECORDS MANAGEMENT

Employee records management is one of the most critical functions of any small or large HR department. Even in the smallest of mom-and-pop shop operations, accurate and ethical record keeping is mandatory. The HR professional must be able to answer questions and establish procedures on the correct way to organize, store, and manage employee records. Most large companies today opt for using a Human Resource Information System (HRIS), which is a sophisticated software program.

A certified PHR or SPHR individual should be able to answer the following questions: What is the correct way to organize employee files? Do employees have access to their files? What government forms do new hires need to fill out? What requirements does the Family and Medical Leave Act have? How do I manage a payroll system? How do we as a company post jobs, manage recruitment, track applicants, and complete EEO reports? How do we track vacation/sick leave/attendance?

Document Management

The employment process generates reams of paperwork, as most of us can attest to: applications, résumés, cover letters, tax forms, insurance applications, exit surveys, and performance evaluations, to name a few. While there are federal guidelines to adhere to that are important to your study for the PHR or SPHR exam, it is important to remember that local and state laws may differ somewhat. You should make yourself familiar with those requirements as well.

Employee records can include most of the following types of documents:

- Job applications, résumés, and educational certification copies
- Disciplinary records
- Family and Medical Leave Act (FMLA) records
- Medical documents and insurance applications
- Payroll
- Performance appraisals and promotions/demotions
- Salary history
- Time and attendance records
- Test records and hiring information

Organizational Documentation Requirements

In addition to employee records, the HR department is responsible for the management of any documentation related to employee performance. These critical documents are necessary to comply with local, state, and federal laws, but they are also critical for the organization as a whole, in case of lawsuits, discrimination claims, hiring and firing practices, and the like.

Employee performance issues should be handled when they occur, with the employee and the employee's immediate supervisor. That is the best case scenario. However, we know that the best case scenario is often difficult to follow. Let's be honest: confrontation is difficult even under the best of cir-cumstances. It isn't easy to tell someone they aren't doing a very good job. It is easier to wait until the annual review comes along and tell them then. The problem with that strategy is that it doesn't work. Situations can become worse if not handled, or for smaller issues, the employee can leave a perfor-mance evaluation feeling picked on: "If they had just told me earlier, I would have been happy to correct it."

When disciplinary action must be taken, it is important that the HR depart-ment has a progressive disciplinary plan in place and that written documenta-tion is taken at each of these levels:

1. Verbal Warning

At this level, the employee has repeatedly demonstrated behaviors or actions that are unacceptable to the manager and the work environment—and these behaviors cause disruption of work and productivity. Example: Joe would get a verbal warning if he repeatedly showed up late for work or he took exces-sively long lunch hours.

2. First Written Warning

At this stage of performance problems, the employee has been warned, yet continues to demonstrate the poor behavior, or it has increased to become an even greater problem. The supervisor typically will write a memo to the employee outlining the problem, stating why it's a problem to the division or unit, and detailing what steps the employee needs to take to rectify the situation. The employee should sign the memo, agreeing to acknowledge the warning and change the behavior. Example: Joe has gone from not only being late to work, but repeatedly calling in sick on Mondays, or coming in late, with the appearance of having been drinking alcohol in excess the prior evening. His performance at his job has been seriously impacted by his behavior.

3. Final Written Warning

When a final written warning is given, the employee has demonstrated an unwillingness to correct the behavior to the satisfaction of the manager or supervisor. The employee should be warned that his job is in jeopardy and that, if immediate changes are not made, he will be terminated from employment. Example: Joe has done nothing to change his behavior since the first written warning was given. In fact, on more than one occasion, a fellow employee has smelled alcohol on Joe's breath. It should be noted in this particular example that if your company has systems in place to assist employees with drug and alcohol problems, the employee should have been referred to the company's employee assistance program (EAP).

4. Suspension and Termination

Company policies vary significantly on the decision-making steps for suspension and termination. Sometimes there is a suspension period, with pay, in order for the employee to assess the situation and find a way to address the problem. It depends on the seriousness of the issue, the employee's work record, or whether it is a personal or emotional problem (or a family issue) that could be resolved quickly. At the suspension stage, an employee would get written documentation on the steps that need to be taken, in a specific period of time, before he can return to employment.

At termination, there should be no surprise to the employee that this action is going to occur. When the disciplinary plan has been followed, the employee has been significantly warned and reprimanded about his unacceptable behavior and has been informed that this was the inevitable outcome. If you have ever had to fire anyone, you know that documentation or not, this is not an easy process for the manager or the employee. Safeguarding employee computers on the employee's exit may be one consideration for the manager, lest the employee think of sabotaging work in progress. It also may be appropriate to have security close at hand when letting an employee go. The HR department should use its best judgment on how to handle termination, keeping in mind the idea of the employee leaving with dignity, not disgrace.

HIGH PERFORMANCE WORK SYSTEMS

In today's workforce, we see an increasingly fast-paced work environment. It is not unusual for a typical worker to be handling multiple tasks on the computer at one time. You could easily have five computer screens open at once: one for a résumé that you are reviewing, another for a cover letter attached to the résumé, one for your email account, one for a Web page tracking a project, and a screen to Google anything that you are researching. And while you are doing that, your assistant could hand you a fax that just came across about the merger in Tel Aviv. There is no doubt that technology has become a huge part of our lives. Twenty years ago we couldn't even fathom how dependent on the Internet and email we would become. Yet now, most of us have not one but multiple email accounts.

Technology and high performance work systems (HPWS) are an integral part of most business operations today. Simply put, an HPWS is a set of HR practices that combine work processes that will maximize employee work performance, knowledge, and skills and manage work flow.

The key concept of an HPWS is that it is a system of interrelated parts that guide work flow, design technology, and management processes. An organization's goal is to ensure these areas are working together to create a seamless work environment that meets its outcomes for both the employee and employer.

In *Managing Human Resources,* by George W. Bohlander and Scott Snell (South-Western College Pub, 13th ed., 2004), the authors cite Ed Lawler's work with the Center for Effective Organizations at the University of Southern California. The main tenets of an HPWS include the following:

1. Shared information
2. Knowledge development
3. Performance-reward linkage
4. Egalitarianism

Project Management

Project management is the process of planning, organizing, managing, and executing a specific assignment that is constrained by time and budget. Each project has a particular life cycle from inception to finish. For HR professionals, managing projects is critical to success and reaches across all of the functional areas of employee workforce management: planning, strategy, employee relations, contract negotiation, and risk management. In each of these areas, there will be projects to deliver at any given point in time. Over the past ten years, circumstances such as tragic school and workplace shootings have made planning for risk management an absolute must for most employers. Developing an action plan for dealing with sexual harassment in the workplace is also a crucial project for an HR department to execute. Revising and updating employee handbooks should be a yearly project.

In project management, you will want to familiarize yourself with each unique stage. There are a variety of models to choose from but most include the following stages:

1. *Initiation*. The beginning of the project is typically called the initiation phase. During this stage, you will receive requests for proposals from those interested in working on the project. If you are building a new building, you would be getting bids from contractors and architects. If you are developing a new career education program, you would be getting ideas from the team members, counselors, and managers working to develop the program. Basically, those who are affected by the project, including customers, will be meeting to discuss ideas about the project. Once the project idea is embraced, it is important to get "buy in," or feedback, about budgets and timelines during this phase.

2. *Planning*. Planning is the next stage in project management. It is crucial that the project manager be organized and skilled in meeting timelines, or your project will be a failure. The project manager should be able to run meetings successfully, manage agendas and multiple calendars, and communicate to each of the stakeholders on the progress of the project.

3. *Execution*. Execution, the next stage of a project, is relatively self-explanatory. Your team has already been created, research has been done, and resources have been acquired. This is where activities are happening: the building is hammered and nailed, the counselors are meeting with the students, and the spreadsheets are being examined. The project manager continues to manage and monitor the timeline, report on progress, and divert resources when problems occur or need to be managed.

4. *Closing*. Closing is the final phase of a project. The customer acknowledges that the project has been done to satisfaction. The CEO accepts what has been delivered. The manager says, yes, everything has been done well and she is happy with it. Basically, all your goals have been met. Often in the closing phase, final reports are written documenting the project activities and resources to be accessed at a later date.

Environmental Scanning

Savvy business managers always know what is going on around them—what the competition is up to, how successful their products are, industry standards, and future trends. This is called environmental scanning—the process by which businesses research information to keep the competitive advantage. In addition, environmental scanning can be done both externally as well as internally. In today's information age, it is an easier process than it once was, but at the same time the amount of information can also be daunting and time-consuming. The challenge is to find what is most appropriate in a given period of time to help you with your decision-making needs.

Environmental scanning can take many different avenues at your place of business. You might be scanning the economy as it relates to economic growth, unemployment, inflation (salaries, for instance), currency, or trend.

Your analysis could include a scan of governmental policies and regulations. This might include issues related to payroll taxes, state debt, political climate, or new legislation.

Other types of environmental scans include legal scans (investigating minimum wage laws, municipal licensing, and worker safety issues); technology scans (researching manufacturing processes or infrastructure issues, such as new roads, airports, hospitals, or schools); and even demographic scans (population size, education level, and income level are all important to an HR manager).

There are a number of models available for analyzing the information that you gather in your environmental scan, which we will discuss in more depth in chapter 3; however, a brief mention of the most common one is appropriate here. The SWOT analysis examines strengths, weaknesses, opportunities, and threats. Strengths and weaknesses are internal to your organization. Opportunities and threats are external to your organization.

Environmental scanning is an important part of being competitive and successful in any industry today, and learning to become more aware of the driving forces around you is essential.

LEADERSHIP CONCEPTS/COMMUNICATION

"Get out of the office and circulate among the troops."   —Abraham Lincoln

Leadership is a difficult subject because there really are no specifics that can be taught. And it is even harder to implement, because it often involves growth, pain, and sometimes failure. Because leadership principles may seem abstract, examples are usually the best way to illustrate where leadership is successful and where it is not.

Numerous theories of leadership have been proposed over the past 60 years or more. There is the Great Man theory in which a leader is born and not made. There are theories based upon traits, behaviors, participative leadership, situational leadership, and contingency leadership. It is important to have a working knowledge of several of these, and then to choose a style of leadership that works best for you and for your company. A popular leadership book, written in 1997, *The Leadership Challenge*, by James Kouzes and Barry Posner, describes a process that is basically transformational leadership.

Contingency Theories

Contingency theories state that there is no one optimal decision-making or leadership style. Instead, it is dependent on various internal and external variables or constraints.

In contingency theories, one examines which constraints are affecting your leadership or decision-making ability. These could be things such as:

- Manager behavior toward employees
- Technology
- Organizational size
- Resources

The effectiveness of the leader, under contingency theory, is contingent on the demands of any particular situation. These theories stress using different styles of leadership depending on the need created in the situation. The most common of these theories is the one by Alfred Fiedler.

Fiedler's Contingency Theory

In Alfred Fiedler's approach, he states that group performance is based on the leader's psychological orientation and three additional variables: group atmosphere, task structure, and the leader's position of power. Fiedler believed that group performance was based on leadership style and what he called "situational favorableness." An interesting part of this theory was the LPC Scale—Least Preferred Coworker Scale. The LPC Scale asks a leader to think of all the persons with whom she has ever worked, and then to describe the one person she worked with the least well. This can be a current coworker or someone with whom she previously worked. Then, she is to rate the worker on several scales, such as friendly or unfriendly, cooperative or uncooperative, guarded or open.

When the scales are scored and averaged, a high LPC score would suggest that the leader has a human relation orientation, while a lower LPC score indicates this leader is more task-oriented. Fiedler's logic is that individuals who rate their least preferred coworker in relatively favorable light on these scales derive satisfaction out of interpersonal relationships; those who rate the coworker in a relatively unfavorable light get satisfaction out of successful task performance.

Path-Goal Theory

Robert House's theory can be described as offering paths to achieve goals. He believed that a leader could affect the motivation, satisfaction, and performance of a group in different ways: by offering performance rewards, helping individuals to identify clear paths to achieve their goals, and removing obstacles to success.

House also described situational factors that affect achievement of these goals, including the subordinate's personality and characteristics of the environment. A common catchphrase from House's theory is *locus of control*, which involves your belief of how much control you have in the situation. If you have an internal locus of control (you believe you control your environment), you prefer a participative leader. If you have an external locus of control (everything is out of your control), you would prefer a more directive leader. If your subordinate believes that he has a high ability himself, he will not like directive leadership.

House believed that there were four styles of leadership:

1. *Directive.* The leader gives specific guidance on performance to subordinates.
2. *Supportive.* The leader is friendly and shows concern for the subordinates.
3. *Participative.* The leader consults with and considers the suggestions of subordinates.
4. *Achievement-oriented.* The leader expects the subordinates to set high-level performance goals and objectives.

Transformational Leadership

For James Kouzes and Barry Posner, the authors of *Leadership Challenge* (Jossey Bass, 2002), the path to success is transformational leadership. Empowering others, modeling the way forward, inspiring a shared vision, and enabling others to act are the tenets behind their leadership philosophy. Other aspects included:

- Sharing a sense of purpose and destiny
- Experimenting and taking risk
- Fostering collaboration and mutual trust
- Setting the example
- Building a commitment to people

Decision-Making Skills and Change Management

You've met them—people who just can't make decisions—whether it is as simple as what flavor of ice cream cone they want or whether they are going to meet you for dinner on Friday night. But in the workplace, we have to make decisions—often very important ones. It is critical to have some insight into your own decision-making skills and to recognize how others make decisions, in order to make change happen at your business. In HR, change management is the name of the game.

The first tenet in any discussion of decision making is that you must develop a belief in other people and understand what they are capable of. A leader shouldn't need to tell talented people how to do their jobs. Trusting and respecting others and staying out of their way is one way to help people make decisions.

Often, we are asked to make decisions when we are already under the gun or when a problem must be resolved quickly. In these situations, it is easiest to just follow your gut or do what you have done before. But there are a few rules that can help you to attack decisions of a large or small magnitude:

1. *Identify what the real problem is.* (Ask for input from others as well.) Is the airline always late because the pilots aren't keeping to their schedule? Or are there too many planes in the air? Ask yourself the who, what, when, where, and how questions. If the problem is very complex, break it down into a series of steps.

2. *Identify the potential causes of the problem.* Is the airplane not as efficient as it used to be? Is it one particular airport that is the problem? Is it an air traffic control situation?

3. *Identify some possible solutions for fixing the problem.* Less planes in the early morning, more in the middle of the day?

4. *Develop an approach that will work at this particular point in time.* If you can't solve it on the spot while a customer is standing right there, resolve it to the customer's satisfaction and take care of it more fully later.

ADULT LEARNING, MOTIVATION, AND TRAINING

Adult Learning Theories

There are as many adult learning theories as there are pages on the Internet, and everyone that you ask will have their own personal favorites and approaches toward adult learning. If you have spent much time in a classroom, it will be readily apparent to you that everyone learns differently however, there are some general categories that learning falls into.

Why is it important for a PHR/SPHR to know about adult learning theories? Because you are concerned with ensuring that your employees are continually updating their skills and training; and some of that learning is going to take place at your workplace. You are going to ask yourself: "Why isn't Steve's approach to training Sarah working? Why isn't she getting it?" She's likely not getting it because he just isn't training her according to her own particular style of learning.

One approach to adult learning is actually quite simple and is based upon the work of psychologist Howard Gardner. In the Multiple Intelligences approach (Armstrong, 1994), there are basically seven types of learning:

1. *Linguistic.* You use words to learn well. It could be written (books, papers) or oral (speeches, lectures). These learners just like words, and you'll see them writing copious notes even when they don't need to.

2. *Logical-mathematical.* You easily see patterns in numbers, can understand cause and effect relationships, relate to the abstract, and like to calculate and test hypotheses. These are usually "accountant types," computer programmers, scientists, and mathematicians.

3. *Spatial*. You are a spatial person and visualize the world around you. You have sensitivity to graphics, color, lines, and shapes and the relationship between those shapes. These are our graphic designers, interior designers, architects, and artists.

4. *Kinesthetic intelligence*. You learn best with hands-on learning. You like to touch and feel things. Using your body and hands to express ideas and feelings is exciting to you. These are typically craftspeople and those who have flexibility and dexterity and enjoy the tactile.

5. *Musical*. You have the ability to hear and distinguish between musical forms, pitch, rhythm, and melody. These are composers, sound technicians, musicians, and music lovers.

6. *Interpersonal*. You have the capability to understand people's moods, emotions, and feelings. You are sensitive to facial expression, tone of voice, gestures, and body language. You easily interpret interpersonal cues. These are the counselors, psychologists, some teachers, and those who can easily influence people to follow their course of action.

7. *Intrapersonal*. You have the capacity for self-knowledge and the ability to act on that knowledge. You have an accurate picture of yourself, your strengths and weaknesses, as well as your moods and motivations. You have the capacity for self-discipline and self-esteem.

As you look over the seven intelligences, try to figure out what your learning style is. Which way do you learn best? Have you always been trying to teach others using your own learning style? Does it work for you? When does it not?

It is important for you to decide how to best approach people that you are training. If your approach isn't working, try another. Interestingly, some students who find it very difficult to study do it better when music is playing. Obviously, they have a musical intelligence. Examine your own intelligence and adult learning style, and remember that others are not always the same as you.

Motivation

No single concept is more controversial than how to motivate people. Theories abound, and researchers have been studying the workforce for decades to determine whether employees motivate themselves or if their managers are responsible for getting them to work harder, smarter, faster. The basic theories give you a foundation for what drives people to perform and how to understand peaks and valleys of productivity. Understanding these peaks and valleys are important to you in planning, training, and working with motivation in the workplace.

Maslow's Old Hierarchy of Needs

Psychologist Abraham Maslow's Hierarchy of Needs is still the most basic and easily understood example of how to describe human behavior and theories of motivation. The steps of the hierarchy follow, with a short description of how they might manifest themselves in the workplace.

1. *Biological and physiological*. These are the most basic human needs and include things such as food, water, breathing, sleep, and comfort. A six-hour training session with no bathroom breaks likely will not result in optimal learning. You'll note that in most well-designed training sessions there are not only frequent breaks (every two hours), but snacks are often provided as "brain food."

2. *Safety*. Once people have their physiological needs covered, they want to be safe from any sort of physical harm. Security and safety manifest themselves in a number of ways. Maslow describes it as a motivation to keep your personal body safe. But it also can be seen as protecting the security of your employment, resources, morality, family, health, and property.

3. *Love/belonging*. This is the need for family, friendship, and acceptance in social groups. One can clearly see how that manifests itself in the workplace. It is the desire to fit in, have friends, and be part of the group.

4. *Esteem*. At this level people are motivated by the desire for respect, recognition, self-confidence, and achievement. This can be seen in the workplace: we all like to be told we are doing a good job, that our work is valuable and worthwhile.

5. *Self-actualization*. When people are satisfied at all of the other levels, they seek to express themselves creatively.

Humans are complex beings. Understanding what motivates people—particularly in the workplace—is difficult at best. But a smart manager knows that it is worth the effort. The job of a manager in the workplace is to get things done efficiently by capitalizing on employee time and effort. To do this, you have to motivate employees. Research shows that employees who are valued and respected are not only more productive, but also more creative.

Other leading theories by noted researchers can be explored by doing additional research on the Internet. Some of the theorists/theories worthy of further study include Douglas McGregor (Theory Y), Frederick Herzberg (commonly called the Hygiene Theory), and David McClelland (Achievement/Motivational Needs Theory).

Training

There are three places that training takes place: the individual level, the task level, and the organizational level. When you had your first job at McDonald's, most of the training was probably done at the task level, with a little organizational philosophy of McDonald's sprinkled in for good measure. Your supervisor trained you how to run the cash register, how to pour the drinks, the appropriate way to greet customers, and how to clock your hours.

For most organizations, it becomes much more complex than the McDonald's approach.

Organizational-level training will likely involve the entire organization or a large division or department. For example, a university in wisconsin conducted a university-wide training program on customer service. Every single person, from the president to the newest hired hourly worker, attended a four-hour customer service training event. At the end, the university implemented "the six-foot rule," which stated that when anyone came within six feet of you with a problem, you had to "own that problem" until it was resolved. It was an excellent organizational training program that saw immediate results.

This training program was implemented after the university determined they had a problem in this area. Often, this is the case with an organizational training program: something goes wrong, and then it needs to be fixed on a global level.

Individual training programs are just as they sound—training that is customized for the person who needs some sort of improvement in one area or another. It might be triggered by a performance review, or it might be initiated by the employee. For instance, an employee thinks that she could do her job a little bit better if you allowed her to take a class on formatting spreadsheets or learning PowerPoint presentations.

Task-level training is at the most fundamental level learning a single job task or skill necessary to do the job well. Jim could train Sally on running the copier. Kim could train Lisa on something that she has been doing poorly.

Developing training programs is key to optimal performance and productivity in your organization, but it is not the answer to all of your problems, nor the only solution. Training programs are covered in more depth in chapter 5.

Communication

Good communication is the cornerstone of any successful employee/employer relationship. It is particularly important to HR professionals. You will be required to communicate effectively—on a number of levels—with everyone from the chief executive officer to customers and constituents, board of directors, and middle- and lower-ranked workers. Choosing successful communication strategies will be very important to you as you evaluate which audience you are addressing.

Employee Communication

Communication delivery methods are normally referred to as upward communication, downward communication, or horizontal communication. Flow of communication can be formal or informal, and it can be internal to the organization or external to the organization.

Real World Note:

Bill Gates, former chairman and CEO of Microsoft, was famous for emailing members of the company at all hours of the day and night–sometimes even at 2:00 A.M. And the employees of Microsoft know that they were free to send Mr. Gates an email at any time with a suggestion or an idea. At Microsoft, it put the "open door policy" on an entirely new level.

Regardless of the delivery method that you will use, the primary purpose must be to provide information and balance the needs and confidentiality of the company with the employee's right to understand what is happening within. The strategy that you use must empower the employee and build trust within the organization. Most employees will tell you that the more they know about the company's vision, goals for the future, and daily operations, the more engaged they are with the process.

Some immediate questions to ask yourself include the following:

- Who am I addressing? Who is my audience? Is there any sensitivity to consider when communicating with this individual or this particular group?

Table 2.1 Communication Delivery Methods

Top-Down Communication	Horizontal Communication	Downward Communication
Intranet announcement closing building early one week	Two secretaries email back and forth about a project.	Staff meetings discussing ongoing projects
PA announcement about a lockdown	Team members on the new software project meet informally after work.	Email from staff member to CEO and vice versa
Organizational newsletters	Joe calls Sally about the custodial needs in a building on campus.	The "open door policy"
Email broadcasts of new job openings and promotions	Don asks Bill to set up a video for him prior to his presentation.	Information training sessions

- What do they *need* to know now? Is there some information that can be presented at a later date?
- What information do I have? What information do I need to collect from someone else?
- Is the information time sensitive?
- What is the best way for the person being addressed to receive this information? For example, if you are used to sending email, but the chairman of the board never reads his email, this probably would not be a good delivery method.

Communicating with Internal and External Constituents

An HR professional is often called upon to communicate with many internal and external partners and constituents. You are wise to develop your skills in giving speeches and presentations, writing professional documents, and communicating persuasively with the public.

As our burgeoning email boxes indicate, electronic communication is rapidly becoming the communication tool of choice for most people. It is prudent to note that it comes with its own special set of guidelines for proper usage. Email should always be professional, written in complete sentences, and checked for correct spelling and grammar. You should be cautious of developing too informal a tone in your email correspondence, although it is generally accepted to begin an email with: "Hi Bill." Your email should have a salutation and a closing, such as "Thank you. I look forward to hearing back from you."

RISK MANAGEMENT

In today's increasingly volatile world, it is unfortunately almost a weekly occurrence to hear about some sort of violence in the workplace. It has no longer become "if" but "when." The smart employer wants to identify any type of workplace risk that could take place and prevent it before it happens. This is the reason for developing a sound risk management program. Risk management is the process of identifying any possible threat and removing or reducing it. Risks come in many possible forms: worker to worker violence, domestic violence, bodily injury, liability for wrongful termination or sexual harassment, losses related to employment issues or insurance claims, and more.

Managing risks involves putting together proper procedural books and insurance plans, removing hazards, and keeping legal documents. HR professionals need to communicate with frontline managers the importance of following procedures when it comes to hiring, safety and security, and what these policies mean to company and personal liability.

Risk management is a very broad topic, which will be further covered in chapter 8, but it includes such items as the following:

- Federal employment legislation
- Occupational Safety and Health Act of 1970
- Employee rights and responsibilities (which include rights to privacy and email accounts)
- Record keeping of all kinds, including workplace injuries and illnesses—and what is considered a work-related injury
- Inspections of food: handling, hazards, and permitting
- Ergonomic issues
- Drugs in the workplace and employee assistance programs (EAPs)
- Fair Labor Standards Act
- Safety and health risks and standards (including mental health issues)
- Environmental standards
- Security measures and prevention of security breaches
- Financial security and risk prevention
- Workplace violence

Obviously, it is nearly impossible to become an expert on such a large list of extremely important items, but the wise HR professional will be skilled in understanding the major legislation and how to properly implement these programs. Knowing where to find information related to each of these topical areas is also extremely important.

CONTRACT NEGOTIATION AND BARGAINING

Individuals and companies negotiate and enter into contracts fairly frequently in the course of business—particularly when there are a good number of employees at the organization represented by a union, like at a university or in a school district. An HR professional knows that it is his job to make sure that all parties feel that they are understood and represented at the bargaining table. Knowing about the fine art of negotiation and the right choices to make in bargaining are imperative.

There are two types of bargaining: collective (or position) bargaining and interest-based bargaining.

Interest-based bargaining, which is sometimes called integrative bargaining, is win-win bargaining. No one has to lose. It is a negotiation strategy in which both parties agree to collaborate to find a resolution. The strategy is to find mutual benefits based on the interests of the disputing parties. When coming to the bargaining table, it is important to take heed of the reasons for the dispute. How did you get here in the first place? It is also important to pay attention to the needs, desires, concerns, and fears that each side is feeling.

Interest-based bargaining usually brings more satisfactory outcomes than position bargaining. Position bargaining is based on fixed opposing views and tends to result in compromise that is not satisfactory to one party, or in no agreement at all. Many times, a compromise results in one party leaving the table angry or with a bitter taste in their mouth.

The first step in the negotiating process is to identify interests: Why do you want that? Why do you need that? What are your concerns? What will happen if you don't get this?

Strategic Planning and Management

MEETING AN ORGANIZATION'S OBJECTIVES

Competition is fierce these days in the business world. If you walk down any supermarket aisle, you will be faced with hundreds of choices of competing brands of chips, soda, and snacks. Turn on the television set, and where you used to have a few network stations, most of us now have 70 or more stations competing for our attention. In today's world, we know that organizations need to be strategic planners and thoughtful decision makers to be successful. Your company likely has many different departments (or if you are working for a smaller company, several individuals) that work together to achieve organizational objectives and goals. As an HR professional, your job is to understand how to incorporate your organization's objectives into your strategic planning and management so that you may participate as a contributing partner in the organization's success.

Strategic Management

For HR professionals, strategic human resource management (SHRM) is the process by which you plan, align, process, and implement the goals in an organization. While studying for your Professional in Human Resources (PHR) or Senior Professional in Human Resources (SPHR) certification, there are several things that you will need to concentrate on related to the strategic management functional areas that will be discussed in this chapter. These include the following:

- Strategic planning
- Decision making and goal setting
- Management functions
- Information processing
- Aligning human capital
- Budgets
- Corporate governance procedures and compliance
- Legislative and regulatory processes

Strategic Planning

You might not be able to predict the future, but a good leader can plan for it. By examining your surroundings, taking calculated risks, and making educated guesses, you might be able to predict changes in the coming years. This type

Real World Note:

For the first time in many decades, colleges and universities now face competition from online universities and training programs offering educational opportunities in the convenience of your own home, on your own time. Kaplan University, University of Phoenix, and Argosy University are just some of the online competitors challenging traditional universities and colleges.

of preparation can help prepare your organization for future successes. Leaders should focus on the matters most important to your organization—the things most closely aligned to your core mission and goals. These are the areas that are important to the future of the company.

Strategic Planning

In the simplest of terms, strategic planning is determining where an organization is going over the next year or more and how you are going to get there. It is worth noting that in the past sometimes strategic planning was also referred to as long-term or long-range planning. Typically, the process is organization-wide, but it can also include specific units, divisions, and departments. Often, it all happens simultaneously. For example, if you were planning to introduce a new systemwide software system at your company, you would plan to implement it at the global level at the same time each individual division would plan for their own changes in process and procedures.

Strategic Analysis

There is no one perfect way to approach strategic planning, but there are some general components that are usually included in the process. First, you need to find out where you are to begin with and to do some analysis of the competition. This is called environmental scanning, and it involves doing a review, or a scan, of the organization's entire internal, external, political, social, economic, and technical environments. As a strategic planner, you will look at all the forces competing in your environment. This review of the strengths, weaknesses, opportunities, and threats is often referred to as a *SWOT analysis*. During your analysis, you will pay particular attention to all of the driving forces affecting change, including the economy, changing demographics, sales, and increasing competition.

While doing your environmental scan, it is important to look at rival firms, customers, newcomers to the industry, buyers, and suppliers. In addition, it would be wise to pay attention to the "substitutes" of your product. Sometimes the greatest threat is not direct competition, but substitutes for the product. What would you buy, for instance, if the store was out of your favorite Tide detergent?

Strategic planning is a dynamic process and not a one-time thing. Good organizations are continually measuring success, planning for the future, and examining new and better ways to improve their products and services in the face of competition.

Strategic Direction

You have decided on who is going to work on your strategic plan, you've done a thorough environmental scan, and now it's time to determine your course of direction. Planners work thoughtfully on setting direction by examining current accomplishments and looking at overall goals for the organization. During this stage, you may be beginning the process for defining your vision and mission statements for the organization, or you may be examining the existing ones to determine if they are on course or if they need modification. Either way, it's good to have an idea of exactly what vision and mission statements are and what part they play in the planning process.

Vision statements are just as they sound, brief written descriptions that should inspire and that communicate the goals of the organization and those they serve. They are forward focused.

Mission statements are more specific descriptions of how an organization will achieve its vision and goals for the future. To be effective, they should describe the company and its unique characteristics and its purpose. Recently, it has also been common to find people who write their own personal mission statements. In about a paragraph, it should describe one's philosophy and goals for the future.

Starbucks lists its mission statement as: "Establish Starbucks as the premier purveyor of the finest coffee in the world while maintaining our uncompromising principles while we grow."

Mt. Holiday, a nonprofit organization for ski enthusiasts in Traverse City, Michigan, describes its mission statement succinctly as: "Provide affordable, educational, and outdoor recreational activities in a safe, clean, and inviting environment for people of all ages through sound business and management practices."

Internal Assessment

Developing a strategic direction involves first doing a thorough analysis of your internal environment. What are the resources and strengths within your organization? What are the challenges and weaknesses in-house? As always, your analysis will certainly depend upon the nature of your business. A university's internal assessment of its environment will be vastly different than that of a product-driven business that sells widgets. However, where they are similar is that they will both examine every functional unit of the corporation. You can collect this information in a variety of ways. Some companies choose to bring in an outside facilitator to meet with focus groups. You can also develop in-house questionnaires and use surveys of customers or consumers. It is important, however, that you analyze the following types of information:

- Current product sales (Are sales up or down?)
- Organizational culture (Is it harmonious or poisonous?)
- Enrollment trends if you are a university or college (Is it higher in certain programs? If so, what have the trends been?)
- Geographic trends (Home sales and other types of sales vary widely by geographic area—is yours keeping up to par with your competitors?)
- Internal technology and computer systems (Do you possess the best technology for your company to be competitive?)

- Equipment and resources (Does your staff have the appropriate equipment and resources to do their jobs well? Nonprofit organizations are notorious for letting these types of items slip by because of lack of funding.)
- Staffing level (Does your company have enough staff to do their jobs well? Are you overworking your current staff to the point of exhaustion?)
- Diversity in your workforce (Do your employees reflect the surrounding community?)
- Strength of your administrative/executive team (Does your team have credibility with stakeholders—including the board, the staff, and the outside community?)
- Turnover rate (What has turnover been like in the past year? Is it always in one area of your organization? If so, you'll need to find out why.)
- Customer satisfaction (How do your customers feel about you? Have you asked them recently?)
- Reputation (What is your reputation with the public? If you don't know, you should.)
- Market timing (Is now the time to market your product? Is there a better time?)

By looking at many of these key areas, you will start to see where weakness and red flags develop. If the turnover at your organization is always in customer service, try to develop a solution for what the problem is. Maybe it is one supervisor, or perhaps it is a lack of resources or a perception of those employees. Once you can identify the problem, you have a better chance of solving it.

External Assessment

The external assessment, unfortunately, is even more challenging than the internal assessment because of the need to touch on such a wide variety of places in the environment. Challenging, but not impossible to do—and you will need to do it. One key tool to help with this is called a STEP analysis, which is an acronym for social, technological, economic, and political.

Social: In a social analysis, you will examine the current target market of your product and social trends. In the late 1980s, the popular singers were Madonna and Prince, and marketing music products to young adults was geared toward their fans. In 2007, Madonna and Prince were featured in AARP magazine because they both were turning 50 (Caroline Kennedy was on the cover of the magazine)! Obviously, there has been a change in social trends! For international corporations, it is even more challenging to examine social trends. Japan led the way for years in the cell phone/camera technology industry. It took some time and marketing, but in the United States those trends have developed into a way of life for Americans with their cell phone/cameras.

Technological: Technology changes at an almost dizzying pace. As Microsoft goes, so goes the rest of the country, it seems. Competitors of Google are trying to line up behind them to get a big piece of the pie. Technology, though, will vary depending upon your industry standards, budget, product, and services. Many companies are choosing to let more and more staff use laptops and work from remote locations. Would that be an efficient practice for your organization? Would production and sales increase if you purchased the latest/greatest automated system? Could you switch to an automated phone system, and how would your customers adapt to that?

Economic: For obvious reasons, economic factors are one of the most challenging items to consider in your analysis. How is the current economy? One needs only to step into a shopping mall at Christmas—full of holiday shoppers with credit cards in hand—to think, "Wow, the economy is going strong." But you may be perplexed by a statement saying holiday shopping is down. Make sure you are examining perception versus reality in the marketplace. How is the unemployment rate in your community? In late 2007, Michigan rated highest in the number of foreclosures. Examining "in the news" items will be central to your analysis. How are interest rates, which are great indicators of home and car sales? In 2008, the high price of gasoline is making a huge impact on buyer behavior.

Political: The political environment is dependent upon your industry as well. For higher education, for instance, state government regulates the budget and often tuition increases. How will that affect a university's bottom line? Other government items to consider are regulations, taxes, and policy changes over a given period. Has the Department of Labor changed the minimum wage? What are the current policies and procedures related to Homeland Security and Safety and how will they affect your future decisions? For international corporations, regulations can change on an almost daily basis—the country of operation and the state department will be where you need to put your attention for current regulations.

Environmental scanning can be challenging, time-consuming, and frustrating, yet it is so worth the effort in setting a strategic plan for your company and developing resources to map your future. Leaders that make the time to address these challenges are rewarded with future success.

Decision Making and Goal Setting

Entire courses are taught on decision making, so what is presented here is a short synopsis of many models that are out there to examine. In short, *decision making* is looking at a set of alternatives and making a choice between them. That's the short version of a complex psychological, cognitive process that the brain goes through in examining alternatives. Sometimes there are no real, rational reasons for the decisions that we make—other than it looks good or feels good at the time: "I'll have the cheeseburger instead of the chicken sandwich." However, it is often much more complex than that. In science, scientists apply the knowledge they have learned in specialized areas—biometrics, for instance—to make informed decisions. For example, medical decision making often involves making a diagnosis and selecting an appropriate treatment—sometimes it is correct, and sometimes it is not. The important part about decision making is gathering enough information to make sure you are making informed decisions and weighing the alternatives along the way.

Decision-Making Style

According to the theories behind the Myers-Briggs Inventory, developed by behavioral psychologist Isabel Briggs, a person's decision-making process depends to a significant degree on her cognitive style. The Myers-Briggs Type Indicator (MBTI) is a popular tool used by career counselors in helping individuals match their personalities with appropriate occupations. The MBTI matches your personal characteristics along a continuum—and the result gives you an individualized profile. The characteristics it measures are extraversion versus introversion, thinking versus feeling, judging versus perception, and sensing versus intuition. The MBTI asserts that all of your personal decision making is based upon on how you relate to this scale. Are you someone who makes decisions with your heart? Or strictly based on fact-based analysis? Are you a person who makes a decision based on your introspective nature?

There are also other cognitive factors that creep into our decision-making processes. Our personal biases toward certain types of people, things, or feelings affect the decisions that we make. As an HR professional, you are wise to examine your own personal biases and decision-making processes before you begin to examine what others are doing. Some common decision-making flaws include the following:

- We tend to make decisions based on past performance and experiences—oftentimes ignoring data that is in front of us that might support a different conclusion.
- We often make decisions based on wishful thinking or optimistic rationalizations. ("I'll go ahead and schedule that trip to Florida even though there is a strong prediction for a hurricane in the next 48 hours—I'll be okay.")
- We tend to accept the first alternative that looks like it might work. ("I'll buy the red sweater for Aunt Hannah; we know she likes red.")
- We tend to place more attention on more recent information and either ignore or forget more distant information. ("Oh, yes, I forgot that every single time I have gone to that restaurant they have awful food. Why did I do this again?")
- We conform to peer pressure. ("Everyone wanted to see that scary movie. Why didn't I tell them I hate horror movies?")

As an HR professional, decision making is going to be an important component of your everyday job. Making sound business decisions will lead to a sound strategic direction and, ultimately, the success of your organization.

Goal Setting

While effective decision making is important to your organization, so is setting appropriate goals for the future. As anyone who has ever set a goal to lose weight after the holidays knows, this isn't always easy. But goal setting is important on several levels in the organization. You will need to set goals to help you with your strategic direction for the future, you will want to set and monitor your own personal goals—daily, weekly, monthly, yearly—and you will want to help others set goals during their annual personnel reviews and during training sessions.

The most tried-and-true goal setting formula is the SMART formula. There are several different ways to use the acronym, but all pretty much mean the same thing:

S—Specific

M—Measurable

A—Attainable

R—Relevant

T—Time Based

Let's say you were conducting a performance review and in talking with Mike, you realize that he's struggling a bit with presenting research data to his supervisor, Julie, in a way that she can understand. You want to help Mike with his goals for the next year, so you brainstorm some ways that he might do this. Using the SMART method for goal setting, you and he might come up with the following goal:

Mike will learn to use the Microsoft Access database software by taking a class at the local community college in the first quarter of next year. Learning Access will help him to further organize his research data and be able to present more coherent reports to his supervisor during the following year.

His goal is definitely specific—he's going to take a community college class in Access. It is measurable—the software will help him create specific reports. It is attainable—as long as the company approves his desire to take the class, it should be. It is definitely relevant to his current problem. And it is time based—he will take it during the first quarter of the year.

The beauty of the SMART goal setting theory is that it is pretty easy to remember and to come up with fairly simple goals that are achievable. The part that most people miss is the time-based portion. Remember, leaving the time portion open-ended often results in the goal falling by the wayside.

Management Functions

You feel like there are never enough hours in the day to complete your job. Management is always asking for more. You don't get paid enough. It's a thankless job, but someone has to do it. We've all felt that way at one time or another. Sometimes it can get overwhelming. As organizations continue to grow and thrive, it is important to revisit from time to time what it is we are supposed to be doing and what our goals are. Sometimes we feel like babysitters just dealing with personnel issues in a given week; other times, we are mired in a budget process or a task analysis. There are really just four essential management functions to direct our work: planning, which we have already covered, organizing, directing, and controlling. Using these functions, you can ensure that your organization's resources are being wisely used to achieve your goals.

Organizing

Managers are responsible for making sure the work happens and for providing a framework for how to get it done. You need to ask yourself these types of questions when organizing your workload: What is it that I need to accomplish today? Who can do it? What resources do they need to do their job well? How much time do we have? Are there any decisions that need to be made before the work can be done? Are there any roadblocks in the way of completing the work?

For example, if Angela is responsible for organizing a fund-raising auction for the chamber of commerce, and she has three months to do it, she would probably revisit this process daily over the course of the month. In one week, she might say to herself, "Today, I need to get the volunteers to the meeting, tell them we've reached 30 percent of our procurement goal and that they need to go back out and seek additional auction items by next week." At her meeting, she would ask questions on how best to keep the work organized and on task, and she would direct the volunteers to get additional auction items and identify any roadblocks that are impeding their process. For instance, perhaps businesses are not donating items to the volunteers and the chamber this year because of a poor economy. Maybe the roadblock isn't the donations, but the volunteers. Have the volunteers just not had time to contact businesses? If so, Angela should redirect their energy to go out again and succeed. In addition, are there resources she can provide to the volunteers to make their jobs easier?

When organizing workload, it is important to consider organizational structure. Who can make the decisions? How is work delegated? In the case above, Angela is working with volunteers. In other organizations, the workload is delegated from one managerial level to subordinates. In addition, is the organization decentralized or centralized? A *centralized organization* is one in which the decision-making authority is concentrated at higher levels in the organization. In contrast, a *decentralized organization* is one in which the authority is delegated at lower levels.

In addition to decision-making authority, it is important to consider the span of control the manager is responsible for. *Span of control* refers to the direct number of employees a manager supervises, or "direct reports" as they are sometimes referred to.

Directing

Managers all possess a certain and unique personal style of developing relationships with employees that work for them. In directing work, it is up to the manager to support, encourage, and help employees achieve their goals. Building partnerships with employees at all levels of the organization is the way to achieve short- and long-term goals.

Controlling

Employees are valuable resources. No one likes to be controlled, but everyone likes to be in control. The control function is the way managers are able to test strategies and plans and, ultimately, implement them. The manager will keep in mind the big picture and long-range plan when surveying progress.

Aligning Human Capital

Your employees are literally the heartbeat of your organization. With proper selection, effective human resource practices, and safe and sensible work environments, employees can be productive cheerleaders for your company. On the other hand, high turnover, low productivity, high absenteeism, or poor sales can suck the lifeblood out of your organization very quickly. Your most important job as an HR administrator is to align human capital—that is, to identify the right people for the right job at the correct time.

Jane might have the right skill set, the right degree, and even the best work experience on paper. But her personality might not fit the job as well as George, who lacks a little of the work experience and can be trained. This is tricky business figuring out the best person and fit for a job. You have to be a manager, a psychologist (almost), and a sleuth and, ultimately, trust your own gut instinct.

There are a number of models to choose from in aligning human capital. In the article "Do you know how many trees there are in New York City's Central Park?" (Robbins and Judge, 2007), there is an alternative approach to conventional wisdom. In the article, it is noted that Amazon.com and Microsoft, both Seattle, Washington–based companies, emphasize intelligence as the primary factor in choosing employees. In the past, at most companies, experience was the determining factor in hiring. These two companies look at intelligence instead and scrutinize college transcripts and SAT scores of potential employees.Microsoft and Amazon believe that their niche in the world is their innovative ideas—and that smart people, regardless of their past jobs, are the most creative and innovative. That's why if you interview for a job there, you might be asked: "How many trees are there in New York City's Central Park?" or "How many gas stations are there in the United States?" The interviewer is looking for how the potential employee will reason their way to the answer.

Cultural Intelligence

In recent years, as our world has become increasingly diverse, it has become important to look for people in our workforce who are sensitive to cultures other than their own. In fact, it has sparked a new term—*cultural intelligence*. Research has shown that some people just seem to have a knack for relating well to people from different cultures. They can communicate better and seem to have an inherent understanding of what is being said. This is important because, when conducting business meetings with those of a culture that is vastly different from our own, misunderstandings can occur and derail the entire process.

As stated earlier, person/job fit is a difficult process, because it is difficult to predict employee behavior. And certainly experience does matter, as does the ability/job fit. As a manager, it is your job to ensure the fit works at many levels—intelligence, ability, skill, and personal. Flight attendants need to have good poise, customer service skills, and friendly personalities; they don't need strong written communication skills. Journalists need reasoning skills and strong attention to detail.

What happens when the fit and ability are not aligned? If you hire someone with far greater abilities than the position calls for, the individual will likely be frustrated very quickly with their job. Similarly, if you hire an individual as an administrative assistant with limited spreadsheet and communication skills, that person might feel inadequate and not have a high level of job satisfaction.

Budgets

This book is not intended to help you design and understand the entire budgeting process. There are whole courses on that. However, what is important to stress here is that you need to learn to develop and manage the HR department in a manner that is consistent with the organization's strategic plans, goals, and processes. You will be expected to provide information for the development of the organization's overall budget, not just the HR department alone. This will include information about salaries, benefits, labor market data, cost of living increases, and the like. It would be wise, if you haven't already done so, to take a basic budgeting and accounting course if you are not familiar with the terminology or to pick up one of those Accounting for Dummies–type books to help you along. We will briefly summarize budgeting and accounting here.

Basic Accounting

In addition to making yourself familiar with basic accounting terminology and budgeting terms, a wise HR professional would also take a short course (most community colleges offer them) in spreadsheets and data collection. Microsoft Excel is the most common spreadsheet tool used today, while Microsoft Access is used for organizing data at a more complex level.

Basic accounting creates reports to summarize business activity. Items you will want to be familiar with include the balance sheet, income statement, and cash flow statement. In addition, you will need to be aware of your organization's fiscal year, which might not coincide with the calendar year. Many organizations operate on a July 1–June 30 fiscal year; others operate their budget aligned with the calendar year. Most government agencies operate under the July-June fiscal year.

The *balance sheet* is a financial picture of an organization at any point in a given time, although it is typically prepared at the end of the month. The balance sheet formula is as follows:

$$Assets = Liability + Capital$$

The *statement of cash flow* provides information about where your money is going in the organization. Is a great deal going to overhead costs? Were administrative expenses highly skewed one month? Were sales down in July? If so, was it on one particular brand of potato chips? This is an important report that allows you to analyze all facets of producing your product (or service). The statement of cash flow can be particularly telling for a new start-up business. Are you spending too much on overhead and not enough on marketing?

The *income statement*, sometimes referred to as a profit and loss statement, is just that. How much did you bring in? How much went out? How much did it cost you to produce your potato chips? How many jars of homeade jelly did you sell? The income statement is composed of revenues, expenses, and net income for a given period of time.

HR professionals need to know the above common accounting terms as well as some frequently used others, which are outlined in table 3.1.

Budgeting

The budgeting process is used to determine the type and amount of resources that you will need to do the job well in the coming year and to accomplish your organization's goals. As most of us can probably attest to from our own home budgeting process, this is not always an easy task. Keeping track of your own spending, your spouse's spending, what you need to save, and what you need to pay on your bills can be complicated. At your organization, the process is probably ten times more complicated than that. Do you need additional employees? Or fewer? Will you need to upgrade technology next year? What is the cost of the software? How about the training time for employees? How much sick leave will be paid out next year? How much vacation time? Basically, budgeting is about how much cash is needed to achieve your goals.

Historical- and Zero-Based Budgets

There are two basic ways to create a budget; the first is based on what was done last year—or a historical-based budget—and the second is a zero-based budget. Budgets based on historic information are a good starting point, particularly if things aren't going to operationally change a lot in the new fiscal year or if most things are just going to increase by a flat percentage rate or be based upon certain salary increases.

A zero-based budget occurs when you are starting from scratch and determining what you need to achieve your goals. If you are creating a brand-new product or service, this would be your process when you are writing your business plan. How much material will you need? What will it cost to produce the item? Will you need to warehouse it? What will the salaries be? Overhead costs? Marketing costs? How many people will you need to hire?

Table 3.1 Common Accounting Terms

Accounting Term	Definition
Accounts receivable	Accounts receivable is money received or owed the business.
Accounts payable	Accounts payable is money owed by the business to suppliers, vendors.
Annual report	An organization's annual report includes the financial statements and accompanying summary of the year in review and plans for the futures.
Assets	Economic resources of a business can be cash or items that can be converted to cash or items such as land or buildings.
Cash basis accounting	Under cash accounting, revenue is only recorded when cash is actually received, and expenses are recorded only when paid out.
Debit	Debit is the left side of an account.
Expenses	Expenses are the cost of the merchandise sold or service used. Reduces owner's capital.
Generally accepted accounting principles (GAAP)	Generally accepted accounting principles are a set of guidelines and procedures that constitute acceptable practices.
Gross profit	Gross profit is sales revenue minus cost of goods sold.
Liability	Liability is money owed by the business to others, such as lenders, the government, or to employees.
Net profit	Net profit is gross profit minus operating expense.
Profit	Profit is all money earned after all expenses have been paid.
Revenue	Revenue is money received from customers for products and services.
Taxable income	Taxable income is the net income of a business upon which the federal, state, and local taxes are based.
Worksheet	A worksheet is a columnar document used to prepare financial statements.

Corporate Governance Procedures and Compliance

Corporate governance is the way organizations and corporations are managed and aligned. Governance of organizations is also a process by which nonprofits are managed, whether they are an all-volunteer or paid staff. The processes by which organizations are structured and managed have significant impact upon employees, shareholders, boards of directors, customers, lenders, and management. In cases of large corporations—such as the Ford Motor Company, an airline, a supermarket chain, or a pharmaceutical company—the decisions made by the company can have a huge impact on the public. When Ford Motor Company laid off thousands of workers in several U.S. plants in 2007, it affected thousands of lives across the country.

For the purposes of the discussion in this book, we can define a corporation as a body formed and authorized by law to act as a unit that has legal rights and responsibilities. While the corporation on its own doesn't make decisions, those in the top levels of the organization can—and do—make decisions, as do their boards of directors.

Key stakeholders in organizations typically fall into the following three categories:

1. *Shareholder*. Shareholders are owners of the corporation. The Green Bay Packers organization, the smallest NFL franchise, is owned by slightly more than 100,000 stockholders (who have over 4 million shares of stock).

2. *Board of directors*. Members of a board of directors can be elected by the shareholders to represent their interests in corporations. In some cases, the person who directs the board has operational responsibilities, such as the CEO (chief executive officer) or CFO (chief financial officer) or an executive director or another officer. These are referred to as "inside directors." In the case of nonprofit organizations, very often the executive director would have operational responsibilities as well as board of director responsibilities. On the other hand, an outside director might be someone who is not employed by the organization, and who does not have operational responsibilities. This would be the case for local civic organizations, such as Rotary Clubs, and women's clubs, such as Soroptimists. It should be noted, however, that board and club members in these types of organizations work every bit as hard—or harder—than paid employees.

3. *Management*. Management includes the executives and officers of a corporation who make day-to-day operational decisions, including the CEO and others in administration.

Legislative and Regulatory Processes

It is easy to believe that we, as private citizens, have no role in the development of federal and local legislation, but that is in fact not true. Local bodies, such as chambers of commerce and citizen action groups, school boards, and local city councils, work hard every year to see that things that are important to our communities are proposed to our legislative bodies. The human resource profession can play an important part in the development of legislation and regulation of employment law. The PHR and SPHR exams are based on federal laws that are important to your work in human resources.

The steps below summarize how the federal legislative process develops something into law:

1. A group of individuals, a business, a professional association, or a congressman has an idea for something and proposes it to the House or Senate.

Real World Note:

The Green Bay Packers organization has been a publicly owned, nonprofit corporation since 1923. A total of 4,749,925 shares are owned by 111,921 stockholders—none of whom receive any dividend on the initial investment. The corporation is governed by a board of directors and a seven-member executive committee.

2. A legislator then sends the idea for the bill to the legislative counsel where it is drafted into language.

3. The bill is then studied by the House or the Senate to determine whether it is likely to pass for a first vote. If it is determined not likely to pass, the bill "dies" at the committee.

4. Bills that look as if they will pass are then studied by a subcommittee. During the committee hearing, the author presents the bill and testimony can be heard in support of and in opposition to the bill.

5. Once the bill has been studied, the committee can make changes to the bill. The subcommittee then votes on whether to return the bill to the full committee for further action.

6. This process continues with votes to change the bill or let it die until it makes it to the legislative calendar and is scheduled for a vote by the full body of the House or Senate.

7. There is a period of debate when members can offer concessions and amendments to the bill that will take affect when and if it is passed.

8. Finally, a vote is conducted.

9. If the full body passes the bill, it must then go to the other body—from the House to the Senate or vice versa—and the process begins again. The bill can be accepted as is and voted to pass as presented. Or it can be tabled or voted down. Bills rejected at this stage are considered dead and will not become law.

10. If the bill passes the second body, but there are major differences that need to be resolved, it goes to another committee to reconcile the differences. If the committee cannot agree to the changes, again, the bill dies and will not become law. If the committee does agree to incorporate changes, both houses of Congress must vote to approve the committee report before it is forwarded to the president for signature.

11. When the president receives the bill, the president has three choices: sign it into law, veto it, or fail to sign it. If the bill is vetoed, Congress may override the veto by a two-thirds vote in each house, in which case the bill passes despite the president's veto. If the president does not sign the bill when Congress is in session, and the bill remains unsigned for ten days, it will become law without the president's signature.

CHAPTER SUMMARY

Strategic human resource management (SHRM) is the process by which you plan, align, process, and implement the goals in an organization. By planning strategically and setting appropriate goals, you help an organization make effective decisions. Strategic planning, strategic analysis (including environmental scans), choosing strategic directions, budgeting, and organizing human capital are all essential elements of SHRM.

REVIEW QUESTIONS

1. During the legislative process, if the president fails to sign a bill, what happens?

2. If you are conducting an environmental scan of your organization, and you are looking at an external assessment of the situation, what are you likely to include in your scan?

3. Fawn works on a community college campus. She has just had her annual performance review. Her supervisor has suggested that Fawn work on improving her written communication skills for the following year. What are some goals she could set that would use the SMART formula?

4. What does the acronym GAAP stand for?

5. What makes up the strategic human resource management (SHRM) process?

6. If an employee has taken the MBTI, and her results were: ESTJ, what does this result mean?

7. You aren't a career counselor, but HR professionals are regularly asked for career advice. Now that an employee has taken the MBTI, and knows that her results were ESTJ, she's asked you if there might be a career path better suited for her, rather than being "stuck" in the payroll office crunching numbers. What would you suggest?

8. What is a vision statement?

9. What does span of control refer to?

10. What is a zero-based budget?

ANSWERS TO REVIEW QUESTIONS

1. During the legislative process, if a bill is not signed by the president, a ten-day waiting period ensues, in which the bill automatically becomes law despite not having the president's signature. If Congress adjourns before the ten-day period is up, the bill will not become law.

2. When doing an environmental scan, you would use both SWOT analysis and a STEP analysis of what is affecting the organization. That is, you will analyze the social, technological, economic, and political environments in an environment scan. You will also use strengths, weaknesses, opportunities, and threats to an organization during the strategic planning process. Note the STEP analysis is also used as part of the internal scan.

3. Specific—emailing her correspondence to her supervisor and enroll in a communications class.

    Measurable—she'll be getting feedback daily from her supervisor as well as in the classroom by way of a specific grade that she needs to achieve to be reimbursed.

    Attainable—we can assume that Fawn's desire to enroll in classes, and her supervisor's trust in her, make the goal attainable to her.

    Relevant—the goal that she has set is timely to her work on a daily basis and shows her desire to improve her skills immediately during the spring semester.

    Time based—she has set a specific time frame, spring semester, for her goal.

4. GAAP stands for generally accepted accounting principles.

5. The SHRM function includes planning, aligning, processing, and implementing the goals in an organization. It is part of the strategic management function for an HR professional.

6. ESTJ means Extroverted, Sensing, Thinking, and Judging.

7. While it is tempting to give professional advice, such as seeking out other opportunities to explore her extroverted side, or to encourage her to stay put because you need her in the payroll department, the most correct answer is for the HR professional to encourage the employee to explore her options with a career counselor.

8. A vision statement is a brief written description that should inspire, and should communicate the goals of the organization and whom it serves. It is forward focused. A mission statement describes the company, its unique characteristics, and its purpose.

9. Span of control refers to the number of people that directly report to a manager.

10. A zero-based budget occurs when you are starting from scratch and determining what you need to achieve your goals.

Workforce Planning 4

WORKFORCE PLANNING AND EMPLOYMENT

In chapter 3, we discussed the strategic planning process and how leaders implement organizational goals and objectives in order to be competitive in today's marketplace. Part of that strategic planning process was doing an environmental scan—both internal and external—of your organization to see what resources you possess and what capital you need to invest in. The chief goal of a human resource planner, relative to strategic workforce planning, is to make sure you have qualified employees who can help to achieve organizational goals. Workforce planning is based on the following:

- Organizational goals and how they relate to current and future staffing needs
- Job analysis of incumbent workers
- The current labor market, training of potential external job candidates

STAFFING ALTERNATIVES

It is a challenging time to be entering into the world of workforce planning. We have a conflux of baby boomers nearing retirement age, yet reluctant to retire. Not only are they livng longer, their retirement nest eggs are often not what they hoped they would be. The Generation Yers, who grew up thinking that the Internet, cell phones, and cable television were the norm, are now the dominant workforce. They are eager for the big paychecks and don't mind changing jobs often.

The "millennials" have surprising attitudes. They believe that nine-to-five jobs interfere with their personal time. They'd like to be able to get the job done whenever, and wherever, they want to. Using a blackberry, cell phone, and a laptop from the park is okay with them, so it should be okay with you, too.

So what is a staffing planner to do? Probably look at alternative staffing methods and a way to please each group of individuals and still meet the demands and objectives of the organization. In other words, be flexible.

Before you embark on your recruiting search for new employees, it is going to be important for you to analyze what you have done in the past and how it's working for you. You'll also need to review your employee demographics and the surrounding community to see if your company reflects the diversity that you wish it to reflect. And, finally, you want to do a thorough job of researching the local and national labor market trends. Only after you have done these things should you try to find qualified candidates for the positions that you seek to fill.

EMPLOYER MARKETING AND BRANDING

Most people are familiar with what a brand is; Tide, Maybelline, Chevrolet, and Kleenex are some examples. And if you have studied marketing at all, you also might know a bit about branding strategies and development. But it sounds a little more complicated when you discuss your business as a brand. Employer branding could be defined, for example, as the image of the organization as a great place to work, in the minds of current employees and other stakeholders in the external market. Developing your branding image and identity is important if you want to communicate with someone about who you are—what your values are and why someone would want to work there, buy there, spend time there.

For example, a church wanting to communicate who it is to its congregation and to potential members made its brand as "the place for all people." The church then defined its core values as being: Welcome, A Place for Dirty Hands, A Place for the Cross, A Place for Story, and A Place for Worship. When you enter this church, you are pretty certain to feel its core brand and values. Have you defined your brand?

Developing your brand and core values is an important recruiting tool. Are there certain companies in your geographic area that when you mention them, people immediately say: "Oh, that's a great company to work for!" Or, in the words of an employee of Genentech, in a *Fortune* magazine article about the best employers to work for: "Wild horses could not drag me away!" That's the company that you want to be! In the Pacific Northwest, it is Microsoft in Seattle and Qualcomm in San Diego. In the Midwest, it is S.C. Johnson, located in Racine, Wisconsin, or Smuckers in Ohio. In the Northeast, favorite companies are Wegman's Supermarket and Ernst & Young, both based in New York. And, some Southern favorite companies include First Horizon National located in Memphis and Children's Health Network in Atlanta. (Source: *Fortune* magazine's 100 Best Companies to Work for in 2007, money.cnn.com/magazines/fortune/bestcompanies/2007/full_list/index.html)

RECRUITMENT SOURCES AND STRATEGIES

Employees are the backbone of the company, so it is imperative that thoughtful consideration be given to the recruitment process. In recent years, thanks to the Internet, recruiting has become considerably different than it used to be.

It can be a blessing and a curse, depending on how you look at the process. On one hand, using the Internet to recruit for employees opens up the opportunity to look at candidates you never would have known about had you just recruited by placing an ad in the local newspaper or through word of mouth, as you might have in the past. Craigslist is one of the hottest internet sites around in 2008. One small non-profit hiring for a communications specialist received 200 applications. On the other hand, using the Internet to recruit can elicit hundreds or thousands of applicants and leave HR staff scrambling to sort out the most appropriate candidates. As an HR manager, you must carefully examine the way you are going to recruit new candidates to your firm, the staff you have to process the applications and interview the applicants, and the recruitment tools you have at your disposal that fall within your budget. Recruiting can be a costly process depending on the position you are seeking to fill.

INTERNAL ASSESSMENT TECHNIQUES

Employers have a number of alternatives for achieving their organizational staffing needs and goals. You can look outside the company for fresh new faces, you can transfer people within the organization or promote the workers already trained in your philosophy, or you can look to alternative staffing methods—like outsourcing or hiring independent contract workers, which has long been popular in the medical field for hiring medical transcriptionists or paralegals in the legal field.

There are a number of ways to go about recruiting candidates for open positions, and one way is called sourcing. *Sourcing* is the process of building a list of potential candidates for the position based upon word-of-mouth, traditional advertising (think newspapers or local websites), and people who you know in the community and are respected in your industry.

Internal Hiring and Workforce Assessment

Of course, your employees are hoping that you are going to look to the incumbent workforce first when you are looking to fulfill your workforce needs. They are already there, they know the company, they have been trained, so what's the problem? Let's first talk about the advantages. No outside recruitment is necessary, which is the first benefit. It sends a message across the organization that you believe employees are valuable and you will reward their contributions. This offers the opportunity to improve employee morale—at certain levels.

But what about the downside? And what are the challenges? Well, let's say three workers at the pharmaceutical plant applied for the new supervisor position. You decide to hire from within. Martin, Kiwi, and RaSonda all work on the line, and they all decide to try for the new supervisory position. Martin has been with the company for 15 years, so he believes he deserves it. RaSonda consistently has the highest production figures, so she feels she deserves it. Yet Kiwi, fresh out of college—only one year with the company—feels she deserves it because she has training in managerial skills. You can sense the recipe for disaster here. One person is going to feel empowered with their new job, yet two might be disgruntled that they didn't get the position and find it difficult to work with their new supervisor. Perhaps in this scenario hiring from outside would be the best solution.

When several people are competing for a position, it can cause a lot of political posturing to ensue and cause even more internal conflict than it would if you hired from outside of the organization. However, let's assume that you are still considering hiring from within. What are the implications for managers?

Promotion and transfer decisions should directly reflect the person's ability to do the job, just as if it were an external hiring decision. As with new employees, you should carefully measure the person's skills and treat them as you would an external hire. Yes, you should even interview the employee. It could also be an opportunity to more closely match an incumbent worker's job fit with the new job. Perhaps an employee has outgrown her current position and is ready for a new challenge that's a better match for the new skills she has learned. You might want to have internal candidates take a skills inventory that measures their knowledge, skills, training, experience, and continuing education that they have participated in. Many companies are making skills inventories a regular part of their Human Resource Information System (HRIS) process. As employees participate in continuing education or training, they can easily add those new skills to their online résumé, and when you are looking to fill a position, you can readily identify the candidates who have upgraded their skills and are now potential candidates.

The following example demonstrates how this might work for you. Let's say Jamie was hired three years previously as an administrative assistant in the Parks and Recreation Department at City Hall. Thanks to an encouraging supervisor, Jamie has diligently been adding a lot of continuing education credits and training over the past three years. She enrolled at the local community college and has taken marketing classes at night. And on company time, with her supervisor's approval, she has learned both PowerPoint and Microsoft Access software to improve her presentation skills. City Hall is a large working environment. As an HR director, you might not know this about Jamie just by passing her in the hallway. But with a coordinated HRIS, you could easily pick Jamie out as a potential candidate for a marketing position that has just opened up, if she added her training to her online resume.

It is important when you are using the internal recruiting method that you do so by a fair and impartial process. The first step in the process is job posting. Almost all companies today have an intranet process for job posting where everyone can view the new and open jobs on the company website. If your company is too small for that, the old-fashioned posting of the position to the bulletin board will do, too.

On the job posting, you will list all of the relevant information related to the position. Obviously, the job title and a brief description of the tasks and responsibilities are first and foremost; the salary range, the position ranking, the dates for the job opening, and the application procedures should also be noted.

It is worth mentioning a couple of points about position rank and the job opening dates. In many companies, there are multiple levels of similar types of positions. One example of this might be administrative assistants who start with a company at a Level 1 and peak at a Level 4. Rewarding internal candidates who have been successful at their jobs and have improved their skills would be an excellent way to promote employee morale and reward improvement. When there is keen competition for moving up the ranks with these types of positions, you will want to be very careful that you have a long enough period of time for applicants to apply and make sure you adhere to closing dates posted on the job opening so as to remain fair and impartial.

External Hiring

Once you have decided that the most appropriate way to fill your new positions, or position replacements, is to use external sources for hiring, there are multiple ways to advertise the position openings. Your next job is to figure out which ones are going to give you the best bang for your buck. Largely, this is going to depend upon the type of position that is open. Finding a new college president is going to be an entirely different process than filling a faculty opening at the college. It would also be a very different process for filling an opening for a dean at the college versus a marketing professional or a vice president's executive assistant. Again, it will be important to examine what has worked in the past and what might work better this time, given newer and faster technology to get the word out.

Speaking of newer and faster technology, it is also pertinent to point out that as you are starting to recruit externally, you should be putting your best face forward to potential candidates. Today, most candidates for professional positions *expect* to have a seamless, streamlined online application process. They expect downloadable applications that they can fill in using Microsoft Word and electronically return to you. The first source they choose to study to research your company is your website. If you are not a technology-savvy firm, you might want to begin researching this for the future, even if it is not possible before this next hire.

Here are some of the common external hiring methods:

- *Word of mouth.* Monster.com still points to the fact that the number one way to get your foot in the door at a company is by networking. It's who you know and who told you about a position. One can never discount the impact of your current employees telling friends, colleagues, and community members about a position opening at your company. And many companies reward employees for employee referrals. This might work at your organization.
- *Media.* Newspaper advertising used to be virtually the only way to get information out about job openings, and people regularly read the

classified ads. As regular print newspapers take a backseat to alternative media, it is important to examine other media options. In some cases, radio ads are one way to advertise, and they are certainly a cost-effective way to get the word out to a large number of people in a short amount of time. However, print advertising can still be the way to go in small towns and for certain position types.

- *Internet recruiting*. Internet hiring took off in the late 1990s with the advent of Monster.com and similar sites. It is worth a cautionary remark to state that you should choose the site carefully. Make sure it is a reputable site with the demographic that you wish to reach. For obvious reasons, it is a good bet for advertising sales and advertising positions. It is also a good choice for recruiting for high-level positions on a national level. The *Wall Street Journal* and the *Chronicle of Higher Education*, for instance, have their own very well-organized sites for posting and seeking jobs. For smaller employers, large volumes of applications could be difficult to manage and sort through. You need to ask yourself if you are prepared for this type of response.

- *Your own website*. Many large employers have their own websites where they regularly list job openings. This is great for potential employees who follow your company closely and wish to work there at some point. Starbucks, Microsoft, Amazon.com, and Google—all coincidentally Seattle-based companies—are known for having started this trend. Many employers have followed suit. These companies have invested in specialized recruiting software that allows applicants to enter information into databases that sort their information for key words, easing the sorting process for identifying potential qualified applicants.

- *Professional organizations*. As an HR professional, you know the value of joining a professional organization. Those are go-to places when doing external recruiting for specialized positions—HR is one of them. In addition, professional conferences are good places to recruit the best of the best candidates who might be looking for new positions.

- *Job fairs*. In one community, the opening of a new, upscale shopping center saw six retail stores opening shortly before the Christmas season. In a wise move, they joined forces, rather than competing for applicants, and held a job fair at a local community college. In that way, potential employees were able to examine each of the six stores, find a fit, and apply for multiple jobs at one convenient site. A win-win for all involved. The job fair format gives employers a chance to meet many applicants during a short window of time. Job fairs are also popular on college campuses shortly before graduation, where students can meet a wide number of employers interested in freshly minted graduates.

- *Colleges and universities*. If you are in close proximity to a local college or university, you would be wise to consider this as a potential recruiting source for your company, if possible. Many employers have designated recruiters that go to colleges on a regular basis to interview applicants and advertise the benefits of the company. Cutco, the maker of fine-quality kitchen knives, has been using college students as salespeople for years now. Many work summers for their entire four years and learn valuable skills in marketing, sales, accounting, and professionalism. Several college painting companies do this as well. Colleges are a good source for entry-level hires in marketing, accounting, finance, para-education, and nursing.

- *Suppliers or vendors*. If your organization uses a number of vendors and suppliers, they might be a good source to turn to when hiring for an open position. Your beer distributor might just be your next best salesperson, and he is already familiar with your company. When you already have a long-term, first-name basis relationship with someone who you know and can trust, it might be an easy recruitment process.

- *Previous contacts*. The old saying "never burn your bridges" applies here. Sometimes individuals who have previously worked for your organization, but left in good standing, are potential hires. They may have had to make a move for various reasons, may have gained new skills, and might be interested in coming back, if the relationship was satisfactory for both parties. In addition, you might remember an applicant who wasn't exactly the right fit for a different position that you interviewed her for, but she left a positive enough impression that you could see her in this new role you are filling. (That happened to this author!)

- *Employment agencies*. Most states have employment agencies that offer free services to job seekers and allow free posting of jobs. Hotels looking for entry-level workers and seasonal staff, or employers seeking to fill large numbers of positions at once might find this an attractive option. Job seekers often benefit from the job counseling and training options and résumé assistance. There is typically no charge for listing jobs with these agencies, who then screen applicants for you.

SELECTION TESTS, TOOLS, AND METHODS

Depending on your industry, you may or may not rely on sophisticated hiring tools and methods. Your company may just require an application, a résumé and a cover letter, and one or two interviews. For others, however, tests and tools are the norm. For some positions, for example, a typing test may be required or some other performance-based task to determine job/person fit. Other organizations have assessment centers (or at least mini-departments or individuals within HR) that measure problem-solving skills, managerial potential, language skills, or team-building skills in potential applicants. The most important thing for you to understand in leading a hiring team is that you must choose tests that are *valid predictors* for success on the job and that are directly related to the job tasks you are hiring for. If someone was to challenge you, could you successfully defend the use of this test for hiring for this position? Are you giving math tests to someone who rarely does math on the job? Are you giving writing tests to laborers who do not have to write as part of their position? If you are, you shouldn't be. Those are the questions to ask yourself.

Screening Tools

The primary candidate selection tools used today are the employment application, the résumé, and the cover letter. There are reams and reams of information out there about résumés and cover letters; indeed, entire websites and hundreds of books are devoted to each topic. Yet still many of us are confounded by the "one right way" to format a résumé and a cover letter. The truth is that as many people as you ask about résumés, the same number of opinions you will get on the topic. What you need to develop is a process by which your hiring managers can quickly sort through job applications and résumés to develop a viable pool of candidates to bring to the interview.

Résumés and Cover Letters

If résumés and cover letters are the primary tools for application to your organization, you will want to develop a process by which they are collected efficiently, sorted effectively, and screened into a small pool of potential candidates. Many companies are purchasing software that allows applications to be sorted by key words in résumés and cover letters. In other companies, it is still done the old-fashioned way—by a relatively subjective process of comparing apples to oranges—because of the lack of uniformity in résumé style and format. We all know that applicants portray themselves in the best possible light. For legal purposes, therefore, it is wise to have applicants also complete an employment application where they all have to answer the same questions.

In screening applications, it is important to have some general characteristics to help you quickly weed out some applications and résumés. Here are a few suggestions:

- *More than the spell-checker*. The English teacher in this author would be remiss if she didn't point out that the first characteristic of a résumé, cover letter, and application ought to be that they have been properly proofread, spell-checked, grammar-checked, and carefully scrutinized for writing fluidity. A candidate who doesn't take these items seriously should not be considered a professional or someone who cares enough to take time with the application process. You might decide that one or two small proofreading problems are no big deal, but major errors should eliminate the candidate from the pool.

- *Accuracy*. Does the flow of information make sense? Are there a lot of gaps in work history? Does the flow of employment history seem logical? For instance, George Petersen has applied for a job as director of your information technology division. He was employed from 1978–1986, but there is no work history from 1987–1992. He has not attempted to make any notations about where he was during that time period (maybe he was in college receiving further training, for instance). Based on this gap in his résumé, George should probably not be considered for the position.

- *Presentation of work history*. Is the work experience presented on the résumé a good match for the position? Are the candidate's skills closely aligned with the job description? Or are skills presented really a "reach"? For example, Ann Snow has applied for a marketing coordinator position at your local chamber of commerce. Her résumé describes a history that has predominantly been working as a secretarial aide, in data entry, or as an administrative assistant. She's probably not ready for that next step into marketing yet, especially if she hasn't experienced the creative, production, and networking components of a marketing job.

- *Length of résumés and cover letters.* Is the résumé overly short? Or excessively long? What about the cover letter. A general rule of thumb is a one-page cover letter and one- to two-page résumé, although you will get many varying opinions on this topic. Academic vitae are usually considerably longer, as is the letter, sometimes each are as long as 5 pages. The cover letter should be specific and to the point, giving you a general feeling for the applicant's communication style and the reasons that you should interview him for the job.

Employment Applications

Employment applications are valid screening tools endorsed by the Equal Employment Opportunity Commission (EEOC). Therefore, they must request information that is directly related to the job advertised. Questions asked must be pertinent to the job and predictors of successful job performance. Applications are important because they are signed by the applicant, who is attesting to the fact that everything he has disclosed on the application is true and accurate.

You may choose one of several types of employment applications. Some are short forms that ask the applicant to fill in just work history and perhaps one or two references. These are useful for jobs with minimal experience required. Longer-form applications ask for longer work histories, education information, training experience, and other related skills. Job-specific employment applications are just that—the form is based on the profession. An architect would be asked for a portfolio, specific projects completed, and references related to the projects. Teachers are usually asked about such things as specific courses taught and curriculum developed.

Preemployment Tests

Preemployment tests have become increasingly popular and are a virtual industry on the Internet. Companies promise all sorts of results in screening out undesirable candidates. There are a number of popular types of tests used in hiring briefly outlined here:

- *Personality tests.* The most popular test of them all is the personality test. It is used to determine a person's psychological profile and whether she is a suitable fit for the job. Often, employers use these tests when looking for managerial types with a gung ho attitude, or for salespeople who are required to be on most of the time. The most popular of these tests is the Myers-Briggs Type Indicator. A similar version is the Kiersey Temperament Sorter (available online in an abbreviated version). Some of these tests can be expensive to administer and score on a company site. If it is a test that is regularly given, employers may opt to have their own staff receive the training to score and interpret the results.
- *Knowledge or proficiency tests.* These tests (also called aptitude tests) are designed to measure an applicant's ability to perform specific job-related tasks, such as typing, language and word usage, and problem solving. One could also classify as an aptitude test having teachers teach a sample class in a job interview (a popular screening method).

- *Honesty/integrity tests*. Although they sound easy to develop, these tests are relatively difficult to measure. They measure an employee's attitude toward such things theft as (is it a theft to steal Post-it Notes, for example?), coming in late to work, taking too long a lunch hour, or squealing on a fellow employee. They also measure attitudes toward drugs and alcohol.
- *Physical ability tests*. An applicant may be asked to demonstrate strength and/or flexibility, if the job demands it.
- *Drug/medical tests*. An applicant may be asked to see a doctor to assess his physical fitness or may be asked for a urine sample to test for drugs in the system.
- *Background checks*. An applicant's driving record, criminal history (in particular, sexual offender history if the applicant is going to work with minor children), or credit history may be checked.

RELIABILITY AND VALIDITY

This section shouldn't attempt to replace a good course in statistical research, but any HR professional who is administering testing as part of the hiring process should become familiar with some important statistical terminology and understand that these criteria are important because of legal requirements.

Reliability

Reliability is the degree to which interviews, tests, and other selection criteria yield similar results over time. For example, unless the interview or test judges the capabilities of a group of applicants the same today as it did last week, the instrument is not reliable. Similarly, a test that yields widely different scores when administered to the same person over a few days is also judged as unreliable.

Validity

Validity is the statistical measure that refers to what a test or selection procedure measures, such as typing ability, and how well it measures it. What is particularly important in personnel selection, however, is that you are measuring something directly related to job performance. You cannot, for instance, routinely give math, writing, typing, and problem-solving tests to all secretarial applicants if all of those items are not directly related to their job. You might, however, give those same applicants a test on listening skills and transcription and on how well they take phone messages.

Criterion-related validity measures how significantly a selection tool correlates with the most relevant job tasks. Performance on a test is compared with actual tasks on the job analysis—using applied mathematics skills, writing skills, or teamwork skills are some examples.

Predictive validity compares a test score given when an employee is first hired with a later test given after the employee has had some training and experience. It should not be used as a punitive measure, but as a tool for learning how the employee has improved. For example: Stella was hired as an entry-level accountant. During her interview, she was given an applied math test, on which she performed adequately enough to be hired. After six months on the job, Stella gained a lot of real-world experience, training, and mentoring from colleagues. When the test was administered again, she scored 100 percent.

Concurrent validity measures a test (criterion measurement) at the same time as the test is given, rather than at a later point as with the predictive test. Stella's applied math test, given at the point of hire, measured that she would perform adequately on the job and with training would likely improve her skill level.

Uniform Guidelines for Selection Methods

The Uniform Guidelines on Employee Selection Procedures were designed with the idea in mind to create a set of standards by which employers could hire in a fair and nondiscriminatory manner. According to the published standards: "These guidelines incorporate a single set of principles which are designed to assist employers, labor organizations, employment agencies, and licensing and certification boards to comply with requirements of Federal law prohibiting employment practices which discriminate on grounds of race, color, religion, sex, and national origin." These standards are available online at www.uniformguidelines.com/uniformguidelines.html#1.

In addition: "These guidelines apply to tests and other selection procedures which are used as a basis for any employment decision. Employment decisions include but are not limited to hiring, promotion, demotion, membership (for example, in a labor organization), referral, retention, and licensing and certification, to the extent that licensing and certification may be covered by Federal equal employment opportunity law."

HR professionals should take particular note that it is mandatory by federal law to keep employment records according to hiring practices. These records are to be organized by sex, race, and ethnic group as dictated by the EEOC: African Americans, American Indians (including Alaskan Natives), Asians (including Pacific Islanders), Hispanic (including persons of Mexican, Puerto Rican, Cuban, Central or South American, or other Spanish origin or culture regardless of race), whites (Caucasians) other than Hispanic, and totals.

These laws were put into place to ensure that unfair hiring practices, referred to as adverse impact, did not occur in the workplace. *Adverse impact* occurs when the selection rate for a protected class is less than four-fifths, or 80 percent, of the selection rate for the group with the highest selection rate.

Real World Note:

In 2005, The Boeing Company settled and won part, but not all, of a federal lawsuit alleging it discriminated against African American employees in its hiring practices. The courts determined that although unintentional, The Boeing Company's policies were under scrutiny for not being as meticulous as they could have been in hiring. Boeing went on record stating that they thought their promotion policies were fair and nondiscriminatory, and encouraged employees to continue to come forward with any concerns.

INTERVIEWING

There is no greater way to strike fear in your heart than to walk into a job interview. Often, it is one lowly candidate and a room full of strangers ready to put her on the hot seat. If you are currently in HR, you likely enjoy this process to some extent—assembling the puzzle of who fits best with what job—and have done quite a bit of interviewing already. However, it is worth noting that job interviews are stressful for interviewers and candidates alike. As the HR professional, you have a short amount of time to find that right candidate for the open position at your company. Your company goals and production likely depend on it. It is your job to make sure you and your hiring managers present an interview environment that portrays your company in a good light and to choose the right type of interview for the job that you are filling.

Typically, a hiring team meets prior to the interview to develop a set of questions that should be asked in the interview. They may also elect to have other items included, such as a real-world scenario role play, a presentation by the candidate, or an in-box test to assess the candidate's ability to think on his feet. There are several types of interviews that you might select, not all appropriate for every situation. There are tools on the Web that can assist you in developing great interview questions and also great tools for applicants to practice their skills prior to the interview. Monster.com has a virtual interview that is useful for employers and applicants alike if you are relatively inexperienced or uncomfortable in developing questions. Below are some interview styles:

- *Behavioral interviews.* The best predictor of future behavior is past performance. Behavioral interviews give applicants a chance to demonstrate how they attacked a problem in their professional life and to tell what steps they used to solve the issue and how successful they were in resolving it. A question might be: "Tell us about a time when you had a conflict within your work unit and what you did to resolve it?"
- *Directive interviews.* In this style of interview, the interviewer has a clear agenda that is followed. Sometimes companies use this rigid format to ensure equality between interviews. By asking each candidate the same series of questions, they can more readily compare the results.
- *Group interviews.* Group interviews allow employers to see how you interact with your peers and what your personality is in relation to others. Disney used to be famous for using this approach when interviewing college students and looking for outgoing personalities to work at their theme parks during summer breaks.
- *Nondirective interviews.* This is a more meandering approach to interviewing and tends to be used by inexperienced interviewers. Candidates are asked broad questions that let them lead the discussion. It is difficult to compare candidates when using this approach.
- *Panel interviews.* This approach allows for several interviewers to interview the candidate at the same time. Colleges and universities often use panel interviews when interviewing administrators; however, more than five on a panel is overkill and can intimidate the candidate.

- *Screening interviews.* Companies use screening tools, such as phone interviews, to ensure that candidates meet minimum qualification requirements. Screening interviewers often have honed skills to determine whether there is anything that might disqualify an applicant from the position. Remember: you do not need to know whether an applicant is the best fit for the position, only whether the applicant is not a match.

- *Hypothetical interviews.* An example might be the following: "You are the last waitress on the evening shift, and it is five minutes before closing. The restaurant is set for the next day's lunch service, and you are ready to call it a night. Two people enter the restaurant wanting a late dinner. What would you do in this situation?"

- *Stress interviews.* In some positions, stress is a regular part of the job. The stress interview intentionally creates and promotes discomfort. The interviewer may have an abrupt or brash attitude. Alternately, the interviewer may stare, be silent, and spend time taking notes. The purpose of this type of interview is to test the candidate's ability to be assertive and handle difficult situations.

- *Structured interviews.* This approach allows the employer to prepare questions in advance to use for all candidates. This method would work when you want a candidate to be able to reflect on some more complex issues that the company is facing and even write down some of the answers before they get to the interview.

In recent years, employers have become more cognizant of the fact that there are certain questions that you can and cannot ask during interviews, lest you appear to discriminate against a potential employee. Gone are the days when you could ask seemingly innocuous questions about family, age, religion, and residency. You will want to carefully scrutinize the questions that your management and hiring team develop for appearance of bias or discrimination. Some sample questions that you cannot ask appear in table 4.1.

Table 4.1 Sample Interview Questions

Interview Questions that You Cannot Ask	Why You Can't Ask It	What Are You Really Asking with This Question?
Do you have a family?	You could appear to discriminate against people with children that might have to spend too much time away from the office. Or conversely, if you ask this of a childless person—and you are a family-centered work environment—you could appear to discriminate against the childless.	If you are really just interested in the candidate on a friendly basis, you'll most likely find out about them when you ask them: "Tell me about yourself." If your question really stemmed from work-life issues and availability, ask a question about the ability to work nights or weekends.

(continued on next page)

How old are you?	You may not discriminate against workers over 40. Only airline pilots are not able to fly over age 70. You *may* ask if the candidate is over the age of 18?	Are you worried that that person can't do the physical work involved in this position? Ask a question related to the physical work instead.
Do you have any disabilities?	You could appear to discriminate against people with disabilities—particularly those that might not be readily apparent, such as mental illness.	If you are interested in their capability to do the work as presented, you may ask: "After reviewing the job description, are you able to perform the essential functions of this job?"
Do you have any religious beliefs that would prevent you from working weekends?	You could appear to discriminate against a certain religious group.	You may ask if the person can work on weekends. If you find that a religious belief does conflict with the work schedule, you should try to find a way to accommodate their religion.

RELOCATION

After you have chosen to hire a new candidate, there may be some additional work necessary to ensure that candidate has a successful transition to the new workplace. Perhaps the best candidate was someone from Pittsburgh, and your home office is in San Diego. Likely, this candidate is going to want some type of compensation for relocating to a new city. Some companies are very generous with relocation offers and practices. In other cases, relocation can be negotiable. Some relocations can be very complicated to manage for the HR office, such as in the case of relocating an entire family to another country. There are a variety of elements that your HR department might want to consider, because this is still part of the recruitment process—you don't want a deal breaker here! Some companies even offer a paid trip for the spouse and/or family to see the area and look for a new home or visit schools; others, such as Frito Lay, even assist with the selling of a candidate's house and purchase of a new one. Payment of moving expenses can be quite costly, especially in a cross-country move, and might be a big negotiating factor for a high-level employee, such as a new vice president.

Some companies choose to outsource this process to a professional group that deals with relocations. This author had the benefit of using one when moving from Wisconsin to Seattle, and it was a godsend. They even sent a packet of information with all the right phone numbers to call for hook up of cable and phone services, garbage pickup, electric services, and the like. I saved a lot of time by not having to research those items myself. As a recruitment and retention tool, your company will want to carefully examine what you can offer potential candidates.

TOTAL REWARDS, RECRUITMENT, AND RETENTION

Total rewards is a buzz phrase for what essentially means all of the tools available to the employer that may be used to attract, motivate, and retain employees. Total rewards include everything the employee perceives to be of value resulting from the employment relationship. Obviously, this is going to vary considerably from individual to individual. It will also depend upon the level of experience and skill of the position you are filling. To a young new mother, child care might be the perk that she is seeking—if your company has it, you are certainly going to highlight this. For someone who has a long commute, flex time or credits for ride sharing might be an appropriate perk that you would highlight in your recruitment phase.

Retention of employees is your obvious goal as an HR professional. You've gone through a lot of work recruiting the new staff member, writing accurate job descriptions, coming up with an appropriate compensation plan and benefits package, and finding the right person/job fit. You want to keep the new employee there!

NEGOTIATION SKILLS AND TECHNIQUES

Negotiation of the employment offer is a two-way street—the HR representative wants to make the best deal on behalf of the employer and to be fair on what the market has to offer, while the employee wants the best offer that meets his personal needs for benefits, family, salary, schedule, and career advancement. Both parties need to be savvy, almost investigative, in learning about what each side is comfortable with.

As a personal example, I remember interviewing for a job as a career counselor with someone who would eventually be my supervisor, and later my vice president. My supervisor let it slip in the interview that they were a few computers short in the department. I keyed in on that. When the HR department called on a Saturday afternoon to make me the offer—which I was very, very interested in—I said I would take it, but only on the condition that there was a computer sitting on my desk when I walked in the first day. I knew, if I didn't mention this, that as the new person, I would likely be the one to wait for the next computer to come in—and it could be months that I would struggle to do my job well. Because I negotiated, there was a computer on my desk when I arrived. I learned later that they took the computer out of a high-tech lab because they wanted me for the position. Negotiation is important to both parties!

One of the goals of the recruitment, hiring, and selection process is not just finding the candidate with the job/person fit, but one who is also going to be able to accept the conditions of employment that you are offering. Much of this can be resolved early on in the recruitment process by giving detailed descriptions of salary range and listing benefits and terms of employment. There is nothing more frustrating then spending months on a job search, weeding it down to one or two candidates, and then suddenly finding a surprise job condition that is a deal breaker. Certainly, you can give room for last-minute negotiations (see the relocation section, for instance, or my computer example above), but you should have a pretty clear idea where you can go with the offers you make.

ORGANIZATIONAL EXIT PROCEDURES

We cannot think of a single executive or manager who likes to terminate an employee. It just is not fun. It is stressful for all parties involved. And in these volatile times when you hear horror stories of people "going postal," it can be very scary. However, your organization needs an organizational exit policy for whatever reason an employee leaves your company. You need this whether employees leave on their own, because they are resigning or retiring, or if you ask them to leave because they are being terminated, downsized, or laid off. The way that you handle an employee's exit from your organization sends a strong message to those who remain in the organization. Coworkers are affected in many different ways when a colleague leaves. For instance, their own workloads could become greater or, in the case of layoffs or firings, they might be fearful for their own jobs.

Voluntary Exits

The HR department is the backbone that makes organizational exits smooth transitions. When employees retire or resign, you are the one that they turn to for guidance. They will need to know such information as what paperwork they need to fill out to start collecting Social Security, when their pension will start to draw, whether they will still have insurance, and how much notice they need to give. These are all questions your division must be able to answer.

When employees resign to take a new position, you have the added responsibility of filling the positions they are leaving. Perhaps a position has needed some tweaking for quite some time—now is the time to figure it out. You might even find yourself deciding to promote or transfer someone into the newly described position (see earlier discussion about internal hiring).

The other way employees might leave your organization is through retirement, which can be an even more stressful time in an employee's life than a resignation. They are leaving something that they have possibly done for 30 or 40 years and moving into a very different time of their life. Not all employees look forward to the golden years of retirement positively. For some, it can be a very scary time. Because of this, many companies have pre-retirement counseling available through their employee assistance program (EAP) and financial counseling available through their retirement programs. Teachers, for example, typically get TIAA-CREF retirement insurance and that company offers a wealth of financial information and advice.

Any way your employees leave the organization, they should be given an exit interview. Sample questions are provided in table 4.2. The exit interview should be a short yet structured process—not a venting session—in which employees are able to share their reasons for leaving the organization and to offer their suggestions for change.

Table 4.2   Sample Exit Interview Questions

Example of an Exit Interview
What is your primary reason for leaving?
What was most satisfying about your job?
What was least satisfying about your job?
Did your job duties turn out to be as you expected?
Did you receive enough training to do your job effectively? (if the person had not been in the job for a very long period of time)
Did you receive adequate support to do your job?
Did you receive adequate feedback regarding your job duties from your supervisor?
Did this company help you to fulfill your career goals?
What would you improve to make our workplace better?
What was the quality of the supervision you received?
Did any company policies or procedures (or any other obstacles) make your job more difficult?
Based upon your experiences, what would you say it takes to be successful at this company?
Did anyone in this company discriminate against you, harass you, or cause hostile working conditions?
Would you consider working for this company again?

Involuntary Exits

Layoffs

The news that a plant is closing or laying off large numbers of workers often sends shivers up our spines. In 2006, Ford Motor Company was one such company that laid off over 25,000 workers in an effort to restructure its failing automotive company. Yet sometimes it is an inevitable part of doing business. The federal government enacted a law in 1988, called the Worker Adjustment and Retraining Notification (WARN) Act, that requires employers with 100 or more full-time workers to give 60-day advance notice in the event of large plant layoffs or closing. The intent was to give those workers adequate time to seek other employment. The various requirements for the WARN Act vary from state to state, so be sure that you know the requirements in your state.

We can expect that Executive Chairman Bill Ford of the Ford Motor Company did not make those decisions lightly in 2006. Thousands of lives were at stake with that decision. A company and its HR representatives must outline the reasons for making these decisions extremely clearly to its employees. In particular, if some of the employees that are being laid off are poor performers, managers should be very certain that they have been documenting this poor performance in performance appraisals prior to the layoff.

Termination

Terminating an employee is difficult enough as it is without also worrying about possible legal issues after the termination takes place. The documenting of any progressive disciplinary issues is crucial to keeping this process from turning into an even larger legal mess. It is important to note that when managers get tripped up on the awkwardness of a termination or try to protect an employee's feelings, they may inadvertently let company policies and legal requirements fall by the wayside.

Progressive discipline is a process for dealing with job-related behavior that does not meet expected and communicated performance standards. The primary purpose for progressive discipline is to assist the employee to understand that a performance problem or opportunity for improvement exists. If, after careful consideration and deliberate documentation of progressive disciplinary processes (see table 4.3), you have determined that just cause warrants termination, you should do it quickly and in a humane manner.

At-will employment is the law that states that either the employee or the employer may terminate the relationship with no liability if there was no express contract for a definite term governing the employment relationship.

Table 4.3   Stages of Progressive Discipline

Disciplinary Stage	Sample Behavior	Action
Verbal Warning	Kelly has repeatedly left her desk to wander around the campus visiting with friends, gossiping, and leaving appointments waiting for her well past appointment times.	Supervisor has verbally warned Kelly that this behavior needs to stop and she should always be at her scheduled appointments on time, not leaving customers waiting for her. Supervisor documents this verbal warning—in written format—in personnel file.
Written Warning	Kelly's performance improves for a time, but then other behaviors replace	Kelly's supervisor writes a memo to Kelly detailing the exact items that are problematic with Kelly's behavior and why, i.e., taking 1½ hour lunches are inappropriate

	the previous behavior—things such as taking late lunch hours, talking on the phone with friends for long periods of time, etc.	because she is not working a full day. Talking on the phone with friends in excess is taking valuable time from her tasks. When possible the supervisor should document dates and times of occurrences. In a meeting, the supervisor presents this memo and Kelly must acknowledge the memo and sign it.
Suspension or Demotion	Ginny has received both a verbal and a written warning for having alcohol on her breath on the job.	Ginny's supervisor should suspend her without pay for one week and order her to seek drug and alcohol counseling or she will be terminated. The supervisor documents this suspension in Ginny's personnel file.
Termination	A colleague has reported that Ginny appears to be under the influence of alcohol on the job.	Supervisor meets with Ginny, who admits that she has been drinking. Supervisor must terminate Ginny immediately.

It is never easy to terminate an employee, but most HR managers can agree on several practices that make the process a little easier. When the employee is informed, it should be in a private setting and done quickly with detailed reasons why this is going to occur. The manager should prepare for the meeting in advance and rehearse how it will be done. If the person is known to have anger management issues or an unstable personality, the manager should take care to have security present or additional staff members close by. The manager might choose to have a representative from HR there as well. A termination meeting should be held in a neutral setting, such as a conference room, and not in a normal work unit where coworkers can see what is happening if the employee loses control of himself. Some additional guidelines are as follows:

- Be brief, matter-of-fact, and come quickly to the point.
- Do not allow the employee to become angry or belligerent. If this happens, stop the meeting immediately and call security.
- Avoid interjecting personal feelings and talking about good and bad behaviors.
- Make sure that you retrieve keys, badges, personal access codes, etc. Do not allow the employee access to computer files or financial statements or any other items that could potentially be destroyed.
- Provide information about severance pay, status of benefits, and coverage.
- Discuss how you will handle inquiries from future employers.

CHAPTER SUMMARY

Workforce planning involves finding the best possible employees to advance an organization's goals. With generational shifts and changes in the economy, workforce planning becomes an even bigger challenge. HR professionals need to look closely at staffing alternatives, brand and core values of an organization, recruitment sources and strategies, and various assessment techniques, screening tools, and interview processes to get the best possible workforce. HR professionals also need to know hiring, retention, and exit procedures to maximize a company's resources.

REVIEW QUESTIONS

1. You are the HR Director for a large firm that creates video games and gaming types of software in a major metropolitan market such as Chicago or Boston. You need to begin sourcing for candidates for two new marketing positions that are opening in the next fiscal year. How would you recruit for this position?

2. You are the hiring manager for a large automobile manufacturing firm seeking to hire new maintenance mechanics. You have advertised the 100 openings at your Birmingham, Alabama, facility. Applications were received by 516 males and 417 females. Thirty-five males were hired and 42 females. Was there any adverse impact in this hiring process?

3. You are the HR manager for a large university. You need to fill vacancies for three adjunct faculty positions. Your supervisor has advised you to use "whatever methods necessary" to hire these three positions out of a pool of 100 applicants. What type of interview methods would you choose?

4. What does "at-will" employment mean?

5. In a job interview, you ask the question: "Can you tell me about the last time that you had to discipline an employee?" This question would be appropriate for what type of interview?

ANSWERS AND EXPLANATIONS

1. Although it is certainly possible that there are internal candidates for this position, and you don't want to discount this, most likely a fresh perspective is probably the best way to fill this position. Young marketing professionals, hip to gaming and the industry, are going to be frequent visitors to sites like monster.com and craigslist.com, enabling you to reach a large number of potential candidates. Job fairs drawing college graduates is also a wise choice for young people with fresh ideas. While advertising in the local newspaper is also a good choice, you also need to ensure the jobs are available online.

2. Adverse impact occurs when the selection rate for the protected class is less than 80 percent of selection rate for the group with the highest selection rate. To calculate whether adverse impact has occurred, you would divide the number of applicants hired by the total number that applied.

3. A screening interview of the top ten candidates, followed by a behavioral interview with the top three candidates, is the best method. By screening the top ten candidates, possibly over the phone, you can immediately weed out the ones who do not work or fit with your university. Then, a second interview—using the behavioral approach—will allow you to see how they approach problems in the classroom. The stress interview is not called for in this approach because classroom teaching is not the "high-stress" type of position that this approach calls for. Nor is the non-directive approach the way to go in this scenario. You want their teaching philosophies, not a meandering conversation.

4. Even if you have neglected to put progressive discipline in place for the work relationship, you may still terminate an employee according to the "at-will" employment law. However, you do set yourself up for potentially being sued for unfair labor practices. C is correct also because the employee also has the ability to terminate the relationship with the employer at will.

5. The correct answer is the behavioral interview. The premise behind the behavioral interview is to assume that past behavior predicts future performance. Asking the applicant how he has disciplined an employee in the past will tell you how he might do so for your company.

Human Resource Development

Human resource development (HRD) is a human resource function housed in an HR department. HRD is a multisystem concept that integrates organizational development (OD) with all of the employees who work in the organization. HRD planning encompasses organizational learning, employee development, training, workforce planning, leadership development, and performance management. It has been suggested that HRD is considered the "soft" side of human resource management (HRM); however, this is a misnomer because HRD impacts an organization's strategic planning goals according to its own vision. Without well-trained employees, nothing can be accomplished.

LAWS AND REGULATIONS

HRD is regarded as a carefully planned *functional* system in the HRM matrix, responsible for complying with federal employment legislation, copyright laws, patent laws, and other legal requirements that directly impact the organizational community. The organization's culture, shared vision, goals and objectives, and strategic planning are impacted by HRD activities. Consideration must be given to federal employment legislation, state laws, and government regulations before any HRD planning can take place. It is a function of HRD to ensure that all activities performed in the organization comply with federal regulations designed to protect workers in employment settings.

To understand how employment decisions are made, federal legislation governing HRD activities must be known. These laws will be discussed more depth in chapter 7. The federal legislation includes the following:

Civil Rights Act (1964)

Civil rights legislation, or Title VII, was created to protect employees under conditions of employment and to safeguard members of protected groups. It prohibits employee discrimination and decisions based on race, color, religion, sex, or national origin. The Civil Rights Act created the enforcement agencies that regulate compliance, the Equal Employment Opportunity Commission (EEOC), and the Office of Federal Contract Compliance Programs (OFCCP).

Exam Note:

For purposes of the exam, there are differences in federal and state laws exist from state to state, and federal law may differ from local government requirements. When laws conflict over the same topic or issue, it is important to understand that the *higher standard* usually applies. In most states, *laws favor the employee.* Sometimes exceptions in the law allow discrimination to take place that is ordinarily prohibited under the law. See "Individual Employment Rights, Issues, and Practices" in chapter 7 for more details on exceptions.

The EEOC is the federal agency responsible for enforcement of Title VII of the Civil Rights Act of 1964. The U.S. Department of Labor (DOL) enforces the provisions of the EEOC. Organizations covered under the EEOC include those that employ more than 15 employees for every workday of 20 or more weeks in a current or preceding calendar year. Inclusion in this category are federal, state, and local governments; public and private educational institutions; employment agencies; labor unions with more than 15 members; and joint labor and management committees formed for apprenticeships and training.

An important feature of the act includes specific record keeping and reporting requirements for all employees. Employment records can be requested by the EEOC or OFCCP. Employers meeting certain qualifications are required to file an annual report to the EEOC by September 30 of each year. Information shared in this report includes specific employment data, such as employment selection practices; benefits planning; race, ethnicity, and gender statistics; disciplinary actions; promotion programs; and attrition and retention figures.

U.S. Department of Labor (DOL)

A federal agency created by Congress in 1913, the DOL serves to protect workers, job applicants, and retirees in the United States. It is the umbrella agency that oversees laws pertaining to workers. Its primary goals are to enforce and improve safe working conditions and to monitor retirement and health benefits, and changes in employment statistics, unemployment, economic indicators, layoffs, new opportunities, and employment discrimination covering wages, salaries, discharge, and unemployment insurance.

Office of Federal Contract Compliance Programs (OFCCP)

The OFCCP is an agency that was created to monitor the activities of federal contractor programs under Executive Order 11246. It mandates that federal contractors holding from $10,000 up to $50,000 in federal contracts must comply under Title VII. Contractors holding more than $50,000 in federal contracts and a minimum of 50 employees are required to develop and implement affirmative action plans. Executive Order 11478 mandates that federal agencies develop and implement affirmative action plans for federal employees. The DOL enforces the provisions of the OFCCP. (See chapter 7 for a broader discussion on these topics.)

Employee Selection

Employee selection is a term commonly used in the search for qualified job applicants. It is an established HRD process implemented through an HR department and facilitated by HR professionals. Job titles associated with the employee selection process include recruiters and employment managers. Employee selection is a *planning* function and requires the organization to research job requirements before interviewing or candidate selection can take place. Selecting the best person for a job is an important HRD function because the selection process impacts the success of the organization at large.

Laws that protect applicants in selection procedures include the following:

- *Uniformed Services Employment and Reemployment Rights Act (USERRA) of 1994.* This act was created to protect and prevent discrimination against all members of the military service and applies to all employers. It does not protect individuals discharged under conditions other than honorable discharge. It is administered and governed by the DOL.

- *Age Discrimination in Employment Act (ADEA) of 1976.* This act prohibits discrimination against any person over 40 years of age. It is an amendment to the Fair Labor Standards Act (FLSA) of 1938 and was amended once again in 1990 by the Older Workers' Benefit Protection Act (OWBPA). The ADEA is administered and governed by the EEOC and covers both public and private employers with 20 or more employees who each work for 20 or more weeks during the current and preceding year. In a union environment, the ADEA is enforced by unions having 25 members or more.

- *Americans with Disabilities Act (ADA) of 1990.* This act is based on the Rehabilitation Act of 1973 and serves to protect qualified workers with disabilities. The act prevents discrimination by providing reasonable accommodations in the workplace to qualified workers. It allows persons with disabilities to participate in company-paid training programs and educational programs and provides accessible facilities to accommodate those in need of special services or training. Further, the ADA requires that adjusting job requirements to fit the needs of the disability must be reasonably accommodated. This is determined by assessing the undue hardship rule for an employer. If the accommodation places an unreasonable or excessive burden on the organization or the employer, an undue hardship exists; therefore, the job may not be reasonably accommodated to fit the needs of the disabled employee.

Common Law

Common law is associated with HRD as a result of unfair labor practices requiring legal decisions by law judges. *Common law doctrines* were written as the result of individual cases adjudicated over centuries and today are an important part of the hiring and selection process. These doctrines are concerned with the employment relationship, from the moment a job applicant is presented with a job description to completing the application process, interviewing, hiring, and providing proper training once an employee joins the organization.

Common law doctrines known to employers include fraudulent misrepresentation, defamation, duty of good faith and fair dealing, employment at will, express or implied contracts, promissory estoppel, respondeat superior, sexual harassment, and constructive discharge. (See chapter 7 for a broader discussion of these doctrines.)

Common law ensures that once a job candidate becomes an employee, the employee will be properly trained by participating in a company-paid or company-sponsored training and development program. The program must be designed to serve, protect, and train employees with the knowledge, skills, and abilities (KSAs) required to perform the job. Further, the job will be performed in a safe environment and where third parties (employees) are not harmed. If improper training exists or no training is offered, and injury to a third party or damage to property can be demonstrated, liability to the employer exists under the law for negligent or no training. The same standard holds true for an organization's performance management system.

Federal Law

Organizational training and development programs are designed to comply with legal requirements discussed earlier in this chapter. Federal legislation governing HRD training activities and written materials associated with training and development publications include the Copyright Act and patents:

- *The Copyright Act (1976).* This act protects professional and original works of its authors; however, two exceptions exist: 1) If an employer hires an employee to create an original company document (e.g., a manual for job training) as part of their job for the company, the employer is named as the owner of the copyright. 2) If a freelance writer, artist, graphic designer, or musician is hired to create a document, the entity that commissioned the work is the owner of the copyright. This is known as a *work-for-hire* exception.
- *Patents.* A patent granted by the U.S. Patent Office allows the inventor exclusive rights to the benefits of a patent for a specified time period. U.S. patent laws are divided into three types:
  1. *Design patents,* which protect new, original, and ornamental designs of manufactured items (limited to 14 years)
  2. *Plant patents,* which protect an invention or discovery of asexually reproduced varieties of plants (limited to 20 years)
  3. *Utility patents,* which protect the invention of new or useful processes by machines, manufacture of or composition of matter, and new or useful improvements to same (limited to 20 years)

ORGANIZATIONAL DEVELOPMENT THEORIES AND APPLICATIONS

Organizational development (OD) is an HRD systems function designed to examine how an organization integrates its employees and management teams to accomplish the goals of the organization. Included in this matrix are human resources, a company's organizational structure, business technology, work processes, and strategic plans. OD defines an organization's *culture* according to how systems, groups, and individuals work together. The culture of an organization is defined by its work environment, leadership style, management groups, employee attitudes, and work motivation. The *climate* of an organization inspires or inhibits employee motivation and performance. OD is derived from a philosophy that motivates employees to perform at peak productivity when organizations consider the needs of their employees.

Job satisfaction surveys have consistently demonstrated that satisfied employees desire work that is challenging, respected, and valued. Studies have shown that if all of these elements are present in a job, employees are less concerned with the amount of money they earn, especially when they feel engaged in the organization's goals and strategic mission. The assumption is made that organizations are in business to make a profit, and OD seeks to create an environment of shared commitment, trust, and values to support this belief.

When dissatisfied employees cause lower levels of achievement and job satisfaction, it is OD's function to identify the problem, diagnose its causes, and seek solutions to resolve the situation. This process is described as an OD intervention. Interventions are designed to gather information about a situation known to be the cause of the problem(s), and its resolution is to remove the obstacle in question. The OD intervention is the solution. An intervention can be defined as a solution to a problem, process, action plan, structure, technological issue, or strategic error. The goal of a strategic intervention is to enact change management through shared knowledge (knowledge management) and create opportunities as a learning organization to resolve the situation through its human capital (employees).

Once the problem/solution has been defined, a strategic OD intervention is implemented through the organization's workforce. The resolution is a change in the organization that will impact the organization's shared values and strategic goals. When OD introduces a strategic change to the organization, it is known as *change management,* or *change management theory.* Change management theory is an OD process that introduces a strategic change in the way a former process was carried out. Similar to homeostasis, an environment that is out of balance with its natural state seeks to regulate the environment in order to maintain its state of balance. When an organization is out of balance because of work-flow problems that surface, it seeks to regain its balance and find solutions to problems to achieve its optimum level of functioning. The process of change management moves the organization forward to remain competitive in the marketplace.

A successful strategic intervention results in greater efficiency and outputs. When the intervention is successful, the organization moves forward again. OD's greatest challenge is to introduce a strategic intervention that the organization's human capital—its employees—will be committed to. In the absence of organizational commitment, the best strategic interventions will fail.

TASK/PROCESS ANALYSIS

While the business of the organization may have its own issues to resolve, OD/HRD strategic interventions are concerned with individuals who work in the organization and how the work is processed through its human capital. Interventions are carefully designed as strategic programs and include affirmative action programs, hiring practices, selection procedures, job satisfaction, performance management, and reward systems.

Two types of OD intervention programs are total quality management (TQM) and techno-structural interventions. Both interventions impact employees and departments at all levels in the organization. Techno-structural interventions analyze how work is conducted in the organization and how employees are involved in the work process. TQM examines all of the resources available to accomplish work tasks. The redesign of work processes, or work flow, is examined by TQM and involves the input and contribution of all employees to analyze work processes and suggest solutions. Quality Circles, Six Sigma, and other high involvement organizations have distinct processes, but are similar interventions, designed to involve employees at all levels in the workforce.

The *quality movement* was started in the 1940s by W. Edwards Deming, who believed that quality is defined by the consumer. Deming, an American, proposed a 14-point plan that focused on management's responsibility to be accountable for work outcomes and internal systems within the organization. Deming's ideas were not well received in America, so he proposed his theories to Japan. Deming was given an opportunity to demonstrate Quality Circles in Japanese organizations, which proved to be highly successful and enthusiastically received. Ironically, Japan was given credit for initiating Quality Circles and introducing them to the American workforce. Deming returned to the United States with his Japanese counterparts, and in the years that followed, Deming and Japanese business leaders were invited to teach American business leaders about the Japanese quality movement and help them to implement Quality Circles in their organizations.

Soon after, Joseph M. Juran supported the principles of the quality movement and proposed, along with Deming's theories, the idea that quality is driven by customer needs and customer satisfaction. If customer needs were identified, a consumer language could be built into the organization's value system to produce quality products and services.

The Juran Trilogy identifies three phases of his model in the quality process:

1. *Quality planning* analyzes quality concerns during the product or service development phase.
2. *Quality control* establishes product and service parameters in the planning and operations phase.
3. *Quality improvements* identify more efficient methods of operation to produce goods and services while reducing waste.

The third early leader and a significant contributor in the quality movement was Dr. Kaoru Ishikawa. He is known for creating the language of analytical tools used to assess work flow and work processes.

Referred to as the *seven tools of quality,* analytical tools were designed and used to demonstrate an organization's work-flow processes and to change them, if needed, to meet the needs of its customers, improve work-flow designs and processes, and remain competitive in the marketplace.

Through the process of statistical analysis derived from analytic principles and physics orientation, and calculations are derived from information gathered from work flow and work processes. Calculations are diagrammed to form a conceptual and visual framework that will be understood by the organization. Following are the seven tools:

1. *Cause and effect diagram* (Ishikawa diagram). A tool designed by Kaoru Ishikawa for analyzing process dispersion, it illustrates the main cause (and subcauses, if known) leading to the effect. It is referred to as a *fishbone chart* because its drawing resembles a fish skeleton.

2. *Check sheet.* This is a data-recording tool designed by the user to visually interpret results of a work flow or process.

3. *Control chart.* This graph compares actual performance with precomputed control data. The performance data consists of groups of measurements in a sequential form of production that seeks to preserve the order. Its purpose is to discover causes of variation in a process versus random variation.

4. *Flowchart.* This graphic planning and control chart is designed to demonstrate relationships between planned performance and actual performance over time. Its purpose is to follow job progress (process) on a graph where one horizontal line represents a time schedule and the other adjacent line represents actual work performance (work flow) of the project.

5. *Histogram.* This graph demonstrates contiguous vertical bars representing a frequency distribution. Groups of items are marked on the *x*-axis, and the number of items in each group is indicated on the *y*-axis. The pictorial nature of a histogram allows visual patterns to be seen that are difficult to define in a table of numbers.

6. *Pareto chart.* A graphic tool for ranking causes from most significant to least significant, this chart is based on the principle that a small percentage of a group accounts for the largest fraction of its impact, or value, otherwise known as the 80/20 principle. In this example, 80 percent of the effects come from 20 percent of possible causes.

7. *Scatter chart.* This graphic technique is used to analyze the relationship between two variables. Two sets of data are plotted on a graph; the *x*-axis is used for the variable to make the prediction, and the *y*-axis is used for the variable that is predicted.

TRAINING AND DEVELOPMENT APPLICATIONS IN HRD

Training and development is an HRD function that seeks to meet the needs of the organization through the training and development of its team members. Each member is trained how to effectively perform her role within the organization and participate in job training programs. Training programs are designed around organizational goals and objectives. A review of training and development programs must first be understood by the behavioral theories that drive training and development processes.

Theories of motivation are briefly mentioned has to support the foundation for the training and development needs of an organization. *Motivation theory* is a psychological construct used in the workplace to train employees to be productive workers. Theories identified below are included to demonstrate how motivation theory is linked to practice in the workplace. (For a broader discussion about motivation theory, see chapter 2). Table 5.1 provides examples of motivation theories and their practical applications in the workplace.

Table 5.1   Linking Motivational Theories and HRD

Theory	HRD Application
Change Process Theory (Lewin)	goal setting, task efficiency
Equity Theory (Adams)	compensation and benefits
ERG Theory (Alderfer)	recognition, employee relations, career development
Expectancy Theory (Vroom)	work effort + performance = reward and values
Hierarchy of Needs Theory (Maslow)	work environment, compensation, benefits, training and development
Job Characteristics Model Theory (Hackman and Oldham)	job analysis, design, enrichment, enlargement
Reinforcement Theory (Skinner)	compensation, incentive, and reward programs
Self-Efficacy/Social Cognitive Theory (SCT) (Bandura)	career development, performance management
Theory of Needs (McClelland)	organizational community, training and development programs
Theory X and Y (McGregor)	employee and labor relations, management practices, organizational culture
Two-Factor Motivation-Hygiene Theory (Herzberg)	job satisfaction, intrinsic and extrinsic rewards

Exam Note:

The ADDIE Model-be familiar with each stage and which order each stage occurs.

Training programs are designed to address short-term needs and technical or immediate needs in the organization. Examples are new hire orientation, on-the-job training (OJT), or computer training. Development programs, comparison, are designed to meet long-term goals for long-range planning, such as a career development programs. The ADDIE model is an instructional method that describes five sequential steps or phases in the training program development process as follows:

- Step 1: *Analysis phase*. Identify problem or situation, gather data, and set target goals for the training program.
- Step 2: *Design phase*. Identify target audience (who will be trained), level of training, and type of training, and establish training objectives.

- Step 3: *Development phase*. Design phase is translated into a presentation model and format; training materials, instructional methods, and how the program will be delivered is decided (e.g., pilot phase, field test, or roll-out program due to time constraints).
- Step 4: *Implementation phase*. Facility and trainers are selected; trainer meetings are scheduled, if program will be a large-scale training program.
- Step 5: *Evaluation phase*. Determine if transfer of training goals has been achieved.

Training and development is an ongoing organizational process designed to teach employees Knowledge Skills Abilities (KSAs) how to remain competitive in the marketplace. *Learning organizations* embody an organization's commitment to train its employees. A learning organization seeks to integrate the organization's talent management with the goals and objectives of the organization. The goal of a learning organization is to share knowledge within the organizational community about internal and external events. Knowledge seeking should be current, relevant to the business, innovative, and in response to environmental events impacting its ability to function effectively.

Knowledge management (KM) is the process of integrating and sharing information across departments, divisions, and locations, depending on the size of the organization. *Cross-functional teams* are designed to implement KM by sharing relevant knowledge and distributing it across departments and locations in a hierarchal system. The process of KM ensures that all relevant data is distributed throughout the organization.

In a day-to-day operation, a learning organization's primary objective is to integrate organizational goals and remain competitive. The desired environment is an optimum level of information exchange where properly trained employees are motivated to bring new information to an organization. *Learning organizations contribute shared knowledge in an organizational community where KSAs contribute to the development of its human capital and organizational objectives.*

Employee Development

Attracting and retaining competent, motivated employees and identifying high potentials for future high-level employees in the organization are key priorities in HRD. A concern in today's learning organization is how to competitively attract high-level talent management (qualified applicants) to meet the needs of the organization while remaining competitive in the marketplace. As an organization establishes a record of success, developing and maintaining high performing work teams that move the organization forward is a competitive objective for employee development trainers.

Employee development is a general term used to describe the professional development of an organization's employees. Career development programs are designed to attract high-potential talent management to become the next generation of decision makers and leaders in the organization. Next generation managers, supervisors, leaders, and key decision makers are important strategic goals in HRD. The HR department works closely with every department in the organization to understand the jobs of its leaders and teams. Large organizations implement strategic staffing programs designed to accomplish this goal. Through the process of job analysis, employment development specialists identify the knowledge, skills, and abilities required to perform jobs assigned to workers. Managers and supervisors participate in questionnaires and organizational surveys to design programs around career planning, promotion, and performance management.

DESIGNING TRAINING AND DEVELOPMENT PROGRAMS

Training programs are designed around organizational goals and objectives. Training programs may include job skills training, supervisory training, management development, career development, coaching and/or mentoring programs, performance management, computer training, TQM, and any number of topics that may be relevant to the organization's strategic goals and operating plan.

Training program development takes place after conducting a *needs analysis,* or *needs assessment.* A needs analysis determines whether a training program will help the organization achieve its goals and overall strategic plan. For example, a manager approaches the HR director and complains that her supervisors are not properly trained. The Training Department is notified by the HR director to conduct a needs analysis (or needs assessment) to determine whether training for supervisors is needed. Included in the decision-making process will be a *cost-benefit analysis (CBA)* to determine if dollars spent to design and implement a training program is cost effective for the entire organization. Upon a thorough investigation and analysis, if it is determined that benefits outweigh costs, the Training Department will be given the task to move forward and explore a *design phase* for this training program.

The design phase is the process used to establish the goals and objectives of the training program. It determines the audience for training and how training will take place, and it targets how development of the program will be completed and by whom. Once this is achieved, the design phase will move into the program development phase.

The *program development phase* considers the organization's entire workforce, even if it is a select group that will be trained. Using supervisors as the example, all supervisors in the identified unit or department will be initially trained. Or all supervisors in the company could be trained. Or a pilot program might be introduced to a select group of supervisors before the organization decides to spend additional dollars rolling out a program to all supervisors in the organization. Other individuals identified for promotion through the scareer development department, HiPos (high potentials), may also participate in the training program. What began as a complaint from one manager may end up as a companywide training program for all of its supervisors and high-potential employees.

An organization's training and development of its human capital is a dynamic and often complex mix of variables successfully achieved through careful planning and development. Careful planning includes a construct known as *employee value proposition,* an organizational term used to describe the characteristics of a job and the employment experiences that attract and retain motivated, high-potential employees to grow with the organization. While HRD shares in the responsibility of developing an organization's high-potential employees, an employee's post-training experience is shared by the team members who must continue to develop this new employee. A controversial dynamic between HRD, the Training Department, and the department where the employee performs the job is called *transfer of training.* It is argued that training and development programs are a waste of time and money when employees complete training and are unable to transfer the new skills to the job. Management complains of time and money spent; however, it is management's responsibility to ensure transfer-of-training skills when employees return to the work site.

TRAINING (INSTRUCTIONAL) METHODS AND MATERIALS

Training methods run the gamut from classroom or seminar training to e-learning or experiential training. Experiential training is designed to be experienced by the individual via demonstration, one-on-ones, or performance.

Training methods and program materials used include the following:

- *Active training methods.* These include case studies, facilitations, simulations, and Socratic seminars (Q&A).
- *Passive training methods.* These include conferences, lectures, and/or presentation-style formats.
- *E-learning.* This includes synchronous, asynchronous, or live e-instruction.
- *Experiential.* These methods include demonstrations, one-on–ones, and performances.

The training environment for these programs can be a classroom, training facility, lecture hall, or seminar at a nearby location, on-site or off-site (e.g., hotel, conference, company retreat). Program delivery methods for training and development programs include:

- *E-learning.* This includes blended learning, distance learning, computer-based training (CBT), and electronic performance support systems (EPSS).
- *On-the-job training (OJT).* This requires performing the job in real time while a mentor or supervisor oversees a trainee's performance.

- *Programmed instruction.* This is self-paced, typically computer- or module-based training, in which participants progress individually or independently, usually within a specified time frame.
- *Simulation training.* This is simulated or interactive training where participants may practice learning new skills in a safe environment before returning to the actual job site or location.
- *Self-study courses.* These are mostly facilitated via computer, online, or in some other format (training manual), are asynchronous in nature, and have timelines or designated deadlines.

Employment Involvement Programs (EIPs)

EIPs are distinguished from traditional OD and company training programs and serve to fill an important need in the organizational community. Unique characteristics derived from EIPs encourage employees to become more involved in their work life. EIPs include a variety of employee programs and increase employee involvement and commitment to the organization. The strategy of an EIP is to increase human capital commitments to organizational goals by seeking feedback from employees and input into decision making. When employees perceive that their input is important, productivity and job satisfaction tends to increase.

Examples of EIPs include company-sponsored group activities, compensation plans, or reward incentives. Climate surveys called SFAs (survey/feedback/action), Quality Circles or TQM, company-paid education, wellness programs, planning committees, clubs, and task forces are additional strategies toward engaging employees in the organization's community.

High Performance Work Systems

High performance work systems, also known as *high performance work teams*, serve to directly involve employees in productivity programs designed to improve company processes, products, and services. Examples of high performance systems include lean manufacturing and self-directed work teams.

TRAINING PROGRAM EFFECTIVENESS: ASSESSMENT, EVALUATION, AND OUTCOMES

Determining if a training program achieved its desired goal(s) and whether dollars spent on a training program benefited the organization are important HRD outcomes. Comparing a program's cost-benefit analysis to its desired goals is evaluated as *the gap between a program's desired outcome versus its actual impact.* The goal of any training program is to improve performance of a job function that will directly impact the strategic goals of an organization. The primary purpose of training is to facilitate knowledge needed to perform a job and to develop the required skills and abilities to carry it out

(KSAs). The desired effect is task performance improvement. When employees are able to successfully apply what they learned in a training program to the actual job, transfer of training has been achieved. It is presumed that the training program was effective if transfer of training occurred. If transfer of training did not occur, the presumption is made that the training program did not accomplish its goals.

Program evaluation is a training and development process for assessing effective (or ineffective) training program outcomes. Several program evaluation models exist; however, the best known model for specifically measuring training program outcomes was developed by Donald Kirkpatrick. The model is designed around a four-step level approach. Measurement at each level is designed to support the objectives of the training program from its initial design phase through the final outcome phase, as outlined below:

- Level 1: *Reaction.* Evaluates participants' reactions to the training program, but not organizational impact
- Level 2: *Learning.* A test measure for participants to determine if learning occurred (focused on the training program itself)
- Level 3: *Behavior.* Job performance measure between six weeks/six months to determine if transfer of training occurred on the job
- Level 4: *Results.* An organizational assessment used to determine if training impacted the business at large (compares initial training objectives to actual results over a specified period of time)

Robert Brinkerhoff extended Kirkpatrick's four-level model to a six-stage evaluation model:

- Stage 1: *Goal setting.* What are the needs and intervention(s) best served by HRD?
- Stage 2: *Program design.* Do activities satisfy Stage 1?
- Stage 3: *Program implementation.* Is program design effective?
- Stage 4: *Immediate outcomes.* Were objectives met?
- Stage 5: *Intermediate outcomes.* Did transfer of training occur?
- Stage 6: *Impact and worth.* Did the program impact the organization in terms of cost and learning?

How is information collected? Evaluation data may be collected in a variety of ways from a number of sources. Typically, data is derived from three groups: participants, training facilitators, and management. Groups may be expanded to include work groups, separate divisions of the organization, and comparisons made between groups. Analysis should include differences in each group assessed to understand why a training program was or was not successful.

Data collection is done by assessing reaction from participants, utilizing check sheets, interviews, surveys, and/or questionnaires. All can be facilitated in person, by telephone, by computer, or through a combination of choices.

Exam Note:

Questions related to program evaluation will likely include Kirkpatrick's evaluation model. Become familiar with method collection, data analysis, and its corresponding levels.

Learning data is typically collected following a course, a test, or a demonstration. For example, if an organization requires ethics education training, the course may be facilitated online and an online post-test will be required to demonstrate completion of the course.

Other learning data methods include:

- *Pre- and post-measures.* Data gathered before and after a program is given. It measures knowledge known before a course and knowledge gained upon completion of a course.
- *Experimental or quasi-experimental designs.* Data gathered utilizing a variety of methods, such as pre/post with a control group, field tests, pre/post with written feedback, anecdotal comments, etc. This design allows for more data to be collected and analyzed and for more in-depth exploration of information.

PERFORMANCE APPRAISAL METHODS

Performance management is an ongoing system of employee feedback about the job the employee performs in the workplace. Its purpose is to develop employees into productive workers and assist them to become effective contributors in the organization. If problems are identified early, they are more likely to be corrected. Performance management feedback is usually given by an employee's direct report. However, this is not always the case, especially if a direct report works from another location or has left the company. When this happens, other individuals will be identified to give feedback to an employee or to conduct the *performance review.* HRD is responsible for training managers and supervisors on how to effectively implement performance management programs. They are *feedback systems* requiring careful planning and training due to the sensitive nature of the employee's performance, how well an employee performs or does not perform on the job, and how an employee perceives his performance compared to feedback received.

Performance coaching is a different kind of feedback. Rather than focusing on actual performance from the previous year, performance coaching focuses on developing employees who are either high-potential employees identified for leadership opportunities or the opposite, as in the case of the poor performance requiring a systematic development of tasks to improve performance. The latter is also known as *corrective feedback*, which sometimes leads to termination.

Performance Appraisal Process

Performance appraisals are generally used as a documentation feedback system assessing job performance in a written format. Feedback is shared between a supervisor and an employee in a formal meeting procedures. A variety of *performance measures* have been developed to more fully assess an employee's work performance over time.

The performance appraisal process is typically rolled out by HRD and comprised of two carefully preplanned steps that take place well in advance of the actual performance review time period:

1. *Training.* Training is a necessary step to ensure consistency and commitment to the review process. Managers and supervisors must be effectively trained on what to say or not say to employees and must be guided by employment laws. What is discussed in the meeting and who should be in attendance during the meeting are planned in advance. If it will be a meeting where negative feedback is shared (e.g., poor performance by an employee), and the employee may react in some undesirable way, another individual, usually from HR, will attend the meeting as well.

2. *Performance assessment.* The performance assessment tool is completed in advance by the supervisor and the employee. Occasionally, a performance review includes a confidential assessment from coworkers, but not always. The review can include past performance, current performance, and future performance, goals, and developmental objectives.

Appraisal Methods

A variety of appraisal methods can be selected for the performance review, but the method is chosen by a key decision maker, such as an HR director, who may present several methods to an executive committee. Once a method has been chosen, the entire organization will use the same method. Exceptions may be that different methods are used for different levels of leadership in an organization; managers and supervisors may be given a different appraisal method than line workers or hourly employees. The appraisal method can take many forms: paper/pencil, computer-driven and scored application, a longer written form, or some other specific type of method.

Examples of specific methods include the following:

- *Behavioral methods.* These can be ongoing or timed, short forms, charts, checklists, comparisons, rankings, rating scales, and/or narratives.
- *Narratives.* These describe an employee's performance in written form. More specifically, narratives can take the form of a critical incident, an essay, or a field review. Critical incidents discuss specific performance issues. These can also include self-evaluation.
- *Essays.* These are designed with greater flexibility; however, caution must be used to properly document what is written about an employee.
- *Field review.* This may be given when an employee is not in direct contact with a supervisor and another individual is given the task of carrying out the review process.
- *360 evaluation.* This is designed to gather feedback from an employee's direct report, coworkers, and other workers that the employee comes into contact with in a working relationship on the job.
- *MBO review.* Management by objectives is typically reserved for managers and supervisors. It is a shared document between a manager and her direct report summarizing objectives and goals from the previous year and whether or not they were achieved.

In some or all of these methods, ratings and feedback are combined to ascertain a numeric score to calculate a performance rating scale. The rating scale identifies an overall summary score that is often used to determine salary increases and if performance levels were achieved.

Appraisal review cycles are usually scheduled once per year. Sometimes a review will be scheduled at the midpoint of the annual cycle. This may occur for several reasons: performance coaching, salary increases, a change in job position, transfers, and/or promotions.

Proper documentation is the most important consideration in the performance review process. Performance appraisals become part of the employee's permanent employment record. Supervisors and managers are responsible for properly documenting an employee's record. If improper documentation is recorded on a performance review or if a heated argument takes place during the review meeting, carefully worded documentation is needed in the event that a lawsuit or inquiry is to happen. Examples of improper documentation may result in a wrongful termination or discharge. Effective training and proper documentation protects the employee and the organization. Poor documentation could result in a major lawsuit against the organization. In some cases, such as a government-contracted organization, improper documentation may result in the shutdown of a business.

MENTORING AND EXECUTIVE COACHING

Career development inside of an organization can take many forms. A large organization with many divisions may house its own Career Development Department. The focus of career development is to identify high-potential employees who can be developed for managerial or leadership positions in the company. Talent management is the process of identifying applicants and employees who demonstrate high performance and commitment to organizational goals and objectives. Career development *coaches* and *mentors* are identified to work with selected employees. Importantly, differences exist in the roles that a coach and mentor fulfill in an organization. A coach is a *thought partner* to an employee for the purposes of career development needs, goal setting, and career planning. A coach may be an internal employee or an independent resource hired as a consultant from an outside organization specializing in executive coaching. A mentor is an internal employee who performs the same or similar work that the employee/mentee was hired to perform. The mentor assists in the development of the employee on the job.

Career development opportunities for employees may include educational opportunities, can be seminars, or retraining for different jobs in the organization. These are usually company sponsored or paid for by the organization. Career development recruiters go outside the organization in search of high-potential employees at job fairs, on college campuses, and through other distribution methods, such as online resources, print media advertising, and employment agencies, where a fee is paid to the agency.

GLOBAL ISSUES

The Internet has played a major role in expanding business opportunities abroad. As businesses expanded into global markets and alliances were formed to create business opportunities in the organization, HRD realized many challenges and opportunities. Multicultural differences exist in the ways that employees communicate globally as a result of different work ethics, languages, communication networks, email systems, and business initiatives. Terms that are familiar in the United States, such as teamwork, informal communication, and cultural practices, have different meanings abroad. It is HRD's role to identify differences and address them within the organizational community so they are not miscommunicated or misinterpreted across organizational boundaries.

Diversity is a key initiative in every organization today, whether or not an organization conducts business abroad. *Diversity awareness* seeks to embrace cultural differences in all employees, encourage open communication, and ensure that discrimination does not take place within the organizational community. *Diversity awareness training* is mandatory in most organizations.

Expatriates and *repatriation* considerations concern employees working for a U.S. organization overseas or those working in a country outside of the United States. American employees who work abroad are identified as *expatriate* employees. Special opportunities and benefits are usually extended to expats, such as housing, language coaching, multicultural mentoring, bonuses, and other benefits. Immediate family members who relocate with the employee are sometimes given extended benefits, such as private schooling and education or travel allowances. *Repatriation* concerns adjustment issues when employees (and their families) return from an overseas job assignment.

CHAPTER SUMMARY

HRD is an integral part of HRM and serves the entire organizational community. OD's function is to analyze change in the organization and examine how organizational systems function with the goals and objectives of the business. OD operates to understand and diagnose problems in the organization relating to its structure, strategic plan, operations, and technology. HRD's role is to provide training and development to the organization's employees, manage the training process, and design management development and leadership programs in a competitive marketplace. Theories of motivation, the ADDIE model, TQM, and performance management are human capital initiatives and key objectives in the HRD process.

REVIEW QUESTIONS

1. What is HRD's function in an organization? How does it relate to HRM?

2. Why is federal legislation an important part of HRD?

3. Briefly describe the Civil Rights Act, EEOC, OFCCP, and DOL.

4. What is OD and how is it different from training and development?

5. Why are common law, the Copyright Act, and U.S. patents relevant to training and development programs?

6. Identify three motivational theories and how they impact HRD programs.

7. What is the Juran Trilogy, and how is it linked to the quality movement?

8. What are "quality circles," and who was Deming?

9. Name two active and two passive training methods.

10. Describe transfer of training.

11. What is a KSA?

12. Describe the ADDIE model.

13. How are knowledge management (KM) and cross-functional teams linked together?

14. Discuss the four components of Kirkpatrick's program evaluation model.

15. What is the difference between a mentor and a coach?

16. Describe a performance management system.

ANSWERS AND EXPLANATIONS

1. HRD is an organized system in the workplace designed to integrate the strategic goals of the organization through the development of its employees. HRD's role is to provide training and development to the organization's employees, manage the training process, and design management development and leadership programs in a competitive marketplace.

2. Consideration must be given to federal employment legislation, state laws, and government regulations before any HRD planning can take place. It is HRD's responsibility to ensure that all activities performed in the organization comply with federal regulations designed to protect workers in employment settings.

3. Civil rights legislation, or Title VII of the 1964 Civil Rights Act, was created to protect employees under conditions of employment, members of protected groups, and prohibits employee discrimination and decisions based on race, color, religion, sex, or national origin. The Civil Rights Act created the enforcement agencies that regulate compliance. They are the Equal Employment Opportunity Commission (EEOC) and the Office of Federal Contract Compliance Programs (OFCCP). US Department of Labor (DOL). A federal agency created by Congress in 1913, the DOL serves to protect workers, job applicants, and retirees in the United States.

4. Organizational Development (OD) is an HRD systems function designed to examine how an organization integrates its employees and management teams to accomplish the goals of the organization. Included in this matrix are: human resources, a company's organizational structure, business technology, work processes, and strategic plans.

   Training and Development is an HRD function that seeks to meet the needs of the organization through training and development of its employees. Each member is trained how to effectively perform their role within the organization and participate in job training programs.

5. Common law ensures that once a job candidate becomes an employee, the employee will be properly trained by participating in a company paid, or company sponsored, training and development program. The program must be designed to serve, protect, and train employees with the knowledge, skills, and abilities (KSAs) required to perform the job. Further, the job will be performed in a safe environment, and where third parties (employee) are not harmed. If improper training exists, or no training is offered, and injury to a third party or damage to property can be demonstrated, liability to the employer exists under the law for negligent or no training. The same standard holds true for an organization's performance management system. It is the employer's responsibility to properly train employees for the job they were hired to perform.

   Organizational training and development programs are designed to comply with legal requirements discussed earlier in this chapter. Federal legislation governing HRD training activities and written materials associated with training and development publications include: the Copyright Act (1976) and patents.

6. Motivation theory is a psychological construct used in the workplace to train and develop employees to be productive workers. Theories are included to demonstrate how motivation theory is linked to practice in the workplace. For a broader discussion about Motivation Theory, please review chapter 2.

7. Joseph M. Juran supported the principles of the quality movement and proposed the idea that quality is driven to customer needs and customer satisfaction. The Juran Trilogy identifies three phases of his model in the quality process: quality planning, quality control, and quality improvements.

8. The quality movement, or Quality Circles, began in the 1940's by W. Edwards Deming who believed that quality is defined by the consumer. Deming, an American, proposed a 14 point plan that focused on management's responsibility to be accountable for work outcomes and internal systems within the organization. Deming's ideas were not well received in America so he proposed his theories to Japan. Deming was given an opportunity to demonstrate Quality Circles in Japanese organizations which proved to be highly successful and enthusiastically received. Ironically, Japan was given credit for initiating quality circles and introducing it to the American workforce. Deming returned to the U.S. with his Japanese counterparts, and in the years that followed, Deming and Japanese business leaders were invited to the U.S. to teach American business leaders about the Japanese quality movement and implement Quality Circles in their organizations

9. Active training methods: case study, facilitation, simulation, Socratic seminar (Q&A), vestibule (a type of simulated learning in a real-life practice environment using actual equipment to gain experience prior to real job implementation. Typically done for hazardous or dangerous type of settings).

    Passive training methods: conference, lecture, and/or presentation style formats.

10. Transfer of training is the technical training term used to describe job skills learned during the training phase are successfully transferred to the job.

11. KSAs, or Knowledge, Skills, and Abilities, are the technical training terms used to describe specific skill sets needed to perform a job. KSAs are also used to design training programs.

12. The ADDIE model is an instructional method that describes five sequential steps or phases in the training program development process. ADDIE is an acronym used to describe the five steps in the training process: (1) Analysis, (2) Design, (3) Development, (4) Implementation and (5) Evaluation.

13. Knowledge management (KM) is the process of integrating and shar-

ing information across departments, divisions, and locations, depending upon the size of the organization. Cross functional teams are designed to implement KM by sharing relevant knowledge and distributing it across departments and locations in a hierarchal system. The process of KM ensures that all relevant data is distributed throughout the organization. The San Diego fires of 2007 are an example of effective KM utilizing cross functional teams.

14. Kirkpatrick's Model is designed around a 4-step level approach and a well known method for training evaluation. Measurement at each level is designed to support the objectives of the training program during its initial design phase through the final outcome phase. The 4 levels include:

    Level 1—Reaction—evaluates participants reaction to the training program, but not organizational impact.

    Level 2—Learning—a test measure for participants to determine if learning occurred (focused on the training program itself).

    Level 3—Behavior—job performance measure between 6 weeks/6 months to determine if transfer of training occurred on the job.

    Level 4—Results—an organizational assessment used to determine if training impacted the business at large (compares initial training objective(s) to actual results over a specified period of time).

15. A coach is a thought-partner to an employee for the purpose of career development needs, goal setting, and career planning. A coach may be an internal employee or an independent resource, hired as a consultant from an outside organization specializing in executive coaching. A mentor is an internal employee who performs the same or similar work that the employee/mentee was hired to perform. The mentor assists in the development of the employee on the job.

16. Performance management is an on-going system of employee feedback about the job they perform in the workplace. It is closely linked to the performance appraisal system for employees typically implemented as an annual review. Its purpose is to develop employees into productive workers and assist them to become effective contributors in the organization. If problems are identified early, they are more likely to be corrected. Performance management feedback is usually given by an employee's direct report.

Total Rewards

In recent years, the phrase *compensation and benefits* has been replaced by a more comprehensive term called *total rewards*. Total rewards (TR), by definition, includes compensation and benefits in addition to personal and professional growth opportunities and a motivating work environment (which includes work/life balance). In most organizations, total rewards is the *single greatest operating expense* for the business and a critical component of the Human Resource Department. Understanding the value of a TR program is an essential task for an HR professional and a significant part of the PHR and SPHR exams. You should expect to develop a firm base of knowledge on local, state, and federal laws related to TR and compensation and benefits. It is important to make special mention up front that laws differ from state to state, and you should make sure you understand the differences between them before you take your exam.

In addition to laws and regulations related to TR, you'll want to understand how incentive plans work, how to adequately compensate your employees based on performance, and how to develop rewards programs.

And finally, it will be important for you to develop a strong understanding of the budgeting and accounting practices associated with a TR program. Two examples would be payroll and benefit reporting.

A general overview of some basic TR strategies—compensation and benefits and work/life balance—and their definitions are listed in table 6.1.

TOTAL REWARDS STRATEGIES

As mentioned in previous chapters, a critical function of HR is attracting, recruiting, and retaining employees. Your TR strategy, in a nutshell, is all of the rewards and compensation—monetary or nonmonetary—that you give to your employees. Monetary compensation includes such items as base pay, incentives, merit pay, medical and dental premiums, pension plans, and paid time off (both vacation and sick/personal leave). It could also include things such as stock options and 401(k) plans. Although it is common to hear complaints about being overworked and underpaid, sometimes it is actually the nonmonetary benefits that are the true attractors to your company, so it is wise to put just as much attention toward these benefits.

In chapter 4, we talked about the importance of developing a brand for your company. Your TR strategy will be an important component of your brand. For instance, it is well known that Starbucks rewards part-time employees with health care benefits. A favorite search engine, Google, was named *Fortune* magazine's best company to work for in 2007 in part because of its unique perks and benefits—on-site gourmet food, gym, laundry facility, and massages are just a few of the perks Google employees receive (see real-world example).

Clearly, competition is the driving force for a company to develop an attractive TR package. Upon closer examination of the *Fortune* article mentioned above, it can be noted that a large portion of the best companies to work for are located in the Pacific Northwest—with the highest percentage being in California.

Table 6.1   Total Rewards Strategies

Compensation	Definition
Base Pay	Wages and salaries alone
Merit Pay	Base-pay with increases based on employee performance or sales figures
Incentives	Cash rewards based on employee performance—such as hitting sales figures by deadlines or quarterly goals
Promotions	Increasing the base pay by a certain percentage rate, based upon past and future performance
Pay Increases	Can be annual increases by a certain percentage rate, based on length of service
Benefits	
Health care/ Wellness	Payment for health, dental, vision insurance payment for sick leave and wellness programs on-site
Paid Leave	Vacation, bereavement, personal leave can include non-monetary compensation but approved time off to attend counseling via employee assistance programs
Retirement	Employee sponsored retirement leave

Developing Your Total Rewards Program

You probably will not be developing a TR program from scratch. More likely, you will be examining the one that you currently have in place and developing strategies for improving what currently exists. There are four phases for implementing a TR program: assessment, design, implementation, and evaluation. In the assessment phase, you begin by examining what you already have in place, what is working for you, and what isn't working for you. In the design phase, you gather data and look at potential rewards strategies that are out there. True, not every company can be Google, but you will gather lots of information and look at the possibilities. In the implementation stage, you begin putting your strategies in place and testing them out—and finally, you will evaluate how well those strategies worked.

The Project Management Team

Before you begin the four-step process for evaluating your TR program, your first task is to develop a strong project management team. You will want to include employees at various levels in the organization to make your team credible. You should choose leaders within your organization, including senior HR professionals with significant project management and TR experience. Others that you might put on your team include the following:

- Top management in your organization
- An outside consultant with experience with similar types of organizations
- Midlevel employees
- Unionized employees
- High-level performers
- Employees with experience in finance, payroll, and employment law
- HR professionals with TR experience
- An employee with experience in policy development

Great care should be taken to develop a project team that is well aware of each individual's role within the team and the importance of the task at hand. It should be noted that, for smaller companies, you might have one person filling several of the roles listed above. Your payroll person might very well be your finance and employment law person all rolled into one. However you develop your team, it should include the best and brightest that your company can assemble. In addition, if you end up with a large project team, you might develop smaller subcommittees that report back to the larger group (e.g., a subcommittee working on health and wellness options, another working on leave issues).

Your project team should develop a *total rewards philosophy* that will serve as its mission statement to develop the best program geared at attracting, recruiting, motivating, and retaining employees.

Phase One: Assessment

Once you have assembled your dream team to begin examining your TR program, you next need to evaluate what you have been doing and brainstorm ideas for improvement. If you have hired a project consultant, he will be crucial to this process and will be able to examine your current practices with a fair and impartial eye. During this phase, you might conduct employee focus groups (again, with an impartial facilitator) and administer surveys. For the focus groups, you will most likely do one for management and one for employees.

Two important components of this process are to look at current industry trends as well as existing practices within the organization. When you examine current practices, it is important to look at the history of your organization and review archived records. Looking at where you have been can give you important clues as to why you are where you are now and where you should be going. Look at your existing databases of information and assemble the following types of reports to glean where you are:

- Turnover rates
- Current salary information
- Actual pay levels versus industry trends
- Past employee surveys
- Current rewards structure

Your project team should ask the following types of questions:

- Do all of your employees have job descriptions? Are they current? Are they accurate?
- Do you have annual/biannual performance evaluations?
- Do you pay overtime?
- How many pay levels are in your current organizational structure?
- Do you have performance-based pay?
- What criteria do you currently use for promotion? (A percentage based upon industry/state standards? Equity? Performance? Seniority?)
- Do you have incentive plans?
- What types of employees receive what current levels of benefits? (e.g., exempt versus nonexempt)
- What are your current performance measures?
- What types of rewards are you using? Are they working for you? Or have they become passé?
- What role will the union play in designing the new system?
- What approval process is needed (via chain of command) to implement the new system? Where are there roadblocks?

Phase Two: Design

In the design phase, your project team will be looking at all of the multifaceted types of rewards your employees receive, such as compensation, benefits, work/life initiatives, professional and personal development, and work environment. In looking at compensation, you should look at base pay, incentive pay, and pay levels. Many organizations have extremely complicated pay level structures depending upon job task, experience, and qualifications. (See the section "Job Pricing and Pay Structures" later in this chapter).

In the design phase, you will want to gather a significant amount of research about your competition: What is luring employees over to your competitors? Do they offer three weeks of vacation compared to your two weeks at start of employment? Or are they offering tuition reimbursement? Do they offer on-site benefits, such as a gym or other wellness programs? What about employee assistance programs? Paid dry cleaning? Free parking? Bus passes?

Has your HR department gathered any data on why employees turned down offers of employment? Even informal data will be important to examine here.

Phase Three: Implementation

Now that you have come up with a design, it is time to put your plan into action. You will want to consider a number of important things in the implementation phase. First, who will be eligible for what rewards? What criteria are you going to use to determine if they are eligible? Things like productivity, customer service, sales figures, profit/loss? In addition to eligibility, you will want to consider the rollout of your TR program. Timing is everything. Will you roll it out prior to outlining some new strategic goals or initiatives? It might help to attract and retain workers. How will you explain the new system to your employees? The more you share at every level of the rollout of a new rewards system the better. Make information available through email and hard copy and in meetings, both large and small. Encourage employees to talk about their feelings and ask questions. Provide information on your intranet and your website. The last thing to consider during the implementation phase is training your employees.

Phase Four: Evaluation

It is often too easy to forget about evaluation of a new system because so much time is spent putting it together. A good correlation is event planning, like a charity auction. Time is taken to put together the event team, recruit interesting donations, and plan the details of the wine and the meal and the table decorations—and you do not want to forget to evaluate how the night went afterward. Was the meal what it was supposed to be? Were people genuinely enjoying themselves? Did the auctioneer keep things moving? It is the same concept when looking at your TR program. In evaluating your program, you will want to revisit what your original objectives were in starting your program. What data do you need to look at to determine if you have met your goals? You'll want to look at surveys, costs, profit/loss statements, recruitment and retention, customer service data, and the like. Taking time to evaluate where you have been makes it much easier to determine where you are going in the future.

ECONOMICS AND THE LABOR MARKET

A careful study of local economics and your current labor market are going to be critical factors in developing a TR package. Almost all states now have websites devoted to employment, unemployment, and labor trends. The Michigan Department of Labor, for example, lists a wealth of information for not only employers but job seekers. The website includes information on current unemployment statistics, along with payroll trends for farm, nonfarm, and industry workers. On Michigan's site, you can also find information on scientific and engineering occupations, job search strategies, and economic forecasts. This is always important, but particularly in an environment where the economy is poor and hiring is difficult. Become familiar with your state's industry and labor trends by reviewing its website.

Organizations may need to review their programs to meet the changing needs of the labor market and to ensure that they are reflective of their own particular environment—urban versus rural. For example, a company that has its headquarters in Dallas, Texas, such as Kimberly-Clark, would have a vastly different environment than one located in New York City or Portland, Oregon. When this author moved from Green Bay, Wisconsin, to Seattle, Washington, I compared cost of living examples from Green Bay to Seattle and found Seattle's cost of living to be one and one-half times greater than Green Bay's. Consequently, I used that information to negotiate salary. When recruiting employees, an organization needs to be cognizant of current market and geographic trends.

While for the most part competition is deemed to be healthy, sometimes it can also be taxing for employers who don't have unlimited resources. Part of the reason the TR package is so important is that, while you might not have the salary that your competitor has to offer, you might have something else to offer that someone would be willing to take a little pay cut for. In major metropolitan areas, for instance, a shorter commute may be much more attractive to an individual than the salary increase.

TOTAL REWARDS: COMPENSATION

The U.S. Department of Labor (DOL) oversees all laws related to employment and compensation. Some of those laws were referenced in chapter 4; however, there are others related to compensation that will be outlined here. These laws were developed to protect workers against unfair labor practices. For an in-depth discussion about all of the laws related to the Fair Labor Standards Act (FLSA), go to www.dol.gov/esa/whd/flsa.

Fair Labor Standards Act of 1938

The FLSA is important to review when studying for the PHR and SPHR exams. Enacted in 1938, it is still the primary law related to employee status and compensation. The FLSA does the following:

- Requires employers to keep meticulous records in all matters of payroll and compensation status. It sets the minimum wage in this country.
- Identifies how to determine who is eligible for exempt status and further defines the difference between administrative, professional, and executive exempt status.
- Determines how to compensate outside sales workers and independent contractors.
- Outlines child labor laws.
- Sets the criteria for paying overtime to employees, how much to pay them, and when an employer is not required to pay overtime.

Exempt Status

Exempt status in the United States generally means that an employee meets certain criteria related to his job and is paid a salary not less than $455 per week (as of January 2008; this figure is not static, so you should check with the DOL for current figure). It is important to note that job titles do not determine exempt status. In order to qualify for exempt status, an employee's specific job duties and salary must meet the DOL's requirements.

Executive Exemption

Executive exemption status is given when an employee is paid a salary not less than $455 per week, AND

- Has the authority to hire and fire employees.
- Has the primary duty to manage the company or a division or subdivision.
- Regularly directs the work of two or more full-time employees.

Administrative Exemption

Administrative exemption status is given when an employee is paid a salary not less than $455 per week, AND

- Has primary duties that are office-related and nonmanual work.
- Has primary responsibilities that include using independent judgment in matters of significance.

Professional Exemption

Professional exemption status is given when an employee is paid a salary not less than $455 per week, AND

- Has primary duties that involve advanced knowledge, predominantly of an intellectual matter.
- Has work that requires consistent exercise of discretion and judgment.
- Has advanced knowledge in a field of science or learning.
- Has advanced knowledge that is customarily acquired by a prolonged course of specialized intellectual instruction.

Computer Employee Exemption

Computer employee exemption status is given when an employee is paid EITHER a salary not less than $455 per week, or on a fee basis, or if compensated hourly, at a rate of not less than $27.63/hour (data retrieved January 2008—check for current requirements), AND

- Has primary duties that include the application of systems analysis techniques and consulting work with users to determine hardware and software issues and functions.
- Is a systems analyst, computer programmer, software engineer, or similarly skilled in the field of computers.
- Has work that involves the design, development, documentation, and/or analysis of computer systems and programs.

In the News:

On May 25, 2007, President George W. Bush signed a spending bill that, among other things, amended the FLSA to increase the federal minimum wage in three steps: to $5.85 per hour effective July 24, 2007; to $6.55 per hour effective July 24, 2008; and to $7.25 per hour effective July 24, 2009.

Minimum Wage

Nonexempt employees must be paid at least the minimum wage for any compensable time. The FLSA sets the minimum wage; however, some states set their wages higher than the federal minimum wage. Not surprisingly, many of the states with higher minimum wage rates are on the western and eastern coasts of the United States, where the cost of living is typically higher than the rest of the country. The FLSA established that 40 hours per week is the maximum amount of time that nonexempt employees may work and requires overtime to be paid for any compensable hours worked over that time.

Overtime

The FLSA requires you to pay your employee overtime if they are nonexempt and work over 40 hours per week at the rate of one and one-half times their current pay (time and a half). And in some states, employees may even be paid double time (working on a holiday might be an example of this), as negotiated by their labor agreements. Exempt employees are not required to receive overtime, but you are not prohibited from paying them overtime. Careful attention should be paid to how, when, and why you execute this practice in fairness to all employees.

Your HR staff should be very knowledgeable about the difference between compensable time and noncompensable time. Compensable time is the time spent working during the week, including being paid for sick leave or vacation leave. For instance, Candy is a nonexempt employee, who works as an administrative assistant in your office. She takes Tuesday afternoon off to attend a doctor's appointment and has requested three hours of personal leave to do so, which you approve. She will still receive her 40 hours of pay for that week. However, if Candy took those same three hours off to visit with her boyfriend, Chip—and got caught—you can dock her pay by three hours.

There are several examples of compensable time that you should also be aware of:

Preparing for the Work Environment

Employees who need to prepare for their work environment by changing their clothing or cleaning up after a shift must be compensated for that time. A health care worker who needs to don surgical scrubs in a sanitized environment when she gets to the hospital would be one example; an employee who needs protective clothing is another.

Travel Time

Traveling to and from work is not compensable time. However, if the travel is a part of the job description, and employees must travel to various sites throughout the day, you must compensate them for their time. An example would be a pharmaceutical sales rep who visits ten doctor offices per day in his sales region.

For nonexempt employees who travel away from home for several days, the FLSA considers that time compensable, but not the time spent on an airplane, train, automobile, bus, ferry, or boat.

Training Periods, Meetings, and Educational Opportunities

You are not required to pay an exempt employee for training, meetings, or educational opportunities that are outside the normal work hours, are voluntary, or are not job related. An example of when you would not be required to pay the employee is in the case of a nonexempt receptionist who is taking courses in chemistry—which is not related to her job description. However, you might opt to pay this individual if she is taking a course to learn about spreadsheets, which would improve her job performance.

Breaks and Meals

You are not required to pay for meal periods longer than 30 minutes. If you require a person to remain at their work station during that time period, however, you must pay them for that time. For example, if Jenny works as a check-in clerk at the community pool, and you require her to be at her station from 12:30–1:00, her only time to eat during the day, you would compensate her for that time.

On-Call Time

On-call time is another tricky one in terms of compensable/noncompensable time. If employees are required to be on-site during the on-call period, you must compensate them for their time. If employees are on-call but at home during the time period, you do not have to compensate them for their time. An employee of a heating and cooling company, for example, might be on-call every other weekend for late-night emergency calls. This worker would not be compensated for their on-call time. In contrast, a nurse who is on-call, but at the hospital waiting for patients, would be compensated for the time.

The Equal Pay Act of 1963

The Equal Pay Act (EPA) of 1963, which is an amended part of the FLSA of 1938, prohibits the discrimination against employees based on their sex. It states that you may not discriminate on the basis of sex by paying wages to employees in an establishment at a rate less than that at which wages are paid to employees of the opposite sex for equal work on jobs, the performance of which requires equal skill, effort, or responsibility, and which are performed under similar working conditions.

It may be interesting to note that during the first nine years of the EPA, the requirement of equal pay for equal work did not extend to persons employed in an executive, administrative, or professional capacity, or for outside salespeople. Therefore, the EPA exempted white-collar women from the protection of equal pay for equal work. In 1972, Congress enacted the Educational

Amendment of 1972, which amended the FLSA to expand the coverage of the EPA to these employees.

Although the EPA has made significant strides toward reducing the pay gap between men and women, women still make on average 76 cents to every dollar made by men in the workforce doing the same work. To remedy that problem, Senator Hillary Rodham Clinton from New York championed the Paycheck Fairness Act in March 2007. Its aim was to narrow the wage gap between men and women. In addition, minority women fare even worse in terms of the salary gap.

JOB PRICING AND PAY STRUCTURES

Salary administration programs are relatively straightforward, yet entire courses are taught in compensation. Basically, what an employer needs to determine are the value of the jobs to the company, what the market is currently paying for those jobs, and the various levels of jobs within that job category. For instance, you might pay technical jobs at four different levels, based upon experience and seniority. You would start with an entry-level position, moving up to professional levels of experience.

As a former job analyst, I know it is critical to spend time making sure job descriptions and tasks match what the incumbent worker is currently doing. In job analysis, you take time observing an employee's tasks, reviewing those tasks for accuracy with the worker, and then analyzing how much time is spent on those tasks and weighing them for critical levels of importance. The ACT company—known mainly for its college entrance exam—has an excellent program called WorkKeys® that is designed to measure job analysis and critical skill levels for jobs. A description of the program can be found online at www.act.org/workkeys.

When pricing jobs, it is also critical to look at the job market. For employees and employers alike, there are wonderful online tools to measure compensation levels in various markets. The Bureau of Labor Statistics also collects and reports data related to compensation.

JOB EVALUATION METHODS

How does a flight attendant's salary measure up against a librarian's salary? Well, the flight attendant has an arguably more risky job; but then, the librarian probably went to school longer and has a master's degree. Comparing worth of jobs is tricky, and you will get as many opinions about job evaluation as the number of people you ask. However, what it usually means that you will be doing is comparing the value of jobs against one another in the company. One could argue that the president's assistant is just as important as he is; however, relative to decision-making capabilities, you will probably want to pay your president more than his assistant. Some factors that you are likely to consider include the following:

- Education level—high school, college internships, bachelor's, master's, or doctorate degree
- Years of experience in the field or significant levels of college training in the field (e.g., a professor might not have hands-on marketing experience but might have a PhD in marketing)
- Training or other factors that give an added edge of expertise
- On-the-job experience (e.g., someone who has worked for six years as a waitress, looking for a job as a maître d')

TOTAL REWARDS: BENEFITS REQUIRED BY LAW

Today's baby boomers no longer take Social Security for granted. There was a time, however, when Social Security was considered a given—the nest egg for the future. As our workforce ages, and workers stay in the workforce longer, there are some skeptics who wonder if Social Security will be there when current generations retire at age 67 or beyond.

Social Security

In its broadest form, the Social Security Act of 1935 was enacted to provide old age assistance and benefits for survivors and dependents of workers. The Old Age, Survivors, and Disability Insurance (OASDI) is for eligible workers upon retirement or disability or for their surviving dependents. Social Security was never intended to be a sole source of retirement income, although it is often thought of that way. In fact, according to Social Security's online website, it was always intended to be one of three sources of income for retirees: Social Security, your own pension plan, and your own savings plan.

The age for retirement is changing. We are healthier than our parents and our grandparents and expected to stay in the workforce longer than they did. Life expectancies are increasing as well; it is not uncommon for people to live to be 100 years of age, nor is it uncommon to see workers in their 70s or even 80s! Consequently, in the early 1980s, the Social Security Administration (SSA) began revising and increasing the ages for full retirement benefits. (See table 6.2 for current ages by date of birth.) The sample benefits for retirement at these ages is available online at www.socialsecurity.gov/retire2/agereduction.htm.

If you were born in 1940, for instance, and elected to start receiving your benefits at full retirement age, your benefit would be around $2,000/month and adjusted yearly for inflation.

Younger workers, in their 20s and 30s, often wonder if Social Security will still be available to them when they retire. In fact, according to Social Security's own website, if changes are not made to the current system, workers in their 20s and 30s could see decreases to their payments in the 26 percent range.

Employers and employees both pay taxes into the Social Security and Medicare systems. The tax rates are based upon laws set by the Internal Revenue Service and the Federal Insurance Contributions Act. You've often heard this referred to as FICA. In 2008, the tax rate is currently 6.2 percent. Disability insurance is taxed at the rate of 90%. If you haven't taken a close look at your paycheck recently, the amount of taxes being paid can be rather staggering when you think about it.

Table 6.2   Retirement Ages by Year of Birth

Year of Birth	Full Retirement Age
1937 or earlier	65
1938	65 and 2 mos
1939	65 and 4 mos
1940	65 and 6 mos
1941	65 and 8 mos
1942	65 and 10 mos
1943–1954	66
1955	66 and 2 mos
1956	66 and 4 mos
1957	66 and 6 mos
1958	66 and 8 mos
1959	66 and 10 mos
1960 and later	67

Source: www.socialsecurity.gov/retire2/agereduction.htm

Total Rewards: Benefits (Employer Elected)

The U.S. Census Bureau states that the amount of uninsured workers is rising in both numbers and percentages. Although, having stated that, workers have come to expect to receive health care coverage in some form in the United States. It is an expensive burden for employers to bear. The costs for medical, dental, and vision insurance can often be a huge percentage of the entire operating budget—depending upon the type of health care plan selected. (Some examples of common employer-elected benefits are listed in table 6.3.)

As this book is going to press during the 2008 presidential elections, the most highly debated topic is universal health care. In a January 2008 *Business First* article, it was reported that almost 80 percent of Americans believe their employers should be required to provide health care. Whether that happens or not remains to be seen, but the reality is that it is a very real expense for an employer, and your options should be carefully considered.

Health and Wellness Programs

In general, more and more companies are opting for preventative programs aimed at health and wellness. The benefits to the employer are obvious. Workers spend less time off work and are more productive. Many wellness programs offer incentives for losing weight and quitting smoking, regular flu shots, counseling for anger management, programs to reduce stress, and opportunities for physical exercise. While on-site gyms are expensive to implement, creative companies can come up with physical exercise programs that aren't as costly, such as yoga, step aerobics, or walking groups during the lunch hour. Other alternatives could be offering discount passes to local fitness clubs or swimming pools. At Pacific Lutheran University in Tacoma, Washington, a group of creative individuals mapped out several different walking paths based on distance. The project was called the "Lute Loop," and staff members regularly met at the lunch hour to walk whatever distance they had the time and energy for that day.

Employee Assistance Programs

Employee assistance programs (EAPs) are employer-sponsored programs designed to assist employees with problems that are not usually job related; some examples might be anger management, financial difficulties, divorce, and grief and education counseling. At a job site this author worked for, a manager was approached by a young employee who experienced an unexpected pregnancy and was struggling with the decision to keep the baby. This was a perfect opportunity to replace the employee to the EAP to get help with a decision so she didn't have to struggle with it alone.

In most EAPs, employees get confidential referrals to the program. And, to ensure anonymity, the receptionists take great care to make sure that Sally isn't waiting in the waiting room at the same time someone else from her company might be there. (Many companies can share EAP counseling resources.) Usually, the employees get a set number of counseling sessions paid for by the employer (six is common), and after that, employees can elect to continue counseling sessions at their own cost.

Table 6.3   Examples of Employer-Elected Benefits

Employee assistance programs	Tuition reimbursement	On-site day care	Paid leave	Paid holidays*
Sick leave	Personal leave	Vacation—can vary greatly from company to company on numbers of day	Relocation assistance— negotiable depending upon level of position	Medical, dental, vision insurances
On-site gyms	Wellness programs— quitting smoking assistance, for example	Pension Plans	Retirement assistance	Financial planning assistance
Parking/ commute assistance	Bus Passes	Religious programs	Dry cleaning pick up	Laundry facilities
Pets at work programs	Flexible scheduling	Telecommuting	Bereavement Leave for close relatives	

*depends upon states

CHAPTER SUMMARY

A total rewards program is one of the most important things that a company can develop for its current and future success. Attracting, recruiting, and retaining a competent workforce should be at the heart of every organization's mission and goals. Developing compensation and benefits plans for your employees is an enormously important—and complicated—task. HR needs to be aware of all of the federal, local, and state guidelines affecting payroll and compensable time. Developing a cohesive program of attractive and affordable benefits will assist an employer in recruiting and retaining employees. Employers should consider health and wellness options, holiday and vacation pay, and personal and sick leave when designing their benefits programs. Similarly, employers should take great care in developing a fair wage ladder within the company and should be aware of all of the components of compensation.

REVIEW QUESTIONS

1. What is the four-step process you should follow in developing your total rewards program?

2. What does it mean if an employee has a reduced FMLA schedule?

3. The Omnibus Budget Reconciliation Act (OBRA) limited executive tax deductions to how much annually?

4. A profit-sharing plan allows employers to contribute deferred compensation based upon a percentage of the company earnings. What is the maximum tax deduction for contributions by the employer?

5. What kind of exemption would a college or university professor meet?

6. Sandy is a receptionist at the local community college. She is a non-exempt employee. She has a 30-minute lunch period, but claims that she doesn't have time to get her work done, so she eats at her desk. Are you required to pay Sandy for the time she spends eating at her desk?

7. An Employee Assistance Program is a program designed to assist employees with non-job related issues, they are affecting employee behavior. Name some of the components of an EAP.

ANSWERS AND EXPLANATIONS

1. The four step process is Assessment, Design, Implementation, and Evaluation, in a continuous loop. It always begins with the assessment phase, because you need to find out where you are first, before you know where you can go.

2. A reduced FMLA schedule means working less during the work week or less during the work day.

3. Executive tax deductions are limited to $1 Million annually. This attractive perk is reserved usually for only the highest levels of senior managers and executives.

4. 25% of the total employee compensation is the maximum tax deduction for contributions by the employer.

5. The correct answer is professional exemption. A college professor would need to have several years of specialized intellectual training, be in a learning field, and primary work would require advanced knowledge in the field.

6. No, you are not required to pay Sandy. You have not required Sandy to stay at her work station; she is choosing to do so. You might work with this employee on managing her time better so that she can take a break.

7. Drug and alcohol counseling, pre-marital counseling, divorce counseling, and smoking cessation programs are all examples of common Employee Assistance Programs.

Employee and Labor Relations

LAWS AFFECTING EMPLOYMENT IN UNION AND NONUNION ENVIRONMENTS

The *employment and labor relations (ELR)* function in HR management oversees company employment policies and employment laws in union and nonunion environments. The rights and responsibilities of an organization toward its employees rely on understanding employment law and executing policies to ensure that all employees are treated fairly. Since the late 1700s, workers and employers have been concerned with fair treatment and nondiscrimination in the workplace. Legislation taking place over the past 220 years in U.S. history demonstrates a progression of laws created to prohibit discrimination and unfair labor practices. To understand how labor practices unfolded, a review of historical events leading up to the present follows.

Employee and Labor Relations History, 1776 to the Present

1790	First union formed in Philadelphia by shoemakers ("cordwainers")
1866	National Labor Union (NLU) founded. Prior to 1866, employee and labor relations grew increasingly violent as organizations worked to organize and workers came together to unionize.
1866	American Federation of Labor (AFL) was formed by Samuel Gompers, which stressed collective bargaining and unionism to protect workers. Up to this time, craftsman were members of the Knights of Labor which stressed social change rather than unionism. When the AFL formed, craftsmen left in hopes of unionization.
1877	The Great Uprising—the first organized, large-scale strike opposing worker abuse by employers.
1886	Haymarket Tragedy, remembered as a violent conflict between strikers, employers, and government interference. The deaths of several policemen resulted and public consensus turned against the labor movement.

Exam Note:

You should expect several questions about historical events, union activities, and legislation approved to protect American workers during the time period regarded as the labor-management movement.

1905	Industrial Workers of the World (IWW), collectively known as the Wobblies, was formed to oppose employer's use of legal injunctions seeking to prevent union organizing activity.
1908	Sherman Antitrust Act (1890), originally formed to prevent monopolies and other restraint of trade activities. In 1908, the Supreme Court amended the act to include unions. The act was amended again in 1914 by the Clayton Act, which removed union protection once again due to the boycott by the National Hatters of North America. This and other union organizing activities were determined to be illegal. The courts determined that participants were liable for these activities.

All of-the events named above occurred during World War I, when government elected to protect unions and labor-organizing activities. Post–World War I, Congress voted to amend protection of unions, until 1926 when the Railway Labor Act was passed.

1926	Railway Labor Act, federal legislation which guaranteed the rights of workers to form unions and bargain collectively. In 1936, legislation approved the airlines' rights to form unions under this act.
1932	Norris-LaGuardia Act, passed by Congress to prevent employers' collective power to use injunctions against union organizing activities, and yellow dog contracts became unenforceable. A yellow dog contract was instituted by employers as a condition of employment not to form or join a union.
1935	A new era unfolded in labor and management, known as the New Deal. Congress sought to mediate the divide between employers and unions. The Social Security Act of 1935 and the Fair Labor Standards Act (FSLA) of 1937 were passed to protect workers, guaranteeing long-term economic protection. The Wagner Act of 1935 further protected the rights of workers to form unions. Employers fought to declare it unconstitutional but the Supreme Court intervened, and in 1937, ruled that the act was constitutional. This ruling and strong support led to an increasing amount of workers joining unions, which peaked in 1950; about 35% of workers joined unions.
1936	Strike at General Motors—a historical event demonstrating the shift in the balance of power between management and organized labor.

1938	Congress of Industrial Unions (CIO) was formed. Previous to this time, craft unions formed the AFL. Industrial workers left the AFL to form the CIO, led by John L. Lewis of the United Mine Workers. This was a significant event because industrial unions were better organized. The CIO became a powerful labor movement in the new industrialized economy.
1938	Fair Labor Standards Act (FLSA) was passed prohibiting abuse in regard to work hours and types of jobs for individuals under the age of 18. The act serves to protect younger workers who might be exposed to possible injury or illness on the job.
1947	Taft-Hartley Act was formed following several post WWII strikes to balance the structure of power between labor and management.
1955	The AFL-CIO was united to form one labor organization.
1959	Landrum-Griffin Act was passed following hearings in Congress of alleged mishandling and abuses of power in union leadership, including corruption. This act ensured a bill of rights to union members preventing abuse of power and control and protecting the financial interests of its members.

Since 1959, U.S. labor laws are still in practice today. More recent legislative activity shifted to employee relations and employment law. HRM is actively engaged and responsible for communicating employment laws and policies to all employees.

1963	Equal Pay Act prohibits discrimination in pay and compensation practices regarding males and females equally qualified for job positions. Practices covered include effort, responsibilities, skills, and working conditions. The act does not cover benefits. Compensation differences are allowed under conditions of merit, quantity and/or quality of production, seniority, and factors not related to sex differences that are required in a job category.
1964	Civil Rights Act (revised) prohibits discrimination based on race, color, religion, sex, or national origin.
1967	Age Discrimination in Employment Act (ADEA) prohibits age discrimination.
1970	Occupational Health and Safety Act was created and established three important departments: OSHA—Occupational Safety and Health Administration; NIOSH—National Institute of Occupational Safety and Health; and OSHRC—Occupational Safety and Health Review Commission. Each department serves to protect workers regarding health and safety on the job.

1990	Americans with Disabilities Act (ADA) prohibits discriminatory hiring practices for American workers with disabilities. Disabilities are defined as physical impairments that substantially limit a life function (e.g., breathing, caring for oneself, engagement with other workers, hearing, learning or concentrating, lifting, speaking, standing, thinking, vision, and/or walking). Reasonable accommodations must be considered for disabled applicants and employees. If the impairment requires a reasonable accommodation and does not create a hardship in the workplace, the employer is responsible for providing accommodations where there is a record of the impairment.
1991	Civil Rights Act (amended) reversed the Supreme Court's conservative decision making (referred to as the "Reagan Court" of the late 1980's) and amended its provisions.
1993	Family and Medical Leave Act (FMLA) was passed to provide unpaid leave and protection for workers to care for self or family members due to the birth of a child, an adoption, or a serious medical condition or recuperation of self or another family member.

INDIVIDUAL EMPLOYMENT RIGHTS, ISSUES, AND PRACTICES

You may recall that this topic is also covered in chapter 5 from an HRD perspective; it is focused on ELR here.

Equal Employment Opportunity legislation and equal opportunity guarantee a safe workplace environment and one that is free of harassment. How employment decisions are made and federal legislation governing HRD activities must be understood. Important federal legislation includes the Civil Rights Act of 1964, the creation of the U.S. Department of Labor (DOL), and the Office of Federal Contract Compliance Programs (OFCCP).

Differences in the law exist from state to state, and federal law may differ from local government requirements. When laws conflict over the same topic or issue, it is important to understand that the *higher standard* usually applies. In most states, *laws favor the employee. Exceptions* in the law allow discrimination to take place which is ordinarily prohibited under the law and include the following:

- *Bona fide occupational qualification (BFOQ).* This allows an employer to exclude certain applicants on the basis of a specific job requirement. For example, if a workplace environment includes chemicals or products that produce an allergic reaction in some individuals (e.g., paint fumes or peanuts), it is legal to exclude certain applicants from an applicant pool based on an allergy or health-related condition (e.g., asthma).

- *Business necessity.* This refers to a condition where an employer requires a specific background of an individual in order to fill an important position in an organization. For example, if a position description includes contract negotiations in Russia, a specific job requirement might include applicants who speak fluent Russian and exclude applicants who do not speak fluent Russian.
- *Seniority systems.* This refers to conditions of length of service to an organization. For example, an employee's length of service to an organization may be a decision-making factor for promotions, start-up projects, layoffs, or possible reassignments. It is important to note this is a legal exception under the law and does not refer to an employee's chronological age.

ELR AND UNION ENVIRONMENTS

Union Structure and Formation

Before a discussion can begin about the structure and formation of a union, it is important to understand what a union is and what it is designed to accomplish. A *union* is a formal organization designed to represent and protect its members in matters of fair labor practices, management policies, and nondiscrimination in employment. By representation of its members through a collective bargaining process, unions negotiate hours, wages, labor practices, and other conditions of employment that are formally written into a document called a *collective bargaining agreement* ("Agreement"). Once the Agreement is ratified through a voting process by its members, the union and management are bound to uphold those policies and entitlements for all union members.

A *union shop* secures the viability of the union and its members. It requires all of its members to maintain union membership as a condition of employment. For example, if an applicant is offered a job at a company, and the job classification is a union position, the applicant will be informed that union membership is a requirement of the job. If the applicant is unwilling to join the union shop, the job must be declined. The applicant may qualify to apply for a nonunion position where union membership is not a requirement of employment.

Note that not all employees working for a company qualify to become union members. Union qualifications are determined by job classification and type of job performed. An organization may employ both union and nonunion members and is ultimately responsible for carrying out the terms of the Agreement. This is typically the work of HRM, where labor relations specialists are hired to manage the working relationships between union and nonunion members, and management and union representatives.

Collective Bargaining Process

The *collective bargaining process* is a meeting that takes place between union officials and company management. The purpose of the meeting is to negotiate terms of the *collective bargaining contract*, a legal document that outlines specific working conditions and benefits for union members employed by a company for a specified period of time. The National Labor Relations Board (NLRB) mandates that collective bargaining agreements facilitated through a collective bargaining process. Union officials and company management are expected to bargain in *good faith*—a union term—which occurs when both sides follow the rules of the collective bargaining process. Bad faith bargaining occurs when either party does not follow the required process and seeks to undermine the other side. Examples of bad faith bargaining are withholding information, stalling, refusing to bargain or discuss proposals, or advancing the bargaining process with a lack of concession on issues considered important by one side or the other.

Collective bargaining tactics include four strategies used by unions in the *negotiating process*: single-unit bargaining, multi-unit bargaining, multi-employer bargaining, and parallel bargaining.

Single-unit bargaining is a meeting that takes place between one union and one employer and is the most common strategy. *Multi-unit bargaining* takes place with one employer housing several different unions. The union negotiates with one employer for all unions employed at the same company—this is also called coordinated bargaining. An example is the airline industry, where each job classification functions as its own bargaining unit (e.g., airline attendants, mechanics, pilots); however, the union will negotiate for all units at the same time.

Multi-employer bargaining is a strategy where a union negotiates with more than one employer at the same time. For example, when the grocery store industry went on strike five years ago, all of its union members, who were employed by different grocery store chains, implemented a strike at the same time. This placed a heavy burden on employers to replace union members with nonunion members in order to keep grocery stores running.

Parallel bargaining includes many strategies with similar goals: leapfrogging, whipsawing, and pattern bargaining. While *parallel* suggests a process that happens simultaneously, it does not occur at the same time. Rather, the union negotiates with one employer at a time, and then uses the outcomes or gains made from one bargaining agreement as leverage at the next company negotiation.

Collective bargaining positions are approaches used in the collective bargaining process. They are identified as positional and principled.

Positional bargaining is a tactic employed to win strategies and includes specific demands made by each side in the negotiating process. The process is known to be adversarial and competitive; also called *hard bargaining* and *distributive bargaining*, one side will gain something from this tactic and one side will lose. Similar to a zero-sum game, one side gives up something so that the other gains something.

Principled bargaining is reserved for problem-solving, strategies. This form of bargaining is conducted in an atmosphere of open negotiation where both parties come together to work out solutions that had not been considered before the bargaining process began. Two types of principled bargaining strategies are integrative and interest-based bargaining (IBB). In the former, both parties come together to look at all of the issues and suggest agreed-to trade-offs on the issues. In the latter, both parties come together on issues because both know that more is to be gained by agreement than disagreement. An obvious example is the viability of a business—if the business is suffering greatly as a result of a strike imposed by the union, both parties understand that without the business, no one will be employed.

Collective Bargaining Agreement

Following the collective bargaining process, the collective bargaining agreement ("Agreement") is formalized in a legal document that outlines specific working conditions and benefits for union members employed by a company for a specified period of time. The employer agrees to abide by those conditions outlined in the Agreement for its members. The NLRB mandates that Agreements include mandatory subjects that are specific conditions of employment, including hours worked, wages earned, other conditions of employment, terms of the Agreement, and any other items related to the Agreement itself.

Clauses that are written into the Agreement are identified as contract administration, dues check off, no strike or no lockout, and zipper clauses. The administration of the Agreement determines how the contract will be administered during the time period of the contract. All policies, procedures, grievances, arbitrations, and resolutions are explained in the contract. If a clause is to be modified during the time period of the contract, a procedure is included in the contract explaining how it is to be carried out. Dues check-off refers to how union members will pay dues to the union organization. No strike or no lockout clause refers to the economic viability of the company and work stoppages. A zipper clause refers to the completion of the Agreement; once negotiations have ended and the Agreement is in place, a zipper clause enforces that changes to the Agreement during the time period of the contract may not be renegotiated.

Topics, or subjects, open for discussion during the negotiation process include mandatory, voluntary, and illegal. *Mandatory subjects* are those items that the NLRA defines as negotiable, such as wages, hours, terms of the Agreement, conditions of employment, and any other bargaining-related questions. Both parties brought to the negotiation are required to bargain on these mandatory subjects. Unresolved mandatory subjects are the only items that may be considered for a strike or lockout. *Voluntary subjects* are any other topics considered lawful, such as management responsibilities and rights, operations procedures, production schedules, and supervisor selection. *Illegal* or *unlawful subjects* may not be included in the negotiating process. Examples of illegal topics include closed shop (except for the construction industry) and hot cargo (a union tactic placing pressure on the company not to do business with a nonunion company).

The Reserved Rights Doctrine is included in the Agreement as a provision covering the rights of management to be responsible for topics not specifically addressed in the agreement.

Disputes will occur during the time period covered under the Agreement for a variety of reasons. When disputes arise, problem-solving solutions are instituted between the union and management to resolve them. Dispute resolution methods and tactics include binding and compulsory arbitration, mediation, court injunctions, lockouts, and boycotts, to name a few.

Binding arbitration is an important resolution process aimed at resolving disputes without litigation and without work stoppage. *Compulsory arbitration* is reserved for those disputes in the public sector where strikes are prohibited. Compulsory arbitration is mandated by legal statute.

Duty of successor employer occurs when a company is acquired by a new company and a union agreement was in place at the time of the sale. The successor employer is identified as the new company. If this happens, the NLRB steps in to decide whether the new company may assume the previous owner's union Agreement. The NLRB investigates several factors before a decision is made: the Agreement itself, the number of employees who remain at the company, differences in the operating plan of the new company, its services and products, and continuity of operations. The new company may not arbitrarily or unilaterally decide to make changes to the Agreement but must renegotiate a new Agreement through the collective bargaining process.

The NLRB governs employee relations activities. Courts serve to interpret and revise legislation as it pertains to employment law. However, ELR is an ongoing process scrutinized under the gaze of the NLRB. Significant court cases and judicial rulings (decisions) in employment law impact HRM practices and are discussed in the next section.

Significant Supreme Court Cases and Decisions in Employment Law

For the exam, you should be familiar with the following Supreme Court cases and decisions:

- *Communication Workers v. Beck (1988).* Beck rights gives rights to the bargaining unit member (employee) to pay a portion of union dues that directly impacts administration of a contract, costs for bargaining, and other organizing activities.
- *NLRB v. Wooster Division of Borg-Warner Corporation (1958).* The Borg-Warner doctrine allows the NLRB to make decisions on how bargaining issues are categorized: illegal, mandatory, or permissive.

- *Circuit City Stores Inc. v. Adams (2001).* Circuit City is commonly referred to in this case. Making compulsory arbitration as a condition of employment was determined to be legal. However, in a similar case, *EEOC v. Waffle House (2002)*, it was further determined that two parties may not contract away the rights of a third party. As such, federal or state legislative branches of government that enforce employee rights may continue to pursue action in cases where illegal discrimination may have occurred, even where compulsory arbitration agreements are required between employee and employer.
- *Excelsior Underwear Inc. v. NLRB.* The Excelsior list is a name and address registry of all employees determined eligible to vote in a union certification election. The list of names is compiled from HR and forwarded to the NLRB, a requirement in the certification process. The NLRB forwards it to the union.
- *NLRB v. Mackay Radio and Telegraph Company (1938).* The Mackay doctrine gives employers rights to permanently replace striking workers during an economic strike.
- *NLRB v. Weingarten (1975).* Weingarten rights allow employees to have representation at an investigative meeting with management if the employee believes that discipline will be discussed at the meeting. An important distinction to note: bargaining unit employees are guaranteed the right to have representation, but nonbargaining employees are not guaranteed this right though representation could take place. In a more recent decision, *NLRB v. IBM Corp. (2004),* it was determined representation would be allowed only for bargaining unit employees.

Unfair Labor Practices

Unfair labor practices (ULP) are those activities an employer or labor organization may use even though they are prohibited under the Wagner Act. Recall this act guarantees employees the right to join a union, participate in the collective bargaining process, and participate in other activities considered legal under the law. Management is prohibited from interfering with employees under this act, whether or not they agree or disagree with these activities.

Several common law doctrines are discussed:

- *Employment at will.* This is the most common and allows both parties (employer and employee parties) in the employment relationship to terminate service for any reason or cause, with or without notice. There have been many contract exceptions put into place since the original doctrine. As a result of the doctrine's erosion by court decisions and statutes over time, exceptions now include express contracts, implied contracts, public policy exceptions, and statutory exceptions.
- *Duty of good faith and fair dealing.* In effect, this provides that both parties enter into the employment relationship by carrying out their roles in fair and honest ways, ensuring that both parties benefit from the contract. It is considered an implied agreement and varies from state to state.
- *Promissory estoppel.* This is an inducement by the employer to have an employee carry out an action that will be rewarded by the employer;

Exam Note:

In particular, Circuit City, Excelsior list, and Weingarten rights are typically questioned on the exam. However, all of the cases named previously are significant and should be reviewed prior to taking the exam. Examinees should also be aware of the role of the NLRB.

however, the employee carries out the action, but the employer fails to reward the employee.

- *Fraudulent misrepresentation.* Similar to promissory estoppel, a misrepresentation by the employer occurs when promises made to a prospective applicant as an inducement to join the company fail to happen for whatever reason after the applicant leaves a former job and joins the company.

- *Respondeat superior.* Literally translated, this means "let the master answer." The employer is ultimately responsible for the actions of its employees. The action(s) must have taken place within the scope of the employee's job duties or during the course of the employee's employment.

- *Constructive discharge.* This is very similar to a hostile work environment created by the employer to motivate the employee to resign from the organization. The courts view this as a cause of action that can be brought against the employer by the employee. Legal standards vary state to state, and the burden is on the employee to show that the employer caused the resignation due to intolerable working conditions.

- *Defamation.* This refers to some form of communication that damages the person's reputation in the community. When it is obvious and deliberate, it is called malicious defamation and most often occurs after the employment relationship has terminated. Defamation is closely related to reference checking when an employer either gives personal information upon inquiry about an employee or receives information about a prospective employee. As a result, reference checks are limited to a brief inquiry, such as name and time of service. *Qualified privilege* refers to employer information given that is job-related only, truthful, and unequivocal.

- *Sexual harassment.* Title VII of the Civil Rights Act of 1964 guarantees that employers will provide a workplace free of sexual harassment. Harassment is divided into two categories: hostile work environment and quid pro quo. In the first, the EEOC defines hostile work environment as "when submission to or rejection of this conduct explicitly or implicitly affects an individual's employment, unreasonably interferes with an individual's work performance, or creates an intimidating, hostile, or offensive work environment." Recent court cases have also held that coworkers, suppliers, or visitors are subject to the law. Quid pro quo is literally translated from Latin to "this for that." This occurs when a coworker asks for sexual favors in exchange for some kind of favorable employment action. Sexual harassment is used as a broad term to cover many unwanted actions in the employment relationship. Written policies stating harassment guidelines and their consequences as a result of harassment allegations should be part of every company's policy and procedure manual.

Employer Policy and Procedure Manual

A company's policy and procedure manual will vary according to the company's business and the state where the company is located. Typically, this manual is given to the employee as an employee handbook. When the employee is hired, a copy of the handbook is usually given to the employee to read and sign. The signature denotes agreement between the employee and employer as to those behaviors and guidelines expected of the employee while working for the company. The contents of both, the manual and the handbook, cover workplace policies, procedures, and rules around effective communications and workplace policies and procedures. Many controversial debates have arisen in recent years when courts ruled in favor of employees as a result of poorly written policy manuals or employee handbooks. In several cases, this resulted in awards to employees costing employers millions of dollars.

FACILITATING POSITIVE EMPLOYEE RELATIONS

Most organizations do not need to have a union in place and prefer to have control of the entire operation of the business. Recall that unions were born when employees were treated unfairly and in discriminatory ways. When membership in union shops became strong, labor and management could no longer ignore powerful union organizations. Management came to the bargaining table as they realized the success of their business rested on treating their employees with respect and dignity. While unions are not as prevalent as they were during World Wars I and II, unions continue today, a testament to their organizing strength and survival. Management continues to negotiate and carry out the terms of collective bargaining agreements today. Even so, most employers prefer to run a nonunion operation.

Treating employees with dignity and respect and offering wages, salaries, benefits, promotions, and other company rewards serves to foster positive employee relations and secure a union-free environment. When workers are treated poorly by a supervisor or management, are offered no incentives for promotion, education, or training, and continue to have things taken away from the working environment as opposed to having more opportunities, workers will become dissatisfied and pursue other measures or jobs to find better working conditions. The rule of thumb that most employers use as a measure to prevent a union election is to offer all employees the same, or similar, benefits and rewards that a union shop would offer. Going beyond these benefits and services by offering even greater noncompensation rewards should be the goal of an organization that seeks to remain union free.

How do employers measure employee satisfaction? Most often employers will analyze employee absenteeism and turnover as a yardstick to decide if changes need to be made in how an organization treats its people. Climate surveys are another measurement tool that reflects satisfaction or dissatisfaction in an organization. Company picnics, holiday gatherings, in-house award programs, service programs, and other perks and benefits serve to treat employees with respect and encourage them to be involved with the organizational community.

Global ELR Considerations

From an ELR perspective, HRM must be cognizant of employment relationships in foreign countries, whether U.S. labor laws conflict with foreign national labor laws, or any cultural differences that may impact the ELR policies of the organization. For example if a union shop is in place in one location, will it impact labor relations in another country or location? Does importing or exporting of goods and services affect ELR? Consideration must also be given to employees sent on overseas assignments (expatriates) hired under an employment agreement, a service contract, or time period. Will the company's employee handbook be enforceable in another country? Are at-will employment agreements enforceable legal documents across international borders?

CHAPTER SUMMARY

HRM is responsible for implementing compliant ELR programs. The ELR function is a cross-functional system that impacts the company at large and all of its employees, whether or not they are members of a union, and whether or not the organization is union free. The history of labor management summarizes the creation of the labor movement and how unions were formed. Unions still in operation today motivate effective labor relations programs and affect how well employees are treated in the workplace. Organizational culture rests with management's philosophy to treat employees with high regard and respect. Positive employee relations programs are strategies to remain union free and foster an organizational community. Legislation governing nondiscrimination in employment is a driving force for the hiring, training, employee selection, and fair labor practices between labor and management. Dispute resolution programs were discussed as ways to resolve work disputes and collective bargaining issues in union environments. Global ELR considerations include organizations having many locations, partners, or expatriates abroad.

REVIEW QUESTIONS

1. What are the EEOC, OFCCP, and NLRB?

2. What role did Congress play during the labor-management movement?

3. Briefly discuss a union organizing campaign.

4. Describe differences in an employer union environment and a nonunion (union-free) environment.

5. What is a collective bargaining agreement?

6. What is management's role in the union negotiation process?

7. What is the difference between binding and compulsory arbitration?

8. Name three dispute-resolution strategies.

9. How does a company facilitate positive employee relations?

10. What is a yellow dog contract and a zipper clause?

11. What are Weingarten rights?

ANSWERS AND EXPLANATIONS

1. The Civil Rights Act of 1964 created the enforcement agencies that regulate compliance. They are the Equal Employment Opportunity Commission (EEOC) and the Office of Federal Contract Compliance Programs (OFCCP).

    The EEOC is responsible for enforcement of Title VII of the Civil Rights Act (1964). The U.S. Department of Labor enforces the provisions of the EEOC. An important provision of the Act includes specific record-keeping and reporting requirements for all employees. Employment records can be requested by the EEOC or OFCCP. Employers meeting certain qualifications are required to file an annual report to the EEOC by September 30 of each year. Information shared in this report includes specific employment data such as employment selection practices, benefits planning, race, ethnicity and gender statistics, disciplinary actions, promotion programs, and attrition and retention figures.

    The NLRB, or National Labor Relations Board, was established by the National Labor Relations Act (NLRA), and serves in response to unfair labor practices.

2. Congress created the U.S. Department of Labor (DOL) in 1913. A federal agency, the DOL serves to protect workers, job applicants, and retirees in the U.S. It is the umbrella agency that oversees laws pertaining to workers. Its primary goals are to enforce and improve safe working conditions; monitor retirement and health benefits, employment statistics, unemployment, economic indicators, layoffs, new opportunities, and employment discrimination.

3. The union organizing campaign is a series of formalized steps required by law to establish a union. Once approved or voted upon, a union is a separate legal entity run by a formal collective bargaining agreement (which is ratified between the union and the business). Through a collective bargaining process, union members negotiate hours, wages, labor practices, and other employment conditions. Once the agreement is ratified by its members, the union and management are bound to uphold those policies and entitlements for all members.

4. In a union environment, a group of employees are held to the provisions of the collective bargaining agreement. A union representative is appointed to ensure that the agreement is carried out at all times. When disputes occur, the union representative meets with the employer before a decision takes place about an employee who is a union member.

    In a non-union environment, there is no formal collective bargaining agreement, and no representative protecting the best interests of the employees. In a non-union environment, there may be representation through HRM, where an employee may go to file a complaint. Usually, benefits are similar; however, in union environments, certain classifications of employees are required to join a union and pay membership dues.

5. A collective bargaining agreement is a formal agreement between two parties (the union and the employer) which seeks to uphold the rights of both parties. The agreement formalizes the relationship between the parties.

6. Management's role in the union negotiating process is to allow union representatives and employees to organize a union and participate in negotiation. Management must not interfere, discriminate, or take part in the organizing campaign; however, it agrees to abide by those conditions outlined in the agreement.

7. Binding arbitration resolves disputes without litigation and without work stoppage. Compulsory arbitration is reserved for disputes where strikes are prohibited. It is mandated by legal statute.

8. Arbitration, meditation, and peer review are three key dispute resolution strategies.

9. Treating employees with dignity and respect, and offering wages, salaries, benefits, promotions, and other company rewards serve to foster positive employee relations.

10. A "yellow dog contract" is used by employers as a condition of employment, and asks employees not to form or join a union. A "zipper clause" refers to the completion of the collective bargaining agreement. Once negotiations have ended and the agreement is in place, a zipper clause enforces that changes to the agreement during the time of the contract may not be renegotiated.

11. Weingarten Rights (established in the 1975 case NLRB v. Weingarten) give employees the right to have representation at a disciplinary meeting. An important distinction to note: bargaining unit employees are guaranteed the right to have representation, but non-bargaining employees are not guaranteed this right. In a more recent decision, NLRB v. IBM Corp. (2004), it was determined that representation would be allowed only for bargaining unit employees.

Risk Management

The public has never been more aware of risk in the workplace than it has in recent years. Unfortunately, workplace and school shootings are on the rise. Routinely, we hear in the news about someone who has "gone postal" at the workplace after a perceived slight by a colleague. And risky behavior doesn't stop at workplace violence. Twenty years ago, we not only didn't worry about someone stealing our identity, it never would have even occurred to most of us how someone could do it—or why they would want to. Now we are keenly aware of guarding our personal information, such as Social Security numbers, our medical information, and anything we do over the Internet.

It is the wise organization that takes great care in developing a program designed to reduce and assess risk. People in diverse fields such as finance, toxicology, medicine, business, psychology, investment management, biology, engineering, systems analysis, and Internet security have been addressing the issues surrounding risk management. In this chapter, we will address risk management as it relates to workplace health and security, privacy issues, and occupational injuries and illness. We will also address safety issues and workplace violence and how you can guard against it and, hopefully, prevent it. For purposes of the PHR and SPHR exams, you will need to have knowledge of how to develop, implement, and assess issues associated with risk management, and the federal laws related to it. In addition, you should be able to understand safety and security risk and potentially violent behaviors in the workplace. The PHR and SPHR exams also require knowledge of health and safety techniques.

What is risk management? *Risk management* is a structured approach to assessing risk in your business and developing strategies to prevent it from occurring. Or, in other words, it's managing the uncertainty of threats from various sources (human, environment, technology, outside entities) by assessing those threats and minimizing or eliminating their potential to do harm to people or your organization.

Risk management strategies are unique to every business. It might involve the threat of a competitor stealing the patent on a new drug that has been researched for decades. Or, to the makers of a drug that you are going to put into your body, risk could be associated with failure of the drug to do its job or with the potential for the drug to harm you in some way. Tylenol's television ad campaign in early 2008 shows a series of Tylenol workers (or actors) declaring their pride in working for the company and their affirmation that they will never forget they make a product that is going into someone's body.

Other risks include financial mismanagement, product loss, computer threats and security breaches, personnel and people risks, record breaches, and natural disasters.

WORKPLACE HEALTH, SAFETY, SECURITY, AND PRIVACY

Every employee has the right to a safe and secure workplace. As dictated by law in the Occupational Safety and Health Act of 1970 (described in detail below), employers must provide for a safe and healthy workplace. But as anyone who has heard or read about the killings at Columbine High School, Virginia Tech, or any of the recent mining disasters knows, this is not always possible. However, employers are required to take all steps possible to minimize and reduce hazards that can potentially cause harm.

Occupational Safety and Health Act of 1970

It was somewhat amazing to the author to think that it took until 1970 to develop a law dealing with occupational safety and health standards, until she witnessed a presentation from a local contingent that had visited China. In the presentation, workers in nearly all walks of occupations routinely performed potentially harmful—even potentially fatal—tasks with virtually no safety measures in place, such as handling dangerous equipment or working with sick patients.

In 1970, the Occupational Safety and Health Act was enacted by Congress and the Occupational Safety and Health Administration was born. OSHA, as it is commonly called, sets the safety standards for all industries.

In 2007, OSHA listed its goals as threefold: 1) strong, fair, and effective enforcement of workplace safety laws; 2) outreach, education, and compliance assistance; and 3) partnerships and cooperative programs.

The main purpose of this act is to underscore that all employers must provide a workforce that is free of hazard and harm, and one that eliminates agents likely to cause death or serious injury. In addition, the act requires all employers to adhere to the laws and standards as outlined in the act and to comply with occupational safety and health standards, rules, and regulations by industry.

Employer Rights and Responsibilities

Employers have the duty to comply with the standards outlined in the Occupational Safety and Health Act and provide workers with an environment safe from harm. It is important to note that HR professionals should keep current with OSHA laws and federal legislation as they pertain to the work environment, because the laws are continually changing—even as this book goes to press (see "In the News" on the sidebar). Table 8.1 outlines employer rights and responsibilities.

Table 8.1 OSHA and Employer Rights and Responsibilities

Employer Responsibilities	Employer Rights
Report to OSHA any fatal accidents within eight hours or any accident requiring hospitalization of three or more employees.	Request identification from an OSHA officer visiting your business.
Provide employees access to medical records upon request.	Accompany the compliance officer as she tours yours business and does the inspection.
Post OSHA that identify potential threats or hazards i.e. in a place where employees gather for lunch or punch time clocks.	Have the assurance that any trade secrets will be held in confidence after the officer has visited your business, i.e., she doesn't share with Coke what Pepsi is doing.
Provide safe tools and equipment and protective gear or clothing.	
Keep accurate records of any workplace injury.	
Provide training on OSHA standards.	
You may not discriminate against any employee that challenges a potential workplace violation of a safety standard.	
Post violations of workplace standards.	

OCCUPATIONAL INJURY AND ILLNESS HAZARDS

Health hazards in the workplace fall into several general categories, as listed in table 8.2.

Occupational Injury and Illness Prevention Programs

As the saying goes, prevention is the key to better health. The same goes for the workplace—assessing your areas of risk and having plans in place to prevent injury and illness should be at the cornerstone of any employer's HR mission.

In March 2008, OSHA sent letters to over 14,000 businesses that were identified as having higher than usual risk of on-the-job injuries. Assistant secretary of labor Edwin G. Foulke, Jr., is quoted as saying: "A high injury and illness rate is costly to employees and employers in both personal and financial

Real World Note:

In March 2008, the Occupational Safety and Health Administration (OSHA) announced the release of *Ergonomics for the Prevention of Musculo-skeletal Disorders: Guidelines for Shipyards,* an industry-specific guidance document that provides practical recommendations to help employers and employees reduce the number and severity of musculoskeletal disorders in the workplace.

"Shipyard work is considered one of the most hazardous occupations, with an injury rate more than twice that of construction and general industry," said Assistant secretary of labor for OSHA, Edwin G. Foulke, Jr. "These guidelines will assist many shipyards in their continued efforts to address and implement ways to reduce work-related musculoskeletal disorders."

terms. Our goal is to make them aware of their high injury and illness rates and to get them to focus on eliminating hazards in their workplace. To help them in this regard, OSHA offers free assistance programs to help employers better protect the safety and health of their employees."

Table 8.2 Occupational Health Hazards

Biological Exposures	Chemical Exposures	Physical Exposures
Anthrax	Toxic metals	Ergonomics, repetitive motion injuries
Asbestos	Exhaust fumes	Excessive noise/hearing prevention
Secondhand smoke	Formaldehyde	Radiation
Needlesticks	Indoor air quality, i.e., "sick building syndrome"	Extreme hot and cold temperatures
Food-borne diseases, e.coli, botulism	Latex allergies	Radio frequency and microwave radiation
Carcinogens	Hazardous waste	On-site preventable falls or physical hazards, such as tripping over an item
Avian Flu	Lead poisoning	Sick coworkers
SARS	Mercury poisoning	Secondhand smoke
Molds and fungus	Toxic chemicals	Stress

Source: http: www.osha.gov

WORKPLACE SAFETY RISKS

The Bureau of Labor Statistics reports that in 2006 there were 5,703 work-related fatalities. The greatest percentage (42 percent) of these were lumped into the category of transportation incidents, followed by contact with objects and equipment (17 percent), falls (14 percent), assaults and violent acts (13 percent), and exposure to harmful substances and environments. (All statistical information is from the Bureau of Labor Statistics at www.bls.gov.)

Some interesting statistics and findings were gleaned from the most current information about workplace safety and are worth noting for consideration at your business:

- Of the 809 fatal falls in 2006, nearly 2 in 5 involved falls from roofs or ladders.
- Of those 5,703 fatalities, 92 percent of them were males.
- A higher percentage of fatal work injuries to women resulted from highway incidents and homicides than for men.

- A higher percentage of fatal work injuries to men were the result of contact with objects and equipment at the workplace (e.g., construction injuries).
- The construction industry had the highest number of injuries, followed by agriculture, forestry, fishing, and mining.
- Education and health services had the lowest numbers of fatalities.
- Fatal injuries were highest for fishers, aircraft pilots and flight engineers, and logging workers in 2006. However, there was a huge increase in the number of fatalities for truck drivers and sales drivers.
- Source: U.S. Bureau of Labor Statistics, U.S. Department of Labor, 2007

WORKPLACE SECURITY RISKS

In the past decade, the potential for security risks has increased exponentially. You only have to visit an airport, school, city government agency, or public utility agency to note all of the security measures in place. It is not uncommon anymore for employees to wear credentials around their necks identifying them as employees, and for hospitals to have extensive security policies in place including measures to safeguard new babies from being kidnapped.

Workplace security risk comes in various forms: financial risk, risk from people, workplace violence, threats from natural disaster, terrorist attacks, computer security breaches, violence, and theft of products or intellectual property. Workplace violence will be addressed as a separate topic in the next section.

Natural Disasters and Terrorist Attacks

In 2001, the United States witnessed the most horrific attacks on its shores when terrorists flew hijacked American planes into the Twin Towers of the World Trade Center and the Pentagon, followed by a thwarted attack on the White House. In 2005, Hurricane Katrina hit New Orleans and essentially wiped out the entire city, which is still being rebuilt as of this writing in 2008. Because the city did not have an adequate plan in place for such a full-scale emergency, citizens had nowhere to go for refuge, hospitals were crowded beyond capacity, and there was little available food, shelter, and resources to assist people in a humane manner. If these two tragedies aren't enough to give most of us a wake-up call about being prepared for the unexpected, the many other natural disasters and terrorist plots since then should be. All companies should be prepared for the unexpected and have a clear plan outlined on how they will help their employees find safe cover and an adequate escape plan in the case of an emergency. To not have a plan in place is naïve. Whether it be for a hurricane, tornado, fire, ice, or earthquake threat, your business should be prepared.

In 2007, after a mass killing at Virginia Tech, a rash of copycat threats sprung up on campuses all over the United States. This was a wake-up call—not only for schools and colleges to examine their evacuation and alert plans, but also for businesses around the country. How are you going to get the word out to your employees in the case of an evacuation? While technology may be on your side in the case of an emergency, it also might not be. A thorough assessment of your alert policies should take place, and you should ask the following:

- Do you have an emergency alert plan? Can you quickly (i.e., in seconds) alert employees of a lockdown or an evacuation?
- Have you examined some of the newest technology to quickly alert employees, such as mass emails to employee computers, text messaging to staff members, and "red-alert" phone messages? Do you have employee cell phone numbers?
- In the case of natural disasters, do you have a policy in place on who should report to duty? Have you identified individuals who are key workers that can manage the threat?
- Have you identified individuals who can handle communications with the media in the case of emergency?
- Do you have a policy in place for how and where employees should evacuate buildings? How will you account for employees after an evacuation? (At one employer, for example, different buildings are evacuated to specific sites—and once there, one key individual is responsible for counting heads.)
- Have you *practiced* your employee evacuation plan? In earthquake-prone areas, duck, roll, and cover drills are appropriate. Have you had a fire drill recently?
- Who makes the decision to evacuate the building? Do you have a back-up plan if that individual is unable or unavailable to make that decision?

Many cities, in the wake of the above-mentioned disasters and emergencies, are now working together with a variety of public and private agencies to develop comprehensive emergency preparedness plans. Usually, they involve cooperative efforts between the police, fire department, nonprofit agencies, and city, local, and state governments.

Computer Security Breaches

Unfortunately, computer hackers are the newest wave of security risks. With most information now stored online, this is a real and grave issue for many companies. Our personal and financial secrets are all there for the next computer hacker to attack with a virus and wipe out or steal out from under us.

WORKPLACE VIOLENCE

The Bureau of Labor Statistics reported that nearly 5 percent of private industry establishments experienced an incident of workplace violence in the past year. While most reported that the occurrence had a negative impact on its employees, most did nothing afterward to change their policies or programs. Surprisingly, the place where the greatest incidence of workplace violence occurred was state government.

Just two months into 2008, a gunman walked into a suburban St. Louis–area city government building and shot and killed six city officials and seriously injured that town's mayor. At Northern Illinois University, just north of Chicago, a former graduate student walked on to the campus—armed with several weapons—and entered a lecture hall and killed five people before killing himself. His girlfriend, who cooperated with the press, said he "wasn't delusional; there was no warning; he was himself. He was normal." But usually when one digs deeper after these horrible incidents take place, there are signs, and there are signals. As an HR professional, it is important to pay attention to the clues.

INCIDENT AND EMERGENCY RESPONSE PLANS

When this author experienced her first earthquake—a 6.8 on the Richter scale—in Seattle, Washington, in 2001, inside a gift shop lined with glassware at a shopping mall, the first thought I had was, What do I do? (Duck under a bench in the middle of the mall.) Where do I go? (Outside, as quickly as possible.) And how do I get there in the dark? (Carefully.) From natural disasters to fire to threats to safety and security, it is important to develop an incident and emergency response plan to help your workers to a secure and safe environment as quickly as possible. Many cities are now developing comprehensive plans that provide for multiple agencies to work together in the event of critical emergencies.

One only needs to remember September 11, 2001, to recall how things can go very right—or very wrong—during a critical emergency. It is imperative that the plan outline all of the critical lines of communication and technology that will be used in the case of emergency.

The Federal Emergency Management Agency (FEMA) is responsible for policies and programs for emergency management at the federal, state, and local levels. This includes the development of a national capability to mitigate, prepare for, respond to, and recover from the full range of emergencies, including natural and technological disasters and national security emergencies.

In 2004, FEMA developed a plan entitled "Are You Ready? An In-depth Guide to Citizen Preparedness," its most comprehensive source on individual, family, and community preparedness. It is available from FEMA, at www.fema.gov, and provides the most up-to-date disaster preparedness information available.

The plan provides a step-by-step approach to disaster preparedness. It includes information about emergency plans, how to identify hazards in your local area, how to develop and maintain an emergency communications plan, and how to prepare your company or family for natural disasters. In the wake of recent disasters—Hurricane Katrina, September 11 terrorism attacks, fatal incidents at the workplace or on college campuses—many cities have examples of their own that you can refer to as well. Other topics that FEMA addresses include evacuation, emergency public shelters, working in conjunction with local service agencies, such as the Salvation Army or Red Cross, how to help animals in disaster, and information specific to people with disabilities.

You will, of course, want to concentrate on the potential emergency situations most critical to your geographic area.

Emergency Planning

The first place to start in developing your emergency plan will be to identify the key individuals who will be responsible in the case of emergency.

Key Staff/Responsibilities

It is crucial to identify the key staff who will implement the emergency plan once you know a disaster/emergency has taken place. Some key elements of the plan that should be addressed include the following:

- Who will make the decision to evacuate the building in the case of emergency? Who are the designated individuals if this person can't be reached, is not present, or is in some way incapacitated? Do you have a reporting line of communication on how to reach one another?

- Do you have staff members designated to take a head count of employees who have been evacuated from the building? For example, at one university outside of Tacoma, Washington, there is a designated staff member in each division who takes roll call outside of a specific landmark known to everyone in the case of an emergency and/or during fire drills.

- Do you have any personnel certified in first aid? Do you have cardiac defibrillators and personnel who can use them?

- Have you identified key individuals to speak to the press and provide public information?

- Have you identified a way that the public can get information about employees' safety and security?

Evacuation Plan

Do you have an evacuation plan at your place of business that would allow all workers to safely evacuate in 15 minutes? You should. And it should be well rehearsed as well. An emergency and evacuation plan is more than just paperwork. A carefully prepared and regularly practiced plan might be the difference between life and death. The Department of Labor's OSHA website has e-guidelines to assist your business in deciding what key elements should be included in an evacuation and how to comply with OSHA standards. The guidelines, which can be found at www.osha.gov/SLTC/etools/evacuation/index.html, cover such topics as when you should or shouldn't evacuate in case of a fire, how to evaluate your business, when and how to train your employees, and the proper way to evacuate in an emergency to lessen the degree of injury or harm.

Your evacuation team should include a diverse group of staff members that are well suited to handle emergency situations and communications.

Your evacuation plan will be determined by the state, county, and facilities where you operate your business.

INTERNAL INVESTIGATION, MONITORING, AND SURVEILLANCE

In just the scope of ten years, we have become a heavily computer dependent world. Where we would have been shocked to have our emails monitored in 1998, we are no longer shocked to learn that emails are monitored by most businesses in 2008. Consider the following found in local news:

> The CEO of The Boeing Company was fired by his board of directors when a savvy IT person noticed a trend in his emails to a female administrator and "leaked" the information of his affair. The CEO had an ethics clause in his contract and while his private life was his own, the board determined that he had violated his contract.

> The Mayor of Spokane, Washington was "outed" by local news media when it was determined that he was cruising gay chat rooms, on his office computer at City Hall. Although the Mayor argued that it was "after hours," he was still using city owned property. The Mayor was recalled from office and has since died.

> A Seattle-based large company monitored the computer of a staff member that was soliciting underage boys, reported him to the police, where he was followed to a motel room and arrested.

And, while NOT in the news, the author heard about someone who was fired from her position at an investment firm for emailing her boyfriend in Germany while on company time.

Monitoring Employees

When, how, and what can you do to monitor and investigate your employees? Most women know the creepy feeling you get in a retail changing room knowing that you are being monitored as you undress. We know it is necessary in the retail industry to avoid theft. There are a lot of reasons that employers monitor their employees; theft of money, products, and equipment are just a few reasons. Other examples include theft of information, research ideas, drugs, or data.

So before we all assume that everyone is a liar and a thief, we should start a discussion about privacy in the workplace and that there is a reasonable assumption that we have privacy. That privacy includes both our personal space and bodies. *All human resource departments should have*

Real World Note:

In Green Bay, Wisconsin, at the James River paper plant in the early 1990s, the body of Thomas Monfils was found at the bottom of a paper vat. He had a large weight tied around his neck. It turned out that Monfils had called Green Bay police with a tip that one of his coworkers, was going to steal a large, expensive electrical cord. The police called security at the plant—and security tried to search him on his way out the door. Kutska refused and was suspended for five days. Kutska was furious that someone snitched on him and set out to find who had done it—and eventually information from the police (incredibly!) released to the coworker led him to the employee and the eventual brutal murder. More than three years later, six employees were finally convicted of the conspiracy and murder. (One would bet that James River now has video surveillance at the plant!)

in place a very clear workplace privacy policy. It should clearly include the following:

- Guidelines for how email, text messages, instant messages, voice mail, and Internet usage is to be monitored.
- When/if Internet usage is acceptable during work hours, lunch hours, and after hours. Is it okay, for instance, for Kathy to search for airfares on her lunch hour or after work? Can Mark email his wife to say he's running late or ask if he needs to stop on the way home for groceries? Most businesses find some of this acceptable, others are much more strict when it comes to short personal messages. You need to decide which is right for your business.
- The employer's right to review data on all office computers.
- Acceptable/unacceptable usage of workplace telephones, pagers, cell phones, automobiles, cameras, etc.

Personal Property Searches

A search may be conducted of personal property when theft is suspected because it has been caught on surveillance or reported by another employee. However, as an employer, you must decide if it is for a legitimate business reason. If you are a retail manager at a clothing store and a sales clerk shows up wearing an outfit that you don't remember her purchasing—you have every right to ask her to produce the receipt and to conduct an audit of inventory. You may ask to search the desk or locker of an employee you suspect has stolen equipment or supplies.

You may not conduct a search of a person's body or ask someone to undress (shockingly, this happens!). In the case of suspecting an employee of hiding something on his body or under his clothing, you should call local police.

Video Surveillance

It is not at all uncommon to find video surveillance in more and more places. Even small stores with relatively few employees find that it is necessary to have video surveillance on the premises. More than one criminal has been caught shoplifting at late-night convenience stores because of cameras on-site. In addition, it can be a safety measure for employees who work alone and are potentially at risk for a predatory crime. For obvious reasons, video surveillance is not appropriate in restrooms or employee changing rooms.

SUBSTANCE ABUSE AND DEPENDENCY

Substance abuse and dependency is a huge problem among the U.S. workforce. 12.8 million people are employed either part- or full-time. The implications of the likelihood for error, accidents, and injuries by people under the influ-ence of drugs or alcohol should be enough to scare any employer into hav-ing a comprehensive drug plan. In addition, there are the increased costs in covering these individuals' sick leave, absenteeism, and decreased productivity. Substance abusers cross all socioeconomic lines, all industries, and are of both genders. They make mistakes operating heavy equipment, or no equipment at all. As an employer, you are responsible for any accident that a substance abuser causes at your workplace—or any customer service issue that occurs because of the employee being high on some substance. Imagine a nurse, high on drugs, being the one caring for your elderly father. Imagine a sales manager selling textbooks, driving from city to city, school to school, who is abusing alcohol and driving with a hangover or while drunk. The implications are mind-boggling. If you are an employer who is a federal contractor subject to the Drug-Free Workplace Act, and a staff member continues to abuse drugs at your workplace, you could be fined and lose potential contracts.

Drug Testing Programs

OSHA recognizes that impairment by drug or alcohol use can constitute an avoid-able workplace hazard and that drug-free workplace programs can help improve worker safety and health. Drug-free workplace programs can help to prevent cost-ly errors, accidents, and injury—particularly in businesses where workers operate heavy machinery. Can you just imagine the sales clerk at Home Depot operating a lift truck filled with heavy lumber while high on drugs?

Once a company decides to implement a drug testing program, it is impera-tive that it is designed to be fair and impartial to all, and it must detail what types of testing will be implemented. In early 2008, a new plan was released by the federal government outlining a strategy addressing the supply of and demand for illegal drugs—and, for the first time, it highlighted the threat of abuse of prescription drugs as well.

Drug-free workplace strategies are known to be powerful tools for prevent-ing and identifying substance abusers. Employers decide to implement drug testing plans for a variety of reasons—early detection, prevention, intervention, and disciplinary reasons. As a plan is implemented, the employer should ask the following types of questions:

- Who are we going to test? All employees or only employees for certain types of positions?
- When will we do the testing? Preemployment? Random? Scheduled?
- What drugs will we test for? Will we test for prescription drugs?
- What will we do with the information once the individual is tested?
- How will the testing be done? Who will conduct it? Where will it be conducted?

It is important to note that before implementing a drug testing program, your organization should make sure that it is complying with any local, state, and federal regulations—as well as the regulations of your employee union, if there is one.

The Department of Labor encourages an employer with a drug testing plan to highly educate its workers with a written policy stating its zero tolerance for drugs in the workplace. You should train your staff on how to implement the policy and how to recognize substance abusers in the workplace. (See some of the common signs found in table 8.3.) You should have a program in place for helping a worker receive counseling in a confidential setting when it is needed.

It is strongly suggested that legal counsel be consulted before creating a drug testing program.

Table 8.3 Signs of Substance Abuse

Inconsistent work performance	Slow pace of work, sporadic, or a manic-type pace
Difficulty concentrating	Excessive fatigue
Silly mistakes, where none occurred before	Errors in judgment
Difficulty making deadlines, where it never occurred in the past	Increased absenteeism or chronic tardiness
Smells of alcohol in the morning	Excessive sick leave
Patterns of absenteeism—i.e., Monday mornings, Friday afternoons	Extended break periods
Mood changes—irritability, moodiness, arguing a lot with coworkers or supervisors	Changes in appearance—sloppy dress, unshaven, uncombed hair, dark circles under the eyes
Physical changes such as slurred speech, dilated pupils, red eyes, sweating a lot, sleepiness	Changes in family relationships, friendships, patterns of money problems

BUSINESS CONTINUITY AND DISASTER RECOVERY PLANS

The 2005 hurricanes along the Gulf Coast proved to the entire United States how very important having a disaster plan in place is to states, cities, and local communities. The sight of thousands of individuals stranded, injured, and dying at the Superdome is something many of us will never forget. It underscores the point that anything can happen and how everything can go so horribly wrong when the plans and systems that you have in place fail.

Equally important as having an emergency preparedness plan in place is paying attention to what happens in the aftermath of a disaster. As of 2008,

New Orleans is still pulling itself up by the bootstraps and recovering from the hurricane. No business or city wants to find itself in similar circumstances. Planning for the aftermath is equally as important and the following points need to be considered:

- How will your business continue to operate after an emergency? If you are a school, for instance, do you have a plan in place for temporary operations for short- or long-term relocation?
- Who will you turn to for assistance in recovery? Do you have shelters identified? Vendors that you can call for assistance?
- Will your customers still be able to be served? How? Even for small emergencies, such as prolonged power outages, do you have emergency generators? Can you operate the cash registers or do you have contingency plans if you can't?

DATA INTEGRITY TECHNIQUES AND TECHNOLOGY

Data integrity sounds like a term coined by a computer geek and sounds much more complicated than it really is. What data integrity means is keeping your data "whole" and managing the integrity of it when it is being retrieved, stored, transferred, or downloaded. It means keeping your data correct and consistent. Think of it in terms of your own medical files. You wouldn't want to transfer doctors and have your new doctor receive someone else's information thinking it represented your health history! It happens!

Information security in our highly computerized world has become increasingly important and critical to our business functions. With more and more online purchasing, banking, and computerized transactions, it is important for businesses to remain vigilant in maintaining secure operations.

CHAPTER SUMMARY

Risk management takes many forms. It involves assessing where hazard and preventable injury, accident, violence, or disaster has the potential to harm your workplace and the employees in it. By assessing your workplace's risks, you can put a plan and policies into place that allow you to address them when they do occur. While planning can never prevent all potential hazards from occurring at your workplace, a plan can help you to react calmly and rationally when something does happen. Part of a risk management program includes developing an emergency preparedness plan, an evacuation plan—in case of fire or other disaster—and a solid plan for resuming business after an emergency happens.

Preventing illness and injury and safeguarding against security risks are other important components to the health and well-being of your business.

Real World Note:

The Wine Alley, in Renton, Washington, didn't skip a beat when the power went out for seven long and cold days during an especially hard winter. Three winter storms hit in a row with the last knocking out power to over a million customers in the greater Seattle area. A couple of savvy business owners knew that, with nothing else to do, people might still be drinking wine! With a generator to power their lights and an old-fashioned handheld calculator and credit card swiping machine, the Wine Alley remained in business, while many others lost all seven days of sales!

REVIEW QUESTIONS

1. What does the Occupational Safety and Health Act of 1970 require?

2. Is an employer required to train employees who regularly work on computers how to reduce neck and back injury or carpal tunnel syndrome?

3. If a supervisor suspects an employee has been spending too much time on the internet during work hours, is it legal for the IT department to search the employee's computer records?

4. Darcy works in an office with George, Molly, and Kevin. Their cubicles are in close proximity to one another. Molly regularly comes into the office when she is ill claiming that she "can't" take time off because she needs the money. Without fail, after Molly comes to work sick one or more of her co-workers also becomes ill. What is this an example of?

5. An employee in a manufacturing plant uses the same repetitive motions throughout her workday and her wrists are beginning to ache, making it difficult to perform certain duties. What is this an example of?

6. What is data integrity?

ANSWERS AND EXPLANATIONS

1. Employers are required to educate employees on safe procedures and train them in proper training methods, they do not actually have to inform employees about all risks in the workplace. In addition, while an employer can eliminate ergonomics issues, at this point in time, they are not required to do so. In the case of fatal accidents, an employer must report any fatal accident or accident that results in hospitalization of three or more employees.

2. The answer is no. They are not required to train employees who work on computers how to reduce neck, back, and carpal tunnel injuries.

3. It is legal IF the employer has a policy stating that her behavior is a violation of company protocol. Depending upon what is found on her computer, and the employee's previous patterns of work, you may decide to either warn her or fire her for her behavior. If the internet sites she has been visiting are of a questionable or obscene nature (pornography, for instance), she would probably be fired immediately.

4. This is a preventable hazard in the workplace. Molly, the sick co-worker, does have sick leave, she is just choosing not to use it. Her supervisor should encourage her to stay home when she is ill, to prevent more of her coworkers becoming ill and more loss of production time.

5. The best answer to this question is (A), a preventable hazard in the workplace. Hopefully, with proper training and placement of Kiki's workstation you can help her to manage and avoid repetitive motion injury.

6. Data integrity is the process by which you enter numbers into an online database; accurately maintain, store, and transfer your data; verify accuracy, correctness, and validity of the data ; and prevent malicious or accidental altering of your documents.

Other Important Labor Laws

Discrimination in the workplace is a major concern for HR professionals. This chapter discusses employment laws and regulations regarding discrimination in the workplace. You will need to understand how the HRM professional becomes involved in a more direct, hands-on approach in the workplace when laws and employment discrimination situations intersect. This chapter reviews the steps that need to be carried out when illegal employment situations arise and how to avoid discrimination and potentially expensive employer/employee lawsuits.

TITLE VII AND THE CIVIL RIGHTS ACT OF 1964

Illegal employment discrimination occurs when employers single out applicants or employees on the basis of age, race, creed, disability, national origin, religion, military duty, sex, or gender. This provision is described under Title VII of the Civil Rights Act of 1964 and is governed by federal employment antidiscrimination laws.

Employment discrimination occurs when employers, employment agencies, unions, or any organization where interviewing and hiring take place discriminates against a job candidate. Discrimination and antidiscrimination laws are enforced at the federal level by the U.S. Equal Employment Opportunity Commission (EEOC). Employers may not discriminate against job applicants or employees in any area of employment, including the following: hiring and recruitment, firing or termination on the basis of age, promotions or demotions, testing and assessment, benefits and company perks, religion and culture, race, sex, or gender, training and development, transfers or layoffs, disability or medically reasonable accommodation(s), compensation, dispensation, or employee classification.

EMPLOYMENT DISCRIMINATION AND ANTI-EMPLOYMENT DISCRIMINATION

Employment discrimination and *anti-employment discrimination* are terms used interchangeably. Discrimination may occur toward employees in many situations: employer to employee, employee to another employee, supervisor to employee, manager to employee, or a sudden change in benefits impacting all employees, to name a few. A historical review of federal laws, unions, and regulations can be found in chapters 5 and 7.

EMPLOYMENT DISCRIMINATION EXCEPTIONS

Extraordinary situations may arise when it appears that an employer is singling out an employee for reasons that might be considered illegal, but in fact, are not prohibited by law. In these cases, employees are not protected from employment discrimination. For example, if a supervisor wants to terminate an employee due to a personality conflict that interferes with the day-to-day operations of the business or interferes with the working relationships and morale of the department, it is unlikely that this would be considered employment discrimination under the law. Why? Because there is no specific provision in law that mentions a personality conflict that can be defined under federal discrimination law.

Discrimination laws were enacted largely to protect employees; however, employers' rights serve to safeguard the protection, continuation, and safety of the business. The employment-at-will doctrine serves to protect both the employer and employee in matters of termination, firing, and giving notice to terminate employment.

AT-WILL EMPLOYMENT

At-will employment law is more often referred to as the *doctrine of employment at will* or the *employment-at-will doctrine* ("Doctrine"). The Doctrine was created by common law and designed to cover all states. Common law is defined as a body of knowledge about a law topic based on court cases and the outcome of those cases. The outcome establishes a precedent whereby all states practice or enforce the Doctrine under the common law principle. *Payne v. Western Atlantic RR* (1884) is the court case that established precedence at the *state* level. *Adair v. United States* (1908) is known as the court case setting precedent at the *federal* level.

According to the Doctrine, in the absence of an employment contract or employment agreement, employees or employers may terminate employment without notice or cause. However, employees and employers may not violate an employment contract or agreement, disregard the law, or ignore regulations or constitutional provisions of public policy as written in the Doctrine when terminating employment.

While the Doctrine does not require employers or employees to give advance notice to terminate employment, employment contracts and employment agreements may specifically state how a resignation is to be carried out. If it is not carried out like this, accrued benefits—such as sick leave, vacation pay, and bonuses—may be placed in jeopardy, including an employee's final paycheck. There may be specific parameters about how final paychecks will be distributed based on whether the employee is laid off, terminated, or enacts the resignation on her own. It is important to note that company benefits are not required by law. Therefore, it is at the discretion of the employer to decide whether accrued benefits will be paid upon termination. Generally speaking, it is based on the goodwill of the employer if benefits are paid upon termination.

Employees are not required to give notice under the Doctrine; however, it is standard practice to give at least two weeks' notice to an employer prior to an actual termination date for many jobs. Once notice has been forwarded to a supervisor or HR, the company will take steps to decide whether the employee should be persuaded to stay, or if the employee is a potential risk regarding security issues because he holds a high position within the organization and has access to sensitive data, or if he might become violent. Either of these reasons may cause the employer to allow the employee to leave before the two-week termination date. Or, if the employee is persuaded to stay, negotiations may begin between the employee and employer to create a new employment agreement or new position within the company. In some instances, a salary increase may result if the employee agrees to stay employed.

Employers may be required to give advance notice of a plant closing, restructuring, downsizing, and layoffs. Notice to terminate employment by an employer was established by the Worker Adjustment and Retraining Notification (WARN) Act, which determined that certain employers are required to warn affected employees at least 60 days in advance of a plant closing or layoff. During this time period, all accrued benefits must be paid regardless of whether an employer elects to release those affected employees prior to the end of the 60-day notification period. State law and the WARN Act override the "no notice" provision described in the Doctrine.

An important exception to the Doctrine exists when an employer is determined to be at fault for terminating an employee for discriminatory reasons. A discriminatory violation will be guided by the Civil Rights Act of 1964, and not the Doctrine. The reason is clear: a discriminatory discharge by an employer is considered an illegal discharge, which is considered to be an exception in the Doctrine.

The three specific exceptions described in the Doctrine are *public policy, implied contract,* and *covenant of good faith and fair dealing.*

Public policy refers to those standards, values, and principles that the court (or legislature) considers to be in the best interest of an individual and the general public. Violations of public policy are resolved through the court system.

Implied contract is the recognized abbreviation for *implied-in-fact contract.* This is an agreement between an employer and an employee(s) that was never *explicitly* documented in writing but *implicitly* agreed to by all parties involved. Examples include a company policy statement, employee manual, performance reviews, a supervisor's promise, or a history of action that may in fact be determined to be an implied contract between the employer and the employee. The inference is drawn that a promise of continued employment or permanent employment may be determined from an implied agreement or conversation.

Covenant of good faith and fair dealing refers to the employer's duty to treat employees ethically, responsibly, fairly, and honestly. It is noted that long-term employees are protected by this exception. Unfair labor practices can result in discrimination, in illegal discharge, or in not granting long-term rewards so that the employer may fabricate reasons to fire or terminate employees of long-standing employment. Coercion, denial of promotions, age discrimination, and retaliatory acts are a few tactics that employers may use to force long-term employees to quit.

All states enforce at-will employment; however, interpretation of the Doctrine is at the discretion of the individual state. It is a common practice for employers to ask employees to sign a document acknowledging that they received the document, to acknowledge the at-will relationship, and to agree to seek alternative resolution to employee disputes before lawsuits may be filed. Further, employees are frequently asked to sign contracts or employment agreements acknowledging receipt of the agreement, understanding of its contents, and intent to follow its terms. A typical example is a company policy manual or a position description.

Employers and employees may waive certain at-will employment rights through contracts and agreements. In a union shop, union-employer collective bargaining agreements may stipulate terms and conditions to terminate or may prevent employers from discharging employees holding membership in the union. For example, company policy may state that any employee who brings a firearm to work will be immediately suspended and/or terminated. If it is a union employee, the collective bargaining agreement may state that the employee will be suspended and a hearing will be held to determine whether the employee should be terminated.

However, if a supervisor fires an employee specifically because the employee turned 40 years old, it's quite likely to be employment discrimination under federal law. Age discrimination against employees who are 40 years old or over is illegal according to the Age Discrimination in Employment Act.

Individual states might prohibit more types of employment discrimination than are governed by federal law. Additionally, certain federal and state laws prohibit discrimination in the form of employer retaliation.

AFFIRMATIVE ACTION AND EQUAL OPPORTUNITY DISCRIMINATION

Introduced in chapter 5, *affirmative action* relates to discrimination that is prohibited in the workplace and how the employment process (hiring, selection and placement, promotion, termination, employee benefits, and pay) is carried out. It is important to note that not all employers will have a union or collective bargaining agreement to protect employees from discriminatory practices.

Affirmative action programs are designed to allow equal employment opportunity for all job candidates and employees regardless of age, race, national origin, religion, sex or gender, and disability. Programs are designed to explain employee rights and to recognize when discrimination has taken place. Under specific guidelines described in affirmative action programs, discrimination is prohibited and is grounds for major lawsuits. Cancellation of government contracts, and in some cases, could result in the shutdown of a business operation. Especially vulnerable are government-contracted organizations and Department of Defense (DOD) contractors.

Important Note:

Most employers do not have unions; therefore, HRM's duty is to inform and train all employees about activities that may result in affirmative action violations and equal employment opportunity discrimination.

ANTIDISCRIMINATION REGULATIONS

Age Discrimination in Employment Act (ADEA)

Age discrimination regards candidate and employee selection specifically prohibited under age discrimination laws. Employees protected under the Age Discrimination in Employment Act (ADEA) include those who are 40 years old and older and who are equally qualified for candidate selection based on knowledge, skills, and abilities (KSAs) when compared to other candidates.

Americans with Disabilities Act (ADA)

This act protects employees with disabilities classified under the ADA and their right to be reasonably accommodated in the workplace as long as reasonable accommodations will not present a hardship in the workplace to the employer or others. It is HRM's responsibility to determine reasonable accommodations for candidates and employees, ensuring employment rights that protect employees with disabilities and prohibit discrimination against them. Even though a work area may be reasonably accommodated, discrimination may still occur if the employee is asked to perform work considered different than other employees performing work in the same job category.

Equal Pay Act (EPA)

The Equal Pay Act of 1963 ensures equal pay for equal work; however, beware—in the United States it is rarely carried out and calculated in ways to demonstrate fairness. It has long been known that females are most frequently discriminated against in this category of the law. While employers are held liable for discriminatorily paying unequal wages, exceptions to the law and wage categories allow this practice to continue. For example, a job category may include a pay range from $50K to $60K. Two candidates are hired for the same job. The male candidate will be offered $55K and the female candidate will be offered $50K. The qualifications for both candidates are equal and both have been hired under the same job category. As shown in this example, the male is paid $5K more than the female candidate. As long as the pay range has been identified, and both salaries fall within this range, then pay discrimination has been protected under the law.

Family Responsibility Discrimination (FRD)

Family responsibility discrimination (FRD) is employment selection discrimination toward job candidates and employees based solely on their obligations to care for family members. For example, an executive secretary needs to leave at a certain time each day in order to pick up her children by 6 P.M. Her supervisor is annoyed because he needs her to work on special projects requiring some evening and weekend work. Overtime pay is offered but the employee can't accept additional job assignments even with a promise of additional pay because of family obligations. Her supervisor wants to replace her because he needs her to work when he has deadlines to meet. In this example, the executive secretary is protected under the law because she is able to continue carrying out the core responsibilities of the job she was hired for.

Harassment

Harassment in the workplace can take many forms. Sexual harassment is one type of harassment at work and includes discrimination based on gender, hostile treatment toward an employee due to gender differences or preferences, and discrimination toward employees who have been identified with AIDS. Statistics demonstrate that females are more often discriminated against (sexually harassed) by males than males are harassed by females. It has long been known that harassment based on sexual orientation—such as gay, lesbian, or transgender people—results in frequent workplace discrimination. Discrimination activities may be covert or overt, and they can also take place away from the work environment. When this happens, it is up to the employee to notify HRM so that proper steps to file a formal discrimination complaint are carried out and an investigation can take place.

Hostile Work Environment

A more subtle kind of harassment, which is not always easily identified, is called hostile work environment. This type of discrimination is considered to be harassment and takes place when a worker can demonstrate that he is treated differently, with hostile aggression, by a fellow coworker, a direct report, or someone who holds power over the employee's job. This may occur due to personality differences, promotions, demotions, or some other event that results in hostile behavior. This is determined by different treatment toward an employee subject compared to the treatment of all other employees who work in the same job category, department, or company. It is the responsibility of the employee to document and detail each hostile act as a formal record for HRM and to file a formal complaint. A formal investigation should be carried out in a confidential manner by an HRM representative, and a determination will be made. It is important to note that investigations may take several months to conclude.

Pregnancy Discrimination Act

Pregnancy, childbirth, and related health conditions are protected under the law. Pregnancy falls under the Family and Medical Leave Act (FMLA) and is considered a medical condition protected under the law. The law provides equal treatment to an employee who is pregnant or to her spouse. It provides for the caring of a newborn or the mother following the birth (or death) of a child. This law protects both parents.

WORKPLACE POLICIES THAT MAY RESULT IN DISCRIMINATION

Dress Codes

Employers have the right to establish a dress code policy. The company's dress code policy can be written or implied and will be considered discriminatory if it adversely impacts or singles out a particular group, class, or individual due to age, national origin, disability, religion, and/or sex. A common error is defining a dress code policy on the basis of sex that results in different policies for each gender. Employers may require that uniforms be worn as a condition of employment. Employers also may require that employees pay for their uniforms, but the employer may not profit from the sale of those uniforms. "Casual Friday" is a typical example of a dress code policy that should be clearly defined by the employer because the word *casual* will be interpreted differently by individual employees.

The airline industry is a typical environment where uniforms are commonly found. Uniforms are considered part of the job and a condition of employment. Displaying company logos is familiar to the public and enhances recognition of airline branding. Airlines may have several different uniforms for each of their employees based on job classification, not by person or gender. This example is a legal practice and would not be considered discriminatory. A highly publicized discriminatory practice occurred recently when a passenger flying on Southwest Airlines was asked to exit the plane as a result of wearing too provocative. While it was not the intent of the airline to single out a particular passenger, it was part of their dress code policy to distinguish *themselves* as a family airline. Unfortunately, this logic backfired and resulted in discrimination charges against the airline.

Interviewing, Candidate Selection, and Hiring

Discrimination could result during the interview and applicant screening process when questions of an illegal nature are asked or pursued.

It is illegal under the Civil Rights Act of 1964 and 1991 for employers to discriminate on the basis of race, creed, color, religion, sex, or national origin. The following examples are questions considered to be illegal in the interviewing, selection, and hiring process:

Race—You May Not Ask…
- What is your skin color?
- What is your race?
- Is your spouse Caucasian/Hispanic/African American/Asian?

Exceptions: There are no fair questions about race in an interview or on an application, but an employer may ask you to voluntarily indicate your race for the purpose of following required guidelines contained in affirmative action programs.

National Origin—You May Not Ask…
- You have an accent; where are you from?
- Where were you born?
- Are you an American citizen?

Exceptions: Employers are required to hire only those employees who may *legally* work in the United States. Employers may ask if you are eligible to work in the United States.

Age—You May Not Ask…
- When were you born?
- When did you graduate from high school?
- How old are you?

Exceptions: The Age Discrimination in Employment Act of 1967 protects workers over the age of 40 from age discrimination in hiring, firing, or promotions and demotions.

About Illegal Interview Questions

While illegal interview questions have been identified, it is not unheard of for interviewers to ask them in such a way as to sound legal. This is a gray area and not always against the law for interviewers (experienced and inexperienced) to ask them.

For example, it is not necessarily illegal to ask about your age or date of birth. Questions may be worded as, "What year did you graduate from high school?" Or, "What high school did you attend?" "May I see your driver's license for verification of identity and eligibility to serve alcoholic beverages?"

But if the candidate is 40 years old or older, it is illegal to ask about age and then decline to hire, *solely on the basis of age*. Again, there are ways that interviewers may structure questions to tweak out personal information or come up with a variety of reasons why a candidate was not hired. If it appears obvious that only young people below the age of 40 work for a company, it is likely that age discrimination or illegal discrimination in hiring has taken place.

Another way for employers to ask questions around race, gender, age, and national origin is to ask for *voluntary* information. This is usually accomplished in a written form; therefore, this practice does not constitute illegal questioning. In most cases, it is to follow the required guidelines of an affirmative action program.

Nepotism

Nepotism means favoring relatives or family members in a workplace setting. This is a tricky category when family members work together and have certain expectations about the working relationships between family members. It is not illegal in employment to hire relatives; however, many issues will surface when favoritism is given to a relative over an equally qualified candidate. An example may include hiring only family members for key positions and hiring minorities in lower positions without the benefit of promotions or other employment practices reserved only for family members. Nepotism is a slippery slope when outsiders are brought into an organization, and its consequences may result in employment discrimination.

Wrongful Termination

Wrongful termination may occur if an employee was terminated solely on the basis of discrimination. Firing an employee solely for a discriminatory reason is illegal.

Criminal Records, Investigations, and Security Clearances

The extent to which employers may consider criminal records in job hiring, discharge, and other employment decisions, while avoiding discrimination, is also mandated by law. Employee rights protection regarding criminal records depends on state laws that allow employers to ask about and consider criminal records for making adverse job and other employment decisions. Examples of adverse decisions include refusal to hire or promote employees based on their *previous* criminal records.

Restrictions vary by state. Overall, employers may not automatically disqualify job candidates solely because they have criminal records. Employers may not ask about or consider a juvenile criminal record to make job or other employment decisions. However, employers typically have the right to ask about and conduct a security investigation in order to make employment decisions based on this information. These are referred to as background checks.

Employers have the right to ask about and conduct an adult criminal record search to make job or other employment decisions. Questions about criminal records, and employment decisions based on same, are limited to convictions only. But this stipulation might not apply if applicants are seeking law-enforcement jobs, mental health work, or jobs where security and safety are needs or concerns.

The type of conviction must be related to the applicant's suitability to perform the job if an employer can make an adverse job or other employment decision based solely on this conviction. Restrictions will vary by state, and some states might not enforce all provisions on employers. A few states have not imposed any restrictions on employers.

Bankruptcy

While bankruptcy is not an employment discrimination law per se, the employment-related provisions make it unlawful for employers to discriminate against employees and job applicants because of bankruptcy or any bad debts they had before filing for bankruptcy and applying for a job.

SEXUAL ORIENTATION, GENDER DIFFERENCES, RACE, AND NATIONAL ORIGIN

A growing number of states prohibit discrimination against gay and lesbian employees. Historically, gay and lesbian employees have found little in the law to protect them from discrimination and harassment in the workplace. However, as acceptance grows toward alternative lifestyles, employers are becoming responsible for providing a workplace that's free of harassment and discrimination based on sexual orientation. On November 7, 2007, the U.S. House of Representatives passed HR 3685, a bill that prohibits employment discrimination on the basis of sexual orientation against gay, lesbian, and bisexual workers. If the Senate votes to pass this bill without a presidential veto, it moves forward to become a new discrimination law identified as the Employment Non-Discrimination Act of 2007.

No federal law prohibits discrimination in private employment, but an executive order specifically outlaws discrimination based on sexual orientation in the federal government.

If a private employer operates a business in a state, county, or city with an ordinance prohibiting sexual orientation discrimination, state law will prevail and the employer must follow the law despite the fact that there is no federal law in place.

State Laws

Seventeen states and the District of Columbia have laws that currently prohibit sexual orientation discrimination in private employment. These states include: California, Connecticut, Hawaii, Illinois, Maine, Maryland, Massachusetts, Minnesota, Nevada, New Hampshire, New Jersey, New Mexico, New York, Rhode Island, Vermont, Washington, and Wisconsin. Some of these states also specifically prohibit discrimination based on gender identity. In addition, the following six states have laws prohibiting sexual orientation discrimination in public workplaces only: Colorado, Delaware, Indiana, Michigan, Montana, and Pennsylvania.

Local Laws

Locally, more than 180 cities and counties nationwide prohibit sexual orientation discrimination in at least some workplaces. To find out whether your state, county, or city has a law prohibiting discrimination on the basis of sexual orientation, contact your state labor department or your state fair employment office. For more information, visit the Lambda Legal Defense and Education Fund website at www.lambdalegal.org, where a state-by-state list of antidiscrimination laws, including city and county ordinances, can be found.

SEXUAL HARASSMENT

Employers are responsible for maintaining a workplace that is free from sexual harassment. This is your legal obligation, but it also makes good business sense. If you allow sexual harassment to flourish in your workplace, you will pay a high price in terms of poor employee morale, low productivity, and employee-generated lawsuits.

The same laws that prohibit gender discrimination prohibit sexual harassment. Title VII of the Civil Rights Act is the main federal law that prohibits sexual harassment. In addition, each state has its own anti-sexual-harassment law.

What Is Sexual Harassment?

Sexual harassment is any unwelcome sexual advance or conduct on the job that creates an intimidating, hostile, or offensive work environment. Any conduct of a sexual nature that makes an employee uncomfortable has the potential to be sexual harassment.

Given this broad definition, it is not surprising that sexual harassment comes in many forms. The following are all examples of sexual harassment:

- A manager suggests to an employee that he will get the promotion if they have sex.
- An attractive office manager is encouraged to wear provocative clothing to attract more customers.
- A male restaurant manager fondles the female waitresses on the job.
- Sexually explicit emails are traded between lawyers in a law firm about their assistants.
- A supervisor's friend from outside the company frequently sends pornographic material via email to his secretary.

The harasser can be the victim's supervisor, manager, coworker, or at any level in the organization. An employer may also be liable for harassment by a non-employee (such as a vendor or customer), depending on the circumstances.

Under Title VII guidelines, sexual harassment is a gender-neutral offense, at least in theory: males can sexually harass females, females can sexually harass males, males can harass males, and females can harass females. A distinction is made among gays and lesbians who were not recognized under the original provisions described in Title VII. However, *statistics show* that the overwhelming majority of sexual harassment claims and charges are brought by women claiming that they were sexually harassed by men.

However, men can be victims of harassment too. For example, if a man's coworkers constantly bombard him with sexually explicit photos of women and sexually explicit jokes, and if this makes him uncomfortable because he is married, this behavior can constitute sexual harassment.

Whether sexual harassment of gays and lesbians is illegal under Title VII is an open question right now and the subject of a lot of debate. The U.S. Supreme Court has never addressed the issue, and lower federal courts and state courts are all over the map with their decisions. Despite the lack of judicial guidance in this area, prudent employers should assume that this type of sexual harassment is illegal as well.

Sexual Harassment Prevention

There are a number of steps that an HR department may follow to reduce the risk of sexual harassment occurring in the workplace. Documentation is one of the most important steps a company can take to investigate claims of harassment.

Real World Note:

California passed a law in 2006 requiring employers that have at least 50 employees to provide supervisors with two hours of sexual harassment training every two years. Connecticut and Maine also require sexual harassment training. Other states strongly encourage employers to provide training, whether or not it is required.

Adopting a clear sexual harassment policy is one of the safeguards to protect employees from discrimination due to harassment. A company policy should be published in the employee handbook, clearly defining sexual harassment and the steps to be taken if it occurs. Having employees complete sexual harassment training annually should be a requirement for all employees, regardless of their position in the company.

Encouraging employees to report suspicious behavior can be facilitated through an anonymous reporting system. Usually a high-level manager, such as a vice president of HR, will receive the complaint and make contact to investigate the claim. All complaints and investigations are considered confidential inquiries in order to safeguard the integrity of the program and encourage employees to report incidents without the threat of retaliation or being harassed for whistle-blowing. Action should be timely and effectively implemented.

The EEOC is the federal agency that enforces sexual harassment laws. To learn more about sexual harassment, refer to the agency's website at www.eeoc.gov.

Small businesses with one to three employees are often exempt from many antidiscrimination laws with the exception of the Equal Pay Act. Local ordinances are usually concerned with companies consisting of five or more employees. It is always a good idea to be current on up-to-date changes in employment law at the local, state, and federal levels. Again, when laws conflict, the higher standard usually prevails.

NONWORK DISCRIMINATION: BREAKS, VACATION TIME, AND LEAVES OF ABSENCE

Nonwork time can be required by law or simply be at the discretion of the employer. When it is discretionary nonwork time, it is usually categorized as a company perk or benefit. Perks and benefits are seen as company-paid or unpaid benefits and not a requirement governed by law. However, discriminatory practices may occur if individuals are singled out compared to others on the job who receive perks and benefits.

For example, if an undesirable employee is on probation, or found to violate company rules or policies, it is not a good idea to deny this employee the same benefits offered to all employees while the employee still works for the company. While the benefit is a perk, discrimination will result if the employee is treated differently and benefits are denied.

Bereavement Leave

Most employers allow one to three days' leave for the death of an immediate family member. However, this is not a law, and it is at the discretion of the company whether bereavement time will be paid time off or approved time off without pay.

Family and Medical Leave Act (FMLA)

The FMLA entitles qualified workers to take unpaid sick leave to care for themselves or family members during a time of hardship when it is difficult to be at the job. However, some companies will offer paid time off if the employee has been employed for a specified number of years.

Leave of Absence

Personal leaves of absence can be paid or unpaid; they may also be denied or not offered until an employee has been working at the company for a required length of time. A medical leave of absence may also be paid or unpaid, depending on length of time, and whether it is offered as a company benefit.

Paid Time Off

Paid time off (PTO) is leave time that includes vacation, personal, and sick leave. It combines all time that an employee may take and is calculated by the number of hours or days allowed. PTO usually requires paperwork and approval by a direct report.

Sick Leave

Sick leave is often a benefit of the company. There is much controversy between employers and employees as to whether unused sick leave time should be paid out at the end of the year. Employers have the option to decide how this time will be accounted for—paid or unpaid.

Vacation Time

General information regarding employee vacation leave benefits are mandated under state and federal laws. This also includes accrued vacation pay.

Work Breaks and Meal Breaks

Work breaks on the job are usually required and referred to as rest, coffee, bathroom, restroom, toilet, snack, or smoke breaks. Meal breaks include breakfast, lunch, or dinner breaks.

Legal Holidays

Legal holidays are most often identified as public holidays. Prior to the beginning of each new year, a company usually lists holidays that will be paid holidays and time off throughout the year. Exempt-status employees are paid a salary and not impacted as much as nonexempt employees, who may elect to work on public holidays and be paid time and one-half or double time to work on these days. Federal workers are entitled to paid holiday leave, but private sector employees are not entitled even though they may be paid.

WORKPLACE INVESTIGATIONS

When conducting a workplace investigation concerning discrimination or harassment, it is important to treat every incident as a serious one. Be sure to document the conversation and information from the first meeting, and follow some basic guidelines.

First, treat every call seriously and treat the informant with respect and sincerity. Reassure the informant that information shared is confidential. There is a tendency to blame the informant; however, the informant is the victim and should be taken seriously. The HR representative should always remain neutral—even when a claim seems frivolous.

Next, make sure that retaliation does not occur against the informant. Retaliation can take many forms: termination, discipline, demotion, pay cut, change in work hours or job responsibilities, or isolating the informant from meetings. Carry out the investigation according to the policy manual and do not skip any details. Be well informed about the law and your role as the employer. Conduct as many interviews as possible; this is the time when all facts and circumstances are most important. Cooperate with all parties, agencies, and representatives. If contacted by the EEOC, write a script about what you will say and how you will say it. Consider hiring an experienced investigator or attorney to represent the company. Once the investigation has concluded, take appropriate action steps to resolve the issues and move forward.

For additional information about conducting an investigation, see *Workplace Investigations,* by Lisa Guerin.

PREVENTING RETALIATION CLAIMS BY EMPLOYEES

When an employee complains about discrimination or harassment—to HR, a government agency, or to another representative—be sure not to punish the informant, or this could be seen as retaliation against the informant. If this happens, legal action against the company and named individuals could result. Be sure to always treat employees with care.

Retaliation Defined

Retaliation is an adverse action that someone takes against an employee because the employee filed a complaint. Employees who participate in an investigation are also protected from retaliation.

Even if the original complaint of harassment turns out to be false under the law, an employee may be able to prove that retaliation happened because of the negative consequences that resulted from the investigation.

Adverse action includes demotion, discipline, firing, salary reduction, negative evaluation, change in job assignment, or change in shift assignment. Retaliation can also include hostile behavior or attitudes toward an employee who complains.

When taking steps toward corrective action, it is important to note that the change should not only include the informant, but it should include everyone. If only the informant is involved, this might be seen as retaliation against the informant.

Preventing Retaliation

Think of retaliation as the flip side of discrimination. As soon as a complaint is filed for discrimination or harassment, the facts and circumstances should be carefully documented because a poor investigation can result in a retaliation claim. Similar to conducting an investigation for discrimination or sexual harassment, it is important to follow an established protocol. Establish a policy about retaliation. Define it and take steps to resolve it. Gather information, conduct an investigation, document all information, remind everyone that the information is confidential, and take action to remedy the situation.

Employee Discipline Problems

An adverse action is retaliatory only if it is taken because the employee complained. You are free to take actions against an employee for other reasons, even if that employee has complained about discrimination or harassment, as in the following examples:

- You can give a negative evaluation to an employee with performance problems.
- You can discipline an employee who is always late to work.
- You can fire an employee who brings a gun to work.

The problem for employers is that some employees will claim that these adverse actions are retaliation—even if they have nothing to do with the employee's complaint.

If you must take adverse action against an employee who has complained, be prepared to show that you have valid reasons for discipline, unrelated to the complaint. These reasons should be supported, if possible, by prior documented warnings to the employee.

EMPLOYEES' RIGHTS

Employment law covers all rights and obligations within the employer-employee relationship—whether relating to a current employee, job applicant, or former employee. Because of the complexity of employment relationships and the wide variety of situations that can arise, employment law involves legal issues as diverse as discrimination, wrongful termination, wages and taxation, and workplace safety. Many of these issues are governed by applicable federal and state law. But, where the employment relationship is based on a valid contract entered into by the employer and the employee, state contract law alone may dictate the rights and duties of the parties.

All employees have basic rights in the workplace, including the rights to privacy, fair compensation, and freedom from discrimination. A job applicant also has certain rights even prior to being hired as an employee. These rights include the right to be free from discrimination based on age, gender, race, national origin, or religion during the hiring process. For example, a prospective employer cannot ask a job applicant certain family-related questions during the hiring process.

In most states, employees have a right to privacy in the workplace. This right to privacy applies to the employee's personal possessions, including handbags or briefcases, storage lockers accessible only by the employee, and private mail addressed only to the employee. Employees may also have a right to privacy in their telephone conversations or voice mail messages. However, employees have very limited rights to privacy in their email messages and Internet usage while using the employer's computer system.

There are certain pieces of information that an employer may not seek out concerning a potential job applicant or employee. An employer may not conduct a credit or background check on an employee, or prospective employee, unless the employer notifies the individual in writing and receives permission to do so. Other employee rights include the following:

- The right to be free from discrimination and harassment of all types
- The right to a safe workplace free of dangerous conditions, toxic substances, and other potential safety hazards
- The right to be free from retaliation for filing a claim or complaint against an employer (these are sometimes called whistle-blower rights)
- The right to fair wages for work performed

CHAPTER SUMMARY

Distinctions were made between discrimination in the workplace and antidiscrimination laws at the federal, state, and local levels. The Civil Rights Act of 1964 and Title VII govern how employees are protected from workplace discrimination. Discharge and termination topics were discussed relevant to at-will employment and the employment-at-will doctrine. Sexual harassment and the different kinds of harassment were discussed along with filing a workplace discrimination claim, conducting an investigation, and workplace retaliation policies. Nonwork time topics, benefits, perks, paid time versus unpaid time, FMLA, and other leave topics were introduced. Employer and employee rights were compared, along with the right to privacy, and situations where employers have the right to investigate employee actions that jeopardize the function, viability, and success of the business.

REVIEW QUESTIONS

1.   Discuss discrimination in the workplace relative to laws that protect the employer versus the employee.

2.   Discuss different kinds of workplace harassment and give an example of each one.

3.   How should employers handle applicants who are convicted criminals?

4.   When are workplace investigations appropriate?

5.   Discuss distinations mode between nonwork time, paid time off, benefits, and public holidays.

6.   What is meant by retaliation?

7.   Briefly summarize what are the three exceptions to the At-Will Doctrine?

ANSWERS AND EXPLANATIONS

1. Illegal employment discrimination occurs when employers single out applicants or employee(s) on the basis of age, race, creed, disability, national origin, religion, military duty, sex or gender. This is described under Title VII of the Civil Rights Act of 1964, and governed by federal anti-discrimination laws.

2. Sexual harassment is one common type of workplace harassment. Sexual harassment takes place when conduct related to sexual inneundo, connotation, explicit directives, photos, e-mails, or any kind of communication of a sexual nature is considered sexual harassment.

   Harassment based on gender, or gender differences (including gay, lesbian or transgender discrimination), is another important type.

   A hostile work environment includes any type of threat, covert or overt, that can be considered hostile with malicious intent.

   It is up to the employee to notify HRM so that proper steps to file a formal discrimination (complaint) are carried out. Once this is done, a formal investigation can take place.

3. Overall, employers may not automatically disqualify job candidates solely because they have criminal records. Employers may not ask about or consider a juvenile criminal record to make job or other employment decisions. However, employers typically have the right to conduct a security investigation before making a job offer. These are typically background checks.

   Employers have the right to ask about and conduct an adult criminal record search to make job or other employment decisions. Questions about criminal records and employment decisions based on same, are limited to convictions only. But this might not apply if applicants are seeking law-enforcement jobs, mental health work, or jobs where security and safety is a need or concern.

   The type of conviction must be related to the applicant's ability to perform the job. Restrictions will vary by state and some states might not enforce all provisions on employers.

4. Workplace investigations are appropriate anytime it is believed that employment discrimination has taken place, the company business may be in danger, sexual harassment has been reported, an employee is harboring a gun, firearm, chemicals, or any type of dangerous weapon that seriously impairs other workers, or has potential to impair others. In most instance, whether or not there has been a formal complaint, workplace investigations are usually appropriate. The question that should be asked is: Is the company business or are employees in danger? If so, then a workplace investigation is always appropriate.

5. Non-work time can be required by law or simply be at the discretion of the employer. When it is discretionary non-work time, it is often catego-

rized as a company perk or benefit. Perks and benefits are not a requirement governed by law; however, discriminatory practices may occur if individuals are singled out compared to receive these perks.

6. Retaliation is any adverse action that an employer takes against an employee after he or she complains about harassment or discrimination. Employees who participate in an investigation of any of these problems are also protected—for example, you can't punish an employee who gives a statement to a government agency that is investigating a discrimination claim.

7. The exceptions to the At-Will Doctire are: public policy, implied contract, and covenant of good faith and fair dealing.

    Public policy refers to those standards, values, and principles that the court (or legislature) considers to be in the best interest of an individual and the general public. Violations of public policy are resolved through the court system.

    Implied contract is an agreement between an employer and an employee(s) that was never explicitly documented in writing but implicitly agreed to by all parties involved.

    Covenant of good faith and fair dealing is the employer's duty to treat employees ethically, responsibly, fairly, and honestly.

International HRM: Global Workforce Training and Development

Companies deliver products and services to customers all over the globe. The phrase *global economy* applies to HRM when dealing with cultural differences in hiring, training, and implementing employment practices in a multicultural workforce. This holds true whether or not a company is considered to be a global organization. Employees, managers, and executives need to be aware of and able to work productively with people who are different from themselves in terms of language, work motivation, training, education, and culture. Universally, employees seek the same things in a job: safety, security, decent wages, and interesting work. However, how employees are trained and what makes a good manager may be different across an international arena. Resolving conflicts, performing a job, and interacting with customers or suppliers may require a different set of skills in an international context.

To be effective, employers across international borders rely on HRM to provide proper training for all employees. Diversity training and diversity awareness programs take into consideration a collective understanding of other cultures and the needs of people from those cultures. Many countries are experiencing a global economy for the first time in their history, and it takes several generations before strong cultural values can be changed and new business practices can be accepted, if they are accepted at all. The U.S. society is known as an individualistic social economy. Individuals are educated and encouraged to pursue individual goals and ambitions without consideration to the family, society, or fellow workers. In many Asian and European cultures, on the other hand, individuals are raised to embrace a collectivistic economy, where family and coworkers take higher priority than individual needs and goals. The U.S. social economy must embrace other cultures to work successfully within their norms, and other cultures must learn how to work in an individualistic culture if their companies hope to survive and thrive in a global economy.

Examples of the HRM needs of a global workforce include the following:

- Managers need to know how to motivate and organize people from a variety of cultural backgrounds.
- Salespeople need to know how to build relationships, negotiate, and sell across cultures.

Exam Note:

A separate GPHR exam is offered through HRCI; however, international topics in chapter 10 are reviewed for the PHR/SPHR exam under Body of Knowledge. Please visit the HRCI website for specific information about the GPHR exam.

- HRD specialists need to understand how to develop best practices that embrace multicultural awareness and simultaneously develop the capabilities of employees in countries other than their own.
- Employees need to be able to work effectively with a wide variety of people.
- Supervisors need to provide effective education and development in other geographies and cultures on client-specific products and processes while maintaining high-quality customer service levels.
- Companies must recognize the opportunities that a global marketplace offers them.

GLOBAL DIVERSITY: CROSS-CULTURAL TRAINING AND DEVELOPMENT

Companies often globalize to take advantage of emerging markets. With the ambitious movement of capital and labor across borders, new issues emerge. One of the most prominent differences in today's business world is the global workforce itself and the way that business is conducted. New technology has driven swift decisions by managers and supervisors who live in different countries, speak different languages, and practice different management principles. The global workforce is made up of the people who exercise the roles and responsibilities designed to carry out the needed work. The type of company also makes a difference. Companies engaged in research, sales, and drug testing often employ technicians, scientists, analysts, and other professionals who work in a country different from where they were born and educated. Job titles, work hours, salaries, tax laws, unions, labor laws, and the local workforce itself are diverse and complex. To further complicate this mix, cultural differences, language barriers, and company benefits must be analyzed and negotiated according to the host company's laws, regulations, and cultural practices.

Diversity programs are not new in the United States, but global diversity presents unique challenges and opportunities. In the United States, diversity is considered a legal issue centered on protecting the rights of workers in protected classes. Diversity is defined by gender, age, sexual orientation, race or ethnic background, and so on. Global diversity means something different—something larger and much more complex.

STAGES OF GLOBAL DIVERSITY

While many companies implement U.S. diversity training in programs such as sexual harassment prevention, they may only be in the first stages of global diversity development. They often neglect to look at the broader issues present in a global economy.

Global/international HR departments must consider the following issues:

- Developing, implementing, administering, and evaluating expatriate and foreign national compensation and benefits programs
- Developing, selecting, implementing, and evaluating flexible work arrangements, diversity programs, and repatriation training
- Implications of a global workforce for work planning and employment
- Business ethics awareness across cultures

Diversity programs are designed for participants to be able to do the following:

- Become aware of expectations that clash with their ethical standards
- Initiate conversations about contrasting business practices and develop best practices that are consistent with their values and expectations
- Understand mixed-culture regulations, patent rights, harassment, and antitrust laws that must be considered, including international contracts with employees
- Navigate in a business world in which a best practice in one culture may be unethical in another so as to learn to uphold ethical standards by addressing underlying needs and expectations of other business partners
- Comply with foreign regulations as they arise on the job

Diversity programs should fit the needs of participants from across industries and functions. Applicable global issues, such as international law, culture, local management approaches, best practices, societal norms, and others, must be considered before a training program can be designed and implemented.

ASSIMILATING NEW EMPLOYEES

In a competitive environment for attracting global talent, companies pay particular attention to how candidates and new hires perceive the company. A well-thought-out and extensive assimilation process often makes new employees more likely to stay. This process should start before the job offer is made, and many companies have assimilation plans for at least the initial six months on the job. This is especially important in group and relationship cultures, since it helps new employees feel welcomed, and it provides the time and structure to establish relationships that will support employees, while encouraging loyalty to the company.

GLOBAL WORKFORCE DEVELOPMENT

Helping employees recognize that they work in a multicultural or a global environment reminds them that they are expected to embrace cultural differences. General awareness programs are a good start. Specific programs targeted to culture-specific needs or functional needs, such as global marketing, e-learning, and program development, serve to foster positive employee relations and cooperation.

Job titles and job responsibilities vary across cultures. Localizing an organization's employee handbook and writing job descriptions to include appropriate differences for various geographies, so employees can read them without feeling left out or misunderstood, are important measures for developing a global workforce.

For example, cultures with a preference for certainty (e.g., preference for structure and rules versus ambiguity) prefer competency-based performance systems. Communicating exactly what is expected, defining specific levels of behavior (e.g., performance-based management system), and assessing all employees against the same criteria feel more fair to many employees. Performance systems that depend on manager discretion can be viewed as biased and unfair.

GLOBAL SELECTION AND RETENTION

Knowing what differentiates successful employees and using recruitment and selection strategies that identify the needed competencies and behaviors reduce the need for introductory skills development, since employees already have the needed skills in place. Smart hiring benefits employees by recognizing those who already have the requisite skills necessary to succeed, and it results in more successful selection and retention efforts.

Global leadership competencies required for success include the following:

- Flexibility to work and manage across cultures
- The ability to be the voice of the local culture to the home office while being the voice of the home office to local employees
- The ability to adapt to cultural differences as they impact business practices

To promote the acquisition of these competencies, the HR function must do the following:

- Define behaviors that are associated with success factors in a company
- Identify internal and external candidates who already practice those success factors
- Provide accurate, reliable, and detailed selection/recruitment data, such as developmental reports and criteria that accurately assess and match job demand with individual achievement (capability)

GLOBAL SUCCESSION PLANNING AND MANAGEMENT DEVELOPMENT

Companies demand talent development and succession management to retain top employees and stay competitive. Linking both development and succession management to leadership competency models leverages investments, expectations, and rewards. Global succession planning seeks to retain individual and collective talent. Defining leadership and management competencies, developing succession plan processes, assessing succession talent, and identifying areas for individual development are part of a global succession plan that ensures the continuation and competitive economics of a global workforce.

HR'S STRATEGIC PARTNERSHIP

HR professionals must strategically align their work with the goals and objectives of the organization and must have a thorough knowledge of global business to meet the demands of a global workforce. What competencies are needed to establish successful companies in new geographies? What are the needs of local workers in host countries? What is the best way to outsource? As a company's strategic plans impact its employees, HR must support and understand the global landscape, from recruitment and hiring techniques employed in other countries to the establishment of contracts and compensation-benefits packages that comply with local laws.

CHANGE MANAGEMENT

Managing change and growth across cultures and geographies requires specific knowledge of the impact of this change and growth on particular cultures. People in different cultures react to change differently. In a change management strategic operation, HR is responsible for instituting change management programs (in concert with an OD department and senior management). In addressing employees before, during, and following this process, HR can address the company's and employees' needs in the following ways:

- Facilitate the charter of change implementation teams
- Provide training for employee communications
- Design and deliver cross-cultural training for multicultural or virtual implementation teams
- Provide change team leader support and data/information from climate surveys, assessment results, and strategic planning initiatives
- Provide the organization with cumulative and historical data on the impact that change will likely have on the company and its employees

KAPLAN

INTERNATIONAL COMPENSATION MODELS AND BENEFITS PROGRAMS

Establishing worldwide compensation and reward systems is a big concern for all global companies. Long-established cultural norms, such as lifetime employment in Japan and industrywide bargaining in Germany, are weakening in response to the pressures of a modern global economy. Hard and fast assumptions about international compensation, such as the notion that pay systems for expatriates provide comfortable salaries and that U.S. compensation practices should be tailored to fit national cultures, do not necessarily hold true in an uncertain economy. The changing global business environment requires that multinational companies constantly review their compensation practices. From a global perspective, substantial differences in how people are paid for work become apparent.

Consider that the same multinational organization operating in both Shanghai and Bratislava may offer very different pay packages to employees in those locations. In Shanghai, pay packages may include housing allowances and bonuses intended to retain scarce critical skills. In Bratislava, pay packages will place greater emphasis on productivity-based gain sharing and base pay (pay packages should be interpreted along the same lines as a compensation package). However, current thinking in a market-based economy suggests that differences will narrow or disappear altogether as global companies deal with similar pressures and challenges. A global economy creates increased competition for customers and requires increased critical skills, while technology operates across international boundaries to form complex global manufacturing and distribution systems.

The French are changing their compensation system gradually, as French voters continue to place a high value on their country's comprehensive social safety net. Also, French managers utilize share-the-work programs to cope with France's high unemployment rate. The British, by comparison, allow more variable systems, including stock options and performance-based schemes. While these changes were generated by similar market-based economies, workers have a say in how they will get paid and have a fair amount of freedom when choosing how to respond.

Different responses to globalization highlight the fact that compensation and reward systems are part of the complex relationship between workers and employers around the world. Added to this complexity are entwined social, political, and economic factors influencing how decisions are made.

CREATING GLOBAL MIND-SETS

A global mind-set seeks to adopt values and attitudes to create a common mental picture for balancing corporate goals, business units, and functional priorities on a worldwide scale. Such a mind-set has enormous competitive advantages. According to Jack Welch, former chairman and CEO at General Electric, "The aim of a global business is to get the best ideas from everyone, everywhere." One cannot hold onto a domestic way of thinking and be successful. This perspective goes beyond "think globally, act locally." Rather, it seems to imply the reverse: "Think locally, but act globally."

Compensation reward systems can become crucial tools to support a global mind-set, or the reverse can happen. Managing compensation and reward systems while competing in worldwide markets has always depended upon understanding economic, social, and political changes in the countries of operation. Successful companies adopt global compensation and reward strategies that align with global mind-sets. Rather than reacting to match local conditions, a global perspective defines the best use of compensation and rewards to compete on a worldwide basis.

HOW EXPATRIATES ARE ALIGNED WITH GLOBAL SYSTEMS THINKING

Expatriates, or *expats*, are U.S. employees who work in foreign locations. Ask compensation directors to describe how international compensation and rewards are managed, and they typically offer one or two responses. Some describe their recent efforts to modify the balance sheet approach for paying expatriates. Most efforts attempt to align compensation costs better with different global assignments. Others consider developmental and longer-term technology transfers and leadership roles to distinguish different national cultures. They point out the importance of localizing compensation decisions within broad corporate principles. The purpose is to align compensation decisions better with differences in national cultures.

Typically, broad corporate principles seem to scratch the surface when it comes to supporting corporate values and global business strategies. More often, local conditions dominate the compensation strategy. The United States has a highly individualistic national culture. In other places, particularly Asia, people are comfortable with more collective values. Security is more important than risk taking, and social sensitivity is important. Executives need to be aware that the national culture is a critical factor when managing international compensation.

In individualistic cultures, if one asks executives about the issue posed above, yet without the word *international*—"Describe how your organization manages compensation practices"—executives talk about initiatives to create a common culture of ownership and performance. They say they want to build flexible, agile cultures through practices such as broadbanding, broad-based stock options, 360-degree assessments, and competency-based projects. Domestically, emphasis is on strategic choice and designing compensation programs to help create a culture sensitive to international markets and performance. Internationally, on the other hand, concern with aligning compensation with different national cultures dominates. Most HR managers believe that competitive advantage is achieved by transforming multinationals into local companies. This view conforms to the conventional wisdom that the only way to manage international compensation is to tailor it to local conditions. The current reality is more a matter of reacting than not acting. From this discussion, it should be assumed that as more organizations move into global markets, higher consideration will be given to global conditions.

CORPORATE RESTRUCTURING

A fundamental change in the direction and strategy for an organization that affects the way in which the organization is structured is called by many names: restructuring, downsizing, outsourcing, divestiture, mergers and acquisitions (M&A), rightsizing, and reorganization. Inclusively, corporate restructuring may involve increasing or decreasing the layers of personnel between the top and the bottom of an organization or reassigning roles and responsibilities. Corporate restructuring often involves reorganizing after a period of unsatisfactory performance and poor results and is often manifested in the divestment or closure of parts of the business and the outplacement, or shedding, of personnel. In this case, *corporate restructuring* is used as a euphemism for *delayering, rationalization, downsizing, rightsizing,* and any or all of the terms named above.

Mergers and Acquisitions, Divestitures, and Integration

We have just been through another round of mergers and acquisitions (M&A) activity, the second strong run of M&A in the last ten years. From huge companies "merging as equals" to smaller companies being swallowed to provide research and development (R&D), a product line extension, or regional consolidation, there has been plenty of activity. Inevitably, these events challenge a company in many different ways, including culture, process, and system integration. The same is true of divestitures, though obviously in a different way. While the fundamental question of merging, acquiring, or divesting is an important strategic decision for most firms, the devil is often in the details of the integration (or separation). Success depends on the thought and due diligence that is given to them in advance and the investment in them during execution.

We will discuss the rationale for and choice between undertaking a merger or acquiring a company, examine negotiation and the various phases of execution and management, as well as look at divestitures. Our focus will be on integration/disintegration and associated issues. We will especially include the role of information technology (IT) and IT integration or separation.

What are the key drivers of M&A or divestiture activity in your company, and how have they changed over the years? Are they due to product line extension, regional consolidation, talent acquisition, IP, customers/distribution, insight into processes, R&D capabilities, preemptive defensive moves, etc.? How do joint ventures fit in the consideration of strategic options?

How do corporations compete with private equity in the M&A space today? Are we entering a period of slower M&A/divestiture activity, or will companies fill the gap left by private equity?

Are you proactive or reactive in your approach? Is M&A or divestiture a strategy in and of itself for your company, or is it simply a tool to implement a wider corporate strategy?

How do you approach M&A and divestiture in terms of metrics and processes? Do you have a process for evaluating deals and M&A or divestiture journeys and results in hindsight?

What key stumbling blocks preventing M&A from hitting their synergy plans have you experienced? How have you mitigated those in future deals? Was IT ever the key issue?

Are different approaches to planning integration required, depending on the type of acquisition? What influence does the strategic goal of the merger or acquisition (or type of M&A) have on the nature, goals, processes, systems, and pace/timing of integration?

How soon is the integration team established? What is its charter, and who determines it? Does anyone create "integration clean teams" that plan for integration?

What factors should determine the planned speed of integration? Some firms move through phases, while others aim directly for the end state—is one or the other approach almost always preferable? What top priorities have to happen quickly?

What processes and metrics do you establish for integration?

What is required for a successful handoff from the M&A/deal/due diligence team(s) to a successful start to integration? Should a designated integration team be formed, or must everyone be engaged in this task?

How do you most effectively link integration plans of different functional areas or business units and ensure they stay coupled during integration?

How long should integration be allowed to last? Which reasons for delays are acceptable, and which are not?

How do you prevent the focus of the newly combined company from becoming too inward during integration? How can you bring real focus to the difficult task of integration without growing an integration culture? Is this a danger? Whose job is this?

How do you ensure you keep an appropriate focus on the people and cultural issues during a procedure that can feel as though it is much more about systems and process integration?

What is the role of senior management during integration? Where should their focus be? How closely are IT integration decisions normally tied to the rest of integration? Should they be more tightly linked?

Dynamics of Divestitures

What are the key considerations for disentanglement in a divestiture? What key factors determine the speed of disintegration? On which elements do you want to move quickly and on which more slowly?

How do you diagnose key dependencies and ensure standalone operations? How do you ensure that only the right types of processes, systems, etc. leave the company in a divestiture?

What are the right ways to anticipate and deal with intellectual property issues? What do divesting organizations generally experience when providing transitional services (IT and other) to acquirers? What are the best practices—the dos and don'ts? What tasks are key for IT in a divestiture?

EXHIBIT A: FIDUCIARY CONCERNS AND HRM

The following text is a letter of communication filed electronically by SHRM to the director of the Office of Regulations and Interpretations on January 30, 2007, regarding fiduciary responsibilities of plan administrators in matters of benefits administration to organizations. Responsibilities include investment advice and explaining plan requirements to employees, shareholders, and others.

Filed Electronically
Robert Doyle
Director, Office of Regulations and Interpretations
Employee Benefits Security Administration
Room N-5669
U.S. Department of Labor
200 Constitution Avenue. N.W.
Washington, DC 20210

Re: Prohibited Transaction Exemption for Provision of Investment Advice to Participants in Individual Account Plans. 71 Fed. Reg. 70, 429 (Dec. 4, 2006) RIN 1210-AB13

Dear Mr. Doyle,

The Society for Human Resource Management (SHRM) appreciates the opportunity to respond to the Department of Labor's Request for Information on the new prohibited transaction exemptions for investment advice provided to participants in individual account plans. The exemptions were added by the Pension Protection Act of 2006 (PPA).

SHRM is the world's largest association devoted to human resource management. Representing more than 210,000 individual members, the Society's mission is to serve the needs of HR professionals by providing the most essential and comprehensive resources available to advance the human resource profession and to ensure that HR is recognized as an essential partner in developing and executing organizational strategies. Founded in 1948, SHRM currently has more than 550 affiliated chapters within the United States and members in more than 100 countries.

SHRM would like to start by applauding the Department for taking the first steps towards issuing guidance that clarifies and expands upon the new prohibited transaction exemptions for investment advice. SHRM strongly believes that participants in 401(k), 403 (b), and other individual account plans need access to high-quality investment advice. Employees are increasingly responsible for investing their own retirement assets, yet many participants lack the knowledge necessary to make prudent investment decisions. Even participants who are relatively knowledgeable may lack the time to make and update investment decisions in a well-informed manner, and it is essential that the Department issue guidance that facilitates investment advice arrangements.

Investment Advice Generally

As a threshold matter, SHRM believes that participants should have access to a broad range of different investment advice approaches. The new PPA prohibited transaction exemptions facilitate advice arrangements that either (i) provide that any fees (including any commission or other compensation) received by the fiduciary adviser do not vary depending on the investment option selected or (ii) use a computer model that meets certain requirements. However, these exemptions are needed only where the fiduciary adviser is a party-in-interest with respect to the plan (or is affiliated with a party-in-interest) and therefore has a potential conflict of interest ("affiliated advice"). There are a number of investment advice approaches that do not raise these prohibited transaction concerns because the investment adviser is not a party-in-interest or otherwise affiliated with a party-in-interest. These approaches range from investment advice arrangements with advisers who have no other nexus to the plan to arrangements that are crafted to rely on Advisory Opinion 2001-09A (the "SunAmerica Letter"). We have some concern that the new prohibited transaction exemptions will come to dominate the investment advice arena, if only because there will be substantial guidance on the contours of the new exemptions. It is imperative that any guidance the Department issues not encourage a "one size fits all" approach to investment advice. For this reason, it is important that the Department clarify and confirm that there are a range of different approaches that plan sponsors may pursue for providing investment advice to participants. As importantly, the Department should address the remaining issues that arise for nonaffiliated investment advice and foster the development of these programs as well.

It is also essential that the Department clarify a plan sponsor's fiduciary responsibilities in selecting an investment advice arrangement. The new PPA prohibited transaction exemption provides that the plan sponsor or other fiduciary has no fiduciary responsibility for advice provided pursuant to one of the new PPA investment advice exemptions (and does not have to monitor any specific advice). Instead, the plan sponsor has limited responsibility "for the prudent selection and periodic review of a fiduciary adviser." There is no guidance directly addressing a plan sponsor's fiduciary responsibilities with respect to investment advice outside of the PPA exemption context. We urge the Department to clarify that these same standards also apply to nonaffiliated advice arrangements. Without this clarification, many common approaches to investment advice will be unattractive to plan sponsors solely because of uncertainty regarding the sponsor's fiduciary role with respect to the arrangement.

SHRM recommends that the Department clarify the guidance related to fiduciary considerations in selecting an investment adviser. It is critical that the Department not create an inference that there is a fiduciary bias against affiliated investment advice. Some plan sponsors will want to be able to hire an affiliated adviser (e.g., as part of a bundled services arrangement). Others will choose to go with an unaffiliated adviser. There should be no inference that an independent third-party adviser is preferable to an affiliated adviser that satisfies a PPA prohibited transaction exemption. The conditions of the exemption are intended to ensure that the advice will not be conflicted advice, and sponsors should be able to assume that this will not be the case. For these reasons, any guidance should clarify that a plan sponsor or other fiduciary need not consider potential conflicts of interest beyond ensuring that the advice program will satisfy a PPA prohibited transaction exemption.

SHRM also recommends that any failure by a fiduciary adviser to satisfy the terms of the exemption does not adversely affect the plan sponsor's fiduciary relief. Although the PPA clarifies the plan sponsor's fiduciary responsibilities in selecting an investment advice arrangement, the PPA imposes a number of conditions in order to rely upon the exemptions. Many of these conditions are within the sole control of the fiduciary adviser (e.g., bad disclosure).

Although the sponsor has a fiduciary duty to monitor the arrangement, a failure attributable to the fiduciary adviser should not adversely affect the plan sponsor's fiduciary relief.

Disclosure of Fee Information

SHRM strongly supports the meaningful disclosure of individual account plan fee information, including wrap fees and revenue-sharing fees. It is essential that plan sponsors and plan participants have accurate and transparent information regarding the fees in a plan, particularly any fees that are embedded in a plan's investment options. Fee transparency is an issue where a plan offers participants access to an investment advice arrangement as well as where a plan does not offer such an arrangement. SHRM understands that the Department is actively working on guidance on fee disclosure that will have an application beyond the advice context, and we are encouraged by the prospect of enhanced disclosure across all individual account plans subject to Title I of ERISA.

Pending issuance of broader guidance on appropriate disclosure of plan fee information, any guidance issued by the Department on fees in the context of investment advice will be important both on its own and because it will be a touchstone for fee disclosure generally. SHRM believes that disclosure is most meaningful for the vast majority of plan participants when that disclosure expresses fees in dollar amounts. To date, much of the fee disclosure has been made in terms of "basis points" and percentages; however, this form of disclosure is abstract and often difficult for participants to evaluate and understand. In addition, it is critical that any fee disclosure reflect and highlight the impact of fees over time. Investment fees may seem modest in the near term but over time may have a dramatic effect in terms of reduced retirement savings. For this reason, it is important that any fee disclosure capture the effect fees have over time (e.g., over a ten-year period). Moreover, the Department should consider approaches that will ensure that fee disclosure is standardized among providers to ensure that participants can easily make an "apples-to-apples" comparison.

KAPLAN

Although fee disclosure is an issue of importance for individual account plans generally, there are a number of unique issues associated with fee disclosure regarding investment advice arrangements. At a minimum, any investment advice fee disclosure must coordinate disclosure under general fiduciary standards with the specific disclosure needed to satisfy the conditions of the PPA prohibited transaction exemptions. It is critical that participants understand both the fees under the plan without the investment advice and the fees if the participant elects to utilize the investment advice arrangement. This is necessary to allow participants to evaluate the cost of the advice. Part of this disclosure is providing clear information regarding the extent to which any fees will be offset or leveled against other fees, for example, where investment management fees are offset against investment advice fees.

Central to fee disclosure regarding advice arrangements is ensuring that any disclosure explains the services that are being provided in exchange for the fees. Many investment advice arrangements effectively include two components: one that provides advice to the participant and one that implements that advice and rebalances a participant's account in accordance with those recommendations. For the former, it may make more sense for fees to be charged on a flat dollar basis. However, most managed account options that provide ongoing rebalancing and management charge based on a percentage of a participant's account. One important function that fee disclosure can serve is to identify the cost of these two functions separately so that participants can reasonably determine whether a particular service is worth the cost.

An issue in the context of affiliated investment advice that is not fee leveled is the extent to which fee disclosure should highlight or otherwise illustrate potential conflicts of interest. In this regard, an affiliated investment adviser may receive additional investment management and/or revenue-sharing payments in connection with the investment advice. However, the very premise of the prohibited transaction exemption for computer-based advice is that this potential conflict is neutralized by the use of an audited and independently certified computer program. Moreover, the PPA requires disclosure of these potential conflicts of interest. As a result, we believe that the plan sponsor or other fiduciary should not be required to provide a numeric disclosure of the total fees paid to a fiduciary adviser in connection with the investment advice. Instead, we believe it is sufficient for the advice disclosure to highlight that the advice may cause the fiduciary adviser to receive additional compensation under the investment funds, including investment management fees and/or revenue-sharing fees. Such disclosure will complement existing disclosures regarding the fees paid in connection with the underlying investment options.

We also note that we see little reason that investment advice fee disclosure should be limited to investment advice arrangements that satisfy one of the new PPA prohibited transaction exemptions. Fee disclosure is essential to all investment advice arrangements without regard to whether the arrangement relies on a statutory prohibited transaction exemption. For this reason, the Department should consider the importance of uniformity of disclosures across different advice approaches. This may be particularly important as more and more plans choose to offer multiple advice programs to participants.

Finally, we note that there is some lack of clarity in the PPA prohibited transaction exemptions regarding the party that bears responsibility for ensuring meaningful disclosure. As mentioned above, the fiduciary adviser is the party that has the requisite information, and we urge the Department to confirm that this is an obligation of the fiduciary adviser and that any failure only affects the fiduciary adviser and not the plan sponsor.

SHRM appreciates the opportunity to submit these comments on the new prohibited transaction exemptions for investment advice. SHRM looks forward to working with the Department to improve and expand investment advice for plan participants.

Respectfully submitted,
Michael P. Aitken
Director, Governmental Affairs
Society for Human Resource Management

REVIEW QUESTIONS

1. What is meant by a global work force and a global economy?

2. How can companies be effective employers across international borders?

3. Discuss diversity training and social differences found in individualistic versus collectivistic cultures.

4. Give at least three examples of a global workforce, describing the need for proper training and development programs.

5. Discuss the implications of similar job titles and responsibilities from a global perspective.

6. Discuss at least four elements considered important in determining global leadership selection and retention measures.

7. Discuss international compensation models and at least two important social and economic factors that must be analyzed across borders when developing compensation plans.

8. Discuss the following quote: "A global mind set seeks to adopt values and attitudes to create a common mental picture for balancing corporate goals, business units, and functional priorities on a worldwide scale."

ANSWERS AND EXPLANATIONS

1. Companies deliver products and services to customers all over the globe. For HRM, a global economy can mean cultural differences in hiring, training, and working in a multicultural workforce. This holds true whether or not a company is considered "global." Employees, managers and executives need to be aware of and able to work productively with people who speak different languages, are motivated differently, and have different training, education, and cultural practices. Universally, employees seek the same things in a job: safety, security, decent wages, and interesting work—but how employees are trained and managed may be different in an international arena. How conflicts are resolved, how to perform a job, and how to interact with customers or suppliers may require a different set of skills than those in the U.S.

2. To be effective, employers across international borders rely on HRM to provide proper training for all employees. Diversity training and diversity awareness programs take into consideration a collective understanding of other cultures and the needs of people from those cultures. Many countries are experiencing a global economy for the first time in their history and it can take several generations for cultural changes to take hold.

3. Diversity training and diversity awareness programs take into consideration a collective understanding of other cultures and the needs of people from those cultures. For example, the U.S. is known as an individualistic social economy: individuals are educated and encouraged to pursue individual goals and ambitions without consideration to the family, society, or fellow workers. In many Asian and European cultures, individuals are raised to embrace a collectivistic economy, where family and co-workers take higher priority than individual needs and goals. The U.S. social economy must embrace other cultures in order to work successfully with these other countries' workers.

4. The following are some examples you could use:

    *   Managers who need to know how to motivate and organize people from a variety of cultural backgrounds

    *   Sales people who need to know how to build relationships, negotiate, and sell across cultures

    *   HRD specialists who need to understand how to develop best practices which embrace multicultural awareness, while simultaneously developing the capability of employees in other countries

    *   Employees who need to be able to work effectively with a wide variety of people

    *   Supervisors who need to provide effective learning and development in other geographies and cultures for client-specific products and processes while maintaining high quality customer service levels

- Companies which recognize the opportunities that a global market place offers them

5. Job titles and job responsibilities vary across cultures. Localizing an organization's employee handbook and writing job descriptions to include geographical and cultural considerations are important in developing a global workforce.

6. Global leadership competencies required for success include:

    - Working and managing across cultures

    - Acting as the voice of the local culture to home office

    - Adapting to cultural differences as they impact business practices

    - Defining behaviors that are associated with success factors in a company

    - Identifying internal and external candidates who already practice those success factors

    - Providing accurate, reliable and detailed selection/recruitment data such as developmental reports and criteria that accurately asses and match job-demand with individual achievement (capability).

7. Establishing world-wide compensation and reward systems is a big concern for all global companies. Restructuring long-established cultural norms, such as lifetime employment in Japan and industry-wide bargaining in Germany, are weakening in response to the pressures of a modern global economy. Hard and fast assumptions about international compensation, such as the notion that pay systems for expatriates provide comfortable salaries and that local (U.S.) compensation practices should be tailored to fit national cultures, do not necessarily hold true in an uncertain economy. An uncertain economy stems from global issues and political events requiring a constant review of compensation practices for multi-national companies. From a global perspective, substantial differences in how people are paid for work become apparent.

8. "Think locally but act globally."

    Compensation reward systems become crucial tools to support a global mindset, or the reverse can happen: formation of major obstacles blocks its path. Organizations competing in worldwide markets have always depended upon understanding economic, social, and political changes. What emerge are companies that adopt global compensation and reward strategies that will be aligned with a global mindsets. Rather than react to match local conditions, a global perspective shifts to define the best use of compensation and rewards to compete on a worldwide basis.

Practice Test: PHR Exam 1

1. Needs assessment determines

   A. optimum staffing levels.
   B. gap between present and desired skills.
   C. funds needed to cover salaries and benefits.
   D. changes in overall mission and goals.

2. Organizational structure is best described with

   A. a pyramid framework.
   B. an organizational chart.
   C. a functional narrative.
   D. job descriptions.

3. Job analysis includes all *EXCEPT* which of the following?

   A. Key tasks
   B. Analysis of time spent doing key tasks
   C. Skills needed for success
   D. Academic background

4. Job descriptions include all *EXCEPT*

   A. job title.
   B. years of experience.
   C. salary range.
   D. education, license, and certifications.

5. Job satisfaction is difficult to measure. It is generally defined as

   A. low turnover rate.
   B. number of long-term employees.
   C. low absenteeism rate.
   D. employee compensation matching expectations.

6. Ideally a firm's workforce should reflect

   A. the general profile of the field.
   B. the general profile of the community.
   C. the general profile of the customer base.
   D. the general profile of the school district.

7. Which of the following are *NOT* principles of the Society for Human Resource Management "Guidelines for Professional Behavior"?

   A. Fairness and justice
   B. Confidentiality
   C. High ethical standards
   D. Promotion of diversity

8. An employee records management system should be able to

   A. manage payroll and leaves and track applicants.

   B. manage payroll and leaves and résumés.

   C. manage payroll and leaves and retention.

   D. manage payroll and leaves and benefits.

9. Employee records can include all *EXCEPT* the following types of documents.

   A. Payroll records

   B. Salary history

   C. Job applications

   D. Position announcements

10. A progressive disciplinary plan *MUST* include

    A. documentation of each step.

    B. only written warnings.

    C. leave without pay.

    D. security precautions.

11. Which of the following is *NOT* a tenet of high performance work systems (HPWS)?

    A. Egalitarianism

    B. Knowledge development

    C. Shared information

    D. Frequent rewards

12. During the initiation phase of a project, the HR professional would typically

    A. choose a project name.

    B. monitor the timeline.

    C. develop a project budget.

    D. document the project activities.

13. During the planning phase of a project, the HR professional would typically

    A. choose a project team.

    B. monitor the timeline.

    C. develop the timeline.

    D. collect ideas from team members.

14. During the execution phase of a project, the HR professional would typically

    A. develop a project budget.

    B. research project options.

    C. create a project team.

    D. monitor the timeline.

15. During the closing phase of a project, the HR professional would typically

    A. monitor the timeline.

    B. document the project activities.

    C. issue the request for proposals.

    D. collect ideas from team members.

16. The SWOT system for environmental scanning stands for

    A. survey, work up options, train.

    B. strengths, weaknesses, options, trials.

    C. survey weaknesses, optimize threats.

    D. strengths, weaknesses, opportunities, threats.

17. Which of the following is *NOT* a theory of leadership?

   A. Transformational leadership
   B. Transcendental leadership
   C. Participative leadership
   D. Contingency leadership

18. Fiedler's contingency theory of "situational favorableness" states that group performance is based upon the leader's psychological orientation and these additional variables:

   A. Leader's power, group atmosphere, and task structure
   B. Leader's experience, group acceptance, and environmental scanning
   C. Leader's compensation, group satisfaction, and interpersonal relationships
   D. Leader's success, group task performance, and task rewards

19. Which of these are *NOT* one of Robert House's four styles of leadership?

   A. Supportive leadership
   B. Directive leadership
   C. Participative leadership
   D. Transformational leadership

20. James Kouzes and Barry Posner describe transformational leadership as

   A. enabling others.
   B. controlling the environment.
   C. managing change.
   D. offering performance awards.

21. Which of the following is *NOT* one of the intelligences described by Howard Gardner's multiple intelligences theory of learning?

   A. Interpersonal
   B. Intrapersonal
   C. Musical
   D. Transformational

22. In Maslow's hierarchy of needs, as each need is satisfied, the next need becomes

   A. dominant.
   B. unnecessary.
   C. fulfilled.
   D. easier.

23. Training needs to take place at which of these three levels?

   A. Task, individual, and organizational
   B. Individual, classroom, and online
   C. Task, fundamental, and universal
   D. Customized, standard, and task

24. Communication can generally be categorized as

   A. formal, informal, or horizontal.
   B. internal, external, or informal.
   C. upward, downward, or horizontal.
   D. sensitive, upward, and downward.

25. Email should always be

   A. as informal as possible.
   B. spell- and grammar-checked.
   C. as formal as possible.
   D. monitored by HR.

26. Which is the following is *NOT* an aspect of risk management?

    A. Workplace violence
    B. Ergonomics
    C. Labor contracts
    D. Federal employment legislation

27. Interest-based bargaining (IBB) for contract negotiation and bargaining

    A. is based on fixed opposing views.
    B. results in a compromise or no agreement.
    C. is sometimes called integrative bargaining.
    D. is often not satisfactory to one party.

28. Strategic human resource management (HRM) is a process by which you

    A. align human capital with institutional direction.
    B. revise corporate goals for compliance.
    C. plan, align, process, and implement organizational goals.
    D. develop corporate governance procedures.

29. Strategic planning determines

    A. where the organization has been.
    B. future direction and steps.
    C. how to beat the competition.
    D. what to report to shareholders.

30. SWOT analysis is a type of environmental scanning that includes the organization's

    A. strengths, weaknesses, opportunities, and threats.
    B. strategies, working conditions, overtime projections, and territory.
    C. strengths, worksheets, organization chart, and task analysis.
    D. strategies, weaknesses, opportunities, and threats.

31. Strategic direction

    A. precedes an environmental scan.
    B. starts with a needs assessment.
    C. concludes with development of a mission statement.
    D. is built on the mission and vision statements.

32. Vision statements include

    A. the mission statement.
    B. a long, detailed description of goals.
    C. a brief description of goals.
    D. the SWOT analysis.

33. Mission statements include

    A. the vision statement.
    B. the risk management plan.
    C. how the company will achieve its vision.
    D. a general description of corporate goals.

34. A span of control refers to

    A. the number of direct reports.

    B. the size of the budget.

    C. the transformational management style.

    D. the length of the job description.

35. Aligning human capital means

    A. having the budget to offer annual merit raises.

    B. providing a safe and secure work environment.

    C. developing an organizational chart.

    D. identifying the right people for the right job at the right time.

36. Cultural intelligence refers to the ability to

    A. speak knowledgeably about fine arts.

    B. speak several languages fluently.

    C. relate to cultures other than one's own.

    D. do SWOT analysis.

37. HR professionals need to provide certain information for the organization's overall budget, including which of the following?

    A. Information on salaries, benefits, and cost-of-living increases

    B. Information on salaries, benefits, labor market data, and cost-of-living increases

    C. Information on salaries, benefits, grant revenue, and cost-of-living increases

    D. Information on salaries and cost-of-living increases

38. The formula for a balance sheet is

    A. Liability = Assets – Capital.

    B. Capital = Assets + Liability.

    C. Assets = Liability + Capital.

    D. Capital = Liability – Assets.

39. A statement of cash flow provides information about

    A. which department has the highest paid employees.

    B. where money is going in the organization.

    C. whether or not your business is a start-up.

    D. whether you are paying too much for marketing.

40. A company's assets include all EXCEPT

    A. cash holdings.

    b items that can be converted to cash.

    C. land or buildings.

    D. employee retirement accounts.

41. The income statement is sometimes referred to as

    A. the bank statement.

    B. the profit statement.

    C. the profit and loss statement.

    D. the net income report.

42. A liability is generally defined as

    A. money owed by the business to others.

    B. outstanding loans.

    C. unpaid employment taxes.

    D. revenue due from customers.

43. Historical-based budgeting is best used

    A. by companies over 50 years old.
    B. by companies that anticipate little operational change.
    C. by companies planning a brand-new product or service.
    D. by companies that plan several retirements.

44. Zero-based budgeting is best used

    A. by companies that are over 50 years old.
    B. by companies that anticipate little operational change.
    C. by companies planning a brand-new product or service.
    D. by companies that plan several retirements.

45. A corporation can be defined as a body formed and authorized by law that

    A. has legal rights and responsibilities.
    B. can make legally binding decisions.
    C. is owned by a board of directors.
    D. is controlled by stockholders.

46. Shareholders or stockholders

    A. manage operations of the company.
    B. elect the board of directors.
    C. approve the annual budget.
    D. choose the chief executive officer.

47. The board of directors

    A. is comprised of the largest stockholders.
    B. represents the stockholders' interest.
    C. is elected by the corporate management.
    D. sets the price of company stock.

48. A centralized organization

    A. has a central administrative office and no branches.
    B. has all employees working in one location.
    C. makes most decisions at higher levels of management.
    D. makes most decisions by staff consensus.

49. A decentralized organization

    A. has administrative staff at each branch location.
    B. has international offices.
    C. makes most decisions by staff consensus.
    D. makes most decisions at lower levels of management.

50. In the context of workforce planning, nepotism refers to

    A. hiring the offspring of an incumbent worker.
    B. length of service for long-service employees.
    C. common characteristics of workers born in the same era.
    D. results generated by regional and national recruitment.

51. A branding image is used to

    A. identify company property and reduce employee theft.

    B. persuade a potential employee to work for your firm.

    C. have a recognizable trademark on every product sold by the firm.

    D. achieve a place on a list of favorite companies to work for.

52. Recruitment strategies need to balance

    A. potential number of applications with staff to sort them.

    B. salary for the opening with amount spent on recruitment.

    C. Internet and other advertising methods.

    D. branding image with word-of-mouth.

53. Sourcing is a process of hiring

    A. only internal candidates.

    B. only external candidates.

    C. through headhunting or executive search firms.

    D. through a variety of recruitment efforts.

54. What is the chief advantage of internal versus external hiring?

    A. It costs less to recruit an internal candidate.

    B. Hiring an internal candidate sends the "right message."

    C. Internal candidates have had a chance to prove themselves.

    D. Internal candidates do not require further training

55. Which is *NOT* a typical candidate screening tool?

    A. Résumé

    B. Cover letter

    C. MySpace page

    D. Application form

56. Which of the following is the *MOST* important screening factor?

    A. Perfect grammar and spelling

    B. Relevance of work history

    C. Gaps in work history

    D. Length of résumé

57. Because they are considered employment tests according to the Equal Employment Opportunity Commission (EEOC), employment applications must request information that is

    A. directly related to the job advertised.

    B. from a list of nationally normed questions.

    C. uniform for all positions in the company.

    D. not already included in the résumé.

58. Which of the following would *NOT* be a typical pre-employment test given to all candidates for a job opening?

    A. Personality test

    B. Knowledge or proficiency test

    C. Integrity test

    D. Psychomotor assessment test

59. The *MOST* popular pre-employment personality test is the

    A.   Kiersey Temperament Sorter.
    B.   Managerial Type Indicator.
    C.   Myers-Briggs Type Indicator.
    D.   Sales Temperament Sorter.

60. An in-box test, where candidates are given a stack of problems typical to the position to prioritize and suggest actions for, is an example of a(n)

    A.   psychological test.
    B.   physical ability test.
    C.   honesty-integrity test.
    D.   knowledge or proficiency test.

61. Honesty-integrity tests

    A.   accurately predict if a candidate would steal office supplies.
    B.   are easy to create and score.
    C.   do not need to be given to all candidates.
    D.   are easy to create but difficult to score.

62. A candidate is asked to lift four boxes of photocopy paper from a hand truck to a countertop in a timed test. This sort of test is called a

    A.   psychomotor assessment test.
    B.   physical assessment test.
    C.   background test.
    D.   proficiency/knowledge test.

63. Reliability of an employment test measures

    A.   whether the candidate can do the job.
    B.   whether the candidate has integrity and reliability.
    C.   whether the test will give consistent results.
    D.   whether the test is long enough.

64. Validity measures how well a test evaluates selection criteria

    A.   when it is given to all candidates.
    B.   it was designed to measure.
    C.   in the quickest amount of time.
    D.   for secretarial applicants.

65. The type of validity that measures how well performance on a test relates to on-the-job performance is

    A.   predictive validity.
    B.   concurrent validity.
    C.   criterion-related validity.
    D.   proficiency validity.

66. The "Uniform Guidelines on Employee Selection Procedures" (UGESP) states that any pre-employment test that selects a protected class at a rate of 80 percent of the group with the highest selection rate is discriminatory. This concept is called

    A.   the Civil Service Commission.
    B.   adverse impact.
    C.   the Rehabilitation Act.
    D.   Title VII.

67. An interview in which the candidate is asked to describe a problem and the steps taken to resolve it is a

    A. screening interview.

    B. panel interview.

    C. behavioral interview.

    D. nondirective interview.

68. Asking all candidates the same questions so that it is easy to compare results is called a

    A. panel interview.

    B. directive interview.

    C. nondirective interview.

    D. stress interview.

69. Giving candidates a list of questions to reflect on and prepare answers for in advance is which type of interview?

    A. Nondirective interview

    B. Behavioral interview

    C. Screening interview

    D. Structured interview

70. Questions asked of candidates must be stated so that only job-related information is collected. Which of the following questions could you *NOT* legally ask at a job interview?

    A. Can you work on Saturdays?

    B. Can you lift 30 pounds?

    C. How tall are you?

    D. Do you have a valid driver's license?

71. *Total rewards* is a phrase used in recruitment that means

    A. salary and benefits of the position.

    B. monetary fringe benefits of the position.

    C. retirement plan options available.

    D. any benefit that can attract, motivate, or retain an employee.

72. Employment at will means that

    A. an employee must give two weeks' notice.

    B. an employee may be terminated for due cause.

    C. an employee may be terminated without cause.

    D. an employee cannot be terminated.

73. All employees who leave the organization should get

    A. an exit interview.

    B. a party.

    C. a retirement pension.

    D. TIAA-CREF counseling.

74. The Worker Adjustment and Retraining Notification (WARN) Act of 1988 requires that employers of 100 or more give a 60-day advance notice that

    A. poor performers will be laid off.

    B. large plant layoffs or closings are planned.

    C. employees must retrain to be retained.

    D. the company plans a stock split.

75. *Total rewards* is a phrase that has replaced the less comprehensive term

    A. *payroll and benefits.*

    B. *compensation program.*

    C. *compensation and benefits.*

    D. *benefits program.*

76. Which of the following is *NOT* a total rewards strategy?

    A. Base pay

    B. Overtime rate

    C. Merit pay

    D. Health care/wellness

77. The phases for implementing a total rewards program are

    A. evaluation, assessment, implementation, design.

    B. design, implementation, evaluation, assessment.

    C. implementation, assessment, design, evaluation.

    D. assessment, design, implementation, evaluation.

78. A total rewards philosophy should guide in the development and implementation of programs to

    A. recruit, motivate, and retain employees.

    B. contain the cost of benefits.

    C. match the philosophy to the corporate culture.

    D. keep the package in line with the external competition for top candidates.

    E. All of the above

79. Information regarding the current reward structure, pay levels versus industry trends, current salary schedule, and turnover rates is gathered during this segment of the total rewards process:

    A. Evaluation

    B. Assessment

    C. Design

    D. Implementation

80. "How do you determine who would be eligible for what rewards?" "How will programs be rolled out?" and "How will you explain the new system?" are questions that are answered in this phase of the total rewards philosophy development process:

    A. Implementation

    B. Evaluation

    C. Design

    D. Assessment

81. Discovering what rewards lure your employees or prospective employees to the competition are part of this phase of the total rewards process:

    A. Design

    B. Evaluation

    C. Assessment

    D. Implementation

82. In this phase of the total rewards process, you compare your original objectives to the plan that has been rolled out and determine further modifications:

    A. Design

    B. Evaluation

    C. Implementation

    D. Assessment

83. What is the primary law related to employee status and compensation?

   A. Equal Pay Act
   B. Americans with Disabilities Act (ADA)
   C. Fair Labor Status Act of 1938
   D. Executive Order 11246 (affirmative action)

84. Which of the following is *NOT* a determiner of exempt status under the Fair Labor Standards Act?

   A. Salary
   B. Ability to hire and fire
   C. Work requiring advanced education
   D. Work involving computer systems analysising

85. A worker who has the authority to hire and fire full-time computer technicians is defined as exempt by

   A. professional exemption.
   B. administrative exemption.
   C. executive exemption.
   D. computer exemption.

86. Unless increased through individual labor agreements, overtime for nonexempt workers is compensated at

   A. double time.
   B. one and one-half time (time and a half).
   C. minimum wage.
   D. compensatory time.

87. Which of the following is compensable time for nonexempt employees?

   A. Time to travel to or from work
   B. Voluntary training outside work hours
   C. Meal periods longer than 30 minutes
   D. Time to change into specialized clothing

88. The Equal Pay Act of 1963 prohibits discrimination of employees based on the employee's

   A. age.
   B. years of service.
   C. sex.
   D. nationality.

89. Which of the following is *NOT* a factor in job evaluation?

   A. On-the-job experience
   B. Years of experience in the field
   C. Education level
   D. Sex of worker

90. Social Security benefits are based on the

   A. Federal Unemployment Tax Act (FUTA).
   B. Old Age, Survivors, and Disability Insurance (OASDI)
   C. Family Medical Leave Act (MFLA).
   D. Retirement Equity Act (REA).

91. Employees spend less time off work and are more productive as the result of health and wellness programs, which can include all of the following *EXCEPT*

    A. personal improvement courses.

    B. flu shots.

    C. incentives to quit smoking.

    D. anger management counseling.

    E. All of the above

92. Employee assistance programs (EAPs) are designed to aid with which types of problems?

    A. Smoking cessation

    B. Financial difficulties

    C. Divorce counseling

    D. Grief counseling

    E. All of the above

93. Nonexempt employees must be paid

    A. time and a half.

    B. minimum wage plus any state adjustment.

    C. minimum wage.

    D. minimum wage for the first 40 hours, then overtime at time and a half.

94. A nonexempt employee must travel to a work-related conference. The travel takes place before and after work hours. The employee will be compensated

    A. for the time attending the conference.

    B. for the time attending the conference plus travel time.

    C. overtime for travel time beyond the 40-hour week.

    D. time and a half for the conference and travel time.

95. The process of defining and reducing possible threats to a company and planning to reduce the amount of harm these threats can cause is

    A. loss prevention.

    B. threat management.

    C. risk management.

    D. emergency action planning.

96. The goals of the Occupational Safety and Health Act (OSHA) of 1970 include all of the following *EXCEPT*

    A. partnerships and cooperative programs.

    B. development of protective gear.

    C. education, outreach, and compliance assistance.

    D. strong, fair, and effective enforcement.

97. Under OSHA laws, which of the following is *NOT* an employer responsibility?

    A. Reporting fatal accidents to OSHA within eight hours

    B. Providing protective clothing and gear

    C. Providing training on OSHA standards

    D. Providing ergonomic equipment

98. Repetitive motion injuries would result from

    A. chemical exposure.

    B. physical exposure.

    C. disease exposure.

    D. biological exposure.

99. What kind of occupational health hazard is secondhand smoke?

A. Biological exposure

B. Chemical exposure

C. Physical exposure

D. Disease exposure

E. Both A and C

100. The *MOST* hazardous industry according to OSHA is

A. construction.

B. shipyard work.

C. general industry.

D. fishing industry.

101. According to OSHA regulations, employers do *NOT* have the right to

A. accompany an OSHA officer on inspection.

B. request identification from a visiting OSHA officer.

C. refuse to allow an OSHA inspection.

D. consult with OSHA on a potentially hazardous situation.

102. Which of these injuries are considered work related?

A. Worker falls on ice in the parking lot.

B. Worker falls at company-sponsored lunchtime yoga class.

C. Worker falls in company restroom.

D. Worker disregards safety procedures and falls from ladder.

103. Which industry had the lowest degree of fatalities in 2006?

A. Airlines

B. Health services and education

C. Logging

D. Fishing

104. How to notify employees of a lockdown or evacuation is part of a company's

A. red alert phone plan.

B. disaster recovery plan.

C. emergency alert plan.

D. risk management plan.

105. The *GREATEST* incidence of workplace violence occurs in

A. post offices.

B. academia.

C. private industry.

D. state government.

106. Which agency is responsible for policy and programs for workplace emergency management?

A. Occupational Safety and Health Administration (OSHA)

B. Federal Emergency Management Agency (FEMA)

C. Department of Labor

D. National Labor Relations Board (NLRB)

107. An emergency plan should identify

    A. key responsible individuals.

    B. how an emergency evacuation decision will be made.

    C. what personnel are certified in first aid.

    D. who will be the liaison to the press and public.

    E. All of the above

108. A clear workplace privacy policy includes

    A. guidelines for monitoring all communications.

    B. a definition of acceptable Internet use.

    C. the employer's right to review data on office computers.

    D. guidelines for acceptable use of company property (cell phones, vehicles, etc.).

    E. All of the above

109. A drug-testing program prevents

    A. abuse of prescription drugs.

    B. unavoidable workplace hazards.

    C. avoidable workplace hazards.

    D. silly errors in data entry.

110. Sloppy appearance, uncombed hair, and dark circles under the eyes can all be signs of

    A. illness.

    B. substance abuse.

    C. Generation X behavior.

    D. a new baby in the household.

    E. All of the above.

111. A disaster recovery plan describes activities that are scheduled to

    A. deliver immediate first aid.

    B. evacuate the building.

    C. move to generator power.

    D. begin after the emergency is over.

112. Jessica works in your human resource department at a major university. She is also taking college courses at night. You have given her permission to make copies of her papers on company equipment and on company time as long as she is prudent about doing so. Once during her lunch hour, you see that she has copied close to 75 pages of a textbook. Because you have given her permission, is Jessica in violation of the copyright law?

    A. No, because you have given her permission to make copies on company time.

    B. No, because as the employer, you have authority over any documents that are copied on company time.

    C. Yes, because she has copied too many pages. If she had only copied two or three pages, she would not be in violation.

    D. Yes, Jessica is in violation of the copyright law whether you have given her permission or not.

113. The originator of the total quality management (TQM) movement is

    A. George W. Deacon

    B. W. Edwards Deming

    C. Kevin John Bennett

    D. Dr. Kaoru Ishikawa

114 SMART is an acronym used in goal setting. Which of these items is *NOT* generally associated with SMART?

A. Action-oriented

B. Attainable

C. Technology

D. Specific

115. *Fiduciary responsibility* is a term for what?

A. Corporate governance

B. The responsibility of those in top levels of the organization to make the best and most prudent decisions on the behalf of shareholders

C. The responsibility of the accounting department

D. The responsibility of the board of directors

116. Jim is the manager of an HR department at a large Internet-based company in the Northwest. Early last year, a top executive, Nick, was asked to submit his resignation because his performance was suffering, largely due to an inappropriate relationship with a coworker. Nick is now looking for a new job. When questioned about why Nick left the position, you are legally able to say what to the reference seeker?

A. You tell the reference seeker the dates of Nick's employment.

B. You tell the reference seeker the truth about why Nick left and that he was asked to submit his resignation.

C. You tell the reference seeker that Nick submitted his resignation on such-and-such date.

D. You hint that Nick was asked to leave, although you never really say so.

117. *Adverse impact* means which of the following?

A. If an HR department legally discloses information about you after your employment, you have been adversely impacted by the disclosure of information.

B. Sixty percent of the hiring in a company is greater than the hiring of protected individuals.

C. The selection rate of the focal group is less than 80 percent of the selection rate of the reference group.

D. A company commits reverse discrimination and hires more Caucasian than minority individuals.

118. A flow chart is

A. the flow of individuals in the organization from top to bottom.

B. the way the work flows through a division or unit in a department.

C. work flow on a specific project.

D. a graphic planning and control chart designed to demonstrate relationships between planned performance and actual performance over time.

119. Herzberg's theory of motivation is sometimes called what?

A. X/Y theory

B. Hygiene theory

C. Expectancy theory

D. Hierarchy of needs

120. Carl, your vice president of marketing, has been asked to lead a team to write a new vision statement. Which of the following is he likely to create?

    A. A statement that describes what the organization is, what it does, where it is going, and how it differs from the competition

    B. A short, catchy phrase that describes what the company is all about

    C. The team's vision in the next fiscal year

    D. Six bullet points that describe the organization's top six goals for the future

121. The four *P*s of marketing are

    A. participation, placement, price, and production.

    B. price, procurement, promotion, and placement.

    C. perception, placement, production, and price.

    D. product, price, place, and promotion.

122. K & J Smith Manufacturing is considering outsourcing its human resources functions. Which of the following are factors to consider?

    A. Lowering costs for the department being outsourced

    B. Reducing human capital

    C. Establishing a case for outsourcing to the board of directors

    D. Sale of assets to the new supplier of services

    E. All of the above

123. Kelly is interviewing receptionists for her dental office. She has interviewed three candidates for the position but is having difficulty deciding between them. They all were just about the same in her mind; no one really stood out. What type of interview bias does she have in her selection process?

    A. Similar-to-me bias

    B. First impression bias

    C. Stereotyping

    D. Average/central tendency bias

124. The administrative team at a local community college is negotiating a new contract with its professional/technical employees. They are using a negotiating process called collaborative bargaining. What is/are another name(s) for collaborative bargaining?

    A. Position bargaining

    B. Mutual gains bargaining

    C. Interest-based bargaining

    D. Collective bargaining

    e. Both B and C

125. The WARN Act of 1988 provided what protection for workers?

    A. Protection for workers in the event of mass layoffs or plant closings

    B. Employer warnings prior to dismissal of employees from their jobs

    C. Ninety-day advance notice if employees will be laid off or a plant closed

    D. Employer-provided training upon a plant closing or employee layoff

126. George has worked 35 years for the Metropolitan School District, and his employer has contributed to his retirement plan for these 35 years. George is now considered fully vested in the retirement plan and can begin to draw his pension. What does *fully vested* mean in this example?

    A. George has contributed the maximum number of years into his retirement plan—35 years.

    B. George's employer has contributed the maximum number of years into his retirement plan—35 years.

    C. George has reached the age of retirement, 62, and can now draw his retirement income.

    D. George has reached the point where he owns the employer's contribution to his retirement plan.

127. By law, OSHA requires employers to have injury and illness prevention plans in place. Which is *NOT* an example of an injury and illness prevention plan?

    A. Emergency response plan

    B. Risk assessment plan

    C. Safety and health management plan

    D. Fire prevention plan

128. The Pregnancy Discrimination Act, passed in 1978, requires Teeko Manufacturing to do which of the following when employee Katie announces that she is pregnant?

    A. Give her 60 days' leave of absence with pay after her child is born.

    B. Provide Katie with her same job after she returns from maternity leave.

    C. Provide Katie with the same benefits and treatment as any employee with a short-term disability.

    D. Give Katie two weeks off with pay after her child is born.

129. Angelina is the newest HRD in your organization. Three months ago, she was charged with developing a training program for six divisions of the organization that are implementing a new software program aimed at streamlining the hiring and benefits program and reducing paperwork. Angelina is in the final stages of evaluating her training program before putting it into action. She's torn between two approaches and has come to you for advice. Which of these do you suggest Angie use?

    A. A combination of lectures, demonstrations, and hands-on training in a computer lab

    B. One-on-one training with individuals and simulation training where trainees can watch you run the software program on a screen in a large auditorium

    C. A series of presentations of the various aspects of the training program to all individuals involved in its use

    D. Simulation training for small groups of people

130. Melissa is a staff member in the accounting department at a large dot-com company in the Northwest. Her supervisor, Liz, has noticed a decrease in the amount of her work and an increase in absences and illnesses. When Liz questions Melissa, Melissa says that she is going through a divorce and indicates that she might be being abused. What should Liz do for Melissa at this point?

    A. Let her have a leave of absence until she can get her act together.

    B. Give her information about counselors that she has heard of in the area.

    C. Refer her to local safe haven agencies that deal with domestic violence.

    D. Refer her to the EAP within the organization.

131. SHRM has six core principles as part of its professional standards. Which of the following is *NOT* one of those six core principles?

    A.   Professional development

    B.   Ethical leadership

    C.   Professional communication

    D.   Fairness and justice

132. Whirlpool, headquartered in Benton Harbor, Michigan, is doing a salary survey of all its salaried employees. Jamal is required to collect the data and report his findings to the CEO and board of directors. One figure in which the CEO is particularly interested is the median salary nationwide for HR directors. What does *median* mean?

    A.   The average

    B.   The middle salary, when the salaries are arranged from highest to lowest

    C.   The salary that occurs most frequently

    D.   The most current data in the middle of the country

133. Which of the following is accomplished in the job analysis process?

    A.   You analyze employee knowledge, skills, and abilities.

    B.   You do a detailed analysis of job descriptions and tasks accomplished.

    C.   You examine core competencies and essential job functions.

    D.   All of the above

134. Which of the following is often the largest operating expense at any organization?

    A.   Recruitment of employees

    B.   Salaries and benefits

    C.   Total rewards

    D.   Vacation and sick leave

135. In total rewards, one type of benefit is typically called work-life balance. Which of the following would be examples of a work-life balance benefit?

    A.   Elder care

    B.   Tuition reimbursement

    C.   Adoption assistance

    D.   Prescription coverage

136. In recent years, Social Security has been a hot topic. When the Social Security Act passed in 1935, what was its original intent?

    A.   To provide a pension for retirement

    B.   To assist employees during the heights of the Depression

    C.   To provide insurance for dependents/survivors upon an employee's death

    D.   To provide unemployment insurance

137. As a result of Americans living longer now than in previous generations, Old Age, Survivors, and Disability Insurance (OASDI) raised the age at which workers may receive their maximum Social Security benefits. If you were born in 1964, at which age will you receive your maximum Social Security benefits?

    A.   62

    B.   65

    C.   66

    D.   67

138. Cathy works at a parts-manufacturing plant in Michigan assembling widgets. Her employer just told her that she can work the rest of the week and then she will be laid off. Her sister, Suzy, lives in Washington state and was also just laid off from an airplane manufacturing company. They made the same salary but are not receiving the same unemployment benefit. Why?

   A. Cathy is older than Suzy, and she's been in the workforce longer.

   B. Each state determines state unemployment insurance (SUI) eligibility requirements within its jurisdiction.

   C. Benefits depend upon the company and its ability to pay its workers SUI.

   D. The cost of living is vastly different between Washington and Michigan.

139. Martin is in management at a large automobile manufacturing company. He hears that Kenny is collaborating with the union and discussing the upcoming contract negotiations. Martin has begun sitting next to Kenny at lunch hour, mocking his interest in the union and the negotiating strategies. Martin is violating which code of conduct?

   A. Employers may not interfere with the rights of employees to organize or engage with a union, according to the National Labor Relations Act (NLRA).

   B. He's discriminating against Kenny, according to the Labor Management Relations Act (LMRA).

   C. He's tampering with the potential collective bargaining agreement.

   D. He's harassing Kenny and in violation of the sexual harassment law.

140. Greta is a carhop at Fast Eddie's Drive-In restaurant. She's very worried about the fact that there are extension cords that she needs to step over to get in and out of the front door to deliver food to patrons. In addition, mouse pesticides are in various places throughout the restaurant. What type of hazards are potentially within this workplace?

   A. Chemical and physical hazards

   B. Safety and biological hazards

   C. Environmental and safety hazards

   D. Health and safety hazards

141. An example of key stakeholders at a company would be which of the following?

   A. Shareholders

   B. Management

   C. Board of directors

   D. CEOS

   E. All of the above

142. The Ford Motor Company laid off workers in several different plants in 2006 and 2007 to recover from lack of sales. This would be an example of which strategic management objective(s)?

   A. Corporate restructuring

   B. Mergers and acquisitions

   C. Reengineering

   D. Workforce reduction

   E. Both C and D

143. A medium-sized health care facility is looking for a first-time office manager at its Shreveport, Louisiana, location. Previously, it operated with six administrative assistants who reported to the HR manager. It has decided to look just within the organization for the new office manager. What is the danger of looking only at internal employees?

    A. They don't have the perspective of other industry viewpoints.

    B. The candidates who don't get the job will be upset to have been passed over.

    C. Lack of diversity in the workforce may result.

    D. Promotion may incur costs.

    E. A, B, and C

144. Some hiring practices include administering aptitude, cognitive, and personality tests. The Myers-Briggs Type Indicator is one such test. What type of test is it?

    A. Aptitude

    B. Personality

    C. Cognitive

    D. Skill

145. If you are using testing in your organization as a predictor for hiring, you must be certain that the tests possess which characteristics?

    A. Content validity and predictive validity

    B. Reliability and content validity

    C. Concurrent validity and success validity

    D. Reliability, construct validity, and content validity

146. A *Seattle Times* article in 2008 ran a detailed article about the compensation plan of the University of Washington's college president. Part of Dr. Emmert's compensation included deferred compensation. What is deferred compensation?

    A. The employee gets a tax-deferred retirement plan.

    B. The employee gets paid after leaving office.

    C. The employee gets paid a commission based on certain criteria.

    D. The employee defers a certain portion of income to charitable organizations.

147. Under COBRA, an employer with 20 or more employees must continue to provide health coverage for employees when a qualifying event occurs. Which of the following is considered a qualifying event requiring the employer to continue coverage for 36 months?

    A. Termination for misconduct

    B. Eligibility for Social Security/retirement

    C. Reduction in hours

    D. Divorce or legal separation

148. A wise manager knows that it is prudent to pay careful attention to stress in the workplace. Bjorn has noticed that recently, Rebecca has been complaining of headaches and stomach problems, has had a number of absences, and has started to isolate herself from others during her lunch hours. Which one of the stages of stress does Bjorn think that Rebecca is experiencing?

    A.   Arousal

    B.   Exhaustion

    C.   Overload

    D.   Resistance

149. A 401(k) is an example of

    A.   nonmonetary compensation.

    B.   monetary compensation.

    C.   deferred compensation.

    D.   Both B and C

    e.   Both A and C

150. Benjamin is researching which performance appraisal processes will be most beneficial to him and his staff when doing their annual reviews. He likes what he sees in the BARS rating system. What does BARS measure?

    A.   It measures whether or not his employees reach the bar that he set for them the previous year.

    B.   It identifies behaviors that the organization has set as desirable and rates employee performance against those set behaviors.

    C.   It identifies key job requirements and creates dimensions by which to measure and rate employee performance.

    D.   It establishes benchmarks at which the employee needs to perform next year.

151. Management and union workers who have just signed a new three-year contract have entered into which of the following?

    A.   Binding arbitration

    B.   Collective bargaining agreement

    C.   Conflict resolution

    D.   Group consensus

152. Your boss has asked you to do an analysis of the relationship between potato chip sales and attendance at the plant and to use that to project future departmental goals. What quantitative tool are you likely to use to show your boss this relationship?

    A.   A PowerPoint presentation that demonstrates a simulation of sales and attendance

    B.   Measures of central tendency

    C.   Simple linear regression

    D.   Average of the attendance at the plant with potato chip sales

153. OSHA regulations require an employer to keep track of injuries and illnesses that are work related. On which of the following would you be required to keep documentation?

    A.   Mark sprained his ankle playing softball during a lunch hour tournament during the workday.

    B.   Cindy worked out in the employer-sponsored gym after work and tore her rotator cuff.

    C.   Esther received a reaction from a flu shot she received at the employee clinic.

    D.   Meg has been suffering from psychological stress related to being sexually harassed by a vice president at the company.

154. Sam has been promoted from HR generalist to HR manager at Sun Press Homes—a large manufacturer of homes in the Midwest. His boss, Henry, tells him he needs to become more familiar with basic accounting terms, which will be a big part of his job. Which of the following is *NOT* likely to be a term that Sam will encounter with his new responsibilities?

    A. Zero-based budgeting
    B. Dividends
    C. Accounts payable
    D. Fiscal year accounting
    E. All of the above

155. The president *MOST* responsible for the Social Security Act of 1935 was

    A. President Franklin D. Roosevelt.
    B. President Theodore Roosevelt.
    C. President John F. Kennedy.
    D. President Lyndon Johnson.

156. Which one of the following is the taxing authority for Social Security and Medicare programs?

    A. IRS
    B. FICA
    C. OASDI
    D. Medicare

157. You are seeking an evaluation process for your company that rates employee performance by getting feedback from customers, supervisors, top management, and team members. Which of the following does so?

    A. Peer review evaluations
    B. Supervisor review/self-evaluation
    C. 360-degree review
    D. BARS

158. At your department store, sales appear to have suddenly plummeted in the jewelry department, but you can't figure out why exactly it has happened. To get to the bottom of the problem, you decide to spend the next week observing each shift and worker in the jewelry department to see what is causing the sales to drop. This would be an example of doing what?

    A. Developing rating scales
    B. Halo error
    C. Using multiple criteria
    D. Critical incidents

159. You are 45 years of age and working at a department store known for hiring young, beautiful women. Without warning, you are let go from your position. You suspect that you have been a victim of discrimination in violation of the Age Discrimination in Employment Act (ADEA). Your state has its own EEO enforcement agency. How long do you have to file your complaint?

    A. 60 days
    B. 180 days
    C. 100 days
    D. 300 days

160. Employee assistance programs do *NOT* provide which of the following forms of assistance to employees?

    A. Training for managers who deal with difficult employees
    B. Anger management classes
    C. Drug and alcohol counseling
    D. Financial counseling

161. Unemployment compensation is typically paid for how long while the recipient must actively be seeking employment?

    A. 90 days
    B. 120 days
    C. 26 weeks
    D. 32 weeks

162. The current baby boom population is working longer than used to be deemed the typical retirement age of 65. However, as the aging population gets near retirement, it becomes more crucial for senior management and HR to develop what type of plan?

    A. Affirmative action plan
    B. Job recruitment plan
    C. Succession plan
    D. Staffing plan

163. Several technical colleges and universities in Wisconsin in the early 2000s attempted to implement a software system designed to improve customer service, streamline financial and human resource processes, and enhance database capabilities. The system they were attempting to implement was

    A. a high-performance work system.
    B. a human resource information system.
    C. a customer service system.
    D. None of the above
    E. Both A and B

164. Which of the following questions is illegal to ask in a job interview?

    A. What year did you graduate from high school?
    B. Do you have a family?
    C. Do you live within the city limits?
    D. All of the above
    E. Both A and B

165. The federal government requires employers to file an enormous amount of paperwork each year and to keep copies of that paperwork for a number of years, depending upon the type of documents. How long is a company required to keep FMLA documents regarding information such as leave dates, hours worked, and disputes over FMLA?

    A. One year
    B. Two years
    C. Three years
    D. Forever

166. According to the job characteristic model, what three factors result in motivated, satisfied, and productive employees?

    A. Meaningfulness of work, task significance, and autonomy
    B. Meaningfulness of work, responsibility for completion of a whole identifiable piece of work, and knowledge of work results
    C. Meaningfulness of work, responsibility for outcomes, and knowledge of work results
    D. Meaningfulness of work, responsibility for outcomes, and fair compensation

167. You are in the process of analyzing the organizational culture within your organization after a large change in upper management. You have over 600 employees, so one-on-one interviews are impractical. What tool might you use to gather information about employee attitudes?

    A.   Employee surveys developed in-house

    B.   Focus groups with an outside facilitator

    C.   A combination of focus groups and surveys, both developed by outside sources

    D.   Anonymous solicitation of feedback

168. Your IT department has tipped you, the HR manager, off to the fact that an individual in your janitorial staff has been sending a number of email and IM messages to pornographic sites. As the employee, does he have privacy rights or can you legally view his email messages?

    A.   Yes, the employee has rights to privacy, and you should not view his email messages.

    B.   No, the employee does not have a right to privacy in this instance. The messages have been sent with company equipment and on company time.

    C.   Yes, the employee does have certain rights to privacy but, in this case, has voided his rights to privacy.

    D.   Both B and C

169. David Quincy, a staff member in your division, has prostate cancer. A claims agent from an insurance company has requested Mr. Quincy's health records and absentee records. Which law prevents you from releasing this information?

    A.   Health Insurance Portability and Accountability Act (HIPAA) of 1996

    B.   The Privacy Act of 1979

    C.   Occupational Safety and Health Act of 1970

    D.   Fair Labor Standards Act (FLSA)

170. Ron is the head of your financial services division. He passed away suddenly of a heart attack, leaving his widow, Nancy, with no health insurance of her own. Is your company required to continue to provide health care insurance to her? If so, for how long?

    A.   No, Ron was the insured. You are no longer required to provide health care insurance for Nancy.

    B.   Yes, you are required to continue to insure Nancy for 36 months.

    C.   Yes, you are required to continue to insure Nancy for 12 months.

    D.   Yes, you are required to continue to insure Nancy for 18 months.

171. What are some causes of involuntary payroll deductions?

    A.   Unpaid back taxes

    B.   Debt garnishment

    C.   Child support garnishment

    D.   Alimony garnishment

    E.   All of the above

172. The Civil Rights Act of 1991 amends which previous act?

    A. Equal Pay Act of 1963
    B. Title VII of the Civil Rights Act of 1964
    C. Age Discrimination in Employment Act of 1967
    D. Occupational Safety and Health Act of 1970

173. Which one of the following issues was a chief focus of the Civil Rights Act of 1991?

    A. Protecting employees from discrimination
    B. Preventing disparate impact
    C. Providing for damages in cases of intentional discrimination
    D. All of the above

174. The EEO-1 form is an annual report the HR division needs to complete by when of each year?

    A. September 30
    B. January 1
    C. December 31
    D. July 1

175. The EEO-1 form does *NOT* list which of the following as race and ethnic categories from which an employee can self-select an ethnicity?

    A. Three or more races (not Hispanic or Latino)
    B. Native Hawaiian or Pacific Islander
    C. American Indian or Alaska Native
    D. White

176. The EEO-1 form requires an employer to group employees by job category. Which of the following is *NOT* a job category listed on this form?

    A. Operatives
    B. Sales
    C. Craft workers
    D. Secretaries
    e. None of the above

177. The EEO-1 form does *NOT* require you to report which of the following information?

    A. Job categories
    B. Marital status
    C. Gender
    D. Race and ethnicity
    E. Both B and C

178. You are interviewing Heather for the position of HR generalist with a team at the hospital. One of the questions that you ask Heather is: "Tell me a time when you had a problem employee, what the issue was, and how you resolved that issue?" This is an example of what type of interview?

    A. Directive interview
    B. Behavioral interview
    C. Nondirective interview
    D. Situational interview

179. Carol is interviewing to be director of development at a local nonprofit. When she enters the interview waiting room, she is handed the set of questions that will be asked during the interview. This is what type of interview?

    A. Situational interview

    B. Behavioral interview

    C. Nondirective interview

    D. Directive interview

180. Kelli is interviewing paralegal candidates for a law firm. As part of the interview process, Kelli asks the following question: "The three lawyers in this firm commonly work on the weekends. On Monday morning, you find the following on your desk: (1) A deposition that needs to be transcribed by Monday at noon, (2) a divorce decree that needs to be filed, and (3) a summons that needs to be served. How would you handle this scenario?" This is an example of what?

    A. An aptitude test

    B. An in-box test

    C. Cognitive ability test

    D. Stress test

181. The Sherman Anti-Trust Act was originally enacted to prevent what?

    A. Organization of unions

    B. Monopolies and other restraint-of-trade activities

    C. Strikes by employees

    D. Free trade

182. The FLSA was enacted to protect which class of workers?

    A. Women

    B. Senior citizens

    C. Workers under age 18

    D. Minorities

183. The carpenters union is negotiating a new contract. There are four types of bargaining that they might use. What are they?

    A. Single-unit bargaining, multi-unit bargaining, multi-employer bargaining, and parallel bargaining

    B. Double-unit bargaining, mutual-gains bargaining, multipurpose bargaining, and parallel bargaining

    C. Single-gains bargaining, parallel bargaining, mutual-gains bargaining, multi-unit bargaining

    D. Compromise bargaining, win-win bargaining, mutual-gains bargaining, single-unit bargaining

184. In 2008, Northwest Airlines and Delta Airlines entered into merger talks. As part of the merger discussion, the airline pilots had separate discussions about how the merger affected their unit. This is an example of what?

    A. Single-unit bargaining

    B. Coordinated bargaining

    C. Multi-unit bargaining

    D. Parallel bargaining

185. In 2007, workers at the grocery store chains Safeway, Albertsons, QFC, and others all threatened to strike at one time. This is an example of what?

    A. Multi-unit bargaining

    B. Multi-employer bargaining

    C. Parallel bargaining

    D. Coordinated bargaining

186. Weingarten Rights, which come from the case *NLRB v. Weingarten* (1975), provided for which of the following?

    A. An employee's right to refuse to be searched on the employer premises

    B. An employee's right to refuse to answer questions that may be discriminatory toward the employee

    C. The employee's right to have representation at an investigative meeting with management, if the employee believes that discipline will be discussed at the meeting

    D. None of the above

187. A landmark ruling in 2001 allows employers to require employees, as a condition of employment, to agree that they will submit all employment disputes, including discrimination claims under state or federal law, to binding arbitration before an arbitrator rather than a judge or jury in a court of law. What was the name of this case?

    A. *EEOC v. Waffle House* (2002)

    B. *Excelsior Underwear Inc. v. NLRB*

    C. *Circuit City Stores Inc. v. Adams* (2001)

    D. *NLRB v. Weingarten* (1975)

188. Suzette has been a troublesome employee since you hired her. She takes extended smoke breaks, has been caught sleeping on the job, and repeatedly doesn't turn in her work on schedule. You've warned her numerous times, but a recent egregious infraction has left you no course but to dismiss her. What do you need to consider before you do this?

    A. You must give her two weeks notice to correct her behavior.

    B. Nothing—employment at will allows you to dismiss her immediately.

    C. She needs to have one day off without pay to consider the consequences of her actions and that dismissal is a probability.

    D. Suzette may file a lawsuit against you for not getting notification of dismissal.

189. Mark and Ginny work at an elementary school. Ginny is married. Mark has repeatedly commented on Ginny's clothing, her eyes, her hair, and her dress. While flattered at first, Ginny reminded Mark that she was married and his comments were making her uncomfortable. Still, Mark is persisting in his comments and has now begun to follow her around school, in the lunch room, and the parking lot. According to the laws on sexual harassment, does this scenario present probable cause of sexual harassment?

    A. Yes, Mark is making an uncomfortable work environment for Ginny.

    B. No, he isn't asking for any special favors relative to his comments.

    C. No, his comments are relatively innocent in complimenting her.

    D. Yes, he is implying that he wants more than a professional work relationship.

KAPLAN

190. Tony is the manager of a fast-food restaurant and he has only young, female waitresses as employees. He's even been heard to say he "likes the pretty young girls" and it's "better for business." Jay applied for a job as a waiter, and Tony didn't hire him, even though he was well qualified and had experience. What is Tony violating in his hiring practices?

    A. Affirmative action regulations

    B. Age discrimination laws

    C. Equal Pay Act

    D. American with Disabilities Act

191. In 2007, the U.S. House of Representatives passed HR 3685. What did this bill prohibit?

    A. Employment discrimination against pregnant workers

    B. Employment discrimination on the basis of sexual orientation against gay, lesbian, and bisexual workers

    C. Employment discrimination on the basis of age against workers over 65

    D. Requiring miners to work longer than usual hours in unsafe conditions

192. Coco works at a bottling plant in Georgia as a line worker. On Monday, she informs her supervisor, Mike, that her father passed away in Virginia and that she needs three days off to attend the funeral. Because the line is shorthanded, Mike denies her request. Is this legal for Mike to do?

    A. Yes, there is no federal law that mandates bereavement leave.

    B. No, Mike is required to give Coco at least one day to attend her father's funeral.

    C. No, Mike is required to give Coco at least three days to attend her father's funeral.

    D. No, Mike is required to give Coco the time she needs to attend her father's funeral, but she must take it without pay.

193. The OFCCP is an agency that was created to monitor the activities of whom?

    A. Health care workers

    B. Government workers

    C. Federal contract workers

    D. Construction workers

194. The chamber of commerce has hired Sally to oversee a specific fund-raising program for the next six months. She has been hired as an independent contractor. The chamber must do which of the following?

    A. Withhold income taxes and Social Security

    B. Not withhold income taxes and Social Security, as these are the responsibility of the independent contractor

    C. Report Sally's earnings to the federal government

    D. Both B and C

195. A small employer with fewer than ten workers interviews Dante for a position as an accountant. Dante is a paraplegic and is in a wheelchair. The small office would make it difficult to accommodate Dante's wheelchair; the company does not have unlimited funds to remodel facilities. What is the employer required to do according to the ADA?

   A. Provide reasonable accommodations to meet Dante's needs.

   B. Put in a wheelchair ramp and modify the office space.

   C. Nothing—this situation would create an unreasonable burden for the employer.

   D. Refer Dante to another employer.

196. Common law doctrine refers to which of the following?

   A. Common law ensures that once a job candidate becomes an employee, the employee will be properly trained by participating in a company-paid or company-sponsored training and development program.

   B. Common law partners receive the same benefits and privileges as marital partners.

   C. Common law includes laws pertaining to fraudulent misrepresentation, defamation, duty of good faith and fair dealing, employment at will, express or implied contracts, promissory estoppel, *respondeat superior*, sexual harassment, and constructive discharge.

   D. Both A and C

197. The term *organizational climate* refers to which of the following?

   A. How systems and processes work together

   B. The climate between managers and staff

   C. The geographic area in which one works

   D. How the organization inspires and inhibits employee performance

198. Amanda is the supervisor of a group of administrative assistants. She is sensing tension in the group, in particular among a group of six individuals in the immediate administrative "pod" where she works. She decides that an organizational intervention is in order. What are the components of an OD intervention?

   A. Complete a survey, conduct interviews, and develop a plan of action.

   B. Identify the problem, diagnose its causes, and seek solutions to resolve the situation.

   C. Enact change management through shared knowledge (knowledge management) and create opportunities as a learning organization to resolve the situation through its human capital (employees).

   D. Both B and C

199. Which of these are two types of OD intervention programs?

   A. Juran trilogy and management by objective

   B. TQM and design intervention

   C. TQM and techno-structural intervention

   D. Techno-structural intervention and management by objective

200. Six sigma is a business process that involves what?

    A. The six objectives for achieving organizational goals

    B. A business management strategy that seeks to remove the causes of defects and errors in manufacturing and business processes

    C. A strategy without a defined sequence of steps and processes

    D. Any strategy that could deal with customer dissatisfaction

    e. Both B and D

201. What are the three components in the Juran Trilogy?

    A. Quality design, quality management, and quality improvement

    B. Quality planning, quality control, and quality management

    C. Quality control, quality design, and quality management

    D. Quality processing, quality control, and quality design

202. A Pareto chart is a graphical representation of what?

    A. The relationship between two numbers

    B. Cause and effect relationships

    C. The 80/20 rule

    D. Quarterly sales figures

203. In a BARS performance evaluation, how is an employee rated?

    A. On a scale from 1–5, based upon certain important dimensions of the job

    B. The sales figures in a given week

    C. Degrees of performance

    D. Both A and C

204. Michelle is an exempt employee. For the past three weeks, she has worked 10–15 hours more per week, sometimes on the weekends, because of an increased workload on a specific project. As her employer, you are required to do which of the following?

    A. Pay her overtime for her hours over 40 hours.

    B. Pay her time and a half for the weekend hours and overtime for the hours worked over 40 hours during the workweek.

    C. You are not required to pay Michelle overtime.

    D. You may pay Michelle overtime, if you have required her to keep track of her hours.

205. Since 1975, increases in Social Security benefits have been based upon what?

    A. Rate of inflation

    B. The economy

    C. The number of people collecting benefits

    D. Cost-of-living adjustments

206. An employee can request FMLA leave for which of the following reasons?

    A.   To travel to China to adopt a child
    B.   To care for an ailing parent
    C.   To visit a child who is in jail
    D.   To place a child in a substance abuse program
    E.   All of the above
    f.   Three of the above

207. Candice has been treated for breast cancer for the last year. During treatment periods, she takes one or two days off during the workweek. This is considered what type of FMLA leave?

    A.   Continuous leave
    B.   Intermittent leave
    C.   Sporadic leave
    D.   Health-needs leave

208. The USERRA of 1994 provides for protection of employees involved in which of the following?

    A.   The witness protection program
    B.   Incarceration for a crime while emplo-yed and awaiting trial
    C.   Being called to active duty while in the reserves
    D.   Returning to college classes

209. Kerry has been working as a consultant for large pharmaceutical sales companies for the past 15 years. She knows the ins and outs of the industry and is frequently called in to other companies to consult on training programs. Kerry might be referred to as

    A.   a field specialist.
    B.   an expert trainer.
    C.   an industry authority.
    D.   a subject-matter expert.

210. Sam and Maggie are employees at a large organization that has a written sexual harassment policy. They are both married to other people and are having an extra-marital affair. He is a vice president; she is an exempt worker. They are not in a direct reporting relationship. Are they in violation of the sexual harassment policy?

    A.   Yes, he is in a position of authority over her.
    B.   No, the relationship is consensual.
    C.   No, she does not report to him.
    D.   Yes, any time two married people are having an affair, it is morally wrong.
    e.   Both B and C

211. Glenda is conducting an exit interview with Charles after he submitted his resignation. It has been clear for some time that Charles has been unhappy with his position at Regal Tool and Die. What is NOT an appropriate exit interview question for Charles?

    A.   Can you tell me why you are leaving the organization?
    B.   Can you tell me what your difficulties were with your supervisor?
    C.   What did you like best about working here?
    D.   If offered, would you ever work here again?

212. As part of the standards for the Society for Human Resource Development (SHRM), HR professionals are expected to do what?

    A. Get their master's degrees
    B. Demonstrate the highest of ethical standards
    C. Continually expand their knowledge of workforce trends
    D. Treat all within their organizations with dignity and respect
    E. Three of the above

213. Robert is a division director at a large coffee company. He regularly meets with his team of 12 and helps guide them as they work on their personal and team goals for the future. He provides direction, gives support, and encourages them along the way. According to the leadership theories you have read, this meets which definition of leadership?

    A. Maslow's hierarchy of needs
    B. X/Y theory
    C. McLelland's theory
    D. House's path-goal theory

214. Miso is helping her staff work on revising their job descriptions. Which of the following are critical components to include in the job description to meet ADA requirements?

    A. Education, certifications, and licenses needed
    B. Physical activity
    C. Mental activity
    D. Nonessential job functions
    E. Three of the above

215. Jan is recruiting for a forklift operator at a large big-box retailer. The last several people who have left this position have reported that they had back injuries from the heavy lifting and equipment used on the job. What is Jan's best course of action?

    A. Leave the description of heavy equipment operation off the job recruitment flyer.
    B. Describe in detail the lifting requirements for the job and the skills necessary for operating heavy equipment on the job.
    C. Wait until the interview to describe the lifting involved in this position.
    D. Report the incidents to OSHA.

216. Kelly has been stationed in Iraq for the past three years on and off. The experience has taken its toll on him. He has sought professional help for posttraumatic stress disorder but has indicated he wants to return to his employment position eventually. Which HR law gives guidance on whether or not you need to accept him back into his position?

    A. ADA
    B. OSHA
    C. FMLA
    D. USERRA

217. Cissy is on military leave performing active duty. She is drawing compensation from the armed services. Under USERRA, do you have to give her compensation from her job as well?

    A. Yes, you have to continue to give Cissy her normal compensation and benefits.

    B. No, you do not have to continue to give Cissy her normal compensation, but you do have to give her COBRA insurance.

    C. No, you do not have to continue to give Cissy her normal compensation, unless she is taking military leave.

    D. Yes, she is able to receive compensation but at a reduced rate.

218. An environmental scan would require you to do which of the following?

    A. Check the global weather conditions for doing business overseas

    B. Examine mathematical models for formulating sales

    C. Do a PET analysis

    D. Do a SWOT analysis

219. A federal piece of legislation designed to restrict the activities of labor unions and prevent walkouts is called

    A. the Taft-Hartley Act.

    B. the Mann Act.

    C. the Ralph Nader Act.

    D. the Sherman Act.

220. In human resource planning, which of the following are important to consider?

    A. The "graying" of the American workforce

    B. Literacy levels of the workforce

    C. The percentage of Hispanic workers in the workplace

    D. Fast-growing occupations

    E. All of the above

221. Many employers use a mentor-mentee relationship with new hires. Kazu plans to propose such a program to the CEO at Teeki Toys Manufacturing. He feels that it will help the new employees assimilate. He has two incorrect statements in his proposal to the CEO. Which of the following is true of mentors?

    A. Mentors should be the same age and gender as the mentee.

    B. Mentors help to make mentees comfortable in their new environment.

    C. Mentors should be older workers and have been on the job for over ten years.

    D. Mentors and mentees should be specifically matched to one another.

    E. Both B and D

222. Performance appraisals are *MOST* used for which of the following reasons?

    A. Discipline of employees

    B. Compensation decisions

    C. Goal identification

    D. Communication

    E. B, C, and D

223. OSHA has developed guidelines for identifying companies that are at high risk for workplace violence. Which one of the following would indicate a company is at high risk?

    A.　No security guards are employed at the workplace (assuming a large workplace).

    B.　Customers regularly abuse employees or use racial slurs or profanity.

    C.　Violence has occurred on the premises.

    D.　Employees have not been trained to handle threatening behaviors.

    E.　All of the above

224. Employee surveillance is *MOST* often used for which of the following reasons?

    A.　Sexual harassment

    B.　Abuse of computer equipment (e.g., misuse of email or the Internet, accessing pornography)

    C.　Theft

    D.　To corroborate personnel issues and employee grievances

225. Title VII of the Civil Rights Act of 1964 identified five protected classes. What are they?

    A.　Race, color, religion, national origin, and sexual orientation

    B.　Marital status, race, religion, and sex

    C.　Race, color, religion, national origin, and sex

    D.　Race, religion, sex, and political orientation

Answers to Questions and Explanations

1. (B) is the correct answer. While all of these differences could generically be considered needs, the needs assessment of core knowledge considers the difference between existing and needed skills.

2. The correct answer is (B). Among the many means of representing an organization, the visualization through a hierarchical organization chart is most useful.

3. The correct answer is (D). Although a certain academic background may be suggested or required in a position announcement, it is not part of job analysis.

4. (C) is correct. Job descriptions include information such as education, licenses, and certification to comply with the Americans with Disabilities Act and minimal level of required experience, but they do not include the salary range.

5. The correct answer is (D). There are many ways to measure employee satisfaction with their positions. The match between expectations and compensation is the most frequently used.

6. The general profile of the community, (B), is correct. An organization increases the ability to attract customers when the workforce mirrors local diversity.

7. The correct answer is (D). The "Code of Ethics and Professional Standards" specifies that all employees must be treated with dignity and respect and given equal employment opportunities. Promotion of diversity is not specified in the guidelines.

8. The correct answer is (B). The document management system may be used to manage payroll, leaves, and résumés. It can serve as the basis to evaluate retention or benefits. Applications of all who applied for a position but were not hired are not usually tracked.

9. The correct answer is (D). Human resources is not required to keep position announcements as part of employee records.

10. The correct answer is (A). A progressive disciplinary plan includes written documentation at all levels, beginning with the verbal warning.

11. Frequent rewards, (D), is the correct answer. High-performance work systems (HPWS) suggest that rewards be tied to performance but does not suggest frequency.

12. The correct answer is (C). The initiation phase of a project life cycle includes gathering bids for the components of the project to develop project budgets. These activities will help the organization determine if the project is viable.

13. The correct answer is (C). Development of the final timeline occurs during the planning phase.

14. The correct answer is (D). As the project is executed, the milestones of the timeline are monitored for satisfactory progress.

15. The correct answer is (B). As the project is closing, the notes are consolidated into a closing final report.

16. The correct answer if (D). Environmental scans help the organization remain competitive. They include an internal assessment of the organization's strengths, a frank analysis of weaknesses, and a realistic review of opportunities for and threats to success.

17. The correct answer is (B). *Transcendental leadership* is a term created as a distractor because it looks like two actual leadership styles: transactional leadership, in which rewards are given to workers who accomplish a goal, and transformational leadership, which brings workers to standards that can have a transforming effect. Don't choose an answer quickly because it looks familiar.

18. The correct answer is (A). One of many leadership theorists, Fiedler considers the power and psychological orientation of the leader as well as the group atmosphere and structure of the task as crucial to group performance.

19. The correct answer is (D). Robert House's path-goal theory suggests a leader should determine goals and direction. He has defined four leadership styles: directive (where the leader gives specific guidance), supportive (where the leader shows encouragement), participative (where the group is involved in decision making), and achievement (where the leader stretches the group with a challenging goal).

20. The correct answer is (A). Transformational leadership focuses on empowering individuals and groups to accomplish goals.

21. The correct answer is (D). Howard Gardner's theory of multiple intelligences includes interpersonal, intrapersonal, and musical intelligences. While the transformational leader may well have transformational intelligence, this is not an intelligence named by Gardner.

22. The correct answer is (A). Maslow has arranged the hierarchy of needs so that as the dominant need is satisfied, the next need becomes dominant.

23. The correct answer is (A). Task-level training is the most basic. Training for individuals is customized to improve their job performance. Organizational-level training is generally reserved for a topic, like "Coping with Stress" or "Customer Service," that affects the entire organization, division, or department.

24. The correct answer is (C). While virtually all the adjectives in answers (A) through (D) could be applied to communication, (C) is correct because it is the only complete answer. Other answers are not fully descriptive because they lack dimensions.

25. The correct answer is (B). Email is less formal than an official memo and more formal than a conversation. Because they can be forwarded to others and legally monitored by an employer, review emails for content, tone, spelling, and grammar before sending.

26. The correct answer is (C). Risk management does not typically involve labor contracts, although it does concern occupational health and safety.

27. The correct answer is (C). Interest-based bargaining (IBB) is sometimes referred to as integrative bargaining, because parties identify common interests and collaborate on the final result.

28. The correct answer is (C). The other answers, aligning goals with mission, revising goals, or developing procedures, are all subordinate to the process of planning, aligning, processing, and implementing the organizational goal.

29. "If you don't know where you are going, you'll end up someplace else." The correct

answer is (B). While a strategic plan is informed by organizational history, takes into account the threat of competitors, and may be reported out to stockholders' meetings, the plan defines the steps to reach future directions.

30. The correct answer is (A). Any of the answers fits the acronym SWOT. This environmental scanning analysis looks at two internal and two external advantages and disadvantages to help plan success: internal strengths and weaknesses, external opportunities and threats.

31. The correct answer is (D). After the external scan, a strategic direction is developed from mission and vision statements to ensure congruency with the organization's goals.

32. The correct answer is (C). Vision statements briefly communicate the organization's goals and how they will be accomplished.

33. The correct answer is (D). The mission statement includes the organization's unique purpose, goals, and how they will be accomplished.

34. The correct answer is (A). Managers make decisions and organize the workload. Their span of control refers to the number of individuals who report to them.

35. The correct answer is (D). Aligning human capital means finding the best person for the position both in terms of technical skills and fit with the organization and team.

36. The correct answer is (C). Cultural intelligence, related to Gardner's interpersonal intelligence, is the skill set needed to relate to individuals different from oneself. This is a useful trait in an increasingly multicultural workplace.

37. The correct answer is (A). The human resource professional's contribution to the budgeting process is information on salaries, benefits, and cost-of-living (COL) increases. Labor market data may drive COL increases, and grant revenue may or may not offset salary expenses.

38. The correct answer is (C). This is one of those questions that depends on the definitions of basic accounting terms and application of common sense. Assets, the total resources of an organization, are equal to the sum of liabilities (money owed) and equity (capital). What you have is what you owe, plus what you won. Assets = Liability + Capital.

39. The correct answer is (B). Cash flow shows where money is going in an organization. The other answers are all issues that can be investigated based on cash-flow information.

40. The correct answer is (D). Employee retirement accounts are managed in trust for employees and are not included as part of the company's assets.

41. The correct answer is (C). The income statement is referred to as the profit and loss statement. It shows how much income was brought in (revenue), paid out (expenses), and the difference, which is the net income for the period.

42. The correct answer is (A). A liability is money owed to others. Answers (B), (C), and (D) may all be components of an organization's liability.

43. The correct answer is (B). Companies that anticipate little operational change often build historical-based budgets on the previous year's budget activity.

44. The correct answer is (C). Zero-based budgeting starts anew to determine the costs to produce a new product or service. In this case, there is enough anticipated

change that a historical-based budget would not be an appropriate forecasting tool.

45. The correct answer is (A). A corporation has legal rights and responsibilities. Depending on how capital was raised, a corporation may be owned by its directors or stockholders. Corporate decisions are not in themselves legally binding.

46. The correct answer is (B). In a public company, shareholders or stockholders elect a board of directors. It, in turn, approves the annual budget and chooses the chief executive officer, who manages the operations of the company.

47. The correct answer is (B). In a public company, the board of directors is elected by the stockholders to represent their interests; directors may or may not be stockholders themselves.

48. The correct answer is (C). No matter the number of locations, a centralized organization makes most decisions at higher levels of management.

49. The correct answer is (D). *Decentralized* refers not to geographical location but to involvement in decision making by all levels of management.

50. The correct answer is (A), hiring a worker who is a member of someone's family.

51. (B) is the correct answer. The branding image helps you attract candidates who will enjoy working for a firm that has your organization's values and mission.

52. The correct answer is (A). Using strategies that will result in a more than adequate number of diverse, qualified candidates will only serve to overwhelm HR staff. You do not need to screen 100 candidates to hire an entry-level receptionist.

53. The correct answer is (D). Sourcing chooses from the many potential strategies those most likely to yield the right number of qualified candidates.

54. Each of the answers is correct to an extent, but (C) is the best answer. No interview will yield the information that the employee has provided through work experience.

55. While (C) is much less likely to be used for screening than the other voluntarily submitted tools, some potential employers are using Web search engines and websites to gain a broader view of candidates.

56. While all these factors are important in screening candidates, most firms would overlook a typographical error or short résumé for a candidate with relevant work history. (B) is the most correct answer.

57. The correct answer is (A). Employment applications must request information that relates directly to the position.

58. The correct answer is (D). If it did not tie into job performance for the open position, a psychomotor test would not be considered appropriate.

59. The Myers-Briggs Type Indicator, answer (C), measures personality traits.

60. The correct answer is (D). The in-box test is an example of a knowledge or proficiency test, predicting how well the candidate will do on the job through simulation.

61. The correct answer is (D). While it is easy to create scenarios or cases for candidates to solve, it is too easy for the candidate to guess what the interviewer wants to hear.

62. The correct answer is (B). Such a lifting test is legal as long as it relates to actual job functions and is not being used to screen out candidates who cannot lift

boxes but whose job does not require lifting.

63. The correct answers is (E), both (C) and (D). Reliability of a test relates to its having consistent length and repeatable results.

64. The correct answer is (B). Validity is often normed by giving the test to incumbent workers with the same job functions and comparing their scores to the scores of candidates.

65. The correct answer is (C). Criterion-related validity measures how well performance on a pre-employment test relates to performance on the job.

66. The correct answer is (B). Adverse impact is determined by comparing test results from protected groups with those of other groups.

67. The correct answer is (C). A behavioral interview asks the candidate to recount a problem and describe the steps taken to solve it. A follow-up might ask how the candidate would resolve it today.

68. Answer (B), directive interview, is correct. This interview format can ensure equity among interviews.

69. The correct answer is (D). A structured interview allows both extraverted and introverted candidates the time to process complex questions and prepare thoughtful answers.

70. The correct answer is (C). You may not ask a candidate's weight or height. You may ask if the candidate would be able to meet a specific requirement of the job.

71. The correct answer is (D). Sometimes nonmonetary rewards, such as the ability to telecommute, will make the difference in recruiting a candidate.

72. The correct answer is (C). The at-will employment doctrine allows employment to be terminated by either party without cause if there is no employment contract.

73. The correct answer is (A). An exit interview provides candid information for the organization about issues the departing employee may have had as well as potential improvements the firm could make.

74. The correct answer is (B). Although it is likely that poor performers would be layoff candidates (answer A), the requirement is to warn all employees that layoff or closure is expected.

75. The correct answer is (C). The area of compensation and benefits has expanded to total rewards.

76. The correct answer is (B). Overtime rate is set at time and a half by the Fair Labor Standards Act of 1938 unless negotiated differently by labor agreements.

77. The correct answer is (D). The process does not end with evaluation, but begins again to ensure continuous improvement.

78. Answer: (E). All of the answers are correct; they are aspects of a successful total rewards program.

79. The correct answer is (B). The assessment process identifies the needs for the reward program to address.

80. Answer (B) is correct. The answers to these questions help determine the details of the program.

81. The correct answer is (A). The design phase also includes looking at the threat of the competitors' practices.

82. The correct answer is (B), evaluation. As you discover potential improvements,

you will begin the development cycle again.

83. While all of these are important to become familiar with, the correct answer is (C), the Fair Labor Status Act of 1938.

84. The correct answer is (A). Salary is not a determiner of exempt status.

85. The correct answer is (C). Executive exemption includes those who hire and fire. That the workers are in computer-related positions does not necessarily mean the supervisor is, too (choice D).

86. The correct answer is (B). Unless modified by labor negotiation, the overtime wage for nonexempt employees is time and a half, as set by the Fair Labor Standards Act.

87. The correct answer is (D). Time to change into specialized clothing, like time required to clean up, is compensable for nonexempt employees.

88. The correct answer is (C). This act was later amended in 1972 to include exempt employees.

89. The correct answer is (D), sex of the worker. Discrimination in compensation or benefit practice is defined as unlawful by Title VII of the Civil Rights Act of 1964.

90. While these are all laws with which one should become familiar, the correct answer is (B), the Old Age, Survivors, and Disability Insurance (OASDI).

91. The correct answer is (E). Self-improvement programs that are unlikely to affect workplace performance are not typical employer-elected benefits.

92. The correct answer is (E). All of the answers are correct and might be typical employer-elected benefits.

93. Answers (A) through (C) are incomplete. (D) is the best answer. Nonexempt employees must be paid at least the minimum wage for the first 40 hours and at least time and a half for hours in excess of 40.

94. The correct answer is (A). Time traveling to the conference outside of work hours would not be covered.

95. The correct answer is (C). The area formerly referred to as "occupational health, safety, and security" has been changed to "risk management" to reflect the prevention and preparation role.

96. The correct answer is (B). OSHA does not develop protective gear. It is the obligation of the employer to provide it.

97. The correct answer is (D). The employer has a concern for ergonomic hazards but is not required to provide ergonomic equipment or fixtures.

98. The correct answer is (B). Repetitive stress injuries result from physical exposure.

99. The correct answer is (E). Secondhand smoke is both a biological (A) and a physical (C) exposure.

100. The shipyard industry, (B), has more than twice the injuries of construction management.

101. Employers do not have the right, (C), to refuse to allow an OSHA inspection. An organization may consult with OSHA on a hazardous situation without penalty so long as it is subsequently corrected.

102. Only falling from the ladder, (D), occurred "on the job" according to OSHA's regulations.

103. Health services and education, (B), had the lowest rate of fatalities in 2006.

104. The correct answer is C, emergency alert plan.

105. More than in national or local government, the greatest occurrence of violence is in state government, answer (D).

106. The Federal Emergency Management Agency (FEMA) is responsible for emergency management. Answer (B) is correct.

107. Answer (E) is correct. An emergency plan should address all of these issues.

108. Answer (E) is correct. All of these elements should be included in the workplace privacy policy.

109. OSHA categorizes impairment by drugs or alcohol as an avoidable workplace hazard, (C). Unfortunately, a drug-testing program won't always catch abuse of prescription drugs or prevent careless errors in data entry.

110. The conditions could be a sign of any of the causes listed; answer (E) is correct. It is important to look for patterns and document findings.

111. Disaster recovery, (D), begins after the emergency is over. (A), (B), and (C) are part of the emergency plan.

112. The correct answer is (D). Yes, Jessica is in violation of the copyright law. In fact, you should never have given her permission to copy another author's work without permission by the author in writing.

113. The correct answer is (B). W. Edward Deming is chiefly remembered as the pioneer in the total quality management (TQM) movement.

114. The correct answer is (C), technology. SMART stands for specific, measurable, attainable or action oriented, and time based.

115. The best answer to this question is (B). It is not only the responsibility of the board of directors but of all top-level executives of your organization.

116. The correct answers is (E), both (A) and (C). Both are legally permissible items of information to disclose. You may not say that Nick was asked to submit his resignation or indicate that he would have been fired had he not chosen to do so.

117. The correct answer is (C), when the selection rate of the focal group is less than 80 percent of the selection rate of the reference group. For instance, say your company has a job opening for an administrative assistant. You received 100 applications. Of the applicants, 95 declare their race as Caucasian, and 5 declare their race as Hispanic. If 40 of the Caucasian applicants are selected and only 1 Hispanic applicant is selected, only 20 percent of the Hispanic applicants were hired versus about 42 percent of the Caucasians, creating adverse impact.

118. The correct answer is (D): a graphic planning and control chart designed to demonstrate relationships between planned performance and actual performance over time.

119. The correct answer is (B), two-factor motivation-hygiene theory. The other theories are associated with (A) McGregor, (C) Vroom, and (D) Maslow.

120. The correct answer is (B), a short, catchy phrase that describes what your company is all about and serves an inspirational purpose both within the company and to your customers.

121. The correct answer is (D). Product, price, place, and promotion are typically referred to as the 4 *P*s of marketing. Sometimes *place* is also described as placement or distribution.

122. All of the choices, (E), are items to consider when outsourcing.

123. The correct answer is (D), average/central tendency bias. In this situation, the interviewer has difficulty making a decision and rates all candidates about the same. In similar-to-me bias, the interviewer overlooks potentially negative characteristics and only hones in on the characteristics that are like the interviewer's own—she went to the same school, dresses like me, has two children, etc.

124. The correct answer is (E); both mutual gains bargaining and interest-based bargaining are examples of negotiating with a win-win strategy for both sides, as opposed to collective or position bargaining, which assume an adversarial, "I win, you lose" philosophy.

125. The correct answer is (A). The WARN Act of 1988 requires employers with 100 or more full-time employees to give 60-day advance notice in the event of mass layoffs or a plant closure. The employer does not have to provide training. However, the advance notice gives employees time to seek training on their own.

126. The correct answer is (D). Vesting, or being fully vested, means the point at which the employee owns the employer's contributions to their pension plan.

127. The answer is (B), risk assessment plan. The other three answers are all examples of illness and injury prevention plans.

128. The correct answer is (C), provide Katie with the same benefits and treatment as any employee with a short-term disability. Answers (A) and (B) are commonly provided but not mandatory.

129. The best approach to this situation is likely (A), a combination of lectures, demonstrations, and hands-on training in a computer lab. This approach will meet the needs of the most learners by using visual, hands-on, and listening skills to learn the new program.

130. The best answer is (D), refer her to the EAP within your organization. While Liz might feel well intentioned about referring her to counselors of whom she's aware or domestic violence programs, the best answer is to refer her to the EAP, which has trained professionals to assist with all of the problems Melissa might be experiencing.

131. The answer is (C), professional communication. While certainly an integral part of the HR duties, it is not one of the six standards, which are (1) professional responsibility, (2) professional development, (3) ethical leadership, (4) fairness and justice, (5) conflict of interest, and (6) use of information.

132. The correct answer is (B). *Median* means the middle salary when the salaries are arranged from highest to lowest. In statistics, the mean/average would be when you add up all of the salaries that Jamal collects and then divide by the number collected. The mode is the value that occurs most frequently.

133. The correct answer is (D), all of the above. Each of these is used as part of a detailed job analysis.

134. The correct answer is (C), total rewards, which includes all forms of rewards, including salaries and benefits, paid time off, 401(k) plans, stock, and incentive plans. It also includes nonmonetary compensation that the employer might provide.

135. The correct answer is (A), elder care. Others would include child care, fitness programs, sick leave, and other paid time off.

136. The correct answer is (C), to provide insurance for dependents/survivors upon employee's death.

137. The correct answer is (D), 67 years of age if you were born in 1964.

138. The correct answer is (B). Each state determines SUI eligibility requirements within its jurisdiction.

139. The correct answer is (A). Employers may not interfere with the rights of employees to organize or engage with a union according to the NLRA. The LMRA refers to the Labor Management Relations Act and deals with employer complaints about union abuse.

140. The best answer to this question is (A), chemical and physical hazards. The pesticides are a potential chemical hazard, and the extension cords are a physical hazard.

141. In corporate governance, the term *key stakeholders* generally refers to shareholders, boards of directors, management, and CEOs. This makes all of these answers correct.

142. The best answer to this question is (E). Reengineering is a way of changing the organizational structure to maximize profit and sales. As part of this process, eliminating jobs could be part of the plan. Reducing labor costs by workforce reduction is also a correct answer to this scenario.

143. The correct answer is (E). (A), (B), and (C) are all hazards of relying strictly on internal talent. There can be value in looking outside of the organization for differing viewpoints and industry talents.

144. The correct answer is (B). The MBTI is a personality test.

145. This is a tricky question. The best answer is (D), because the question asked about using the tests in relation to hiring. Reliability measures the tests' ability to be consistent over time. Content validity measures their relationship to a part of the job for which the applicants are being tested—typing skills for a data entry job, for instance. And construct validity measures the connection between the test and being successful on the job. In other words, if your data entry clerk candidate, who is graded on number of entries per day, scores 90 percent versus someone who scores 30 percent, she is more likely to be successful on the job. Concurrent validity measures success at the same time a test is being taken (e.g., a driver's education test).

146. The correct answer is (A), tax-deferred retirement plan.

147. The correct answer is (D). Divorce or legal separation is the only event that requires 36 months of coverage. (A) requires no coverage. Answers (B) and (C) require 18 months of coverage.

148. The correct answer is (B), exhaustion. The symptoms of the exhaustion stage are physical signs such as headaches, fatigue, and stomach problems; emotional symptoms such as depression and isolation or general moodiness; and cognitive issues such as being poorly organized or showing poor judgment.

149. The correct answer is (D). 401(k)s are considered both monetary compensation and deferred compensation.

150. The correct answer is (C), it identifies key job requirements and creates dimensions by which to measure and rate employee performance.

151. The correct answer is (B), collective bargaining agreement. A collective bargaining agreement is between the union and

the employer for a specified period of time—in this case, three years.

152. The correct answer is (C), simple linear regression. This line graph represents the relationship between one variable and another and predicts future activity.

153. The correct answer is (D). Meg has been suffering from psychological stress related to being sexually harassed by a vice president at the company. The other choices, while happening on work time, are not specifically related to the job. Mental illness is not considered work related unless you can find a psychiatrist who attests to its being work related. Because the sexual harassment is happening only while she is on the job, it is likely that you could find a health care official to state that it is work related and requires documentation.

154. The correct answer is (B). *Dividends* is a finance term that is not commonly used in simple accounting and likely will not be a part of Sam's responsibilities. He likely will encounter the other terms in his new position.

155. The correct answer is (A), President Franklin D. Roosevelt.

156. The correct answer is (A), the IRS. When the FICA law was enacted, the responsibility for collection was shifted from the Federal Insurance Commission to the IRS.

157. The correct answer is (C), 360-degree review. Such evaluations include input from superiors, subordinates, internal and external customers, and coworkers but do not include a self-evaluation component.

158. The correct answer is (D), critical incidents. This method of performance evaluation focuses the evaluator's attention on specific behaviors on a job. This method would work well in this case to

see if one employee is doing something, in particular, that is causing a drop in sales.

159. The correct answer is (D), 300 days in states with EEO enforcement agencies, 180 days in states without EEO enforcement agencies. This is a good reminder to become familiar with the laws in your state.

160. The correct answer is (A): EAPs usually do not offer training for managers who deal with difficult employees. EAPs typically offer the other types of assistance.

161. The correct answer is (C), 26 weeks.

162. The correct answer is (C), succession plan. This plan seeks to identify individuals who might move into higher level positions—and be groomed for those positions—as executives and managers retire. It is important to note that a wise succession plan also includes the option of hiring from outside the organization when someone retires.

163. The correct answer is (E), both A and B. The system was computerized, making it a typical HRIS, but it also centralized all management functions.

164. The correct answer is (E). You may ask if someone graduated from high school if it is a requirement of the job for an entry-level position. However, you may not ask what year they graduated in an attempt to "age" someone. You may not ask if someone has a family, no matter how innocuous you feel the question is. It could be construed as an attempt to discriminate against someone with or without children. You may ask the question about residing within the city limits if it is a requirement for employment.

165. The correct answer is (C), three years for an employer with over 50 employees.

166. The correct answer is (C), meaningfulness of work, responsibility for outcomes, and knowledge of work results.

167. The best answer for this question is (C), a combination of focus groups and surveys, both developed by outside sources. Outside resources are likely to be more effective in this particular scenario to demonstrate the appearance of impartiality in the results.

168. The answer to this question is (D), both (B) and (C) are correct. While employees do have certain rights to privacy, the employee has provided a compelling reason for you to suspect unprofessional activity in the workplace, access his email records, and reprimand him for his behavior.

169. The answer to this question is (A). HIPAA prevents discrimination against individuals with preexisting conditions when hired.

170. The answer to this question is (B). Yes, under COBRA, within 30 days of a qualifying event—the death of a spouse—you are required to continue to provide the health care option for Nancy for 36 months.

171. The answer is (E). All of the above are examples of involuntary wage garnishments that an employer is required to withhold from employee paychecks.

172. The correct answer is (B), Title VII of the Civil Rights Act of 1964.

173. The correct answer is (D), all of the above. The main focus was to prevent disparate impact and intentional discrimination, as well as provide guidelines in awarding damages in cases of discrimination.

174. The correct answer is (A). The EEO-1 form, which includes race and ethnicity reports as well as job categories, must be completed by September 30 of each year.

175. The correct answer is (A). Three or more races (not Hispanic or Latino) is not a category on the EEO-1 form. Two or more races, however, is a choice.

176. The correct answer is (D). Secretaries is not a job category listed on the EE0-1 form. Administrative support workers is a category.

177. The correct answer is (B). Marital status is not a category that is reported on the EEO-1 form.

178. The correct answer is (B). A behavioral interview is one in which you pose scenarios and ask for a response from the interviewee, assuming that the candidate will demonstrate how they overcome problems and resolve issues.

179. The correct answer is (D), directive interview. In this interview style, a set of questions is prepared ahead of time, and the same set is asked of all candidates. Sometimes employers share them up front and allow candidates a chance to think about them before entering the room. Other times, candidates are asked to think "on the fly."

180. The correct answer is (B), an in-box test. Candidates demonstrate how they might prioritize information in a sample real-world situation.

181. The correct answer is (B). The Sherman Anti-Trust Act of 1890 was enacted to prevent monopolies and other restraint-of-trade activities.

182. The correct answer is (C), workers under age 18.

183. The correct answer is (A). Single-unit bargaining, multi-unit bargaining, multi-employer bargaining, and parallel bargaining are four types of collective bargaining.

184. The correct answer is (B), coordinated bargaining. Coordinated bargaining occurs when a specific job classification—in this case airline pilots—functions as its own bargaining unit.

185. The correct answer is (B), multi-employer bargaining. The strategy is to use multiple employers to place pressure on the unions and deter potential strikes.

186. The correct answer is (C), the right to have representation at an investigative meeting with management, if the employee believes that discipline will be discussed at the meeting.

187. The correct answer is (C), *Circuit City Stores Inc. v. Adams* (2001). This legislation proved important for a number of reasons, most importantly because the Supreme Court addressed the assertion that arbitration agreements are inherently unfair.

188. The best answer is (B), nothing. Employment at will allows you to dismiss her immediately. While Suzette very well could express an interest in suing you, you have documented previous infractions, and employment-at-will law allows either the employer or the employee to separate from the relationship without notice.

189. The best answer to this question is (A). Yes, Mark is creating an uncomfortable work environment for Ginny. While sexual harassment can be a gray area, Mark's persistence after requests to cease and desist have made Ginny's work environment hostile, a requirement under the law.

190. The best answer is (A), affirmative action regulations. Tony has a clear pattern of hiring only individuals of a certain age and gender and did not hire a qualified candidate of the other gender.

191. The correct answer is (B), employment discrimination on the basis of sexual orientation against gay, lesbian, and bisexual workers.

192. The correct answer to this question is (A). No federal law mandates bereavement leave. Many employers, however, allow one to three days of bereavement leave, with pay, in the event of the death of an immediate family member. Wise employers also know to spell out in employment manuals what constitutes an "immediate" family member and whether or not it includes the parents of one's spouse, etc.

193. The correct answer is (C), federal contract workers. "It mandates that federal contractors holding $10,000 or more (up to $50,000) in federal contracts must comply under Title VII. Contractors holding more than $50,000 in federal contracts and a minimum of 50 employees are required to develop and implement affirmative action plans. Executive Order 11478 mandates that federal agencies develop and implement affirmative action plans for federal employees."

194. The correct answer is (D). The organization does not have to withhold income taxes and Social Security for an independent contractor, but it does need to report her earnings to the federal government.

195. The best answer is (A), provide reasonable accommodations to meet Dante's needs. It would be considered undue hardship on a small employer to remodel the facilities to accommodate one employee's needs. However, the employer might be able to accommodate a portable wheelchair ramp to assist his getting into the building. The office might not ultimately be able to accommodate his needs.

196. The correct answer is (D), both (A) and (C) are examples of common law doctrine.

197. The best answer to this question is (D), how the organization inspires and inhibits employee performance. Organizational climate is part of the overall organizational culture.

198. The correct answer to this question is (D). Both (B) and (C) are components of an OD intervention, the main components being to seek answers and provide solutions.

199. The correct answer is (C), TQM and technostructural intervention. Both interventions impact employees and departments at all levels in the organization. Technostructural interventions analyze how work is conducted in the organization and how employees are involved in the work process. TQM examines all of the resources available to accomplish work tasks.

200. The correct answer is (E), (B) and (D) are both true. Originally developed by the Motorola corporation, six sigma was originally designed to improve manufacturing processes and *defects*. A defect is defined as anything that could lead to customer dissatisfaction. Six sigma was heavily influenced by the processes of TQM.

201. The correct answer is (B), quality planning, quality control, and quality management.

202. The correct answer is (C), the 80/20 rule. Simply put, 80 percent of something is caused by 20 percent of something else. For example, 80 percent of the sales are generated by 20 percent of your sales force. In addition, a Pareto chart can help pinpoint where you have 80 percent of your problems and your greatest return on improvement if you can identify the 20 percent causing the problems.

203. The correct answer is (D). (A) and (C) are both correct. In the BARS rating system, a certain job dimension—such as data entry—is rated on a scale based upon performance.

204. The best answer to this question is (C). You are not required to pay Michelle overtime because she is an exempt employee. However, if you choose to do so, the employee must be required to keep track of her hours.

205. The correct answer to this question is (D), cost-of-living adjustments. According to the Social Security websites, "A COLA increases a person's Social Security retirement benefit by approximately the product of the COLA and the benefit amount. The exact computation, however, is more complex. Each Social Security benefit is based on a 'primary insurance amount,' or PIA. The PIA in turn is directly related to the primary beneficiary's earnings through a benefit formula. It is the PIA that is increased by the COLA, with the result truncated to the next lower dime."

206. The correct answer is (F), three of the above. Leave would likely not be granted to visit a child in jail, but the other answers meet FMLA requirements.

207. The correct answer is (B), intermittent leave. During intermittent leave, the employee is absent for multiple periods of time, not necessarily in a continuous pattern, regarding the same reason and/or illness.

208. The correct answer is (C), reservists called to active duty. This act provides for reentry into the workforce and protection of one's job while called to active duty.

209. The correct answer is (D). A subject-matter expert is someone who is considered an expert in the field.

210. The correct answer is (E). Both (B) and (C) are the best answers, if the employees were not asked to sign a morality clause, which some employers do have in place.

211. The correct answer is (B): Can you tell me what your difficulties were with your supervisor? While you want to give an individual exiting your organization a certain amount of latitude to share feelings about what was good or could be improved, you do not want the exit interview to turn into a complaint session against the employee's supervisors.

212. The correct answer is (E), three of the above. While a master's degree, (A), does meet the requirements of professional development—required of the field—it is not explicitly required.

213. The correct answer is (D), House's path-goal theory. His theory posits that leadership's role is to guide, encourage, and direct those along the way.

214. The correct answer is (E), three of the above. Nonessential job functions, (D), are not included in the job description, and listing them is not an ADA requirement.

215. The best answer is (B), describe in detail the lifting requirements for the job and the skills necessary for operating heavy equipment on the job. You wouldn't leave this crucial piece of information off of the job description, nor would you wait until an interview to tell someone about it. You might wish to make sure all of the safety equipment necessary is in place to make sure you prevent any further injuries. The previous personnel could have been performing their positions incorrectly.

216. The correct answer is (D), the USERRA (Uniformed Services Employment and Reemployment Act) of 1994.

217. The correct answer is (C). No, you do not have to continue to give Cissy her normal compensation, unless she is taking military leave. You must, however, continue to offer benefits at the rate she received before active duty, not COBRA.

218. The correct answer is (D). Do a SWOT analysis—strengths, weaknesses, opportunities, and threats.

219. The correct answer is (A), the Taft-Hartley Act.

220. The correct answer is (E), all of the above. The average age of workers is rising; the United States is increasingly becoming more diverse, including rising numbers of Hispanic workers; and an increasing number of workers are illiterate or have English as a second language.

221. The correct answer is (E). Answers (A) and (C) are incorrect statements. Mentors can and should be any age or gender and do not have to mirror the mentee. Similarly, a person can be a mentor after relatively any amount of time on the job as long as the employee can offer coaching and advice.

222. The correct answer is (E). While three of the four answers (B, C, and D) are good components of performance appraisals, research shows that most often, they are used for compensation decisions. Discipline does not normally belong in a performance appraisal.

223. The correct answer is (E): all of the above indicate a company at high risk.

224. The correct answer is (C), theft.

225. The correct answer is (C), race, color, religion, national origin, and sex.

Practice Test: PHR Exam 2

1. Under the USERRA of 1994, an employee who is called to military duty must receive which of the following accommodations?

   A. They continue to accrue seniority.

   B. Get the raises and promotions that they would have received had they remained in their positions.

   C. Leave of absence for 10 years.

   D. Provisions to continue to take online classes while they are in active service.

   E. None of the above

2. Stanley has been serving as a reservist for the military in Iraq for the past three years. There is one condition by which Stanley will not be reinstated to his job that you have been holding while he has taken his leave of absence.

   A. He has suffered devastating injuries making him no longer able to perform the duties which he performed in the past.

   B. He is suffering from post-traumatic stress disorder, making his thought patterns and his mental health will make it difficult for him to do his job.

   C. He received a court martial.

   D. He received a military reprimand from his commanding officer.

   E. None of the above

3. You are a consultant doing a revision of job descriptions throughout a large direct marketing organization. While doing your job analysis, you should most likely consult with which of the following?

   A. The HR staff.

   B. The subject matter experts

   C. The supervisors of the positions you are analyzing.

   D. All of the above.

   E. B and C.

4. The EEO-1 form has several components to it. Which are included on the form?

   A. Reporting of various types of positions at the company

   B. The number of persons, either male or female in the positions at your company.

   C. Race and ethnicity.

   D. All of the above.

   E. None of the above

5. In 2002, President George Bush enacted a rarely used power to restrict union activities by longshoremen. President Bush was enacting what important labor legislation?

   A. The Mann Act.

   B. The Wagner Act.

   C. The Sherman-Taft Act.

   D. The Taft-Hartley Act.

   E. None of the above

6. An important component of a HR Professional's responsibilities includes:

   A. Ensuring that compensation programs are compliant with all federal, state, and local laws and regulations.

   B. Ensuring that compensation programs are complaints with state laws and regulations.

   C. Checking credit reports and background checks for all applicants to jobs.

   D. Checking transcripts and grade reports for all applicants to jobs.

   E. None of the above

7. Criminal background checks are:

   A. Mandatory for hiring in all positions.

   B. Must comply with FCRA requirements.

   C. Be related to the position applied for.

   D. Only done when an applicant is going to work with children.

   E. None of the above

8. You are the HR Director for a non-profit agency that works with the elderly. You are hiring a new agency director. May you or may you not use a polygraph test when hiring this employee?

   A. No, the EPPA prohibits the use of polygraph testing in the hiring process for any job.

   B. Yes, because this director is working with at-risk population.

   C. Yes, you may use polygraph testing at any time.

   D. No, because polygraph testing is used only very limited circumstances.

   E. None of the above

9. The EPPA Act of 1988 allows polygraph testing for which of the following groups:

   A. Hospitals, nursing homes, security guards, the FBI.

   B. FBI contractors, national security workers, armored car workers, pharmaceutical sales.

   C. Teachers, college administrators, security workers, pharmaceutical distributors.

   D. Government workers, national defense contractors, teachers, DMV workers.

   E. None of the above

10. John is developing a training program for his accounting staff. His boss, Keri Sue, tells him to look into the ADDIE Model. ADDIE stands for what?

    A. Act, Design, Do, Initiate, Evaluate

    B. Analysis, Design, Develop, Implementation, Evaluation

    C. Associate, Delegate, Demonstrate, Initiate, Evaluate

    D. Acquire, Demonstrate, Delegate, Initiate, Educate

    E. None of the above

11. The Acquired Needs theory is attributed to what individual?

    A. Abraham Maslow

    B. Karl Jung

    C. J. Stacy Adams

    D. David McClelland

    E. None of the above

12. BF Skinner's theory of reinforcement is based upon which of the following?

    A. Classical Conditioning
    B. Reinforcement Conditioning
    C. Operant Conditioning
    D. Negative Conditioning
    E. None of the above

13. An effective HRIS would have the following components?

    A. A database of stored information
    B. Reduce paperwork
    C. Consolidate processes and systems.
    D. All of the above.
    E. None of the above

14. The teachers in your local area are negotiating contracts for the new school year. Administration and the teachers union are approaching the table as adversaries. What type of bargaining process are they using?

    A. Integrative Bargaining
    B. Collective Bargaining
    C. Traditional Bargaining
    D. Arbitration Bargaining
    E. None of the above

15. The Freedom of Information Act provides that any person has the right to request access to federal agency records or information. What is a possible exception to this rule?

    A. Properly classified as secret in the interest of national defense or foreign policy.
    B. Related to medical history.
    C. Investigatory records compiled for law enforcement purposes.
    D. All of the above.
    E. None of the above

16. As of July 2007, workers covered by the FLSA are required to earn not less than what minimum wage?

    A. $6.75
    B. $5.85
    C. $7.89
    D. $8.50
    E. None of the above

17. Kellye is divorcing his wife, Trina, who was awarded child support and alimony in the divorce agreement. The courts have ordered that what happen to Kellye's wages and by law, you are required to comply with?

    A. Wage deductions
    B. Wage garnishment
    C. Wage compliance
    D. None of the above
    E. All of the above

18. Merit pay negotiated between and employee and a employer is also known by what other name?

    A.   Hitting-the-bar pay
    B.   Goal-reaching pay
    C.   Pay-for-performance
    D.   Project pay
    E.   None of the above

19. The Title VII of the Civil Rights Act of 1964 identified which five protected classes?

    A.   Gender, Race, Religion, Sex, Disability
    B.   Disability, Color, Race, Sex, National Origin
    C.   Gender, Color, Sex, Religion, Disability
    D.   Race, Color, Religion, National Origin and Sex
    E.   None of the above

20. By mutual agreement, Gary, and his employer have agreed that he will resign his employment and receive pay for the remaining two months of his contract. This agreement is known as:

    A.   Negotiated pay buy out
    B.   Severance pay
    C.   Accelerated pay
    D.   Protected pay
    E.   None of the above

21. Your CEO has asked that you calculate the direct and indirect costs of your wellness initiatives implemented last year and to divide those by the benefits received by the employees. What is he really asking for?

    A.   Risk assessment
    B.   Request for proposal
    C.   Needs analysis
    D.   Return on investment.
    E.   None of the above

22. A management strategy for an organization, based upon on quality, and the participation of all its members aimed at customer satisfaction was developed using which approach?

    A.   Total Rewards Management
    B.   Best Satisfaction practices
    C.   Total Quality Management
    D.   Customer Services Approach
    E.   None of the above

23. You are the first full-time paid director of a non-profit foundation. Your board of directors has asked you to analyze the budget from the ground up, not using previous budgets submitted by non-paid, volunteer workers. You have been asked to develop which kind of budget?

    A.   A zero-based budget
    B.   Balanced budget
    C.   Bottom-up budget
    D.   Needs-based budget
    E.   None of the above

24. During contract negotiations, the teacher's union failed to notify management of the intent to renegotiate a contract in a suitable time before it expired and could be renegotiated. This is an example of what?

   A. Position bargaining

   B. Interest-based bargaining

   C. Bad-faith bargaining

   D. A grievance.

   E. None of the above

25. Roxanne works in a chemical plant and has noticed mold in the bathrooms, heating vents and around air conditioning units. She has developed breathing problems both on the job site and off the job site. Roxanne has been exposed to what type of environmental hazard and violation of OSHA standards?

   A. Ergonomic hazard

   B. Biological hazard

   C. Physical hazard

   D. Chemical hazard

   E. None of the above

26. Which of the following are considered a category of OSHA violations?

   A. Willful

   B. Serious

   C. Other-than-serious

   D. All of the above

   E. None of the above

27. OSHA laws cover a wide-range of health and safety issues, that you must be familiar with for your industry and general health standards. Which of the following is a statue that OSHA covers?

   A. Asbestos Emergency Response Act of 1986

   B. Safe Drinking Water Act of 1977

   C. Solid Waste Disposal Act of 1976

   D. All of the above

   E. None of the above

28. If you believe your employer has discriminated against you because you exercised your safety and health rights or other protected activity, you have how many days, according to the OSH Act to file a complaint?

   A. Indefinitely.

   B. 30 days

   C. 60 days

   D. 90 days.

   E. None of the above

29. The Clean Air Act was developed mainly to reduce which of the following?

   A. Secondhand smoke

   B. Air pollution

   C. Reduce asbestos in buildings

   D. All of the above.

   E. None of the above

30. Which of the following do you <u>not</u> have to record and report to OSHA?

    A. Mental illness, that is not work-related.

    B. Contagious diseases—such as tuberculosis.

    C. A fender-bender in a motor vehicle on company property, while employee is commuting to-and from work.

    D. None of the above.

    E. All of the above.

31. Which of the following acts prohibits federal agencies from sharing information about individuals?

    A. Fair Credit Reporting Act

    B. Equal Pay Act

    C. Age Discrimination in Employment Act

    D. Privacy Act

    E. None of the above

32. Which of the following acts established the EEOC?

    A. Occupational Safety and Health Act.

    B. Title VII of the Civil Rights Act of 1964

    C. Equal Employment Opportunity Act of 1972

    D. Age Discrimination in Employment Act.

    E. None of the above

33. The Age Discrimination in Employment Act of 1967 prohibits discrimination against persons of what age or older?

    A. 40

    B. 50

    C. 60

    D. 65

    E. None of the above

34. Which of the following established that hiring selection processes be job related and if using selection tools, that they be valid predictors of job success and job tasks?

    A. Equal Employment Opportunity Act

    B. Uniform Guidelines on Employee Selection

    C. Title VII of the Civil Rights Act

    D. Labor Management Reporting Act

    E. None of the above

35. According to which act, in the absence of an employment contract or employment agreement, employees or employers may terminate employment without notice or cause?

    A. Age Discrimination Act

    B. Employment at Will Doctrine

    C. Equal Opportunity Act

    D. Privacy Act

    E. None of the above

36. Which of the following is an example of a question that you should <u>not</u> ask during a job interview?

 A. Do you live in town?

 B. Do you have a family?

 C. Why did you leave your last position?

 D. Are you eligible to work in the United States?

 E. All of the above

37. In the United States, sexual harassment of gays and lesbians is illegal under Title VII. Is this currently true or false?

 A. True. It is illegal.

 B. False, it is currently not illegal.

 C. False, it is currently not illegal, but is being considered by the Supreme Court.

 D. True. It is illegal, in some states.

 E. None of the above

38. The Family and Medical Leave Act requires employers to provide which of the following?

 A. 1–3 days of leave upon the death of a close family member.

 B. 3–5 days of leave upon the death of a close family member.

 C. 5–7 days of leave upon the death of a close family member.

 D. Does not require employers to provide bereavement leave.

 E. None of the above

39. According to the job characteristic model, what three psychological states of a job-holder result in motivated, satisfied and productive employees?

 A. Meaningfulness of the work, task significance, and autonomy

 B. Meaningfulness of work, responsibility for completion of a whole identifiable piece of work, and knowledge of work results

 C. Meaningfulness of work, responsibility for outcomes, and knowledge of work results

 D. Meaningfulness of work, responsibility for outcomes, and fair compensation

 E. None of the above

40. Factors to consider when investigating whether sexual harassment is hostile or offensive include all of the following <u>except</u>:

 A. Frequency of the misconduct

 B. Whether the person is male or female

 C. Severity of the misconduct

 D. Whether it interferes with work performance

 E. None of the above

41. A chart that shows the reporting relationships between employees in an organization and the flow of information at a company, is often called what?

 A. A flow chart

 B. A Responsibility Chart

 C. An organizational chart

 D. None of the above.

 E. All of the above

KAPLAN

42. Glenda is looking at a document that includes the following information: Title of the position, department, reporting lines, supervisory responsibilities, exempt status, salary range, a percentage of the duties performed on the job. What is she looking at?

    A.   A resume.

    B.   A job analysis

    C.   A position summary

    D.   A job description

    E.   None of the above

43. SHRM lists all of the following <u>except one</u>, as part of their professional standards. Which one is it?

    A.   Conflict of interest

    B.   Fairness and justice

    C.   Fiscal responsibility

    D.   Ethical leadership

    E.   None of the above

44. 1) You will conduct yourself with professional integrity and not engage in activities that are actual, apparent, or potential conflicts of interest with the company. 2) You will adhere to published policies on conflicts of interest within the company. 3) You will refrain from using your position for personal or financial gain of any kind, or the appearance of such. 4) You will refrain from giving preferential treatment in any human resources processes including hiring. These 4 statements are all examples of <u>what standard in</u> SHRM's standards.

    A.   Conflict of interest

    B.   Fairness and justice

    C.   Fiscal responsibility

    D.   Ethical leadership

    E.   None of the above

45. Job applications, FMLA documents, insurance applications, and salary histories are all examples of what?

    A.   Employee records

    B.   Job records

    C.   Benefit records

    D.   None of the above

    E.   All of the above

46. Verbal warning, written warning, suspension, and termination are examples of what?

    A.   The firing process.

    B.   The corrective process

    C.   Progressive discipline

    D.   All of the above.

    E.   None of the above

47. A university implemented a new software system called, "Student Action" that tracks admissions, registration, financial aid, as well as personnel records. This is an example of what?

    A.   Document management system

    B.   Human Resource Best practices

    C.   Personnel management

    D.   High Performance Work System

    E.   None of the above

48. The process of planning, organizing, managing and executing a specific assignment that is constrained by time and budget is called what?

    A.   Project management

    B.   Time management

    C.   Risk management

    D.   Assignment management

    E.   None of the above

49. What are the four phases of project management?

    A. Analysis, Design, Delivery, and Execution.

    B. The beginning, the middle, the end, and the post-mortem.

    C. Scanning, Planning, Sending, and Ending.

    D. Initiation, Planning, Execution, and Closing

    E. None of the above

50. The process by which businesses research information to keep the competitive advantage is commonly called what?

    A. Research analysis

    B. Environmental scanning

    C. Competitive scanning

    D. Competitive analysis

    E. None of the above

51. What item might you examine when doing an environmental scan?

    A. Current technology trends

    B. Governmental regulations

    C. Demographics

    D. All of the above

    E. None of the above

52. Stan used a SWOT analysis when he did the environmental scan for his company. What is SWOT an acronym for?

    A. Standards, Weights, Opportunities, Trends

    B. Strengths, Weaknesses, Opportunities, Threats

    C. Strengths, Weaknesses, Opportunities, Trends

    D. Standards, Weaknesses, Opportunities, Threats

    E. None of the above

53. Don is doing an analysis of what constraints are affecting George's decision-making, and his behavior toward employees. This type of analysis describes what type of theory from leadership?

    A. Path-Goal Theory

    B. Hierarchy Theory

    C. Leadership Theory

    D. Contingency Theory

    E. None of the above

54. Alfred Fiedler's contingency theory included a LPC-scale? How did Fieder define "LPC"?

    A. Leader, performer, co-worker

    B. Least preferred co-worker

    C. Least preferred constraint

    D. None of the above

    E. All of the above

55. Who is the author/theorist responsible for the Path-Goal Theory?

    A. Robert House

    B. Abraham Maslow

    C. Alfred Fiedler

    D. Kouzes & Posner

    E. None of the above

KAPLAN

56. Which of the following are examples of Gardner's multiple intelligences?

    A. Kinesthetic, Musical, Reading, Mathematics,

    B. Hands-on, Spatial, Interpersonal, Hearing

    C. Musical, Sensory, Interpersonal, Mathematics

    D. Linguistic, Spatial, Interpersonal, Musical

    E. None of the above

57. You observe that Katie, one your assistant manager's that you are considering promoting, has an uncanny ability to understand people's mood, emotions, and feelings. By your study of multiple intelligences, you know that people with this ability easily can influence people to follow their course of actions. Katie is exhibiting what type of multiple intelligence?

    A. Kinesthetic

    B. Logical

    C. Interpersonal

    D. Intrapersonal

    E. None of the above

58. Michael and Conrad, two project assistants, are emailing back and forth about a project for an upcoming event at their office. This is an example of what type of communication?

    A. Internal communication

    B. Project communication

    C. Bottom-up communication

    D. Horizontal communication

    E. None of the above

59. The process by which you plan, align, process, and implement the goals in an organization is called what?

    A. Strategic planning

    B. Strategic management

    C. Both of the above.

    D. None of the above.

    E. All of the above

60. The process of determining where an organization is going over the next year or more, and how you are going to get there is called what?

    A. Strategic planning

    B. Strategic management

    C. Both of the above.

    D. None of the above.

    E. All of the above

61. Strategic planning is also sometimes referred to by what other term:

    A. Long-term planning

    B. Long-range planning

    C. Short-term planning

    D. Both A and B.

    E. None of the above

62. Sandy is doing an analysis of the sales of her jams and jellies that she sells and doing planning for the future. She is paying particular attention to what product customers buy if her product is not in stock—in other words, her competition. What is Sandy doing?

    A. A product analysis

    B. An environmental scan

    C. Sales analysis

    D. Competitive analysis

    E. None of the above

63. A community college, near Seattle has this on its website: "Renton Technical College prepares a diverse student population for work, fulfilling the employment needs of individuals, business and industry." What is this an example of?

    A. A diversity statement
    B. A vision statement
    C. A mission statement
    D. None of the above.
    E. All of the above

64. A brief written description that should inspire, communicate the goals of the organization and whom they serve, which is forward focused is what?

    A. A diversity statement
    B. A vision statement
    C. A mission statement
    D. None of the above.
    E. All of the above

65. Julio is examining several things in his department: turnover, looking at customer service surveys, how diverse his team is relative to the surrounding community, and staffing needs and resources. What is Julio doing?

    A. An internal assessment
    B. Strategic planning
    C. Social analysis
    D. External assessment
    E. None of the above

66. The direct number of employees a manager supervises, or "direct reports" as it is sometimes referred to is also called what?

    A. Work unit
    B. Span of control
    C. Employee relations
    D. None of the above
    E. All of the above

67. A financial picture of an organization on any point in given time, is called what?

    A. Cash flow statement
    B. Debit statement
    C. Income statement
    D. Balance Sheet
    E. None of the above

68. What is sometimes referred to as a profit and loss statement?

    A. Income statement
    B. Cash flow statement
    C. Balance Sheet
    D. None of the above
    E. All of the above

69. SFM Pet Manufacturing has just mailed its constituents its financial statements and accompanying summary of the year in review and plans for the futures. What is this called?

    A. Year-end summary
    B. Annual Report
    C. Stockholders Report
    D. Gross Profit Statement
    E. None of the above

70. Melissa has just asked Heather to produce a report that lists Gross profit minus operating expense. What accounting operation is she asking Heather to figure for her?

    A. Net profit statement

    B. Liability statement

    C. Profit statement

    D. Taxable income statement

    E. None of the above

71. Which of the following is NOT a type of organizational structure?

    A. Product-based organizational structure

    B. Functional organizational structure

    C. Matrix Organizational structure

    D. Design Organizational structure

    E. None of the above

72. Phyllis, your division unit coordinator, has asked you to look at each one of your nurses' KSAs when deciding where they should be placed on the unit team structure. Phyllis is asking you to look at what?

    A. Knowledge, Skills, and Attitude.

    B. Kindness, Speed, and Attendance.

    C. Knowledge, Skills, and Abilities.

    D. Knowledge, Skills, and Attendance

    E. None of the above

73. When religion, sex, or national origin is "reasonably necessary to the normal operation" of the business—it meets what definition to be exempt from the Title VII of the Civil Rights Act.

    A. Bona fide occupational qualifications.

    B. Diversity exception

    C. Disparate impact

    D. Protected classes exemptions.

    E. None of the above

74. Your business has been going smoothly this year. You expect the staffing levels to stay relatively the same, and you are projecting that sales are going to remain relatively constant and expenses similar to this year. What type of budget should you prepare for your board of directors?

    A. Historical budget

    B. Zero-based budget

    C. No budget at all, let them refer to last year's

    D. Balanced budget

    E. None of the above

75. A body formed and authorized by law to act as a unit which has legal rights and responsibilities, is also called a what?

    A. An organization

    B. A legal unit

    C. A corporation

    D. A governmental agency

    E. None of the above

76. Analyzing the social, technology, economic, and political environments in an environment scan is also called what?

   A. A SWOT analysis

   B. A STEP analysis

   C. A strategic planning analysis

   D. A technology analysis

   E. None of the above

77. What type of worker is not required to receive overtime pay?

   A. Part-time workers

   B. Full-time workers

   C. Exempt workers

   D. Both A and B.

   E. None of the above

78. You are looking for summer help at your ice cream store. The next door neighbor has 6 kids under 18 willing and able to work. Which of the following can you NOT hire?

   A. Kerry, who is 16 years of age

   B. Ryan, who is 13 years of age

   C. Cassie, who is 14 years of age

   D. Jimmie who is 15 years of age

   E. All of the above

79. Child labor laws are very strict about the hours that children may work during the school year. Between which hours may a youth work?

   A. 7:00 A.M. to 7:00 P.M.

   B. 8:00 A.M. to 8:00 P.M.

   C. 9:00 A.M. to 9:00 P.M.

   D. 12:00 noon to midnight

   E. 11:00 P.M. to 4:00 A.M.

80. Which of the following jobs is deemed too hazardous for anyone under the age of 18?

   A. Mining

   B. Working with chemicals

   C. Working unsupervised with machinery

   D. All of the above

   E. None of the above

81. During the legislative process, if the president fails to sign a bill, which of the following options will happen?

   A. The bill fails and does not become law

   B. After a 10 day waiting period, the bill becomes law without the president's signature.

   C. Both houses of Congress must pass the bill by a two-thirds majority.

   D. The bill is returned to the president for his signature.

   E. None of the above

82. Candy, is a staff member in the Human Resources office, working as a generalist. At your suggestion, she has taken the MBTI, and her results were: ESTJ. She's asked you to interpret the results for her. Is she:

   A. Eclectic, Serious, Thinking, Judging

   B. Eccentric, Sensing, Thinking, Judicious

   C. Extroverted, Serious, Thoughtful, Judging

   D. Extroverted, Sensing, Thinking, Judging

   E. None of the above

KAPLAN

83. When disagreements occur between union and management in an organization, they are typically resolved using what process?

    A. Dissolution
    B. Dispute
    C. Abatement
    D. Grievance
    E. None of the above

84. Natasha was given a test on English Speaking Skills upon her hire at the garment factory. Then, she was enrolled in English-as-a Second Language classes delivered on her job site. Six months later, she was given a second test to see if her language skills had improved. This is an example of using what?

    A. Predictive validity
    B. Construct validity
    C. Language validity
    D. Measurement validity
    E. None of the above

85. Mark has promised Amanda that if she attends a conference with him, and intimates to her, that if she slept with him, she will get better working hours in the future than the rest of her colleagues. This is an example of what legal term?

    A. Zipper clause
    B. Quid pro quo
    C. Yellow Dog
    D. Job bidding
    E. Dating

86. You need to hire a new Vice President of Institutional Advancement. You are in the process of building a list of potential candidates for the position based upon word-of mouth, people that you know in the community and are respected in your industry. This process is called:

    A. Networking
    B. Sourcing
    C. Outsourcing
    D. Fishing
    E. Headhunting

87. A pre-employment test designed to measure an applicant's ability to perform specific job-related tasks, such as in typing, language and word usage, or problem solving is called what?

    A. A job design test
    B. A work test
    C. Proficiency test
    D. Timed test
    E. None of the above

88. The degree to which interviews, tests, and other selection criteria yield similar results over time is called what?

    A. Reliability
    B. Validity
    C. Security
    D. Predictive
    E. None of the above

89. Lisa has been given a test prior to employment in which she needs to demonstrate her ability to quickly develop a memo to an outside constituent to your company. Which statistical measure is important relative to this test?

    A. Predictive validity
    B. Criterion-related validity
    C. Concurrent validity
    D. None of the above
    E. All of the above

90. When the selection rate for a protected class is less than 4/5th or 80% of the selection rate for the group with the highest selection rate is called:

    A. Adverse impact
    B. Stereotyping
    C. Diverse impact
    D. Profiling
    E. None of the above

91. You are interviewing Joy for a position as your new executive assistant. As part of the interview, you ask the following question: "Please tell me a time when you experienced a personnel challenge, with someone that reports to you, and how you resolved that conflict." This is an example of what type of question?

    A. A biased interview question
    B. A directive interview question
    C. A non-directive interview question
    D. A behavioral interview question
    E. None of the above

92. Lizabeth is conducting Steve's performance appraisal, and she has a list of his key job requirements from the job description she created last year. From this she is taking 1–5 job dimensions to rate his performance. Lizabeth is using what?

    A. A BARS scale
    B. A scorecard
    C. A BORS scale
    D. A gap analysis
    E. None of the above

93. Barbara has been offered the position of Event Coordinator for the non-profit foundation where you are the HR coordinator. It is up to you to discuss with her the benefits associated with her job. You tell her she gets 21 days vacation, paid holidays, 14 days of personal leave, and a bus pass, if she chooses to utilize this. Her salary will be $40,000 per year. You have just discussed what with Barbara?

    A. The perks of her job.
    B. Total Rewards
    C. Administrative rewards
    D. Compensatory model
    E. None of the above

94. A tool designed by Kaoru Ishikawa for analyzing process dispersion where the chart resembles a fish skeleton, is also called by what name?

    A. A control chart
    B. A cause and effect chart.
    C. Diagram chart
    D. None of the above
    E. All of the above

95. A graphic planning and control chart designed to demonstrate relationships between planned performance and actual performance over time is also called what?

    A. A flow chart

    B. A cause and effect chart.

    C. Diagram chart

    D. None of the above

    E. All of the above

96. Donald Kirkpatrick developed a 4 step training model for program evaluation. The second step in his model is what?

    A. Learning

    B. Results

    C. Reaction

    D. Behavior

    E. None of the above

97. A performance evaluation designed to gather feedback from an employee's peers, supervisors and individuals that the employees comes into contact with in a working relationship on the job is called what?

    A. A 360 degree evaluation

    B. A behavioral evaluation

    C. A field review

    D. A ranking evaluation

    E. None of the above

98. An inducement by the employer to have an employee carry out an action that will be rewarded by the employer is called what?

    A. Respondeat Superior

    B. Promissory estoppel

    C. Implied contract

    D. Job enrichment

    E. None of the above

99. Jennifer has been asked to determine the impact the city will feel should an earthquake or other natural disaster occur. She is being asked to complete what?

    A. Emergency Management Plan

    B. Risk Assessment

    C. Risk Management

    D. None of the above

    E. All of the above

100. This court case gave rights to the bargaining unit member (employee) to pay a portion of union dues that directly impact administration of a contract, costs for bargaining, and other organizing activities. Which Supreme Court case what it?

    A. Brown vs. The Board of Education

    B. NLRB v Wooster Division of Borg-Warner Corporation (1958)

    C. Excelsior Underwear, Inc. v. NLRB

    D. Communication Workers v. Beck (1988)

    E. None of the above

101. This court case determined that the NLRB could make decisions how bargaining issues are categorized: illegal, mandatory, or permissive.

    A. NLRB v. Weingarten (1975)

    B. NLRB v Wooster Division of Borg-Warner Corporation (1958)

    C. Excelsior Underwear, Inc. v. NLRB

    D. Communication Workers v. Beck (1988)

    E. None of the above

102. Federated grocers threatened to strike in late 2007. The grocers represented several major chains of grocers in the country. What court case should the stores be familiar with in the case of a pending strike?

    A. NLRB v. Mackay Radio and Telegraph Company (1938)

    B. NLRB v Wooster Division of Borg-Warner Corporation (1958)

    C. Excelsior Underwear, Inc. v. NLRB

    D. Communication Workers v. Beck (1988)

    E. None of the above

103. Corky was suspected of stealing out of the company cafeteria. In meeting with his superiors, about the suspected theft, he brought a friend who was a lawyer with me to the hearing. Which court case, determined that Corky could have representation in this meeting?

    A. NLRB v. Mackay Radio and Telegraph Company (1938)

    B. NLRB v Wooster Division of Borg-Warner Corporation (1958)

    C. Excelsior Underwear, Inc. v. NLRB

    D. NLRB v. Weingarten (1975)

    E. None of the above

104. What electronics store was involved in a lawsuit about employee rights relative to arbitration agreements?

    A. Fry's

    B. Best Buy

    C. Circuit City

    D. Radio Shack

    E. None of the above

105. Which industries had the lowest degree of fatalities in 2006?

    A. Airline pilots

    B. Health services and education

    C. Logging workers

    D. Fisherman

    E. None of the above

106. The Sherman Anti-trust Act, was originally enacted to prevent what:

    A. Organization of unions.

    B. Monopolies and other restraint of trade activities.

    C. Strikes by employees

    D. Free trade.

    E. None of the above

107. As a result of Americans living to be longer than in previous generations, THE OASDI raised the age in which workers may receive their maximum social security benefit. If you were born in 1964, at which age will you receive your maximum social security benefit?

    A. 62

    B. 65

    C. 66

    D. 67

    E. 60

108. Which federal act, relative to document retention, requires a company to track compensation records for three years?

    A. Title VII of the Civil Rights Act

    B. Employee Retirement Income Security Act

    C. Davis Bacon Act

    D. None of the above

    E. All of the above

109. What are the standards established for financial accounting commonly called?

    A. FAAC

    B. FAAB

    C. FCAP

    D. GAAP

    E. None of the above

110. If you are using testing in your organization, as a predictor for hiring, you must be certain that the tests possess which characteristics?

    A. Content validity and predictive validity.

    B. Reliability and content validity.

    C. Concurrent validity and success validity.

    D. Reliability, construct validity, and content validity.

    E. None of the above

111. Jasmine Manufacturing owes $25,000 dollars to Samson Manufacturing for previous business dealings. When Bobbi Sue does the financial statement for this year, she will list the $25,000 as what?

    A. An asset

    B. A liability

    C. An audit

    D. Revenue

    E. None of the above

112. Job Satisfaction is difficult to measure. It is generally defined as:

    A. Low turnover rate

    B. Number of long-term employees

    C. Low absenteeism rate

    D. Employee compensation matching expectations

    E. None of the above

113. Justin is developing a communications strategy for this department. In doing so, before he presents his message to the CEO he should ask himself which of the following questions?

    A. Who is my intended audience?

    B. Is the information to be developed in a certain time frame?

    C. Who in the department will be developing and delivering the message?

    D. All of the above.

    E. None of the above

114. Fred is developing a HPWS. Which of the following is NOT a part of high performance work systems (HPWS)?

    A. Egalitarianism

    B. Knowledge development

    C. Shared information

    D. Frequent rewards

    E. None of the above

115. Employee surveillance is most often used for which of the following reasons:

    A. Sexual harassment.

    B. Abuse of computer equipment, i.e., email, internet, and pornography

    C. Theft

    D. To corroborate personnel issues and employee grievances

    E. None of the above

116. In small town America, sometimes the employees at a company do not reflect the community's diversity. For which of the following reasons would an employer want a more diverse workplace?

    A. A diverse workforce can be more creative.

    B. To avoid lawsuits.

    C. Increases the pool of candidates

    D. Both A and C.

    E. All of the above

117. Initiating, planning, executing, controlling, and closing a project describes which of the following?

    A. Leadership.

    B. Project management.

    C. Transformational management.

    D. Workforce management.

    E. None of the above

118. Melanie is doing a job analysis of Theresa's job as a direct marketer. She should do which of the following:

    A. Focus strictly on Theresa, not the job.

    B. Focus strictly on the job, not Theresa.

    C. Focus strictly on the tasks in Theresa's job description.

    D. None of the above.

    E. All of the above

119. OSHA has developed guidelines for identifying companies that are at high risk for workplace violence. Which one of the following would indicate a company at high risk?

    A. No security guards employed at the workplace (assuming a large workplace).

    B. Customers regularly abuse employees or use racial slurs or profanity.

    C. Violence has occurred on the premises.

    D. Employees have not been trained to handle threatening behaviors.

    E. All of the above indicate a company at high risk.

120. The president most responsible for the Social Security Act of 1935 was:

    A. President Franklin D. Roosevelt

    B. President Herbert Hoover

    C. President Calvin Coolidge

    D. President Thomas Jefferson

    E. President Richard Nixon

KAPLAN

121. What is deferred compensation?

    A. Tax-deferred retirement plans.

    B. The employee gets paid after they leave office.

    C. The employee gets paid a commission based on a certain criteria.

    D. The employee defers a certain portion of their income to charitable organizations

    E. None of the above

122. Dr. Kirby is working on a long-term plan for her chiropractic office. In her planning she would probably <u>not</u> ask herself which of the following questions?

    A. What am I paying my employees?

    B. Where do we want to be in the future?

    C. Where is the office right now?

    D. How will we get where we need to go?

    E. None of the above

123. Maggie was born in 1940. What is her full retirement age?

    A. 65

    B. 65 and 6 months

    C. 66

    D. 66 and 6 months

    E. 50

124. The SSA of 1935 established the first of what programs?

    A. Medicare

    B. Retirement

    C. Tax

    D. Unemployment insurance

    E. None of the above

125. A large banking company has a wide variety of benefits and programs to meet its diverse population's needs. This is known as what?

    A. Diversity benefits plan

    B. Wellness plan

    C. Cafeteria plan

    D. None of the above

    E. All of the above

126. COBRA lists which of the following as "qualifying" events?

    A. Child enters college

    B. Death of a spouse

    C. Divorce

    D. All of the above

    E. None of the above

127. The FLSA established which of the following?

    A. Minimum wage

    B. Child labor laws

    C. Compensation laws

    D. A and B.

    E. None of the above

128. You are have 50 or more employees at the worksite where you are the HR Director. FMLA requires you to pay unpaid leave to which of the following?

    A. Employees within 75 miles of the worksite.

    B. Employees within 50 miles of the worksite.

    C. Employees within 25 miles of the worksite.

    D. Employees within 100 miles of the worksite.

    E. None of the above

129. Dianne is a small employer just starting out. She asks you, an experienced HR professional, which benefits are mandatory for her to provide by law. Which of the following is <u>NOT</u> mandatory?

    A. Christmas Holidays

    B. Social Security

    C. COBRA

    D. FMLA leave

    E. None of the above

130. Coco's father passed away, and she asks her boss for three days bereavement leave. They are shorthanded and the boss denies her request. Is this legal?

    A. Yes, there is no federal law that mandates bereavement leave.

    B. No, Mike is required to give Coco at least one day to attend her father's funeral.

    C. No, Mike is required to give Coco at least three days to attend her father's funeral.

    D. No, Mike is required to give Coco the time she needs to attend her father's funeral, but she must take it without pay.

    E. None of the above

131. OSHA has a provision called the "General Duty" clause. What does this refer to?

    A. Employers are required to examine the general duties and work hours of its employees

    B. Employers are required to be aware of employees exhibiting potentially violent and risky behaviors

    C. Employers are required to be aware of potential safety violations

    D. None of the above.

    E. All of the above

132. You are likely to hear the term "intellectual property" at which of the following workplace settings?

    A. A library.

    B. A college.

    C. A medical facility.

    D. All of the above.

    E. None of the above

133. Which one of the following issues was a chief focus of the Civil Rights Act of 1991:

    A. Protecting employees from discrimination.

    B. Disparate impact.

    C. Provide for damages in the cases of intentional discrimination.

    D. All of the above.

    E. None of the above

134. Greg is interviewing Buffy for a job at a large well-known delivery service. He assumes that she is unable to lift heavy boxes because she is a woman. This is an example of what type of interview bias?

    A. Negative impression bias

    B. Average bias

    C. Stereotyping

    D. None of the above

    E. All of the above

135. You are called by the HR Department of a local company to interview for a job. They give you 4 possible time slots to interview: 10:00 A.M., 11:00 A.M., 1:00 P.M., or 2:00 P.M. You know about the phenomena called: "Recency Bias". Which time slot do you choose?

    A. 10:00 A.M.

    B. 11:00 A.M.

    C. 1:00 P.M.

    D. 2:00 P.M.

    E. None of the above

136. Ellen interviews 8 candidates for a position on her team. One of those candidates, Owen, had a very annoying habit during his interview. Ellen can't seem to get past that one thing, even though Owen had a number of other good aspects to his interview. Ellen is demonstrating which interview bias?

    A. Stereotyping

    B. First impression

    C. Horn effect

    D. Nonverbal

    E. None of the above

137. George, your supervisor, readily admits that he's a little behind the times when it comes to internet posting of jobs, yet he knows that this is probably the best way to advertise his upcoming position for a marketing coordinator. You tell him which are some popular places to advertise to get a good return on recruitment?

    A. monster.com, Craigslist, godaddy.com

    B. monster.com, Craigslist, eBay

    C. monster.com, Craigslist, Google

    D. monster.com, Career Builder.com, and Craigslist

138. Which of the following is NOT a Total Rewards strategy?

    A. Base pay

    B. Overtime rate

    C. Merit pay

    D. Healthcare/wellness

    E. None of the above

139. Information regarding the current reward structure, pay levels vs. industry trends, current salary schedule and turnover rates is gathered during this segment of the Total Rewards Philosophy development process.

    A. evaluation

    B. assessment

    C. design

    D. implementation

    E. None of the above

140. What is the primary law related to employee status and compensation?

    A. Equal Pay Act

    B. Americans with Disabilities Act (ADA)

    C. Fair Labor Status Act of 1938

    D. Executive Order 11246 (Affirmative Action)

    E. None of the above

141. Which of the following is NOT a determiner of exempt status under the Fair Labor Status Act?

    A. salary

    B. ability to hire and fire

    C. work requires advanced education

    D. work involves computer systems analysis

    E. None of the above

142. Which of the following are compensible time for non-exempt employees?

    A. time to travel to or from work

    B. voluntary training outside work hours

    C. meal periods longer than 30 minutes

    D. time to change into specialized clothing

    E. None of the above

143. Employees spend less time off work and are more productive as the result of health and wellness programs which can include all BUT:

    A. Personal improvement courses

    B. Flu shots

    C. Incentives to quit smoking

    D. Anger management counseling

    E. None of the above

144. A non-exempt employee must travel to a work-related conference. The travel takes place before and after work hours. The employee will be compensated:

    A. for the time attending the conference

    B. for the time attending the conference plus travel time

    C. overtime for travel time beyond the 40 hour week

    D. time and a half for the conference and travel time

    E. All of the above

145. The goals of the Occupational Safety and Health Act of 1970 (OSHA) include all <u>except</u> which of the following?:

    A. Partnerships and cooperative programs

    B. Development of protective gear

    C. Education, outreach and compliance assistance

    D. Strong, fair and effective enforcement

    E. None of the above

146. The greatest incidence of workplace violence occurs at which of the following?

    A. post offices

    B. university campuses

    C. private industry

    D. state government

    E. All of the above

147. During recent national disasters in the United States, most of us learned that which agency is responsible for policy and programs for workplace emergency management?

    A. Occupational Safety and Health Administration (OSHA)

    B. Federal Emergency Management Agency (FEMA)

    C. Department of Labor

    D. National Labor Relations Board (NLRB)

    E. None of the above

148. Juanita asks you to develop a clear workplace privacy policy. Which of following would this policy include?

    A. guidelines for acceptable use of company property (cell phones, vehicles, etc.)
    B. definition of acceptable internet use
    C. the employer's right to review data on office computers
    D. All of the above
    E. None of the above

149. Sloppy appearance, uncombed hair, dark circles under the eyes can all be signs of:

    A. illness
    B. substance abuse
    C. Generation-Y behavior
    D. a new baby in the household
    E. addiction to late-night television shows

150. Strategic Human Resource Management (SHRM) is a process by which you:

    A. Align human capital with institutional direction
    B. Revise corporate goals for compliance
    C. Plan, align, process and implement organizational goals
    D. Develop corporate governance procedures
    E. None of the above

151. You have been studying for your PHR certification, so you know when your CEO mentions the importance of "aligning human capital" that she means:

    A. having the budget to offer annual merit raises
    B. providing a safe and secure work environment
    C. developing an organizational chart
    D. identifying the right people for the right job at the right time
    E. None of the above

152. HR professionals need provide certain information for the organization's overall budget. This would include:

    A. Information on salaries, benefits and cost of living increases.
    B. Information on salaries, benefits, labor market data and cost of living increases
    C. Information on salaries, benefits, grant revenue and cost of living increases
    D. Information on salaries and cost of living increases
    E. All of the above

153. A company's assets include all EXCEPT the following:

    A. Cash holdings
    B. Items that can be converted to cash
    C. Land or buildings
    D. Employee retirement accounts
    E. None of the above

154. Historical Based Budgeting is best used:

    A. by companies over 50 years old

    B. by companies which anticipate little operational change

    C. by companies planning a brand new product or service

    D. by companies who are planning a succession plan

    E. None of the above

155. Zero-based Budgeting is best used:

    A. by companies over 50 years old

    B. by companies which anticipate little operational change

    C. by companies planning a brand new product or service

    D. by companies who are planning a succession plan

    E. None of the above

156. A corporation can be defined as a body formed and authorized by law which:

    A. has legal rights and responsibilities

    B. can make legally binding decisions

    C. is owned by a Board of Directors

    D. is controlled by stockholders

    E. All of the above

157. A centralized organization

    A. has a central administrative office and no branches

    B. has all employees working in one location

    C. makes most decisions at higher levels of management

    D. makes most decisions by staff consensus

    E. None of the above

158. The Copyright Act of 1976 states that the law protects the author for the life of the author, plus how many years?

    A. 50 years

    B. 70 years

    C. 100 years

    D. There are no lifetime limits.

    E. 200 years

159. You have commissioned Sheila to write a series of articles about your company as part of her job description—public information officer. Sheila is looking for a new job. She states that "she" owns the material and can use it as part of her application materials. Based upon your knowledge of the Copyright Law, is this true or not?

    A. Yes, it is true. She is the author of the material, so she does own it.

    B. No, it is not true. Because the work was created as part of her job description, the employer owns the material.

    C. The Copyright Law does not address this situation.

    D. The material is public domain, so none of the above apply.

    E. All of the above apply.

160. You have developed a training program for the technicians at your organization. They are required to demonstrate competence on the skill before passing to the next level. What is this type of training called?

    A. Performance-based

    B. Experience-based

    C. Technician-based

    D. None of the above

    E. All of the above

161. Harvard University is widely known for using examples of real-life situations and examples for business students to learn the how's and how-not-to's of the way things should be done in business. Harvard uses what type of training method?

    A. Demonstration Method
    B. Experience Method
    C. Socratic Method
    D. Case Study Method
    E. None of the above

162. Jung Pharmaceuticals uses an appraisal system where feedback is given from the supervisor, the subordinate, and customers. They are using which type of performance appraisal system?

    A. Round-the-clock
    B. 360-evaluation
    C. 520-feedback
    D. None of the above

163. Learning Organizations have which of the following characteristics?

    A. Systems thinking
    B. Communications thinking
    C. Universal thinking
    D. Design thinking
    E. All of the above

164. A chart that graphically represents what is normally called the 80/20 rule is called what?

    A. Org Chart
    B. Pareto Chart
    C. Histogram
    D. 100-degree chart
    E. None of the above

165. What is the name of the motivation theory that basically states people are motivated strictly by the reward they will receive at the end?

    A. X/Y Theory
    B. Acquired Needs Theory
    C. Maslow's Theory
    D. Vroom's Theory
    E. Pavlov's Theory

166. Online learning is an example of what type of training?

    A. Vestibule training
    B. Computerized training
    C. Passive Training
    D. Active Training
    E. None of the above

167. You need to determine how one variable affects another in your organization, when you are doing your needs analysis. What statistical tool might you use to measure this?

    A. T analysis
    B. Qualitative analysis
    C. Data-systems analysis
    D. Correlation coefficient
    E. None of the above

168. What measures one variable against another when doing a statistical analysis?

    A. Simple linear regression
    B. Qualitative analysis
    C. Data-systems analysis
    D. Correlation coefficient
    E. None of the above

169. You happen to know that Mike scored exceedingly well on the assessment test that you gave him in the pre-hire period. You are now interviewing him for the job. What is this phenomena called?

    A. Stereotyping

    B. Psychic effect

    C. Knowledge-of-predictor effect

    D. None of the above

    E. All of the above

170. Maura works in the research division of your organization, makes $22,000 per year supervises several staff members, and spends most of her time working on intellectual materials. She is what type of employee?

    A. Exempt, based on administrative exemption

    B. Exempt, based on computer exemption

    C. Exempt, based on the research exemption

    D. Non-exempt, based upon salary exemption

    E. None of the above

171. Organizations, like people, go through various life cycles. The stage that describes when the organization has plateaued and has most of the resources it needs is called what?

    A. Decline

    B. Maturity

    C. Growth

    D. End

    E. None of the above

172. Organizations, like people, go through various life cycles. The stage that describes when the organization tries to find funding and employees are sometimes paid below their position description is called what?

    A. Decline

    B. Maturity

    C. Growth

    D. Start-up

    E. None of the above

173. The area of business responsible for managing systems, email, internet usage, phone usage, software and data is usually called?

    A. Information Technology

    B. Systems Technology

    C. Computerized Technology

    D. Communications Technology

    E. None of the above

174. Organizations, like people, go through various life cycles. The stage that describes when the organization is typically inefficient and bureaucratic is called what?

    A. Decline

    B. Maturity

    C. Growth

    D. Start-up

    E. None of the above

175. The process by which multiple individuals rate a candidate on their performance is called what?

    A. Multiple-rater bias

    B. Inter-rater reliability

    C. Both A and B

    D. None of the above

    E. All of the above

KAPLAN

176. Farrah, who has cerebal palsy, is protected by what law which prohibits health insurance companies from discrimination against individuals with pre-existing conditions?

    A. COBRA
    B. FEMA
    C. COLA
    D. HIPAA
    E. None of the above

177. Which organization provides a free service to help employers determine if their workplace is a safe environment?

    A. OSHA
    B. ERISA
    C. WARN
    D. HIPAA
    E. None of the above

178. Doug sent his three female co-workers an email that included some less than flattering descriptions of women. This was the first time he did it. According to the law, is this considered sexual harassment?

    A. Yes, anything that co-workers finding sexually demeaning is considered sexual harassment.
    B. Yes, he has created a hostile work environment.
    C. No, a single incident of unwanted behavior—unless it was particularly offensive or intimidating does not constitute sexual harassment.
    D. No, offensive emails are not considered sexual harassment.
    E. None of the above

179. Whistleblowing is an example of what type of workplace issue?

    A. Privacy Rights.
    B. Ethics
    C. Confidentiality
    D. All of the above.
    E. None of the above

180. Marissa has just finished a challenging assignment that has taken many weeks to plan for and complete. She is pleased with herself and treats herself to a special lunch with co-workers. Marissa is experiencing what type of reward?

    A. Extrinsic reward
    B. Intrinsic reward
    C. Monetary reward
    D. Culinary reward
    E. None of the above

181. Gavin's supervisor has just asked him to consider a third party contract with three soft drink providers in the company's cafeteria. He's been asked to get RFP's from all three. What is an RFP?

    A. Return from Provider
    B. Request from Provider
    C. Research for Proposal
    D. Request for Proposal
    E. None of the above

182. Which of the following is an example of a third party contract?

    A. An agreement for a cleaning service to provide cleaning services.

    B. An agreement with a temp agency to provide employment services.

    C. An agreement with an outsourcing firm to provide contract services.

    D. All of the above.

    E. None of the above

183. You are a job analyst hired by a firm to help them prepare up-to-date job descriptions for everyone working in their marketing department. As part of the analysis, you need to meet with the SME's at the job site. What is an SME?

    A. Sales Management Employees

    B. Subject Matter Expert

    C. Supervisors, Managers, and Employees

    D. Supervisors, Managers, and Executives

    E. None of the above

184. Tommy is an employee at your organization who has worked there for six years. He feels satisfied by his job and the recognition he has received there. He recently stated that he'd like to enroll, at his own expense, in a leadership program. However, it may take a couple of hours a month of company time. In Maslow's Hierarchy of Needs, he would state that Tommy is at what level of the continuum?

    A. Social

    B. Self-Actualization

    C. Esteem

    D. Happiness

    E. None of the above

185. Jesse is a manager that believes that most employees are in need of constant direction, or that they are basically lazy if you don't motivate them. He is what type of manager?

    A. A dictator

    B. Theory Y manager

    C. Theory X manager

    D. Powerful manager

    E. None of the above

186. The theory that describes how behavior can be changed by behavior modification is called what?

    A. Classical Conditioning

    B. Positive Conditioning

    C. Negative Conditioning

    D. Operant Conditioning

    E. None of the above

187. A television news station has assembled a group of individuals together to ask them about the delivery of their six o'clock evening newscast? They are using what type of process for getting feedback?

    A. Focus Group

    B. Survey

    C. Climate Study

    D. All of the above.

    E. None of the above

188. Regarding dress codes, it is illegal for a company to force a female employee to wear a skirt while she is on company time.

    A. True, it is illegal for a company to require a female to wear a skirt

    B. False, it is not illegal for a company to require a female to wear a skirt as long as it is not discriminatory.

    C. Neither A or B is true.

    D. False, it is not illegal, but it is discriminatory.

    E. None of the above

189. Your strategy as CEO of your company is to make sure that all employees know that you are visible and open to access and dialogue. Your philosophy is commonly known as MBWO. What does this acronym stand for?

    A. Management by Work Objectives

    B. Management by Walking Around

    C. Marketing by Work Opportunity

    D. Making Business Work Onsite

    E. None of the above

190. A common phenomena that HR professionals witness is when new hires are paid a wage greater than the incumbent workers, even though they have similar skills and education. What is this called?

    A. Wage Compression

    B. Workforce Compression

    C. Level 5 Compression

    D. None of the above

191. The theory that concludes that leaders are "born" and not-made, i.e. that you are innately possess leadership skills is also called what?

    A. The Clinton Theory

    B. The "Great Man" Theory

    C. The "Great Leader" Theory

    D. Inherent Leader Theory

    E. None of the above

192. Describing the essential functions of a job, when writing a job description, is required to keep you in compliance of what?

    A. The KSA Act.

    B. The NRA Act

    C. The ADA Act

    D. The ROI Act

    E. None of the above

193. In your organization, employees report to two managers, one is responsible for the product—potato chips—the other manager is responsible for marketing those potato chips in the southwest region of the United States. This would be an example of which type of organizational structure?

    A. Matrix

    B. Divisional

    C. Marketing/Management

    D. Product Based

    E. None of the above

194. Colette is a supervisor at a college that delivers most of its curriculum online. She communicates with her faculty predominantly via email and the internet. This would be an example of what type of organizational structure?

    A. Matrix
    B. Seamless
    C. Marketing/Management
    D. Product Based
    E. None of the above

195. You need to collect a large amount of information from your employees in a short amount of time. Which is the best method of collecting this information?

    A. Interviews
    B. Focus Groups
    C. Both A and B.
    D. Surveys
    E. None of the above

196. You are developing a training program for your administrative assistants and exempt employees. You have decided to use a mix of classroom lecture and on-the-job training. What might be something to consider when developing each training module?

    A. Adult learning theory
    B. Diversity
    C. Opportunity theory
    D. Human Development theory
    E. None of the above

197. The Federal Enforcement Agency that oversees issues related to privacy in the workplace is which of the following?

    A. Department of Justice
    B. Department of Labor
    C. EEOC
    D. Both A and C.
    E. None of the above

198. The Oneida Tribe operates a casino in the Midwest. They give preference to hiring Indian applicants and employees living on the reservation. Is this a legal practice?

    A. No, you may not discriminate against non-Indian applicants.
    B. Yes, you may give preference to Indian employees based on the EEOC Act.
    C. Yes, you may give preference to Indiana employees based upon Title VII.
    D. Both B and C.
    E. None of the above

199. Official documents that are issued by which the President of the United States manages the operations of the Federal Government are called Executive Orders. These become law in how many days?

    A. 30
    B. 60
    C. 90
    D. 120
    E. 150

200. The seven categories of race and ethnicity which you are required to report in EEO Surveys include which of the following?

    A.   Black or African-American, Asian, White, Ukrainian

    B.   American Indian, Native Hawaiian or Other Pacific Islander, Ukrainian

    C.   Native Hawaiian or Other Pacific Islander, Latino, Eskimo

    D.   White, American Indian, Native Hawaiian or Other Pacific Islander, Asian

    E.   All of the above

201. You are interviewing a member of the armed services, who recently returned from Iraq? Which of the following is an <u>inappropriate</u> question to ask her?

    A.   Were you honorably discharged?

    B.   What branch of the service did you serve in?

    C.   Both A and B.

    D.   None of the above.

202. You are interviewing a member of the armed services, who recently returned from Iraq? Which of the following is an <u>appropriate</u> question to ask her?

    A.   Were you honorably discharged?

    B.   What branch of the service did you serve in?

    C.   Both A and B.

    D.   None of the above.

203. According to federal law, employers are <u>not</u> held responsible for their employee's harmful actions, if they were unaware of those actions.

    A.   This statement is true.

    B.   This statement is not true.

    C.   This statement is not true, whether the employer is aware or unaware of the actions by the employees.

    D.   This statement is not true, unless they can prove their lack of awareness in court.

    E.   None of the above.

204. Title VII, The Civil Rights Act, was enacted in what year?

    A.   1952

    B.   1964

    C.   1970

    D.   1935

    E.   1981

205. In 1886, a violent conflict between strikers, employers, and the government occurred. This was called what?

    A.   The Famous Railway Strike

    B.   The Great Uprising

    C.   The Millworkers Strike

    D.   Haymarket Tragedy

    E.   The Chicago Fire

206. This Act was originally acted to prevent monopolies. It was:

    A.   Sherman Antitrust Act

    B.   The Mann Act.

    C.   Industrial Workers of the World Act.

    D.   The New Deal.

    E.   None of the above

207. Bonnie has left your workplace and is applying for new jobs with state government. Your HR office has been receiving inquiries about her employment with your agency. She left your agency on less than favorable circumstances. You must be very careful to not give information about Bonnie that would cause damage to her reputation in her community. What is a term that defines this?

    A. Liable
    B. Fraud
    C. Defamation
    D. Good faith
    E. None of the above

208. OSHA laws state that an employer must do which of the following?

    A. Post violations of workplace standards.
    B. Provide employees with the latest and greatest safety equipment, even if the cost is a burden to the employer.
    C. Report violations that require hospitalization of an employee.
    D. All of the above.
    E. None of the above

209. In 2008, OSHA identified which of the following industries as a particularly hazardous occupation?

    A. Construction
    B. Mining
    C. Teaching
    D. Shipyard
    E. None of the above

210. What is one of the newest types of security risks that an employer must be guarding against?

    A. Anthrax.
    B. Poisoning of water systems
    C. Terrorism
    D. Computer Security breaches
    E. All of the above

211. Which agency developed the following publication in 2004: "Are you Ready? An In-depth Guide to Citizen Preparedness"?

    A. Office of Homeland Security
    B. FEMA
    C. Department of Labor
    D. OSHA
    E. None of the above

212. A job description would probably NOT include which of the following?

    A. The person's educational credentials
    B. Job Title
    C. Years of experience
    D. Essential duties and functions
    E. None of the above

213. You are identifying the basic skills necessary to do certain jobs on your campus. You are likely doing what?

    A. Writing job descriptions.
    B. Doing a job analysis.
    C. Identifying workers who need further training.
    D. None of the above.
    E. Both A and B

214. Carl has repeatedly been performing poorly at his position as a maintenance mechanic. His supervisor, Charlie, has been following the steps of progressive discipline as his company prescribes. At what stage is Carl one step away from termination?

    A.   Final Written Warning

    B.   Suspension

    C.   Prosecution

    D.   Verbal Warning

    E.   None of the above.

215. Eva expects her subordinates to set high goals and objectives in her department at the hospital. She is known as what type of leader?

    A.   Transformational

    B.   Directive

    C.   Supportive

    D.   Achievement-Oriented

    E.   None of the above

216. Nancy is the type of supervisor who is friendly and shows concern for her employees, but doesn't really give much direction. She is known as what type of leader?

    A.   Transformational

    B.   Directive

    C.   Supportive

    D.   Achievement-Oriented

    E.   None of the above

217. Which are three important tenets of Kouzes and Posner's model of transformational leadership?

    A.   Model the way

    B.   Empower others

    C.   Inspiring a shared vision

    D.   All of the above

    E.   None of the above

218. In your two-day seminar on the new automated processing system at your manufacturing plant, you may sure to provide employees with frequent rest breaks, including lunch, and small snacks and water to keep them comfortable. You do this because you know about Maslow's Theory of Basic Human needs. Which level are you helping to satisfy for your employees?

    A.   Biological and Physiological

    B.   Safety

    C.   Esteem

    D.   Self-Actualization

    E.   None of the above

219. You observe that Micki, a new receptionist at your travel agency, has been sending out emails to customers addressed as follows: "Hey, how ya doin?" She has offended two customers already. You take this has a training opportunity to teach Micki about communication? Which of the following should you ask her to start asking herself before she sends another email to her customers?

    A.   Who is my audience?

    B.   Should I observe any sensitivity in communicating with this person?

    C.   Is this communication formal enough for the workplace?

    D.   All of the above

    E.   None of the above

220. Which of the following is <u>NOT</u> a decision-making flaw?

   A. Making a decision based on wishful thinking.

   B. Making a decision on past performance.

   C. Making a decision based on current celebrity trends.

   D. Making a decision based upon peer pressure.

   E. None of the above

221. In large major metropolitan areas, that are rich in diverse populations of people, wise managers know to be mindful to what relatively new phenomena?

   A. Cultural intelligence.

   B. Multiple intelligence.

   C. Both A & B.

   D. Emotional intelligence.

   E. None of the above

222. This is the net income of a business upon which the federal, state and local taxes are based.

   A. Capital

   B. Taxable income

   C. Annual Report

   D. Assets

   E. None of the above

223. Revenue is only recorded when cash is actually received and expenses are paid. This is called what?

   A. Cash basis accounting.

   B. Profit and loss statement.

   C. Debit accounting.

   D. All of the above.

   E. None of the above

224. What is the first step in the legislative process to develop something into law?

   A. A legislator sends the bill to congress.

   B. A bill is drafted by the House or Senate.

   C. A person writes a letter to his or her congressperson

   D. A group, individual, or business proposes an idea for something to the House or Senate.

   E. None of the above.

225. The SHRM certification is a _____ test.

   A. Way too long

   B. 3 hour

   C. 4 hour

   D. 5 hour

   E. Both A and C.

Answers to Questions and Explanations

1. Answer: (A). They continue to accrue seniority and other benefits and thought they are continuously employed.

2. Answer: (C). Court martial, dishonorable discharge, and going AWOL are all reasons to forfeit your rights for future employment.

3. Answer: (E). It's both (B) and (C). In some instances HR staff will have very little knowledge and experience with individual job duties. The supervisor and the subject matter experts—the ones doing the job—have much greater first hand knowledge of the position.

4. Answer: (D). All of the above. EEO-1 requires reporting of ethnicity, job positions and breakdown between males/females within those positions.

5. Answer: (D), the Taft-Hartley Act.

6. Answer: (A). This ensures that compensation programs are compliant with all federal, state, and local laws and regulations.

7. Answer: (B). Complying with FCRA requirements is essential.

8. Answer: (D). Polygraph testing is used only very limited circumstances, such as positions involved with national security, pharmaceuticals, or armored car services.

9. Answer: (B). FBI contractors, national security workers, armored car workers, pharmaceutical sales.

10. The correct answer is: (B). Analysis, Design, Develop, Implementation, Evaluation

11. Answer: (D). The Acquired Needs theory is attributed to: David McClelland.

12. Answer: (C). Operant Conditioning is the idea that behavior can be changed through positive and negative reinforcement.

13. Answer: (D). All of the above are important to an effective HRIS System.

14. Answer: is (C). Traditional Bargaining is also called Position Bargaining.

15. The best answer is (D). All of the above, if the disclosure of medical history reveals a distinct invasion of privacy.

16. Answer: (B). According to the Department of Labor, $5.85 is the minimum wage as of July 2007.

17. Answer: (B). Wage garnishment is a legal procedure in which a person's earnings are required by court order to be withheld by an employer for the payment of a debt such as child support.

18. Answer: (C). Merit pay is also called pay-for-performance.

19. Answer: (D). Race, Color, Religion, National Origin and Sex are all considered protected classes under Title VII.

20. Answer: (B). Severance pay, which is often offered upon termination of an employment contract, is not mandatory and is strictly at the discretion of the employer and based on the length of service to the company.

21. Answer: (D). He is looking for a return on investment into the program. as opposed

to the benefits the employees are receiving. For example, less commute time, more time to exercise, less time off work because of better health initiatives, etc.

22. Answer: (C). Total Quality Management is based upon the teachings of W. Edwards Deming.

23. Answer: (A). A zero-based budget is one where your total income minus your total expenses equals $0. In a zero-based budget you must assign every dollar of income to an expense (or savings) category.

24. Answer: (C). Bad-faith bargaining, in this particular case, fails to give adequate notice in time for the contracts to be properly negotiated.

25. Answer: (B). Mold, bacteria, dust, and viruses are also considered biological hazards according to OSHA.

26. Answer: (D). All of these are considered categories of OSHA violations, no matter the level of severity.

27. Answer: is (D). All of the above are covered, along with at least 12 other acts related to health and wellness.

28. Answer: (B) 30 days. If evidence supports the worker's claim of discrimination, OSHA will ask the employer to restore the worker's job, earnings and benefits.

29. Answer: (B). While asbestos and second-hand smoke have legislation of their own, cleaning up air pollution was the primary goal of the act.

30. Answer: (E). All of the above. Mental illness, not related to the job, or certified as such by a health professional, does not have to be reported. Tuberculosis also does not have to be reported UNLESS it is specifically related to an employee's position. Nor does a car accident on company property have to be reported when the staff member is commuting to and from work.

31. Answer: (D). The Privacy Act of 1974.

32. Answer: (B). Title VII of the Civil Rights Act of 1964. The Equal Employment Opportunity Act of 1972, established that employees may have to prove disparate impact, if they feel that they have been unjustly discriminated against.

33. Answer: (A). The correct answer is age 40 or older.

34. Answer: (B). Hiring tools need to be valid and reliable predictors of job success and job task must be matched to job requirements.

35. Answer: (B). Employment at Will Doctrine, which provides for both the employee or employer to terminate employment at any time.

36. Answer: (B). Do you have a family? You may ask the residency question, for example, if that requires the individual to live within the City limits, which is common in major areas for police and firefighters. It is also legal to ask if a worker is eligible to work in the United States.

37. Answer: (B). False. It is currently not illegal according to federal law. Although some states have specific guidelines in place protecting gays from sexual harassment, you should check local laws and regulations.

38. Answer: (D). Many employers do allow 1–3 days of leave upon the death of a close family member. Most employers take great care to specify in employee handbooks, what specifically constitutes "close" family—so that it doesn't extend to cousins and distant relatives.

39. Answer: (C). Meaningfulness of work, responsibility for outcomes, and knowledge of work results.

40. Answer: (B). Although the more common examples of sexual harassment is male against female, it does occur the other way around, and also with same sex individuals.

41. Answer: (C). An organizational chart.

42. Answer: (D). The <u>process</u> of job analysis would look at the each of these things that then form the job description.

43. Answer: (C). Fiscal responsibility is not one of the listed guiding principles. The professional standards are based on the following principles: professional responsibility and development, ethical leadership, fairness and justice, conflict of interest and use of information.

44. Answer: (A). Conflict of interest.

45. Answer: (A). Employee records must be tracked with the employee record management system.

46. Answer: (C). Progressive discipline.

47. Answer: (D). High Performance Work System organizes work and paper flow at multiple levels.

48. Answer: (A). These are all components of project management.

49. Answer: (D). Initiation, Planning, Execution, and Closing are the key phases of project management.

50. Answer: (B). Savvy business managers always know what is going on around them—what the competition is up to, how successful their products are, the industry standards and future trends, the purpose for the environmental scan.

51. The correct answer is (D) all of the above, in addition to many others.

52. Answer: (B). Strengths, Weaknesses, Opportunities, Threats are the components of a SWOT analysis.

53. Answer: (D). The effectiveness of the leader, under contingency theory, is contingent upon the demands of any particular situation.

54. Answer: (B). The Least Preferred Coworker scale asks a leader to think of all the persons with whom she has ever worked, and then to describe the one person she worked with the least well. This can be a current co-worker or someone whom they previously worked with. Then, they are to rate them on the following scale such as friendly or unfriendly, cooperative or uncooperative, guarded or open.

55. The correct answer is (A) Robert House.

56. Answer: (D). Linguistic, Spatial, Interpersonal, Musical are four of the seven multiple intelligences that Gardner lists in his theory. The others are: logical-mathematical, kinesthetic, and intrapersonal.

57. Answer: Katie is (C) Interpersonal, and would likely be a good candidate for the promotion.

58. Answer: (D). Horizontal communication. One can assume so, since both Michael and Conrad have similar job titles.

59. Answer: (B) Strategic management.

60. Answer: (A). Strategic planning.

61. Answer: (D) . Both A and B are both synonyms for strategic planning.

62. Answer: (B). An environmental scan is a method in which you pay attention to the "substitutes" for your product if it is not available.

63. Answer: (C). A mission statement.

64. Answer: (B). This is an example of how to write a vision statement.

65. Answer: (A). Julio is doing an internal assessment of his work environment.

KAPLAN

66. Answer: (B). Span of control is the "reach" of how far your managerial responsibility goes.

67. Answer: (D). The balance sheet is typically prepared at the end of the month. The balance sheet formula is as follows: Assets = Liability + Capital.

68. Answer: (A). Income statements help track how much money went in and how much went out.

69. Answer: (B). Annual Report.

70. Answer: (A). The net profit statement shows gross profit minus operating expense.

71. Answer: (D). Design Organizational structure is the fake; the other three are very valid organizational structures.

72. Answer: (C). Knowledge, Skills, and Abilities are the KSA that Phyllis is asking you to examine.

73. Answer: (A). Bona fide occupational qualifications. (BFOQ).

74. Answer: (A). Budgets based on historic information are a good starting point, particularly if things aren't going to change a lot (operationally) in the new fiscal year, or are just going to increase most things by a flat percentage rate or based upon certain salary increases.

75. Answer: (C). All of the choices are tempting, but a corporation is the only one authorized to act as a unit, with related legal rights and responsibilities.

76. Answer: (B). A STEP analysis is the only choice to incorporate all of those elements into an environmental scan.

77. Answer: (C). Exempt workers.

78. Answer: (B). Ryan, who is 13 years of age, is the one you cannot hire. The 14- and 15-year-olds you may hire, however, they may

work no more than 3 hours per day or 18 hours per work week.

79. Answer: (A). 7:00 A.M. to 7:00 P.M.

80. Answer: (D). All of the above are tasks that minors are not allowed to do, by law.

81. Answer: (B). During the legislative process, if a bill is not signed by the president, a 10-day waiting period ensues, in which the bill automatically becomes law despite not having his signature. If Congress adjourns before the 10-day period is up, the bill will not become law.

82. Answer: (D). Extroverted, Sensing, Thinking, Judging are the result.

83. Answer: (D). If the disagreement remains unresolved at this grievance process stage, the dispute can go to an arbitration process.

84. Answer: (A). Predictive validity.

85. Answer: (B). Quid pro quo is Latin for "this for that," which suggests an even exchange—even though his request is highly inappropriate.

86. Answer: (B). Sourcing is the process of gathering names of potential candidates when recruiting for a new position.

87. Answer: (C). Proficiency or Knowledge test.

88. Answer: (A). Reliability.

89. Answer: (B). Criterion-related validity. What is most important in this question, is making sure that the criteria, in this case writing ability, is directly related to a task that she is going to be performing the job.

90. Answer: (A). Adverse impact.

91. Answer: (D). A behavioral interview question, where the applicant must demonstrate how their previous behavior in a

certain situation, might be applied in her future performance.

92. Answer: (A). The BARS Scale—behaviorally anchored rating scale—is what you would use to evaluate the employee's performance based on his job dimensions.

93. Answer: (B). Total Rewards—all of these are part of her total rewards package.

94. Answer: (B). A cause and effect chart.

95. Answer: (A). A flow chart.

96. Answer: (A). Learning is the second step. Step 1 is Reaction, Step 2, is Learning, Step 3, is Behavior, and Step 4 is Results.

97. Answer: (A). A 360 degree evaluation gives you a full sense of an employee's all-around job performance.

98. Answer: (B). Promissory estoppel is a legal term that stands for incentivizing employees' performance.

99. Answer: (B). Risk Assessment. Risk Management is the entire area of safety and security plans, and an emergency management plan would be developed after you have done a risk assessment.

100. Answer: (D). Communication Workers v. Beck (1988).

101. Answer: (B). NLRB v Wooster Division of Borg-Warner Corporation (1958).

102. Answer: (A). NLRB v. Mackay Radio and Telegraph Company (1938). This court case gave employer rights to permanently replace striking workers during an economic strike.

103. Answer: (D). NLRB v. Weingarten (1975). Weingarten Rights give employees the right to have representation at an investigative meeting with management if the employee believes that discipline will be discussed at the meeting.

104. Answer: (C). Circuit City. The case was Circuit City Stores v. Adams, 2001.

105. Answer: (B). Health Service and education had the lowest degree of fatalities in 2006.

106. Answer: (B). The Sherman Anti-trust act of 1890 was enacted to prevent monopolies and other restraint of trade activities.

107. Answer: (D) 67.

108. Answer: (C). Davis Bacon Act

109. Answer: (D). GAAP—Generally Accepted Accounting Principles

110. Answer: (D). This is a tricky question. The best answer is (D), because the question asked about using the tests in relation to hiring. Reliability measures the tests ability to be consistent over time. Content validity measures a part of the job for which they are being tested—typing skills for data entry, for instance. And, construct validity measures the connection between the test and being successful on the job, i.e. your data entry clerk, who is graded on number of entries per day—if she scores 90% vs. someone who scores 30% is likely to be more successful on the job. Concurrent validity measures success at the same time a test is being taken, i.e. a driver's education test.

111. Answer: (B). A liability.

112. Answer: (D). Employee compensation matching expectations

113. Answer: (D). All of the above. Justin should know as much as possible before he gives his presentation, including his audience, the proposed project specifications, and who will be carrying out the objectives.

114. Answer: (D). High performance work Systems (HPWS) suggest that rewards be tied to performance, but do not suggest frequency.

115. Answer: (C). Theft is the most common reason.

116. Answer: (D). Both A and C. Different people bring different perspectives and ideas, as well as opening up the number of people available for a given position.

117. Answer: (B). Those are the components of project management.

118. Answer: (B). Focus strictly on the job, not Theresa.

119. Answer: (E). All of the above indicate a company at high risk.

120. Answer: (A). President Franklin D. Roosevelt was responsible for the Social Security Act of 1935, which was part of his New Deal economic policies designed to help the country through the Depression.

121. Answer: (D). The employee defers a certain portion of their income to charitable organizations

122. The best answer to this question is: (A). What am I paying my employees? However, note that this might be a part of the "where are we now" question as well.

123. Answer: (B). 65 and 6 months is the full retirement age.

124. Answer: (D). The first federal unemployment insurance program was also part of Roosevelt's Social Security Act.

125. Answer: (C). Cafeteria plan.

126. Answer: (D). All of the above. (A) would be considered a qualifying event, because of the child would be a dependent, who is no longer covered.

127. Answer: (D). Both minimum wage and child labor laws were key elements of the FLSA.

128. Answer: (A). Employees within 75 miles of the worksite.

129. Answer: (A). Holiday leave is not mandatory.

130. Answer: (A). There is no federal law that mandates bereavement leave.

131. Answer: (B). Employers are required to be aware of employees exhibiting potentially violent and risky behaviors, and to act accordingly.

132. Answer: (D). All of the above. Intellectual property can incorporate any potentially confidential information or intellectual information developed.

133. Answer: (D). All of the above. The main focus itself was to provide guidelines against disparate impact and intentional discrimination, as well as provide guidelines in awarding damage in cases of discrimination.

134. Answer: is (C). Stereotyping. He assumes she cannot lift the boxes merely because she's a woman, without knowing anything about her experience or qualifications for such a job.

135. Answer: (D). 2:00 P.M. is the right choice. Assuming that the interview team will convene following the last interview, the Recency Bias effect basically assumes that the team remembers what the most recent candidate—in this case the last one—stated in their interview rather than the earlier candidates.

136. Answer: (C). The Horn effect is when the interviewer concentrates on a specific characteristic of the interviewee's candidacy. It could be just about any characteristic.

137. Answer: (D). Monster.com, Career Builder, and Craigslist are the correct resources. Godaddy.com is a place to register internet domain names, Google is a search engine, and eBay is used mainly to buy and sell merchandise.

138. Answer: (B). Overtime rate.

139. Answer: (B). The assessment process identifies the needs for the reward program to address.

140. Answer: (C). While all of these are important to become familiar with, the correct answer is C, the Fair Labor Status Act of 1938.

141. Answer: (A). Salary is NOT a determiner of exempt status.

142. Answer: (D). Time to change to specialized clothing, like time required to clean up, is compensable time for non-exempt employees.

143. Answer: (A). Self-improvement programs that are unlikely to affect workplace performance are not typical employer-elected benefits.

144. Answer: (A). Time traveling to the conference outside of work hours would not be covered.

145. Answer: (B). OSHA dies not develop protective gear, although it regulates use. It is the obligation of the employer to provide it.

146. Answer: (D). More than national or local government, the greatest occurrence of violence has historically been in state government.

147. Answer: (B). Federal Emergency Management Agency (FEMA).

148. Answer: (D). All of the above.

149. Answer: (B). All of these features can be related to substance abuse, and an employer should know the signs. .

150. Answer: (C). Plan, align, process and implement organizational goals.

151. Answer: (D). Identifying the right people for the right job at the right time.

152. Answer: (A). Information on salaries, benefits and cost of living increases would be important to the company's overall budget.

153. Answer: (D). Employee retirement accounts.

154. Answer: (B). For companies which anticipate little operational change, a historical based budget can give an accurate representation of what the company will achieve.

155. Answer: (C). Companies planning a brand new product or service can benefit more from a zero-based budget, because it's harder to predict what will happen with the new elements.

156. Answer: (A). Corporations have legal rights and responsibilities, given that they are established by law.

157. Answer: (C). Most decisions at higher levels of management (or in a "centralized" place in the company).

158. Answer: (B). After 70 years, you may use an author's work without permission.

159. Answer: (B). No, it is not true. Because the work was created as part of her job description, the employer owns the material.

160. Answer: (A). Performance-based training.

161. Answer: (D). Case Study Method.

162. Answer: (B). 360-evaluation.

163. Answer: (A). Systems thinking.

164. The Answer: (B). Pareto Chart.

165. Answer: (D). Vroom's Expectancy Theory.

166. Answer: (C). Passive Training.

167. Answer: (D). Correlation coefficient.

168. Answer: (A). Simple linear regression.

KAPLAN

169. Answer: (C). Knowledge-of-predictor effect

170. Answer: (D). Non-exempt, based upon salary exemption.

171. Answer: (B). Maturity.

172. Answer: (D). Start-up.

173. Answer: (A). Information Technology.

174. Answer: (A). Decline

175. Answer: (B). Inter-rater reliability—the process for reducing bias.

176. Answer: (D). HIPAA.

177. Answer: (A). OSHA

178. Answer: (C). No, a single incident of unwanted behavior—unless it was particularly offensive or intimidating does not constitute sexual harassment.

179. Answer: (B). Ethics issues.

180. Answer: (B). Intrinsic reward. A feeling of self-satisfaction—although the culinary reward was nice, too.

181. Answer: (D). Request for Proposal.

182. Answer: (D). All of the above are third party contracts.

183. Answer: (B). The Subject Matter Expert is the person that knows the most about the job you are analyzing, the employee himself.

184. Answer: (B). Self-Actualization. He is satisfied at the other level and is seeking opportunities on his own to bring him to a higher level.

185. Answer: (C). Theory X manager—based upon McGregor's x/y theory of management.

186. Answer: (D). Operant Conditioning.

187. Answer: (A). Focus Group.

188. Answer: (B). False; it is not illegal for a company to require a female to wear a skirt as long as it is not discriminatory. A company has the right to tell employees how formal or informal clothes should be in the workplace and at off workplace sites (for example, an off-site black tie event).

189. Answer: (B). Management by Walking Around—the philosophy that employees should see you and be able to talk with you "While you are walking around" at the workplace.

190. Answer: (A). Wage Compression.

191. Answer: (B). The "Great Man" Theory.

192. Answer: (C). The Americans with Disabilities Act.

193. Answer: (A). Matrix.

194. Answer: (B). Seamless

195. Answer: (B). The best answer for this question, given the limited information that you have is: (B) Focus Groups—which would allow you to reach a cross-section of employees in a short amount of time. Employee Surveys could be costly and time-consuming to develop, unless you had unlimited resources to do so.

196. Answer: (A). Adult learning theory.

197. Answer: (A). Department of Justice

198. Answer: (C). Yes, you may give preference to Indiana employees based upon Title VII.

199. Answer: (A). 30

200. Answer: (D). White, American Indian, Native Hawaiian or Other Pacific Islander, Asian. These are four of the seven categories.

201. Answer: (A). "Were you honorably discharged?" is an inappropriate interview question.

202. Answer: (B). "What branch of the service did you serve in?" is an appropriate interview question.

203. Answer: (C). This statement is not true, whether the employer is aware or unaware of the actions by the employees.

204. Answer: (B). 1964

205. The Answer: (D). Haymarket Tragedy.

206. Answer: (A). Sherman Antitrust Act (1890), amended in 1908 and 1914.

207. Answer: (C). Defamation is when some form of comment can damage a person's reputation or status in the community or in the workplace.

208. Answer: (A). Employers are only required to report accidents that require hospitalization of three or more employees, not a single employee. Health and Safety equipment must be provided at reasonable cost to employer.

209. Answer: (D). Shipyard.

210. Answer: (D). Computer Security breaches, although each item listed are potential issues in risk management.

211. Answer: (B). FEMA.

212. Answer: (A). This is somewhat of a trick question. The credentials that the person holds, is not necessarily one and the same as what is needed for the job. For instance, you may have hired a Ph.D., but a Master's Degree is perhaps all that is necessary for that position.

213. Answer: (B). Doing a job analysis.

214. Answer: (B). Suspension, is one step away from termination.

215. Answer: (D). Achievement-Oriented, according to the theory espoused by Robert House.

216. Answer: (C). Supportive, according to the theory espoused by Robert House.

217. Answer: (D). All of the above. Kouzes and Posner espouse modeling, empowering, and inspiring as key elements of their theory of transformational leadership.

218. Answer: (A). Because food and sleep are very body-oriented needs, feeding them and letting them take breaks where they can unwind are taking care of biological and physiological needs.

219. Answer: (D). All of the above

220. Answer: (C). Making a decision based on current celebrity trends.

221. Answer: (A). Cultural intelligence.

222. Answer: (B). Taxable income.

223. Answer: (A). Cash basis accounting.

224. Answer: (C). A group, individual, or business proposes an idea for something to the House or Senate.

225. Answer: (D). Both A and C. Good luck on the exam!

Practice Test: SPHR Exam 1

1. Evaluating activities that address employee training and development needs include

   A. performance appraisals.
   B. talent management.
   C. performance management.
   D. the unique needs of employees.
   E. All of the above

2. Typically, HRD programs are designed around compliance issues. *Compliance* specifically refers to

   A. union bargaining agreements.
   B. applicable federal and state regulations.
   C. local laws.
   D. Both B and C
   E. organizational needs.

3. A needs assessment analysis is conducted to

   A. identify strategic planning goals.
   B. establish HRD development activities and priorities.
   C. target organizational problems.
   D. gather information to make organizational decisions.
   E. None of the above

4. The primary goal for designing and implementing employee training programs, such as computer assisted training, harassment prevention, and leadership development, is to

   A. obtain feedback about a training program.
   B. identify the best training method(s) for the situation.
   C. increase individual and organizational effectiveness.
   D. design an employee development survey.
   E. All of the above

5. To evaluate the cost-benefit analysis of an employee training program, metrics are typically used to demonstrate whether or not a program contributed to the organization's strategic goals. Methods used to measure program effectiveness include all of the following *EXCEPT*

   A. ranking and rating scales.
   B. surveys.
   C. pre-testing.
   D. post-testing.
   E. anecdotal information.

6. Participant surveys, interviews, and employee attitude questionnaires are designed to

   A. solicit employee information in a confidential manner.

   B. receive feedback on how well a training program impacted individual employees.

   C. obtain feedback from employee direct reports (e.g., supervisors, managers, directors).

   D. obtain feedback on how effectively a training program met the needs of the employee and the organization.

   E. All of the above

7. Talent management refers to

   A. identifying talented employees.

   B. attracting talented applicants.

   C. training high-potential employees for upper management positions.

   D. assessing employees who will stay with the company.

   E. identifying employees who can be developed for long-term assignments and future promotions.

8. Talent management programs are designed around

   A. attracting high-potential employees to meet the demands of organizational goals.

   B. hiring high-potential applicants.

   C. developing talented employees who are eager to move up in the organization.

   D. meeting an organization's strategic plan based on its talent pool.

   E. None of the above

9. Performance appraisals are used to

   A. reward employees.

   B. identify problem employees.

   C. fire lazy employees.

   D. evaluate an employee's performance on the job.

   E. evaluate an employee's performance on the job and determine salary increases.

10. The performance appraisal process is the responsibility of

    A. HRD.

    B. management.

    C. supervisors.

    D. employees.

    E. All of the above

11. Selecting and developing the most appropriate performance appraisal program for an organization is largely the responsibility of

    A. HRM.

    B. management.

    C. supervisors.

    D. employees.

    E. All of the above

12. Implementing a successful performance appraisal program is conducted by a variety of training methods, including

    A. computer-assisted training.

    B. face-to-face interviews.

    C. meetings with managers and supervisors.

    D. All of the above

    E. Both A and B

13. Performance appraisal methods include

   A. face-to-face interviews.

   B. paper-and-pencil assessments.

   C. computer-scored inventories.

   D. MBOs.

   E. All of the above

14. A 360-degree appraisal method is a feed-back tool primarily used for assessing the performance of

   A. line supervisors.

   B. management employees.

   C. department chairs.

   D. union employees.

   E. bad employees.

15. Performance appraisals are conducted

   A. annually.

   B. twice per year.

   C. when a promotion is pending.

   D. as often as needed.

   E. All of the above

16. MBO, a performance appraisal method, is designed to

   A. focus on individual performance while contributing to the organization's broad-range goals.

   B. focus on individual performance goals only.

   C. target major strengths and identify weak performance areas.

   D. review the past year's performance.

   E. plan for the following year's performance goals.

17. ADA, ADEA, USERRA, and EEOC are acronyms that refer to

   A. Title VII.

   B. nondiscrimination in employment.

   C. federal, state, and local laws and regulations related to HRD activities.

   D. discrimination in employment.

   E. None of the above

18. The difference between an HRD program and an OD program is that

   A. an HRD program is a training and development program, while an OD program is an organizational program.

   B. an OD program focuses on intervention, and an HRD program focuses on employee development.

   C. an HRD program focuses on compliance, and an OD program focuses on goal setting.

   D. an OD program focuses on process improvement, and an HRD program focuses on talent management.

   E. All of the above

19. ADA is a federal program designed to protect

   A. employees with disabilities.

   B. employees with occupational needs.

   C. organizations employing workers with disabilities.

   D. organizations with hazardous work conditions.

   E. None of the above

20. The purpose of the EEOC is to

    A. offer unemployment compensation to employees who have been laid off from work.

    B. calculate the amount of wages an unemployed worker receives after losing a job.

    C. provide equal employment opportunities to hourly workers.

    D. ensure compliance and equal employment opportunities for all U.S. citizens.

    E. direct the employment activities of organizations in the United States and abroad.

21. Career development is to leadership as

    A. talent management is to promotion.

    B. performance management is to performance appraisals.

    C. mentoring is to executive coaching.

    D. executive coaching is to talent management.

    E. All of the above

22. Performance management methods include all of the following *EXCEPT*

    A. process improvement.

    B. goal setting.

    C. management by objectives.

    D. job rotation.

    E. promotions.

23. E-learning is designed to take advantage of

    A. computer-based instruction.

    B. a uniform way to deliver training programs to employees.

    C. a large organization having multiple locations to train employees in an asynchronous environment.

    D. training large numbers of employees who cannot meet face-to-face in one location.

    E. All of the above

24. Global issues in HRM refers to

    A. expatriates.

    B. international law.

    C. economic conditions.

    D. only those organizations conducting business on the Internet.

    E. A, B, and C

25. Mentoring is to executive coaching as

    A. training and development is to performance improvement.

    B. process improvement is to promotions.

    C. teaching is to training.

    D. All of the above

    E. None of the above

26. An organization's culture is defined by its

    A. employees.

    B. strategic plan.

    C. organizational goals and objectives.

    D. values.

    E. None of the above

27. Title VII was originally created to

    A. protect the rights of employees who were not members of a union shop.

    B. protect employees with disabilities.

    C. ensure fair treatment for all job classifications.

    D. ensure nondiscrimination in employment for male and female employees.

    E. None of the above

28. A training method designed to allow an employee to learn a new task requiring considerable knowledge and skill before returning to the work site to perform the job is called

    A. mentoring.

    B. coaching.

    C. OJT.

    D. RT.

    E. task/process analysis.

29. The specific requirements to perform a task or procedure are called

    A. job rotation.

    B. OJT.

    C. KSAs.

    D. MBO.

    E. None of the above

30. A key difference between mentoring and executive coaching is that

    A. an executive coach is a professional trained to work with employees on performance improvement issues.

    B. a mentor is a trained professional in a specific field.

    C. there is no difference.

    D. a mentor works in the same field and serves as a teacher or guide to the employee, whereas similar work experience is not a requirement in the coaching relationship.

    E. None of the above

31. Human resource development (HRD) is a human resources function

    A. typically found in a human resource department.

    B. housed in a training department.

    C. considered to be the "soft side" of HRM.

    D. Both A and C

    E. None of the above

32. HRD is a multisystems concept that

    A. integrates organizational development (OD) with all of the employees who work in the organization.

    B. encompasses organizational learning, employee development, and training and development.

    C. includes workforce planning, leadership development, and performance management.

    D. impacts an organization's strategic planning goals under a shared vision.

    E. All of the above

33. HRD is an organized system in the workplace designed to

   A. integrate the strategic goals of the organization through the ongoing development of its employees.

   B. train its employees.

   C. diagnose training problems in the workplace.

   D. create training programs that ensure compliance with employment laws and regulations.

   E. None of the above

34. A strategic HRD alliance with the organization encompasses all of the following key concepts *EXCEPT*

   A. organizational development, organizational learning, and training and development.

   B. needs assessment, job analysis, talent management, and performance appraisals.

   C. career and leadership development, employee behavior, and motivation theory.

   D. None of the above

   E. All of the above

35. HRD is regarded as a carefully planned functional system in the HRM matrix that is responsible for

   A. nonlegal requirements directly impacting the organization.

   B. complying with federal employment legislation, copyright laws, patent laws, and other legal requirements that directly impact the organizational community.

   C. the organization's culture, shared vision, goals and objectives, and strategic planning.

   D. communicating legal requirements impacting federal employment legislation, state laws, and government regulations before any HRD planning can take place.

   E. Both B and D

36. It is HRD's responsibility to ensure that all activities performed in the organization comply with federal regulations designed to

   A. protect workers in employment settings with more than 25 employees.

   B. guarantee nondiscrimination in employment.

   C. protect workers under conditions of employment under Title VII.

   D. foster trust and ongoing development of its employees in work settings.

   E. All of the above

37. To understand how employment decisions are made, federal legislation governing HRD activities must be known. Federal legislation in employment settings includes

   A. the Civil Rights Act (1964).

   B. Title VII.

   C. laws affecting members of protected groups.

   D. laws enforcing nondiscrimination and deterring decisions based on race, color, religion, sex, or national origin.

   E. All of the above

38. The Civil Rights Act created the enforcement agencies that regulate compliance. They are the

   A. Equal Employment Opportunity Commission (EEOC) and the Office of Federal Contract Compliance Programs (OFCCP).

   B. OFCCP and the U.S. Department of Labor.

   C. EEOC and the Americans with Disabilities Act (ADA).

   D. OFCCP and the ADA.

   E. None of the above

39. The U.S. Department of Labor enforces the provisions of the EEOC. Organizations covered under the EEOC include

   A. organizations employing more than 15 employees for every workday of 20 or more weeks in a current or preceding calendar year.

   B. federal, state, and local governments.

   C. public and private educational institutions.

   D. employment agencies, labor unions with more than 15 members, and joint labor and management committees formed for apprenticeships and training.

   E. All of the above

40. An important feature of the Civil Rights Act includes specific record-keeping and reporting requirements for all employers. Employment records can be requested by

   A. the EEOC or OFCCP.

   B. employers meeting certain qualifications, who are required to file an annual report to the EEOC by September 30 of each year.

   C. the U.S. Department of Labor.

   D. Both A and C

   E. None of the above

41. Information shared in this required report includes

   A. specific employment data, such as employment selection practices and benefits planning.

   B. race, ethnicity, and gender statistics.

   C. disciplinary actions and promotion programs.

   D. attrition and retention figures.

   E. All of the above

42. A federal agency created by Congress in 1913, this agency serves to protect workers, job applicants, and retirees in the United States and serves as the umbrella agency overseeing laws pertaining to workers.

    A. OFCCP
    B. DOL
    C. EEOC
    D. All of the above
    E. None of the above

43. When differences in state laws exist from state to state and federal law differs from local government requirements, conflicts in the law regarding the same topic or issue will *MOST* often be resolved

    A. where the law favors the employee.
    B. where the higher standard exists.
    C. where exceptions in the law allow for discrimination to take place.
    D. on a case by case basis.
    E. All of the above

44. Exceptions in employment law include all of the following *EXCEPT*

    A. Bona fide occupational qualification (BFOQ)
    B. business necessity.
    C. seniority system(s).
    D. ADA.
    E. A, B, and C

45. Which exception below allows an employer to exclude some applicants on the basis of a specific job requirement?

    A. BFOQ.
    B. Business necessity
    C. Seniority system(s)
    D. Americans with Disabilities Act
    E. None of the above

46. Which exception below describes a condition where an employer requires an applicant with a specific background to fill an important position in an organization?

    A. BFOQ
    B. Business necessity
    C. Seniority system(s)
    D. ADA
    E. All of the above

47. When is it okay to base a decision on seniority?

    A. When the employee is old and needs to retire
    B. When the employee will be terminated for insubordination
    C. When the situation regards conditions of length of service to an organization
    D. When the employee is selected for a promotion or start-up project or has won an age-related class action suit against the company
    E. All of the above

48. Which agency below was created to monitor the activities of federal contractor programs under Executive Order 11246, mandating that federal contractors holding $10,000 or more (up to $50,000) in contracts must comply under Title VII?

   A. Office of Federal Contract Compliance Programs (OFCCP)

   B. Department of Defense (DOD)

   C. Equal Employment Opportunity Commission (EEOC)

   D. Department of Labor (DOL)

   E. None of the above

49. Employee selection is a planning function implemented by a human resource department. The process of searching for qualified job applicants is guided and facilitated by

   A. OD.

   B. HRIS.

   C. compensation and benefits.

   D. HRD.

   E. None of the above

50. Selection tests are used to identify the most qualified job candidates for a job. The practice and use of selection procedures are closely monitored by

   A. the EEOC and the OFCCP to ensure that discrimination and unfair hiring practices do not take place.

   B. the DOL to ensure that exceptions are allowed.

   C. the Uniformed Services Employment and Reemployment Rights Act (USERRA) of 1994.

   D. the HR director.

   E. All of the above

51. Laws that protect applicants in selection procedures include the following:

   A. Uniformed Services Employment and Reemployment Rights Act (USERRA)

   B. Age Discrimination in Employment Act (ADEA)

   C. Fair Labor Standards Act (FLSA)

   D. Older Workers' Benefit Protection Act (OWBPA)

   E. All of the above

52. Age Discrimination in Employment Act (ADEA), passed in 1976, prohibits discrimination against any person

   A. over 50 years of age.

   B. over 40 years of age.

   C. under 62 years of age.

   D. Both A and B

   E. None of the above

53. In a union environment, ADEA is enforced on unions with the following:

   A. 99 members or more

   B. Fewer than 25 members

   C. More than 25 members

   D. At least 50 members

   E. It depends on the union bargaining agreement.

54. The Americans with Disabilities Act (ADA) of 1990, based on the Rehabilitation Act of 1973, serves to protect qualified workers with disabilities. The act prevents discrimination by requiring that employers provide reasonable accommodations to qualified workers, including adjusting job requirements to fit the needs of the disability. Whether to accommodate is determined by assessing the

    A. undue hardship rule in terms of the employer's resources.

    B. reasonable accommodation request.

    C. excessive burden placed upon the disabled employee.

    D. employee's disability.

    E. None of the above

55. Common law is associated with HRD as a result of unfair labor practices requiring legal decisions by law judges. Common law doctrines were written as the result of unfair labor practices adjudicated over

    A. centuries.

    B. collective bargaining agreements.

    C. congressional acts.

    D. the past 50 years.

    E. None of the above

56. Common law doctrines are concerned with the

    A. employment relationship.

    B. employer relationship.

    C. policies concerning nondiscrimination.

    D. All of the above

    E. None of the above

57. Examples of common law doctrines include all of the following *EXCEPT*

    A. fraudulent misrepresentation, defamation, duty of good faith, and fair dealing.

    B. employment at will and express and implied contracts.

    C. promissory estoppel, *respondeat superior*, sexual harassment, and constructive discharge.

    D. All of the above

    E. None of the above

58. Common law doctrines ensure that once a job candidate becomes an employee, the employee will be properly trained by participating in a company-paid or company-sponsored training and development program. Training programs must be designed to

    A. facilitate positive working relationships with peers.

    B. serve, protect, and train employees with the knowledge, skills, and abilities (KSAs) required to perform the job.

    C. be performed in a safe environment where third parties (employees) are not harmed.

    D. generate profit for the organization.

    E. A, B, and C

59. If improper training exists and injury to a third party occurs,

    A. liability to the employer exists under the law for negligent (or no) training.

    B. the burden is on the employee to prove negligence.

    C. the burden is on the employer to prove compliance.

    D. there is no liability if an employee signs a "do not sue" contract at the time of hiring.

    E. None of the above

60. Federal legislation governing HRD training activities and written materials associated with training and development publications includes

    A. the Copyright Act (1976).

    B. patents.

    C. employer-owned copyright material.

    D. work-for-hire exceptions.

    E. All of the above

61. U.S. patents are divided into three types:

    A. Art patents, plant patents, and utility patents

    B. Technology patents, art patents, and design patents

    C. Utility patents, plant patents, and design patents

    D. Design patents, manufacturing patents, and technology patents

    E. None of the above

62. Organizational development (OD) is an HRD systems function designed to

    A. integrate human resources, a company's organizational structure, business technology, work processes, and strategic plans.

    B. examine how an organization integrates its employees and management teams to accomplish the goals of the organization.

    C. define an organization's culture according to how systems, groups, and individuals work together.

    D. All of the above

    E. None of the above

63. Organizational culture is defined by

    A. the work environment.

    B. leadership style.

    C. management groups.

    D. motivation.

    E. All of the above

64. Organizational climate inspires or inhibits employee motivation. OD derives its philosophy from this model and is based on the belief that

    A. motivated employees perform at peak productivity when organizations consider the needs of their employees.

    B. job satisfaction is the key to employee performance.

    C. salary is a key factor in employee performance.

    D. All of the above

    E. None of the above

65. Job satisfaction surveys have consistently demonstrated that

    A. salary is the most important motivator regarding job satisfaction.

    B. satisfied employees desire work that is challenging, respected, and valued.

    C. employees are less concerned with the amount of money they earn when they feel included in the organization.

    D. shared commitment and trust are not important job satisfiers.

    E. Both B and C

66. OD interventions are designed to gather information about a situation known to be the root cause of an organizational issue and its resolution. An OD intervention can be defined as a solution to a problem, process, action plan, resolution, structure, technological issue, or strategic error. The goal of an OD intervention is

    A. to enact change management through shared knowledge, also known as knowledge management.

    B. to create opportunities as a learning organization.

    C. to resolve the situation through its human capital (employees).

    D. All of the above

    E. None of the above

67. Change management theory is

    A. an OD process that introduces a strategic change in the way a former process was carried out.

    B. a strategic management process.

    C. a solution to a problem.

    D. an intervention of change management.

    E. None of the above

68. OD/HRD strategic interventions concern

    A. individuals who work in the organization.

    B. how the work is processed through its human capital.

    C. interventions carefully designed to move the organization forward to meet its goals and objectives.

    D. All of the above

    E. None of the above

69. OD/HRD strategic programs include all of the following *EXCEPT*

    A. affirmative action programs.

    B. hiring practices and selection procedures.

    C. job satisfaction, performance management, and reward systems.

    D. programs that resolve issues in the organization regarding its human capital.

    E. None of the above

70. Two types of OD intervention programs that include quality are total quality management (TQM) and techno-structural interventions. Techno-structural interventions analyze

    A. how work is conducted in the organization and how employees are involved in the work flow process.

    B. all of the resources available to accomplish work tasks.

    C. the input and contribution of all employees.

    D. interventions designed to involve employees at all levels in the workforce.

    E. None of the above

71. The quality movement was started in the 1940s by

A. Joseh M. Juran.

B. Japanese leaders.

C. W. Edwards Deming.

D. American workers who believed that quality is defined by the consumer.

E. Dr. Kaoru Ishikawa.

72. Deming proposed a 14-point plan that focused on

A. performance issues in American companies.

B. management's responsibility to be accountable for work outcomes and internal systems within the organization.

C. manufacturing issues in Japanese organizations.

D. quality circles.

E. motivating employees with leadership opportunities.

73. Joseph M. Juran supported the quality movement and proposed the idea that

A. quality is driven by customer needs and customer satisfaction.

B. a consumer language could be built into the organization's value system to produce quality products and services.

C. motivation should be driven by customer satisfaction.

D. Both A and B

E. All of the above

74. The Juran Trilogy identifies which three phases of the quality process?

A. Quality, planning, and control

B. Planning, control, and improvements

C. Quality control, worker motivation, and consumer satisfaction

D. Management support, worker motivation, and quality circles

E. Planning, control, and worker satisfaction

75. Dr. Kaoru Ishikawa, a significant contributor to the quality movement, is known for creating

A. the language of analytical tools used to assess work flow and work processes.

B. the seven tools of quality.

C. the needs of the consumer.

D. Both A and C

E. Both A and B

76. A tool designed by Dr. Kaoru Ishikawa for analyzing process dispersion illustrates the main cause leading to its effect; it is a cause-and-effect diagram. It is *MOST* easily recognized as a

A. fish bone chart resembling a fish skeleton.

B. check sheet designed to interpret work flow.

C. flowchart designed to demonstrate relationships between planned performance and actual performance.

D. graph comparing performance with precomputed data.

E. None of the above

KAPLAN

77. A graph showing contiguous vertical bars representing a frequency distribution of items on the *x*-axis against the number of items on the *y*-axis is called a

    A. Pareto chart
    B. histogram
    C. scatter chart
    D. work flow distribution
    E. All of the above

78. A graphic tool used to rank causes from most significant to least significant is termed a

    A. cause-and-effect diagram.
    B. scatter plot.
    C. Pareto chart.
    D. 80/20 principle.
    E. Peter principle.

79. Training and development is an HRD function that seeks to meet the needs of the organization by designing programs and tools around

    A. the organizational goals and objectives.
    B. the training needs of the workforce.
    C. strategic planning.
    D. organizational outputs.
    E. All of the above

80. Motivation theory is a psychological construct used in the workplace to

    A. train and develop employees to be productive workers.
    B. support the ambitions of motivated workers.
    C. identify ways to motivate high-potential employees.
    D. assist supervisors in the hiring and selection process.
    E. All of the above

81. In terms of linking motivational theory to OD and training and development programs, which early theory is *MOST* noted for emphasizing worker productivity, labor relations, and management practices?

    A. Change process theory
    B. Expectancy theory
    C. Theory X & Y
    D. Job characteristics model
    E. Self-efficacy/social cognitive theory

82. Training programs are designed to address

    A. short-term goals that address technical or immediate needs in the organization.
    B. development programs designed to meet long-term goals for long-range planning.
    C. both short-term needs and long-term goals.
    D. compliance programs designed to meet employment laws and regulations governing employee rights.
    E. All of the above

83. The ADDIE model describes five sequential steps or phases in the training program development process. Which of the following steps is *NOT* included in the model?

A. Step 1: Analysis phase—Identify problem or situation, gather data, and set target goals for the training program.

B. Step 2: Design phase—Identify target audience, level of training, and type of training, and establish training objectives.

C. Step 3: Development phase—Design phase is translated into a presentation model and format, training materials are developed, and means of program delivery are decided.

D. Step 4: Instructional method phase—Facility and trainers are selected and meet to determine best training method for the program.

E. Step 5: Evaluation phase—Has transfer of training goals been achieved?

84. Training and development is an ongoing organizational process primarily designed to

A. facilitate new knowledge, skills, and abilities (KSAs) for employees.

B. remain competitive in the marketplace.

C. describe the process of an organization's commitment to train its employees.

D. integrate the organization's talent management with the goals and objectives of the organization.

E. All of the above

85. The goal of a learning organization is to

A. share knowledge within the organizational community about internal and external events.

B. seek knowledge that is current, relevant to the business, innovative, and responsive to environmental events.

C. impact its ability to function effectively.

D. All of the above

E. Both A and B

86. Knowledge management (KM) is the process of

A. integrating and sharing information across departments, divisions, and locations.

B. designing cross-functional teams to implement KM by sharing relevant knowledge and distributing it across departments and locations in a hierarchal system., depending on the size of the organization.

C. distributing relevant data throughout the organization.

D. All of the above

E. None of the above

87. A recent event where KM was implemented effectively using cross-functional teams organized across multiple departments was

A. Hurricane Katrina.

B. the San Diego fires of 2007.

C. 9/11.

D. the NYSE.

E. Microsoft Corporation.

88. In a day-to-day operation, a learning organization's primary objective is to

    A. create cross-functional teams that are well organized.

    B. integrate organizational goals and remain competitive in the market-place.

    C. achieve an optimum level of informational exchange where properly trained employees are motivated to bring new information to an organization.

    D. contribute shared knowledge.

    E. Both B and C

89. Attracting and retaining competent, motivated employees and identifying high-potential employees for future high-level positions in the organization is

    A. a key priority in HRD.

    B. a concern in today's learning organization.

    C. a competitive way to attract high-level talent and establish a record of success.

    D. a way to develop and maintain high-performance work teams that move the organization forward.

    E. Both A and D

90. *Employee development* (ED) is a general term used to describe

    A. the professional development of an organization's employees.

    B. career planning for employees.

    C. career development programs designed to attract high-potential talent management.

    D. Both A and C

    E. All of the above

91. Next-generation managers, supervisors, leaders, and key decision makers are

    A. an important strategic goal in HRD.

    B. the sole responsibility of the HRD department.

    C. invited to work closely with HRD to implement strategic staffing programs.

    D. trained to perform jobs assigned to other workers, managers, and supervisors.

    E. Both A and C

92. Training and development programs are designed around

    A. organizational goals and objectives.

    B. job skills training.

    C. supervisory training.

    D. management development training.

    E. any number of topics that may be relevant to the organization's strategic goals and operating plan.

93. Training program development takes place after conducting a needs analysis, or needs assessment. A needs analysis is conducted to determine

    A. if a training program will help the organization achieve its goals.

    B. the viability of the organization's overall strategic plan.

    C. if dollars spent to design and implement a training program have been cost-effective.

    D. whether a training program should move forward to its design phase.

    E. None of the above

94. The design phase of a training and development program includes all of the following *EXCEPT*

    A. the process used to establish the goals and objectives of the training program.

    B. the decision as to whether a training program should move forward to the design phase.

    C. the determination of the audience for training.

    D. the consideration of how training will take place.

    E. the targeting of how development of the program will be completed and by whom.

95. The program development phase considers the organization's

    A. entire workforce, even if only a select group will be trained.

    B. select supervisors in the identified unit or department and whether they should be initially trained.

    C. HiPos and other identified employees.

    D. strategic mission and values.

    E. Both A and D

96. An organization's training and development of its human capital

    A. is a dynamic, often complex mix of variables successfully achieved through careful planning and development.

    B. includes careful planning and a construct known as an *employee value proposition,* a term used to describe the characteristics of a job and the experiences that attract and retain motivated, high-potential employees.

    C. is a key initiative for the organization at large.

    D. is shared by the team members who must continue to develop and mentor its new team member(s).

    E. None of the above

97. A controversial dynamic between HRD, its training department, and the department where the employee performs the job is called

    A. KSAs.

    B. KM.

    C. transfer of training.

    D. TQM.

    E. synchronous learning.

98. It has been argued that training and development programs are a waste of time and money because

    A. employees complete training and are unable to transfer new skills to the job.

    B. management complains of time and money spent.

    C. management expectations are unrealistic.

    D. supervisors are inexperienced mentors.

    E. None of the above

99. Training methods run the gamut from classroom or seminar training to e-learning and experiential training. Training methods and program materials used to deliver training programs include all of the following *EXCEPT*

    A. active training methods such as case study, facilitation, simulation, Socratic seminar (Q&A), and vestibule.

    B. passive training methods such as conference, lecture, and/or presentation-style formats.

    C. email methods such as synchronous, asynchronous, or live e-instruction.

    D. experiential training such as demonstration, one-on-one, and performance.

    E. All of the above

100. Program delivery methods for training and development programs do *NOT* include

    A. training taking place at a nearby location, on-site or off-site.

    B. blended learning.

    C. distance learning.

    D. self-instruction.

    E. EPSS.

101. Simulation training is interactive training where participants may practice learning new skills

    A. before returning to the actual job site or location.

    B. via computer, online, or in some other format.

    C. in a safe environment.

    D. both on the job and off the job.

    E. Both A and C

102. Employment involvement programs (EIPs) fill an important need in the organizational community. Unique benefits derived from EIPs include the

    A. encouragement of employee involvement and commitment to the organization.

    B. increase in human capital commitments to organizational goals.

    C. seeking of feedback from employees and input into organizational decision making.

    D. Both A and B

    E. None of the above

103. Examples of EIPs include all of the following *EXCEPT*

   A. reward incentives.

   B. company-sponsored group activities.

   C. nonpolitical contributions.

   D. company-paid education.

   E. wellness programs.

104. The primary purpose of developing a high-performance work system is to

   A. create high-performance work teams.

   B. involve employees directly in productivity programs.

   C. improve company processes, products, and services.

   D. create self-directed work teams.

   E. None of the above

105. Determining if a training program achieved its desired goal(s) is an important HRD outcome. The comparison of a program's cost-benefit analysis to its desired goals is evaluated as

   A. the gap between a program's desired outcome versus its actual impact.

   B. differences between program costs and benefits gained.

   C. the impact of transfer of training skills and program outcomes.

   D. All of the above

   E. None of the above

106. The goal of any training program is to

   A. improve performance of a job function.

   B. directly impact the strategic goals of an organization.

   C. facilitate knowledge needed to perform a job and develop the required skills and abilities to carry it out (KSAs).

   D. apply what was learned in a training program to the actual job.

   E. All of the above

107. Program evaluation is a training and development process for

   A. determining program success and improvements.

   B. assessing effective (or ineffective) training program outcomes.

   C. supporting the objectives of the training program.

   D. measuring the design phase through the outcome phase.

108. The best known four-step model for specifically measuring training program outcomes was developed by

   A. W. Deming.

   B. R. Brinkerhoff.

   C. Harvard School of Management.

   D. Kirkpatrick.

   E. J. Juran.

109. The Kirkpatrick model of program evaluation is designed around a four-step approach. Measurement at each level is designed to

    A. support the objectives of the training program during its initial design phase through the final outcome phase.

    B. evaluate participants' reaction to the training program but not its organizational impact.

    C. determine if transfer of training occurred on the job.

    D. compare initial training objective(s) to actual results over a specified period of time.

110. Program evaluation data may be collected from a number of sources. It is typically derived from which three groups?

    A. Work groups, training facilitators, and supervisors

    B. Participants, training facilitators, and management

    C. Separate divisions of an organization, comparing each group to itself and other groups

    D. Individual data, group data, and senior management data

    E. None of the above

111. Data collection is gathered using the following methods *EXCEPT*

    A. interviews.

    B. surveys.

    C. questionnaires.

    D. check sheets.

    E. in-person data gathering.

112. Learning data is usually collected following a course, test, or demonstration. For example, if an organization requires ethics education training, the course may be facilitated online, and an online completion exam will be a requirement of the course. The *BEST* learning data method used to determine successful completion of the course would be

    A. pre/post-measure.

    B. post-measure.

    C. experimental design.

    D. quasi-experimental design.

    E. All of the above

113. The primary reason for using an experimental or quasi-experimental design is to allow for

    A. the collection of anecdotal information that may be valuable.

    B. flexibility in the research.

    C. more data to be collected and analyzed to explore information in more depth.

    D. the inclusion of a control group.

    E. All of the above

114. Performance management is an ongoing system of

    A. performance coaching.

    B. employee feedback about the jobs they perform in the workplace.

    C. assisting employees to become effective contributors in the organization.

    D. identifying employee performance problems early so they are more likely to be corrected.

    E. All of the above

115. Performance feedback is usually given by

    A. an employee's direct report.

    B. the person in charge of the work group where the employee performs the job.

    C. a manager.

    D. a supervisor.

    E. A, C, and D

116. Who is responsible for training managers and supervisors how to implement performance management programs effectively?

    A. HRD

    B. HRM

    C. Payroll

    D. A department head

    E. None of the above

117. The difference between performance management and performance coaching is

    A. the difference between actual performance and performance demonstrated from the previous year.

    B. the difference between required performance and actual performance.

    C. the difference between developing employees strengths and addressing weaknesses.

    D. the difference between actual performance and employee development.

    E. the difference between performance goals and performance objectives.

118. Performance appraisals are *MOST* often used as

    A. a documentation feedback system that assesses job performance in a written format.

    B. feedback shared between a supervisor and an employee in a formal meeting.

    C. performance evaluations and performance reviews.

    D. a measure to more fully assess an employee's work performance over time.

    E. a gauge to assess employees for promotions.

119. The performance appraisal process is typically comprised of

    A. a prepublished guide that can be purchased by a company to implement a performance appraisal system.

    B. several steps carried out by HRM and implemented by department managers.

    C. carefully constructed preplanned activities taking place well in advance of the actual performance review.

    D. training all employees so that a consistent system can be put into place.

    E. All of the above

120. A variety of appraisal methods can be selected for the performance review, but the method selected is the decision of

    A. a key decision maker, such as an HR director, who may present several methods to an executive committee.

    B. senior management that votes on the method best suited for the organization.

    C. HRD.

    D. each department head.

    E. All of the above

121. Exceptions in the performance appraisal process may be that

    A. an employee is terminated for cause, requiring an exit interview.

    B. different methods are selected for different levels of leadership.

    C. different methods are used for hourly employees than salaried employees.

    D. a performance appraisal may be given for extenuating circumstances, such as a promotion or a demotion.

    E. B, C, and D

122. The appraisal method can take many forms *EXCEPT*

    A. paper/pencil tools.

    B. a casual conversation taking place between an employee and a supervisor.

    C. computer-driven and scored applications.

    D. a written format, such as MBO, that includes goals and objectives.

    E. All of the above

123. Examples of specific assessment methods include all of the following *EXCEPT*

    A. short forms.

    B. checklists.

    C. comparisons.

    D. rankings or rating scales.

    E. All of the above

124. Narratives describe an employee's performance in written form and can take the form of a(n)

    A. critical incident.

    B. essay.

    C. field review.

    D. All of the above

    E. None of the above

125. While critical incidents discuss specific performance issues, essays allow greater flexibility. However, the evaluator must be cautious about

    A. providing proper documentation.

    B. what is written about an employee.

    C. whether or not it is a field review.

    D. the confidentiality of feedback derived and shared.

    E. None of the above

126. A 360-degree evaluation is designed to gather feedback from an employee's

    A.   social circle at work.

    B.   work group.

    C.   direct report, coworkers, and any or all other workers with whom an employee comes into contact on the job.

    D.   coworkers who give feedback about the employee and how the employee carries out the responsibilities of the job.

    E.   Both C and D

127. In some performance appraisal methods, ratings and feedback are combined to arrive at a numeric score to calculate a performance rating. The rating scale identifies

    A.   an overall summary score.

    B.   a score used to determine salary increases.

    C.   if performance levels were achieved.

    D.   All of the above

    E.   None of the above

128. The need for proper documentation is an important consideration in the performance review process. If improper documentation is recorded on a performance review at a government-contracted agency, or if a heated argument takes place during the review meeting, the end result may be action taken against the organization in the form of

    A.   an investigation.

    B.   a business shutdown.

    C.   wrongful termination.

    D.   cancellation of the contract.

    E.   All of the above

129. A large organization with many divisions may house its own career development department. The primary focus of career development is to

    A.   identify high-potential employees who can be developed for managerial or leadership positions.

    B.   identify applicants and employees who demonstrate high performance and commitment to organizational goals and objectives.

    C.   identify selected employees who need to work with a coach or mentor.

    D.   Both A and B

    E.   All of the above

130. The difference between an internal coach and mentor is that

    A.   the coach can be a "thought partner" to an employee while a mentor cannot.

    B.   the mentor acts as a guide, or teacher, on the job, and a coach assists the employee with goal setting.

    C.   the mentor works with the employee for the purpose of career development planning while the coach remains neutral.

    D.   a mentor performs the same job as an employee, and the coach performs a different job.

    E.   None of the above

131. Career development recruiters search outside the organization to find high-potential employees, using job fairs, college campus searches, and other

    A. competitive distribution methods.

    B. ad agencies.

    C. online resources.

    D. print media.

    E. None of the above

132. As businesses expand into global markets and alliances formed to create business opportunities, HRM encounters many challenges and opportunities *EXCEPT*

    A. the Internet has played a major role in expanding business opportunities abroad.

    B. more multicultural differences exist now that employees communicate globally.

    C. work ethics, language barriers, communication networks, email, and other business initiatives have different conceptual meanings.

    D. interpreting differences within the organizational community so they are not miscommunicated or misinterpreted across organizational boundaries.

    E. None of the above

133. Diversity is a key issue in every organization, and diversity awareness seeks to

    A. have employees embrace cultural differences..

    B. encourage open communication.

    C. ensure that cultural discrimination does not take place within the organizational community.

    D. offer diversity training as a mandatory training initiative in most organizations.

134. Expatriates are workers

    A. who work for an organization overseas.

    B. who work in a country outside of the United States.

    C. who are U.S. citizens who work abroad.

    D. who accept overseas assignments in special circumstances.

    E. and their families who live abroad.

135. Repatriation concerns

    A. adjustment issues when employees return from an overseas job assignment.

    B. adjustment issues when families of employees return to the United States from an overseas assignment.

    C. applying for work visas in a foreign country.

    D. administrative paperwork when employees return from an overseas job assignment.

    E. All of the above

136. HRD is an integral part of HRM and serves to develop

    A. human resource team members.

    B. new employees who need to be trained.

    C. employees identified for training and development as part of talent management, and other promotable employees.

    D. the entire organizational community.

    E. None of the above

137. OD's function is to analyze change in the organization and how organizational systems are integrated in conjunction with the goals and objectives of the business. OD operates to understand and diagnose

    A. problems in the organization relating to its structure.

    B. threats in the organization relating to its competitive environment.

    C. systems in the organization relating to its structure, strategic plan, operations, and technology.

    D. how people and systems work together in the organization.

    E. Both C and D

138. HRD's role is to provide training and development to the organization's employees, and OD's role is to diagnose organizational structures and systems working together. HRD and OD combine efforts to support

    A. training employees and managing and designing management development and leadership programs in a competitive marketplace.

    B. theories of motivation which align with the organization and its strategic goals so that proper training and development programs can be identified.

    C. human capital initiatives and key objectives in the HRD process.

    D. training and development of human capital that supports key initiatives in the organization.

    E. Both A and B

139. The ADDIE model is an acronym for

    A. analysis, design, development, implementation, and estimation.

    B. analysis, design, development, implementation, and evaluation.

    C. analysis, discussion, design, implementation, and estimation.

    D. analysis, development, discussion, implementation, and evaluation.

    E. All of the above

140. The ADDIE model is used in HRD, OD, and other departments where a training program is needed. Several key developers work together to create a design and its final implementation. The model is *MOST* often identified with

    A. HRD development specialists.
    B. training and development instructors.
    C. instructional designers.
    D. None of the above
    E. All of the above

141. The ADDIE model is *MOST* often used because it

    A. represents a dynamic interaction based upon flexible guidelines for building effective training and development tools.
    B. is an instruction system design (ISD) model based on continuous feedback and flexibility to adapt training goals while meeting the needs of the organization and its employees.
    C. allows for formative feedback while instructional materials are being created.
    D. attempts to save time and money by identifying training problems while they are relatively simple to fix.
    E. is designed to use observational evaluation of training methods as a guideline to measure training program effectiveness as its final outcome.

142. Which step of the ADDIE model is described below?

    "Training program content assets were created in the design phase. Programmers worked to develop and integrate technologies needed to roll out the training program. Test developers performed technological feedback and monitoring of training procedures. The project was reviewed and revised according to feedback given by managers, supervisors, and employees enrolled in the program."

    A. Analysis
    B. Design
    C. Development
    D. Implementation
    E. Evaluation

143. The *MOST* successful training programs are evaluated by

    A. transfer of training.
    B. feedback from supervisors.
    C. how many employees successfully complete the training program.
    D. feedback from employees who completed the training program.
    E. the ADDIE model.

144. Title VII of the Civil Rights Act (1964) was designed to

    A. guarantee equal employment opportunity for all eligible persons applying for a job.
    B. make businesses accountable for disparate impact on and nondiscrimination toward protected classes.
    C. guarantee nondiscrimination in employment toward applicants and employees on the basis of race, color, national origin, religion, and sex.
    D. All of the above
    E. None of the above

145. Illegal employment discrimination may occur when

   A.   employers single out applicants on the basis of age, race, creed, disability, national origin, religion, military duty, sex, or gender.

   B.   employers, employment agencies, unions, or any organization hires a job candidate in a way that results in employment discrimination.

   C.   antidiscrimination laws are enforced at the federal level by the U.S. Equal Employment Opportunity Commission (EEOC) but ignored at the state level.

   D.   employers discriminate among job applicants or employees if the job can only be filled by a male or female.

   E.   All of the above.

146. Discrimination may take place in all of the following employment areas *EXCEPT*

   A.   promotions.

   B.   company benefits.

   C.   company perks.

   D.   medical accommodations.

   E.   None of the above

147. Employment discrimination can occur toward employees in all of the relationships or situations described below *EXCEPT*

   A.   vendor to employee.

   B.   employee to employee.

   C.   supervisor to direct report.

   D.   a change in benefits.

   E.   None of the above

148. Antidiscrimination laws may intersect or conflict at the federal and state level. In cases where employment laws conflict, which standard is the employer obligated to follow?

   A.   Only federal law

   B.   Only state law

   C.   Only laws of the state where the organization has its business license

   D.   Either federal or state law

   E.   Whichever law imposes the higher standard

149. Extraordinary situations may occur when an employer is singling out an employee for reason(s) that could be considered illegal but, in fact, are not prohibited by law. In those cases, employees are

   A.   protected by law.

   B.   not protected from employment discrimination.

   C.   may be protected or may not be—it depends on the situation.

   D.   All of the above

   E.   None of the above

150. When a supervisor wants to terminate an employee due to a personality conflict that interferes with the day-to-day operations of the business or interferes with the morale of the department, it is

    A. unlikely that this action would be considered employment discrimination.

    B. subjective and considered a biased action under the law.

    C. unlikely that this action would be considered discrimination, since no specific provisions under law discuss personality conflicts.

    D. not discrimination, because personality conflicts are legal under federal discrimination exceptions.

    E. None of the above

151. Discrimination laws were enacted largely to protect

    A. employers.

    B. employees and employers.

    C. employees.

    D. employers' rights to safeguard the protection and continuation of the business.

    E. All of the above

152. The employment-at-will doctrine serves to protect the employer and employee in matters of termination, firing, and

    A. discrimination in employment.

    B. giving notice to terminate employment.

    C. not giving notice to terminate employment.

    D. Both A and C

    E. Both B and C

153. The at-will doctrine was created by common law and designed to cover all states. Common law is

    A. a body of knowledge based on court cases and their outcomes.

    B. the outcome that establishes a precedent where all states enforce the doctrine under the common law principle.

    C. based on case law and establishes precedence at the state level.

    D. decided at the federal level.

    E. a guideline used when deciding how to terminate an employee.

154. According to the common law doctrine, in the absence of an employment contract or employment agreement,

    A. employees or employers may terminate employment using the two-week notice rule.

    B. employees and employers may terminate employment without notice or cause.

    C. employees and employers may terminate employment with cause to prevent future lawsuits.

    D. employers may terminate employment for any reason.

    E. employees may terminate employment with or without cause.

155. When the at-will doctrine includes specific provisions as to how a termination is to be carried out,

    A. it is a violation of the employment contract or agreement to disregard the law, ignore regulations, or violate constitutional provisions of public policy as written in the doctrine when terminating employment.

    B. employment is at will; therefore, employees and employers may terminate employment at any time and without notice.

    C. employees must carry out provisions of the at-will agreement, but employers may terminate an employee at any time for just cause.

    D. employers and employees may not violate any provision of the agreement unless it is known that discrimination has taken place.

    E. All of the above

156. Separately from the employment-at-will- doctrine, employment contracts and employment agreements may specifically state how a resignation is to be carried out. If a resignation is not carried out according to the employment agreement, employers have discretion to

    A. withhold accrued benefits such as sick leave, vacation pay, and bonuses.

    B. deny an employee's final paycheck.

    C. deny benefits according to provisions described in the employment agreement.

    D. pay benefits upon termination.

    E. All of the above

157. It is considered standard practice for employees

    A. not to give notice under the at-will doctrine because it is not required.

    B. to give at least two weeks' notice to an employer prior to an actual termination date.

    C. to allow two weeks lead time so the employer can decide if the employee should be persuaded to stay.

    D. to give notice, unless the employee has a high position in the company.

    E. to give notice so the employer may decide whether or not to terminate the employee.

158. The requirement to give notice of terminating employment was established by the

    A. Worker Adjustment and Retraining Notification (WARN) Act

    B. Civil Rights Act of 1964

    C. Age Discrimination in Employment Act (ADEA)

    D. Americans with Disabilities Act (ADA)

    E. Civil Rights Act of 1990

159. Which of the following three specific exceptions are well known and described in the employment-at-will doctrine?

    A. Public policy, implied contract, and Americans with disabilities

    B. Public policy, implied contract, and covenant of good faith and fair dealing

    C. WARN Act, ADEA, and BFOQ

    D. None of the above

    E. All of the above

160. Standards, values, and principles that the court considers to be in the best interest of an individual and the general public

    A. fall under the public policy provision in the employment-at-will doctrine.

    B. are implied in the employment contract.

    C. refer to the covenant of good faith and fair dealing.

    D. refer to all three exceptions to the employment-at-will doctrine.

    E. have nothing to do with the employment-at-will doctrine.

161. An implied contract under the employment-at-will doctrine is recognized as an implied-in-fact contract. This type of agreement between an employer and an employee

    A. is not explicitly documented in writing but is implicitly agreed to by all parties involved in the employment relationship.

    B. could be demonstrated in a company policy statement, employment manual, or performance review.

    C. may result from a supervisor's promise or suggestion.

    D. may result in a history of action between the employer and employee.

    E. All of the above

162. The covenant of good faith and fair dealing refers to the employer's

    A. duty to treat employees ethically, responsibly, fairly, and honestly.

    B. biased treatment of long-term employees due to age discrimination, denial of promotions, or avoidance of paying long-term rewards.

    C. obligation to treat long-term employees responsibly, preventing discrimination or unfair labor practices due to age, promotions, or illegal layoffs.

    D. maltreatment of long-term employees, denying long-term benefits, earned promotions, or bonuses.

    E. All of the above

163. All states enforce at-will employment. However,

    A. interpretation of the employment-at-will doctrine is at the discretion of the states.

    B. interpretation of the employment-at-will doctrine is at the discretion of the legislature.

    C. interpretation of the employment-at-will doctrine primarily rests with federal law.

    D. interpretation of the employment-at-will doctrine is decided by the employer.

    E. interpretation of the employment-at-will doctrine is at the discretion of the courts.

164. In a union shop, collective bargaining agreements may stipulate terms and conditions to terminate employees. Which of the following statements is TRUE?

    A. Employers may be prevented from terminating employees holding membership in the union.

    B. Employers may overrule a collective bargaining agreement if a union member brings a firearm to work.

    C. Employers may immediately suspend and/or terminate a union shop employee for just cause.

    D. Employers may not overrule a collective bargaining agreement before a hearing is held to determine whether an employee should be terminated.

    E. Both A and D

165. Under the provisions of the Age Discrimination in Employment Act (ADEA),

    A. age discrimination refers only to employees who have been terminated after age 40.

    B. employers may not fire employees age 40 or older.

    C. terminating employees for cause beyond the age of 40 is illegal.

    D. employees 40 and older are protected by law.

    E. discrimination in employment due to age is illegal.

166. Affirmative action defines discrimination that is prohibited in the workplace and

    A. describes how the employment process must be carried out according to its provisions.

    B. specifies nondiscriminatory practices in hiring, selection, and placement.

    C. excludes promotion, termination, benefits, and pay.

    D. ensures nondiscrimination in the hiring process through employer affirmative action programs.

    E. ensures equal employment opportunities for qualified workers.

167. Affirmative action programs are designed to

    A. provide equal employment opportunity for all job candidates and employees.

    B. demonstrate equal opportunity regardless of age, race, national origin, religion, sex, gender, and disability.

    C. explain employee rights if discrimination has taken place.

    D. prohibit discrimination in hiring practices and avoid expensive lawsuits.

    E. Both A and B

168. Guidelines described in affirmative action programs protect

    A. nonunion members from discrimination in employment.

    B. union members, who are exempt from an affirmative action program because of the collective bargaining agreement.

    C. all employees in the event of a shutdown of a business operation.

    D. all employees in the event of a cancellation of government contracts.

    E. None of the above

169. Affirmative action programs are designed to eliminate discrimination in employment. Examples of discrimination may include all of the following *EXCEPT*

    A. only hiring employees under the age of 25.

    B. hiring only men in a job category.

    C. excluding candidates due to national origin, race, or religion.

    D. hiring gender-specific candidates due to sexual preferences required by the job.

    E. not hiring nonclassified, unprotected job candidates for specific job categories, such as white males.

170. Age discrimination means candidate and employee selection that is specifically prohibited under age discrimination laws. Employees protected under the Age Discrimination in Employment Act (ADEA) include those

    A. who are 40 years old and equally qualified for selection as other, younger candidates.

    B. who have equivalent KSAs and experience when compared to other candidates.

    C. who may be overlooked for promotion opportunities based on age or gender.

    D. Both A and B

    E. Both B and C

171. Employees with disabilities as described under the Americans with Disabilities Act (ADA)

    A. have legal rights to be reasonably accommodated in the workplace.

    B. have rights to reasonable accommodations in the workplace that do not present a hardship to the employer or others.

    C. do not automatically qualify to be reasonably accommodated.

    D. may still be discriminated against if asked to perform work considered different than work performed by other workers in the same job category.

    E. All of the above

172. Equal pay for equal work is ensured by

    A. the Equal Pay Act of 1963.

    B. Title VII.

    C. ADEA.

    D. FLSA.

    E. the Civil Rights Act of 1964.

173. The Equal Pay Act of 1963 ensures equal pay for equal work; however, it is known that female workers frequently have lower pay as compared to males who hold the same positions and titles and perform the same job duties. This practice is considered legal when comparing

    A. pay ranges.

    B. BFOQs.

    C. promotions or title changes.

    D. similar jobs with different job classifications.

    E. All of the above

174. Family responsibility discrimination (FRD) occurs when discrimination during employment selection is directed toward

    A. candidates solely on the basis of their obligations to care for family members.

    B. females who still have young children at home.

    C. nonexempt employees.

    D. candidates for exempt jobs who will earn higher salaries.

    E. candidates who don't have the ability to work nights and weekends.

175. Harassment in the workplace can take many forms and include all of the following *EXCEPT*

    A. sexual harassment.

    B. discrimination based on gender.

    C. treatment resulting in a hostile work environment for an employee.

    D. higher work expectations for some employees over others in the same job category.

    E. None of the above

176. Sexual harassment statistics demonstrate that

    A. females are more often discriminated against due to sexual harassment by males than males are by females.

    B. harassment based on sexual preference and gender identity results in frequent workplace discrimination.

    C. discrimination activities may be covert or overt.

    D. harassment can occur away from the work environment.

    E. All of the above

177. A relatively subtle kind of harassment not always easily identified is

    A. sexual harassment.

    B. hostile work environment.

    C. sending email about an employee meant to denigrate the worker's reputation and effectiveness.

    D. setting higher expectations for one employee than for all others in the same job category.

    E. All of the above

178. A hostile work environment is a type of discrimination considered to be harassment when a worker can demonstrate that

  A. the employee is treated differently and with hostile aggression by a fellow coworker.

  B. the employee is treated differently by a direct report in a manner that suggests hostile aggression.

  C. the employee is treated differently by someone who holds power over the employee's job.

  D. a personality conflict results in perceived hostile aggression by a coworker.

  E. All of the above

179. Employees who feel discriminated against or perceive they are treated differently than other employees should do all of the following *EXCEPT*

  A. report the behavior to HR.

  B. report the behavior to a supervisor.

  C. document each incident of harassment.

  D. confront the aggressor.

  E. request a formal investigation.

180. The best way to ensure a workplace that will be free from harassment is to do all of the following *EXCEPT*

  A. develop a clearly written formal workplace harassment policy.

  B. allow workers to contact HR in a confidential manner.

  C. conduct a formal investigation.

  D. publish the results of an investigation to discourage this practice in the future.

  E. terminate the aggressor if the harassment is a violent act.

181. A formal investigation is carried out when

  A. an employee requests it.

  B. an HR director decides there is sufficient evidence to warrant an investigation.

  C. an employee has documented incidents of harassment.

  D. an employee reports harassment—all reports of harassment should be taken seriously and investigated.

  E. All of the above

182. A formal investigation should be carried out in a confidential manner by

  A. a representative from HRM.

  B. a company-selected investigator.

  C. a trusted company official.

  D. the HR director.

  E. All of the above

183. Allegations of harassment that result in a formal investigation should be

  A. immediately acted upon, with a resolution reached as quickly as possible.

  B. thoroughly investigated, possibly over several months, before reaching a conclusion.

  C. investigated by a company attorney.

  D. resolved within a two-week period.

  E. taken seriously, unless the aggressor or employee who filed the complaint leaves the company.

184. Pregnancy, childbirth, and related health conditions are protected under

    A. Title VII of the Civil Rights Act.

    B. ADA.

    C. FMLA.

    D. ADEA.

    E. WARN Act.

185. The law ensures equal treatment of an employee who is pregnant and

    A. of her spouse for the purpose of caring for a newborn.

    B. of the mother following the birth of a child.

    C. of the caregiver.

    D. None of the above

    E. All of the above

186. A company's dress code policy can be written or implied but may be considered discriminatory in all of the following conditions *EXCEPT*

    A. if it adversely impacts a particular group.

    B. if it is related to class.

    C. if it affects an individual due to age.

    D. if it affects employees differently due to national origin or religion.

    E. None of the above

187. A common error is attempting to define a dress code policy

    A. on the basis of sex.

    B. that results in different policies for each gender.

    C. that requires uniforms to be worn as a condition of employment.

    D. that requires employees to purchase uniforms to promote brand name awareness, causing the company to profit from their sale.

    E. All of the above

188. "Casual Friday" is a typical example of a dress code policy that should be

    A. clearly defined as a dress code policy by the employer, since *casual* will be interpreted differently by individual employees.

    B. clearly identified as a dress code policy.

    C. eliminated from employee handbooks.

    D. made an option and not a formal dress code policy.

    E. None of the above

189. Uniforms are considered part of the job and a condition of employment as long as

    A. the company does not profit from the sale of uniforms.

    B. uniforms are required for all employees.

    C. the company does not discriminate with regard to who may or may not wear a uniform.

    D. the uniforms do not involve gender differences.

    E. All of the above

KAPLAN

190. It is considered discriminatory to impose a dress code policy on all of the following *EXCEPT*

    A. the public that uses a company's products or services.

    B. employees of a certain gender.

    C. employees of a certain religion.

    D. when it is necessary to single out an employee for using bad judgment.

    E. employees wearing ethnic clothing.

191. Discrimination could result during the applicant-screening process when

    A. questions of an illegal nature are asked or pursued.

    B. candidate selection is based on the ability to speak English.

    C. selection is based on race or gender.

    D. All of the above

    E. None of the above

192. The following examples are considered illegal in the interviewing, selection, and hiring process *EXCEPT* when

    A. the information is voluntarily indicated in an application.

    B. a company's affirmative action plan requires it to follow hiring guidelines.

    C. American citizenship is a requirement of the job.

    D. the ability to speak another language is a requirement of the job.

    E. None of the above

193. Which question below is legal to ask in an applicant interview?

    A. When did you graduate from high school?

    B. I like your accent; do you mind sharing where you are from?

    C. Are you are eligible to work in the United States?

    D. In what part of the country were you born?

    E. May I see your driver's license to verify eligibility?

194. Favoring relatives or family members for promotions and raises may be interpreted as what, depending upon the situation?

    A. Illegal

    B. Legal

    C. Nepotism

    D. Discrimination

    E. All of the above

195. Wrongful termination may occur if an employee is terminated

    A. solely on the basis of discrimination.

    B. for attending jury duty or leaving work for a court hearing.

    C. for taking advantage of FMLA benefits.

    D. as a result of violating the company's written company policy manual.

    E. All of the above

196. Employee rights protection regarding criminal records depends on

    A. the extent to which state laws allow employers to ask about criminal records for making employment decisions.

    B. adverse decisions.

    C. a bias toward not hiring employees based on previous criminal records.

    D. Both A and C

    E. None of the above

197. Overall, employers may not disqualify job candidates *EXCEPT* under which of the following condition(s)?

    A. Solely because they have criminal records

    B. Making a job offer contingent upon the results of asking about a past juvenile criminal record

    C. On the basis of a security investigation

    D. On the basis of a background check

    E. None of the above

198. Employers have the right to ask questions about criminal records and make employment decisions based on the answers in all of the following cases *EXCEPT*

    A. the questions are limited to convictions only.

    B. when applicants are seeking law enforcement jobs.

    C. applicants are seeking mental health-related work.

    D. where security and safety is a need or concern.

    E. All of the above

199. A learning organization includes all of the following elements *EXCEPT*

    A. systems thinking.

    B. team learning.

    C. defining a shared vision.

    D. mental models.

    E. All of the above

200. Excluding a job candidate based on a prior criminal conviction

    A. must be related to the applicant's suitability to perform the job before the conviction is considered.

    B. is sometimes okay; restrictions vary by state, and some states might not enforce all provisions on employers.

    C. is sometimes okay; a few states have not imposed any restrictions on employers.

    D. is okay when it relates to workplace security issues.

    E. is okay with crimes relating to security issues for which the applicant was found to be guilty.

201. Employment-related provisions make it unlawful for employers to discriminate against employees or job applicants because of

    A. bankruptcy.

    B. any bad debts.

    C. any bankruptcy history they had before filing for bankruptcy and applying for a job.

    D. bankruptcy, divorce, or liens against their home.

    E. All of the above

202. Historically, gay and lesbian employees have found little in the law to protect them from discrimination and harassment in the workplace. However, as acceptance grows toward alternative lifestyles,

    A. employers are responsible for providing a workplace that is free from harassment.

    B. discrimination based on sexual orientation warrants a workplace investigation.

    C. alternative lifestyles remain undefined and unprotected by the law.

    D. adverse impact on the basis of affectional preference may result in discriminatory action whether or not an employee is gay or lesbian.

    E. None of the above

203. On November 7, 2007, the U.S. House of Representatives passed HR 3685, a bill that prohibits employment discrimination

    A. on the basis of sexual orientation.

    B. against gay, lesbian, and bisexual workers.

    C. against those who participate in alternative lifestyles, including divorced, separated, or married couples.

    D. Both A and B

    E. None of the above

204. If the U.S. Senate votes to pass HR 3685 and the president does not veto it, it will move forward to become a new antidiscrimination law called the

    A. Employment Discrimination Act of 2007.

    B. Employment Non-Discrimination Act of 2007.

    C. Civil Rights Act of 2007.

    D. Revised Title VII Act of 2007.

    E. Executive Order HR 3685.

205. When a private employer operates a business in a state, county, or city with an ordinance prohibiting sexual orientation discrimination,

    A. state law will prevail, and the employer must follow the law despite the fact that there is no federal law in place.

    B. federal law will prevail, and the employer must follow that law despite the fact that a state or local law is in place.

    C. the higher standard will apply, whether it is local, state, or federal law.

    D. Both A and C

    E. All of the above

206. Who or what is responsible for maintaining a workplace that is free from sexual harassment?

    A. State law

    B. The employer

    C. Federal law

    D. The HR director

    E. The legislature

207. The same laws that prohibit gender discrimination also prohibit sexual harassment. Which of the following statements is TRUE?

   A. Title VII of the Civil Rights Act is the main federal law that prohibits sexual harassment.

   B. The Civil Rights Act of 1993 prohibits sexual harassment.

   C. The Employment Non-Discrimination Act of 2007 prohibits sexual harassment.

   D. HR 3685 prohibits sexual harassment.

   E. All of the above

208. Sexual harassment is recognized as

   A. any unwelcome sexual advance by a coworker.

   B. behavior on the job that creates an intimidating, hostile, or offensive working environment.

   C. conduct of a sexual nature that makes an employee uncomfortable.

   D. various behaviors that may create a hostile work environment.

   E. All of the above

209. All of the following examples may be considered forms of sexual harassment *EXCEPT*

   A. a manager suggests to an employee that the employee will get a promotion if she has sex with the manager.

   B. An attractive office manager is encouraged to wear provocative clothing to attract more customers.

   C. Two coworkers decide to become intimate together, even though company policy discourages it.

   D. Sexually explicit emails are traded between lawyers in a law firm about their secretaries.

   E. A male restaurant manager is hostile toward the female waitresses who are overweight.

210. The harasser is identified as the person violating the policy toward another employee. The harasser can be all of the following *EXCEPT*

   A. the victim's supervisor.

   B. the victim's spouse.

   C. the victim's subordinate.

   D. a vendor or customer.

   E. a coworker.

211. Sexual harassment is considered a gender-neutral offense. Under this definition, it can be assumed that all of the following will be recognized under the provisions of Title VII *EXCEPT*

   A. males harassing females.

   B. gays harassing lesbians.

   C. females harassing males.

   D. females harassing females.

   E. males harassing gays.

212. Statistics show that the majority of sexual harassment claims and charges

    A. are brought by women who claim they were sexually harassed by men.
    B. are brought by men who claim they were sexually harassed by women.
    C. result in statistics that aren't reliable, since so many claims are never investigated.
    D. result in statistics that aren't reliable, since many women fear retaliation if they file a claim against male coworkers.
    E. result in statistics that aren't reliable, since many men don't report claims of sexual harassment.

213. The steps an HRM department may take to reduce the risk of sexual harassment include all of the following *EXCEPT*

    A. documentation, since it is not a good idea to have confidential information in a file where others may see it.
    B. not investigating claims of harassment if the victim feels threatened by the harasser.
    C. adopting a clearly defined sexual harassment policy that all employees are required to read and sign.
    D. requiring employees to complete sexual harassment training every year.
    E. requiring senior officers of the company to complete harassment training.

214. California passed a law in 2006 requiring employers who have at least x employees to provide supervisors with two hours of sexual harassment training every two years.

    A. $x = 50$
    B. $x = 25$
    C. $x = 100$
    D. x = all employees
    E. x = 2 or more

215. Which agency enforces sexual harassment laws?

    A. State agency
    B. Federal agency
    C. EEOC
    D. Legislature
    E. Government

216. Small businesses with one to three employees are usually exempt from many antidiscrimination laws *EXCEPT*

    A. the Equal Pay Act.
    B. Title VII.
    C. the Civil Rights Act.
    D. laws dealing with union shops.
    E. ADEA.

217. When laws conflict,

    A. federal law prevails.
    B. state law prevails.
    C. the higher standard usually prevails.
    D. local ordinances prevail.
    E. the Civil Rights Act prevails.

218. Nonwork time, breaks, vacation time, and leaves of absence may be required by law or

    A. be at the discretion of the employer.

    B. if the nonwork time is discretionary, be categorized as a company perk or benefit.

    C. be company paid but not a requirement governed by law.

    D. dispensed to individuals according to their job rank and title.

    E. be decided by company officers.

219. If an undesirable employee has been placed on probation for violating company rules or policies,

    A. benefits may be withheld.

    B. it is not a good idea to deny this employee the same benefits offered to all employees.

    C. while the employee still works for the company, it is best to treat the employee the same as all other employees regarding benefits.

    D. benefits are discretionary and discrimination is unlikely to occur if benefits are denied.

    E. All of the above

220. Employers typically allow one to three days' leave for the death of an immediate family member. However, it is at the discretion of the company whether or not bereavement time will be paid time off or approved time off without pay. Immediate family members include all of the following *EXCEPT*

    A. stepmother.

    B. father-in-law.

    C. grandfather.

    D. grandmother.

    E. the family dog.

221. The Family Medical Leave Act (FMLA) entitles qualified workers to

    A. take unpaid sick leave to care for themselves or family members.

    B. take paid sick leave to care for themselves.

    C. take time off when it is difficult to be at the job while caring for a family member.

    D. Both A and C

    E. All of the above

222. A leave of absence can be paid, unpaid, or denied; it usually depends upon

    A. how long an employee has been working at the company.

    B. the company benefit program.

    C. whether or not it is a medical leave.

    D. Both A and C

    E. Both A and B

223. Paid time off (PTO) is leave time that is best defined as

    A. an employee's accrued vacation time.

    B. personal time and sick leave.

    C. all of the time an employee may take away from the job, calculated in terms of the number of hours or days allowed.

    D. a discretionary benefit for which reasons an employee may take time off are decided upon by the employee's supervisor.

    E. absence approved by a direct supervisor.

224. Sick leave pay is a benefit of the company. If an employee receives *x* number of days per year but doesn't take it, the employee often feels justified in being paid for time not taken. Controversy between employers and employees centers around

    A. whether unused sick leave time should be paid regardless of time taken, or lost at the end of the year.

    B. whether employers ultimately have the option to decide how this time will be disposed of and whether it will be paid or unpaid.

    C. whether employees may bank unused sick time hours into the following year.

    D. trust, motivation, and loyalty.

    E. None of the above

225. Generally, most companies offer vacation time with a job. Vacation time is considered a benefit and not a requirement by law. Employees usually feel that any unused time should be either paid or banked into the following year. Employers, however, typically advise that

    A. employees take earned vacation time or risk losing the time and compensation.

    B. waiting until the end of the year to request vacation time is not justification for banking it if the request is denied.

    C. for the well-being of the individual, taking planned vacation time is mandatory.

    D. accruing vacation time may be warranted under certain conditions.

    E. the disposition of vacation time is at the discretion of the employer.

Answers to Questions and Explanations

1. Answer: (E). HRD programs focus on developing employees to meet organizational objectives. Identifying individual strengths and performance goals that target training needs for employees, while simultaneously satisfying organizational needs and objectives, is the primary objective of an HRD department.

2. Answer: (D). *Compliance* refers to legal matters covered by employment law and driven by federal, state, and local law enforcement agencies.

3. Answer: (B). HRD conducts a needs analysis to prioritize employment development activities for the organization and its employees. When specific problems occur in departments that impact employee performance and training, a needs analysis is conducted to identify what will be needed to develop a training program with specific performance goals in mind.

4. Answer: (C). Increasing individual and organizational effectiveness are primary outcome goals of an organization's training and development programs.

5. Answer: (E). Anecdotal information is not a specific measurement tool designed to measure outcomes and calculate statistics, as found in (A), (B), (C), and (D). While anecdotal information may be interesting and informative, it is additional information that may be collected to explain other events that may have impacted the outcome of specific measurement studies.

6. Answer: (E). Participant surveys, interviews, and employee attitude questionnaires are designed to gather a variety of data that explains employee attitudes, how they feel about the job, the organization's working environment, and whether a training program meets the needs of the organization and its employees.

7. Answer: (E). While (A), (B), and (C) touch upon the breadth of talent management as an employment resource, (E) encompasses the true intent of talent management to identify talented, high-potential employees who can be developed for long-term assignments and future promotions.

8. Answer: (A). (A) is the best answer because a key goal in talent management theory is to be able to identify and attract high-potential employees who can be developed to meet organizational demands.

9. Answer: (D). Performance appraisals are designed to measure an employee's performance on the job. Other reasons for conducting performance appraisals can be more specific, such as rewarding an employee for good performance, firing an employee for poor performance, and determining salary increases based on performance.

10. Answer: (E). The HRM department is responsible for identifying a performance appraisal system that an organization will use to evaluate employees' performance on the job. An organization's performance appraisal system encompasses the input

of key positions in the organization, from HRD to the direct report who supervises an employee, to the employee who will be given the appraisal. The performance appraisal process is the responsibility of everyone involved in the performance appraisal system.

11. Answer: (A). It is typically the responsibility of the HRM department to identify a performance management system that will satisfy the needs of the organization and all of its employees.

12. Answer: (D). Successful implementation of a performance appraisal program requires training, feedback, and meeting with managers and supervisors to understand the unique needs of the organization so that an effective appraisal method can be identified.

13. Answer: (E). Performance appraisal methods include a variety of task-driven tools designed to focus on key performance goals for the job an employee was hired to perform. (A), (B), (C), and (D) identify four specific kinds of performance appraisal methods that can be used to measure performance on the job.

14. Answer: (B). A 360-degree performance appraisal method is designed to gather feedback about an employee from more than one source. Since managers typically interact with superiors, peers, and subordinates, feedback is gathered from work associates to gain a complete picture about a manager's work performance and interactions with others on the job. Answers (A), (C), and (E) might be given a 360; however, the general theory driving a 360 instrument is about receiving feedback from a variety of workers with whom an employee works and interacts to carry out the job function properly.

15. Answer: (D). While most employees receive a performance appraisal once a year, appraisals may be given for a variety of reasons and may occur at any time. Examples are new hires; probationary employees; and employees who will be promoted, demoted, or terminated.

16. Answer: (A). MBO, or management by objectives, focuses on an individual's performance goals in relation to the organization's overall strategic plan. More typically, MBOs are reserved for those who work in a management capacity and are responsible for the organization's revenue goals in the area that they manage.

17. Answer: (C). The acronyms refer to employment legislation: ADA, Americans with Disabilities Act; ADEA, Age Discrimination in Employment Act; USERRA, Uniformed Services Employment and Reemployment Rights Act; and EEOC, Equal Employment Opportunity Commission.

18. Answer: (B). As explained in the answer, OD, organizational development, focuses on organizational intervention and implementation of systems designed to interact together. HRD, human resource development, focuses on the training and development needs of employees.

19. Answer: (A). ADA, Americans with Disabilities Act (1990), was designed to protect Americans with disabilities from discrimination in the workplace. The law applies to employers with 15 or more employees.

20. Answer: (D). The Civil Rights Act (1964) established the EEOC, which prohibits discrimination on the basis of race, color, religion, gender, or national original and covers employers with 15 or more employees.

21. Answer: (A). Career development describes how individuals develop their career in a typical organizational hierarchy, leading to a management, or leadership, position. Talent management seeks

to attract and identify high-potential employees suitable for promotion in the organization.

22. Answer: (A). *Process improvement* refers to an organization's operations; *performance management* refers to an individual's performance in the organization.

23. Answer: (E). While e-learning refers to computer-based instruction, its goal is multifaceted, encompassing efficient ways to deliver training and instruction to employees throughout the organizational system and locations.

24. Answer: (E). Global issues concern international threats and opportunities that impact employees and the business operations at large. Expatriates, or expats, are U.S. employees who work in a foreign country for an American company. International law includes those laws that impact U.S. employees and employers conducting business abroad. Economic conditions concern the viability of the company conducting business in the United States and abroad.

25. Answer: (A). Mentoring and executive coaching have separate goals, yet both are de-signed to help individuals improve performance and identify personal and professional goals and objectives. Training and development and performance improvement are also separate objectives, yet both are designed to develop and/or improve performance on the job.

26. Answer: (D). Organizational culture is defined by the organization's values, beliefs, and mission, reflected in the behavior and environment of those who work for the organization.

27. Answer: (E). Title VII of the Civil Rights Act (1964) was created to protect employees from sexual harassment in the workplace. Two types of harassment were defined: quid pro quo and hostile work environment.

28. Answer: (C). OJT, on-the-job training, is designed to allow employees and potential employees a real work environment for training. Employees are able to demonstrate knowledge of their training while actually performing the job, and potential employees have an opportunity to try out the job before deciding to accept a job offer.

29. Answer: (C). KSA is a common acronym to describe the knowledge, skills, and abilities required to perform a job function or task.

30. Answer: (D). As explained in the answer above, mentors are typically found in the workplace and work with others of similar work backgrounds. Mentors have experience beyond those whom they are mentoring. Coaches may or may not be employees in the organization but are hired to work with individuals (employees) on performance issues, goals, and objectives. Coaches are often used for high-potential employees that the organization believes will succeed with proper guidance.

31. Answer: (D). HRD is part of the human resource function and establishes the training and development needs of the organization's employees. It is considered the "soft side" of HRM because it is indirectly rather than directly involved in achieving revenue goals. The training department is housed in a human resource department, not the other way around as stated in (B).

32. Answer: (E). HRD is housed in the HRM branch of an organizational chart. It is primarily concerned with (A) through (D). With well-trained employees, effective training programs, and proper identification of training needs, the HRD function positively impacts the organiza-

tion's mission, values, culture, and strategic plan.

33. Answer: (A). The key word in this answer is *ongoing*. HRD must continue to evaluate its training programs in terms of the current goals and objectives of the organization.

34. Answer: (D). All of the concepts identifed in (A) through (C) are impacted and controlled by HRD. A strategic alliance ensures the successful implementation and cooperation of the entire organization to embrace the training and development function for its employees.

35. Answer: (E). HRD is intended to meet compliance requirements regarding federal legislation and other important laws impacting employees and employers. Before any HRD planning can take place, HRD must understand these requirements. Then planning or development of training programs can take place, ensuring nondiscrimination in employment practices.

36. Answer: (C). Title VII of the Civil Rights Act (1964) guarantees a workplace that is free from discrimination and protects employees on the job.

37. Answer: (E). Title VII was founded under the Civil Rights Act of 1964. Guaranteeing nondiscrimination in employment, federal legislation covers members of protected groups. Examples of protected groups are individuals eligible to work who have disabilities; individuals over the age of 40; and individuals who are members of protected groups that can be identified by race, color, religion, sex, or national origin.

38. Answer: (A). Both the EEOC and the OFCCP are acronyms identifying enforcement agencies that regulate compliance with nondiscrimination employment laws for eligible employees in the United States. Eligible employees are those who are qualified and able to perform the job function(s) they were hired to carry out.

39. Answer: (E). This question references the number 15 for the minimum membership of unions and the minimum number of employees working for an organization. It is generally assumed that organizations with fewer than 15 employees will treat employees the same; however, it cannot be guaranteed according to the guidelines set forth.

40. Answer: (A). Only the EEOC or the OFCCP may request specific record-keeping and reporting requirements. Such requirements are usually identified as an affirmative action plan.

41. Answer: (E). The data included in this report is designated in (A), (B), (C), and (D) and must be accurate, quantifiable, and meet the reporting requirements of the EEOC and the OFCCP.

42. Answer: (B). The U.S. Department of Labor (DOL) was created in 1913 to serve the labor movement, which established the social and economic achievements of American workers. The first Labor Day was celebrated September 5, 1882, in New York City. Samuel Gompers is known as the original founder, president, and long-time leader of the American Federation of Labor (AFL).

43. Answer: (B). The higher standard regards those laws that serve to protect the American worker (and those who have a legal right to work in the United States). The higher standard imposes the most protection when laws conflict at the federal or state level.

44. Answer: (D). Exceptions are situations that allow discrimination to take place due to business necessity. BFOQ, or bona fide occupational qualification, is person-specific and refers to situations

where a specific requirement exists that excludes others in the same group. A business necessity is job related and becomes necessary for the safety of the organization and its employees. Seniority systems apply in those situations when it is okay to allow preferential treatment based on seniority. The Americans with Disabilities Act (ADA) is not considered an exception; it is designed to protect workers with disabilities.

45. Answer: (A). Described in #44, a BFOQ allows employers to discriminate on the basis of a specific job requirement.

46. Answer: (B). Described in #44, a business necessity allows discrimination to take place when it regards the safe operation of the business.

47. Answer: (C). Described in #44, an exception based on a seniority system regards those conditions that make it necessary to discriminate on the basis of conditions of length of service.

48. Answer: (A). The OFCCP requires contractors to comply with Executive Order 11246 regarding Title VII of the Civil Rights Act of 1964. It mandates development of affirmative action plans for the purpose of increasing inclusion of protected classes in the workforce.

49. Answer: (D). *Employee selection* is the term generally used to describe the process of searching for qualified job applicants. Its function is housed and managed in a human resource department.

50. Answer: (A). The question specifically refers to the practice and use of selection procedures. This is a compliance issue, so the best answer is (A), since the EEOC and OFCCP monitor unfair hiring practices.

51. Answer: (E). All of the acts named in (A) through (D) protect workers in specific

situations when they might otherwise be discriminated against in an unfair selection procedure.

52. Answer: (B). ADEA specifies that it applies to employees over 40 years of age.

53. Answer: (C). In a company environment where a union shop exists, ADEA is enforced for union members where there are more than 25 employees who hold union membership in the organization.

54. Answer: (A). Undue hardship favors the employer; an accommodation will be considered or implemented only if it does not unreasonably place the employer and workers in harm's way or cause the employer to spend inordinate dollars to accommodate the disabled employee.

55. Answer: (A). Common law doctrines are concerned with legal decisions made by judges over centuries on individual cases that served to establish legal precedence for future cases involving unfair labor practices.

56. Answer: (A). Common law doctrines, as noted in #55, serve to set precedence in legal cases concerning unfair labor practices. The doctrines are directed at the employment relationship. Examples of unfair labor practices covered by the doctrines are found in question #57 below.

57. Answer: (D). Unfair labor practices described in the doctrines are noted in (A) through (C). For a broader discussion of the terms noted in this question, review chapter 7, "Employee and Labor Relations," under the subtitle "Unfair Labor Practices."

58. Answer: (E). Programs for the purpose of job training must be free from harm and foster positive working relationships in the program and on the job. The program must contain opportunities for practice, comply with all laws, be nondiscrimina-

tory, and include all KSAs needed to perform the essential features of the job successfully.

59. Answer: (A). Employers are responsible for providing safe working conditions for all employees. If improper training exists and injuries occur, liability for those injuries exist under the law. For a broader discussion of workplace safety, compliance with OSHA standards, and conducting employee accident investigations, please review chapter 8, "Risk Management."

60. Answer: (E). The publication of HRD training activities, manuals, and other written materials is protected under the Copyright Act (1976). Workplace patents are covered under the U.S. Patent Act and include three types: design, utility, and plant patents. Differences between employer-owned copyright material and written work created by a freelance author are known as work-for-hire exceptions. Work that is created for someone else is owned by the person who commissioned the work, not the person who is considered the author of the work.

61. Answer: (C). Utility patents protect the invention of processes, machines, or composition of matter for 20 years. Plant patents protect the invention of asexually reproduced plant matter for 20 years. Design patents protect the invention of newly created, original, and ornamental designs for 14 years.

62. Answer: (D). OD considers the entire organization and how people and systems will work effectively together. OD considers the strategic goals of the organization and seeks to integrate objectives through the process of needs analysis and implementation of interventions designed to align with the broad-range goals of the organization. Included in this mix are (A), (B), and (C) described above.

63. Answer: (E). Organizational culture is defined by a mix of complex, intangible assets regarding the environment, values, and beliefs practiced by its leaders and management groups and evidenced by the motivation of its employees. An organization's culture is reflected in the behavior and feedback of all employees throughout the organization.

64. Answer: (A). An organization's climate is created by its culture; it includes behavior, motivation, leadership style, management practices, and opportunity for advancement that may or may not be present. Bureaucratic influence in the organization is also impacted by an organization's climate and management style. Suffice it to say that motivated employees perform best when organizations consider the needs of their employees.

65. Answer: (E). Job satisfaction surveys are given to test the employment climate in an organization. If attrition and retention are threats to the organization as evidenced by high turnover, job surveys, if well designed, will identify reasons why employees are not satisfied, respected, or valued. When employees feel included in the social community of the organization, salary becomes less of an issue in maintaining high job satisfaction.

66. Answer: (D). OD interventions are not training programs; rather, they exist to find solutions to organizational problems that threaten the efficient flow of work through integrated systems management. Performance improvement, learning organizations, quality management, and shared knowledge are a few factors that are commonly discussed in an OD intervention designed to diagnose and implement solutions to organizational problems.

67. Answer: (A). Change management theory considers how a current process that no longer works is carried out, by whom it

is carried out, and how to introduce a strategic change in the way that it is carried out. Once defined, usually through a needs analysis study, a strategic change is introduced as an intervention specifically designed to resolve the issue and move the process forward again.

68. Answer: (D). In a joint effort with key individuals who are responsible for carrying out the work of the organization in an efficient manner, strategic interventions are designed by the OD arm of the organization. Strategic interventions are carefully designed to be carried out by the organization's leaders and management.

69. Answer: (E). Strategic programs that have been designed and created by OD/HRD include all of those described in (A) through (D). These programs are considered strategic because they are designed to work in concert with the goals and objectives of the organization's business plan.

70. Answer: (A). Techno-structural interventions address how work gets done through the involvement of employees. Redesigning work flow processes is a major goal of techno-structural interventions. TQM is another type of techno-structural intervention, as are six sigma and high-involvement organizations. All are intended to be long-term involvement OD interventions.

71. Answer: (C). Deming, an American, is credited with introducing the quality movement in Japan. He proposed the philosophy in answer (D). Joseph Juran and Dr. Ishikawa followed in Deming's footsteps.

72. Answer: (B). Deming placed the burden of quality on management because it was ultimately accountable to the consumer, whom Deming believed defined quality. Deming held that management was able to control internal systems and work outcomes that communicated quality to the consumer.

73. Answer: (D). Juran believed that quality begins with the consumer and defining customer needs. Once identified, needs could be translated back to the business so that products and services could be developed that satisfied the needs of the business and the consumer.

74. Answer: (B). Quality planning addresses quality concerns during product development; quality control follows the planning process and guidelines that were originally developed in the planning phase; and quality improvement is an ongoing process of product, operations, and waste management improvement.

75. Answer: (E). Check sheets, histograms, cause-and-effect diagrams, scatter charts, stratification, and Pareto charts are a few analytical processes developed by Ishikawa that were widely used by organizations in the quality movement.

76. Answer: (A). The fish bone chart is also known as the cause-and-effect diagram or Ishikawa diagram and is often used in brainstorming sessions as an information-gathering tool.

77. Answer: (B). The purpose of using a histogram is to illustrate random occurrences and analyze whether or not a pattern emerges.

78. Answer: (C). Pareto charts are often recognized as graphical representations of the 80/20 rule, such that 80 percent of the problems are caused by 20 percent of the reasons. Vilfredo Pareto was an Italian economist. Pareto charts arrange data in descending order.

79. Answer: (A). While all potential answers might arguably be correct, the primary goal of a training and development

department is to meet the goals and objectives of the organization through proper training of its workforce.

80. Answer: (A). Motivation theory concerns how people are motivated to do what they do. In a work situation, motivation theory is used to identify how to train workers to be productive and satisfied employees.

81. Answer: (C). Theory X & Y, a well-known theory proposed by Douglas McGregor, assumes that there are two types of management styles toward employees. *X* are those managers who believe that employees need constant direction and need to be micromanaged. *X* employees need job security most of all. *Y* managers believe that employees are motivated by work that is both challenging and satisfying. *Y* employees naturally seek responsibility if they are motivated by work that is satisfying.

82. Answer: (E). Collectively, training programs are designed to meet organizational goals and objectives while also conforming to compliance laws and regulations regarding nondiscrimination in employment for all employees.

83. Answer: (D). Step 4 is the implementation phase. All of the preceding work comes together in this stage for a presentation and training of the trainers, if they will be needed. Facilities, classroom style, mode of training, and materials are introduced and implemented.

84. Answer: (A). KSA is a familiar training and development acronym. Required knowledge, skills, and abilities are determined to meet organizational goals and objectives. The key to determining whether a training outcome is successful is whether or not transfer of training occurs on the job.

85. Answer: (D). Learning organizations are concerned with current informational exchange that is shared within the organizational community and outside the working environment; their purpose is to seek knowledge that impacts the organization's ability to remain competitive in the marketplace.

86. Answer: (A). Knowledge management is the business process of sharing knowledge across the organizational environment so that all sectors of the business groups can be integrated into informed cross-functional teams.

87. Answer: (B). Communication was shared using knowledge management across multiple departments in an organized manner during the 2007 San Diego fires. Preplanning allowed each sector to act in accordance with a business plan that was organized prior to the event. Historical catastrophic events, such as Hurricane Katrina, 9/11, and several Florida hurricanes, taught valuable lessons to communities about how to mobilize rescue teams effectively during a community-wide crisis.

88. Answer: (E). For KM or informational exchange to be successful, it is important to be able to understand organizational goals so that information shared is relevant to the business environment.

89. Answer: (E). Both (A) and (D) describe the primary functions of a successful HRD department.

90. Answer: (D). ED is concerned with attracting high-potential employees who can be professionally developed in carefully planned in-house career development programs.

91. Answer: (E). Through the efforts of HRD in gathering information from managers, supervisors, and organizational leaders in preparation for the next generation of

high-potential talent management, effective training and development programs can be created around the needs of the entire organization.

92. Answer: (A). It cannot be stressed enough that the primary purpose of an organization's training and development program supports the needs of the entire organization. By developing effective training programs, successful transfer of training skills can take place to support the goals of each department.

93. Answer: (A). Although (C) is important, the correct answer is (A), since (C) does not give enough information. For (C) to be the correct answer, it needs to include a cost-benefit equation answering a question such as "Will dollars spent designing and implementing a training program be more cost-effective than dollars it is supposed to save or earn?" or "Will the return on revenue (or cost savings) be greater than the cost of training itself?"

94. Answer: (B). Answer (B) is correct, since moving forward to the design phase precedes the design phase and is not part of the design phase. This is associated with the ADDIE model of training. Answer (B) is part of the analysis phase described in the ADDIE model.

95. Answer: (E). The program development phase, Step 3 of the ADDIE model, looks at a broad scope of the impact the program will have on the entire organization, even if the program is intended for a select group of individuals.

96. Answer: (A). As organizations are constantly in motion and change is constant, an important task of an HRD department is to understand the ebb and flow of the organization at large so that the right mix of talents and backgrounds complement and fit into the organizational climate and culture. A well-run training and development department takes into account all of these variables and includes them in the training effort.

97. Answer: (C). Transfer of training is one of the best measures of training evaluation. The key questions are "Did transfer of training successfully take place at the end of the training program?" and "If not, why not?" This tension between HRD and the organization is a constantly changing dynamic due to a variety of variables not found in the training program itself, such as KSAs, candidate selection, management style, leadership, KM, and worker motivation.

98. Answer: (A). The reasons are found in question 97, which points to whether or not transfer of training successfully took place.

99. Answer: (C). While online training programs may be synchronous, asychronous, or delivered via live e-instruction, they are not typically part of an email format. *E-learning* is the correct term, and it is usually accomplished by logging into a website with a password where class participants have been enrolled in advance and where online units or modules are sequentially published as part of a course or seminar.

100. Answer: (D). Self-study should not be confused with self-instruction. Self-instruction is not a recognized program delivery method, but self-study is. Self-study is intended to be directed and controlled by the learner, but the learner needs to communicate with a trainer or mentor to complete the training program.

101. Answer: (E). Simulation training is typically found in situations requiring a high degree of risk to the participant and possibly placing other workers or the work site itself in harm's way. Simulation training is used as an interactive training method where participants can practice learning

new skills in a simulated environment where no harm will come to them or to others.

102. Answer: (D). When employees feel connected to an organization, either through community activities or on-site social activities, they are more likely to be committed to the organization and to demonstrate greater employee satisfaction.

103. Answer: (C). Political and nonpolitical contributions are not part of an EIP program. EIPs are directly linked to employee benefits and rewards.

104. Answer: (B). High-performance work systems directly involve workers in the productivity process. It is felt that directly involving employees in productivity programs promotes high involvement, motivation, retention, and commitment to organizational goals and objectives.

105. Answer: (A). This is the primary purpose of the evaluation process in an organization's training and development department. If costs to produce a training program outweigh its actual impact, then the training program did not achieve its goals. If transfer of training occurred based on metrics established at the time a program was designed, actual impact was achieved.

106. Answer: (C). KSAs are the target goals of organizational training programs, and transfer of training is the primary outcome. Answer (D) speaks to the principle of transfer of training; however, it speaks to outcomes rather than goals.

107. Answer: (B). Program evaluation may be determined through several means: employee evaluations, transfer of training, company surveys, and statistical reporting. Note that these are not all of the ways that program evaluation can be carried out. The evaluation method is largely determined by the type of training that was implemented.

108. Answer: (D). The Kirkpatrick model is best known for measuring training program outcomes. It is based on a four-step model; each level must be achieved before moving to the next level.

109. Answer: (A). The four-step approach in Kirkpatrick's model is reaction, learning, behavior, and results.

110. Answer: (B). It is felt that participants, training facilitators, and management provide the most valuable feedback to determine whether or not successful training was achieved.

111. Answer: (E). In-person interviewing is valuable in terms of gathering anecdotal information; however, data collection is a quantitative approach to gather information that is measurable. The difference between an interview and in-person data gathering is that interviews, to be measurable, must contain a specific set of questions asked of all participants, otherwise known as the structured interview.

112. Answer: (A). A post-measure would be an acceptable choice to confirm that the program was completed; however, a pre/post-measure determines the difference between what knowledge was known before a course was completed and how much knowledge was learned upon completion of the course. The question asks for the best learning data method, so the best answer would be (A), not (B). Experimental design is not appropriate for this type of training, and a quasi-experimental design combines a variety of methods usually reserved for other kinds of studies.

113. Answer: (C). Experimental and quasi-experimental designs may have control groups, anecdotal data, and more complex kinds of data gathering that would

be required of a study where more in-depth information is needed.

114. Answer: (B). Performance management is a planned employee appraisal program facilitated by a human resource department. While there are numerous appraisal feedback systems that can be implemented, their primary purpose is to give feedback to employees about job performance.

115. Answer: (E). Most often, performance feedback is a two-way communication between the employee and the supervisor or direct report. Sometimes a direct report leaves the company, and another designated person facilitates the performance appraisal. Rarely will the appraisal be completed by someone in absentia without the benefit of a meeting between the employee and another person; however, it sometimes happens that the employee is asked to complete a form and a designee will complete it in absentia.

116. Answer: (A). HRD is the human resources arm of training and development. If the company is small and does not have a separate HRD department, a representative from human resources will assume the training and development role.

117. Answer: (D). Performance management addresses how an employee performs on the job; performance coaching addresses how an employee can improve performance, which is commonly called employee development.

118. Answer: (A). Performance appraisals can be utilized for a variety of reasons; however, their primary purpose is to be used as a documentation feedback system that assesses job performance. A record of performance is an important part of an employee's permanent employment record. Documentation is important for historical verification of past and present performance. It is often a predictor of future performance, but not always.

119. Answer: (C). The process of a performance appraisal system takes place over several months, completed well in advance of the actual performance review meeting, and is most often conducted annually.

120. Answer: (A). While every employee, supervisor, and manager is involved in the performance management process, it is the decision of the HR director and senior management to decide which performance system is best suited for the organization.

121. Answer: (E). The performance appraisal process is designed to be used in a variety of situations that serve to document and allow feedback to employees about their job performance.

122. Answer: (B). The appraisal method is never casual; it is always a set of pre-planned activities that have been designed well in advance of the actual meeting between an employee and a direct report. Casual conversations may take place to confirm a meeting or a question; however, the appraisal method and process are formal and concrete.

123. Answer: (E). Answers (A) through (D) describe different kinds of assessment methods found in a performance appraisal system. A short form may be one page that includes a rating and brief description for each item; a checklist allows similar characteristics to be measured for like jobs; comparisons measure a desired level of performance versus actual performance; rankings compare employees as part of a statistical analysis across departments, job categories, and organizations; and rating scales allow for a numbered ranking sometimes used to determine salary increases.

124. Answer: (D). Narratives allow for feedback that is additional information not specifically found on a rating or ranking system. They can take many forms and are used to describe specific instances of performance, whether the evaluation is for a promotion, demotion, lateral move, or termination.

125. Answer: (A). Proper documentation is essential in a performance review of any kind. If the review is for a critical incident, the supervisor must take care that anything completed in writing is reviewed by a representative from HR before a meeting takes place. A word or phrase may be found to be discriminatory according to the law. Legal action could result from documentation not properly formed.

126. Answer: (E). A 360-degree feedback evaluation method is designed to give information to an employee about how others perceive that person in the workplace. It is ideally designed to provide feedback from direct reports, peers, and subordinates, but not always. This is why it is called a 360-degree evaluation. The employee can read how others experience the working relationship in a variety of situations on the job. Feedback from others is built into a report where comments are combined in a confidential grouping, not allowing for identification of each feedback person.

127. Answer: (D). In a comprehensive feedback system, all of the above are used to calculate a final score. The score is used to determine salary increases. These pay increases should not be confused with a COLA, a cost-of-living adjustment. All employees will receive the same COLA increase (based on a percentage) if one is given at the time of a performance appraisal, but not all employees will receive a salary increase nor will employees receiving an increase get the same amount.

128. Answer: (E). All of the above could result in the event of a mismanaged performance review if the company is found to be negligent or discriminatory.

129. Answer: (A). A career development (CD) department may include answers (A) through (C); however, the primary focus of a CD department is to identify high-potential employees who can be developed for larger assignments and promotions.

130. Answer: (B). Mentors provide a background of similar experience and provide advice based on previous similar experiences. A coach assists employees with performance issues and goal setting but is trained in a different discipline than that of the person being coached.

131. Answer: (A). Competitive distribution methods include answers (B), (C), and (D) but also include conferences, professional meetings, networking, employment agencies, and any other distribution method where potential applicants may be found.

132. Answer: (E). In this question, the exception is not known. If it were, it could be anything from the current global economy, financial conditions of the company, or any threats to the viability of its business services.

133. Answer: (A). Embracing cultural differences promotes awareness and acceptance of different cultural backgrounds of employees. Communicating diversity awareness includes communicating that the organization accepts cultural differences and does not tolerate discrimination toward any employee. While (C) speaks to the discrimination issue, it does not include all of the elements of diversity awareness.

134. Answer: (C). Answer (C) is the most complete answer and fully describes who is an expatriate. A similar term is *expat.*

135. Answer: (A). Repatriation includes all of the elements in answers (B), (C), and (D); however, repatriation concerns itself with the employee, successful reentry back into the United States, and readjustment issues that may occur as a result of living overseas for work.

136. Answer: (D). HRD is an integral part of the entire organizational community. It includes all of the elements of (B) and (C), but HRD is responsible for numerous other training and development activities that serve to train employees for job assignments.

137. Answer: (E). OD's role is to serve the organizational community by resolving issues within its operational systems and in how individuals and groups interact within those systems. It is an integrative system that seeks to resolve performance improvement processes and work flow.

138. Answer: (D). The intent of this question is to probe the test taker's understanding of the separate roles that HRD and OD play in the organization. They appear to be similar in nature and interface together when a training program or process improvement is needed. When this occurs, a needs analysis study is designed, and a training program is created through the combined efforts of HRD and OD. HRD guides training and development programs in the organization, and OD focuses on operating systems and work flow.

139. Answer: (B). Answer (B) describes the five major tenets of the ADDIE training model. Within each tenet is a description of the process that follows. It is a sequential model; one step cannot be accomplished without completing the previous steps.

140. Answer: (E). It is important to understand that careful planning, design, and implementation of a training program requires the cooperation of several key individuals and departments. The ADDIE model is often selected as an initial framework so that everyone who is a stakeholder in this process understands the design process from a theoretical viewpoint.

141. Answer: (A). The ADDIE model allows for flexibility and change in the design and implementation process.

142. Answer: (D). The answer is (D) since the program has already been developed and now is in its initial implementation phase.

143. Answer: (A). Transfer of training is the key goal and outcome of training and development programs.

144. Answer: (D). Title VII of the Civil Rights Act (1964) guaranteed equal employment opportunity on the basis of eligibility to work in the United States and nondiscrimination in employment for protected classes of people. It ensured that businesses would be held accountable for discriminatory employment practices.

145. Answer: (A). Answer (A) is the best answer since it does not describe a reason for an exception. Answer (B) cannot be verified as an illegal act, answer (C) is false, and answer (D) describes an exception to the law.

146. Answer: (E). Discrimination could result from any one of the items described in answers (A) through (D).

147. Answer: (E). Each scenario described in this question could result in discrimination, even if it does not involve the immediate organizational community, as in answer (A).

148. Answer: (E). When laws intersect or conflict, it should not be presumed that the federal law enforces the higher standard. Organizations must adhere to the higher standard, whether it is stipulated by federal, state, or local law.

149. Answer: (B). An exception may occur, such as a BFOQ (bona fide occupational qualification), making it necessary to hire and select particular individuals based on the necessary qualifications for the job.

150. Answer: (A). While there are no provisions in the law for a personality conflict, there are provisions that describe situations in which the day-to-day operations of the business are placed in jeopardy due to extraordinary situations. In those instances, it is difficult to prove discrimination took place. In such situations, careful documentation is necessary.

151. Answer: (C). It could be argued that all of the answers in this question are correct; however, laws were enacted as a result of discriminatory practices taking place against individuals of minority classes and unsafe working conditions in manufacturing dating back to the 1800s.

152. Answer: (E). In the absence of an employment agreement, the employment-at-will doctrine allows both the employee and employer the freedom to terminate employment at any time and without cause. Contingent on the way an employment agreement is written, the at-will doctrine serves to protect employers and employees in matters of termination.

153. Answer: (A). Common law is the outcome of legal decisions made by judges over a period of centuries. Common law serves as a guiding legal principle in matters of employment discrimination and illegal employment practices.

154. Answer: (B). Answers (A), (C), (D), and (E) are plausible; however, answer (B) is the explanation described in the at-will doctrine and the best answer to this question.

155. Answer: (A). Due to many exceptions written into employment agreements since 1959, the intent of the at-will doc-

trine has been eroded over time. However, if an employment agreement or contract modifies the employment-at-will relationship, the law must still be followed. If an employee signs an employment agreement that includes exceptions to employment-at-will, the burden is on the employee to seek clarification of the agreement or risk being held to it.

156. Answer: (E). Apart from the at-will doctrine, if employment agreements specifically state how terminations are to be carried out and the employee signs the agreement, employers have discretion to terminate according to the terms of the agreement or contract.

157. Answer: (B). Although it is not required according to employment at will, it has become standard practice for employees to give two weeks' notice of termination.

158. Answer: (A). The WARN Act (1988) requires 60 days' advance notice to employees in the case of large layoffs or plant closings. It only applies to employers with 100 or more full-time employees or employers with 4,000 or more employees including full-time, part-time, seasonal, subsidiaries, and independent contractors. Exceptions to the 60-day rule are natural disasters, such as Hurricane Katrina, or business necessity.

159. Answer: (B). Exceptions were written into the employment-at-will doctrine beginning in 1959, when court decisions and statutes began to modify the agreement. Public policy exceptions occur when employees act in the best interest of legal statutes or the law. Whistleblowers are an example of a public policy exception. Implied contracts are situations where a conversation or written document establishes an understanding between the employer and employee but where no formal contract has been signed. The covenant of good faith and fair dealing determined that the contractual relation-

ship suggests an obligation to act in a fair and honest manner, ensuring that both parties to the contract will carry out the terms of the agreement.

160. Answer: (A). The question describes one of the three exceptions noted in the employment at-will doctrine. Public policy is the exception described in the question. Answers (B) and (C) describe the other two exceptions, and answers (D) and (E) are false.

161. Answer: (E). The implied contract, one of the three exceptions to the employment-at-will doctrine, recognizes situations that can occur in the employer/employee relationship in which an implied contract is suggested but no formal contract was written. Answers (A), (B), (C), and (D) are examples of implied contracts.

162. Answer: (A). Answer (A) describes the intent of the covenant of good faith and fair dealing, one of the three exceptions to the employment-at-will doctrine. Answers (B), (C), and (D) describe instances that relate to the covenant, and answer (E) is incorrect since only (A) defines the principle of the covenant.

163. Answer: (A). Each state has the discretion to interpret the employment-at-will doctrine according to the employment laws of the state and the situation. Answer (D) may seem plausible since the employer does have a duty to uphold the tenets of the at-will employment agreement.

164. Answer: (E). In an organization where a union shop exists, employers must uphold the collective bargaining agreement. Even in a case of just cause, a hearing must be held before a termination can take place. The employee may be suspended until a hearing takes place; however, the employee may not be terminated until a hearing is held to determine whether the union shop employee should be terminated.

165. Answer: (D). The provisions of the act state that employees who are 40 or older are protected by law. Answers (A), (B), (C), and (E) describe situations that may or may not occur due to age but are not covered by the act.

166. Answer: (E). Answer (E) addresses the intent of the affirmative action program. The other answers describe considerations that are addressed by an affirmative action program.

167. Answer: (E). Answers (A) and (B) describe what affirmative action programs are designed to include. Answers (C) and (D) are examples of what may happen if affirmative action programs are not carried out.

168. Answer: (E). None of the answers describe affirmative action guidelines. They in fact describe situations that may require consideration under an affirmative action program. Affirmative action programs are designed to prevent the employer from using discriminatory employment practices and to protect the employee from employment discrimination.

169. Answer: (D). Answer (D) is an exception in the affirmative action process if it can be demonstrated that gender-specific preferences are required by the job. The other answers describe potential discriminatory hiring practices that would be considered violations under the law, unless an exception can be demonstrated.

170. Answer: (D). Answers (A) and (B) address specific provisions covered by ADEA. Answer (C) is incorrectly stated (ADEA addresses employees qualified to work who are 40 and older).

171. Answer: (E). Answers (A) through (D) describe the basic provisions of ADA.

172. Answer: (A). The Equal Pay Act (1963) addresses gender differences and ensures that compensation is equal for males and females for jobs that are similar in terms of requirements, skills, labor, responsibilities, and working conditions.

173. Answer: (E). Although the intent of the Equal Pay Act (1963) was to address equal pay for equal work regarding gender, answers (A) through (D) describe compensation practices that are legal under the law. Therefore, pay differences are allowed to exist in all of the situations described in this question.

174. Answer: (A). This question is self-explanatory regarding family responsibility discrimination and candidate selection. Answer (A) describes the conditions under which family responsibility discrimination is found.

175. Answer: (E). The question asks for an exception to the answers provided; however, all of the possible answers given are considered forms of workplace harassment and would be considered discriminatory employment practices.

176. Answer: (E). All of the answers describe potential workplace sexual harassment situations. Answer (D) describes a situation that would still be considered harassment under the law, since discrimination may occur away from the work environment.

177. Answer: (B). Answer (B) describes a type of sexual harassment covered by law. A hostile work environment can take many forms and be unnoticeable in many instances. An employer may hire attractive females who are unqualified for the job, bypassing other qualified candidates or hire younger employees and bypass older ones. Alternatively, there may be casual joking in the workplace that others find offensive or other scenarios that would fall under the category of a hostile work environment.

178. Answer: (E). All of the examples in the answer choices would be considered harassment under the law.

179. Answer: (D). The question asks for an exception, and the answer is (D). Confronting the aggressor should not be pursued, since retaliation may ensue. Although retaliation is also illegal, the best protocol to take in any harassment situation is to report the incident(s) to a confidential representative appointed by the HR department. Most of the time, the representative is the HR director, unless the organization is so large that another representative is selected.

180. Answer: (D). The question asks for the exception, and the answer is (D). Publishing results of the investigation violates the confidentiality clause that may be found in a workplace harassment policy manual. Unless the perpetrator or organization is sued and the outcome is made public, either through the court system or in the public domain, all information about a harassment allegation should remain confidential.

181. Answer: (D). While all of the answers given are plausible and should result in investigative action by HR, the best answer is (D). All reporting of harassment should be taken seriously and investigated. It is not up to the employee or HR director to decide whether or not harassment should be investigated; if there is a harassment allegation, an investigation needs to take place.

182. Answer: (E). Depending upon the organization, a company representative will be selected to investigate the matter of harassment. Investigation is done confidentially and documented in a report facilitated by the HR department.

183. Answer: (B). Answer (B) is the best answer, as it raises two important processes in the investigational protocol. While it is ideal to resolve the matter as quickly as possible, some investigations may take several months to conclude.

184. Answer: (C). Answer (C) describes the Family Medical Leave Act, which covers conditions of pregnancy, childbirth, and other related health conditions.

185. Answer: (E). The law ensures the support of caregivers in the event an employee has a family medical condition requiring time off from work to care for family members.

186. Answer: (E). In all of the answers choices, there are no exceptions. A dress code policy would be considered discriminatory if it any of the answers.

187. Answer: (D). Profiting from the sale of employee-required uniforms and requiring the employee to pay for them is an error.

188. Answer: (A). Many employers have a casual day and describe it as part of a formal dress code policy in the employee policy manual. *Casual* will have a variety of meanings to different employees and should be clearly defined.

189. Answer: (E). Uniforms may be a condition of employment under any of the circumstances in the answer choices as long as they are nondiscriminatory.

190. Answer: (D). Companies may not impose a dress code policy for answers (A), (B), (C), and (E); that could be considered discriminatory. Answer (D) would not be discriminatory if an employee uses bad judgment in selection of dress.

191. Answer: (D). All of the answers given except (E) may result in discriminatory hiring practices according to Title VII of the Civil Rights Act (1964).

192. Answer: (D). The question asks for an exception. Answer (D) would be considered nondiscriminatory if the job requirements called for the ability to speak a particular language to perform a necessary task of the job.

193. Answer: (C). Eligibility to work in the United States is a requirement for jobs with most U.S. companies. All of the other questions would be considered illegal during an applicant interview. Answer (E) can only be asked following an offer of employment.

194. Answer: (C). Nepotism is favoring a family member in a business situation but is not considered illegal. If a promotion was denied to an employee in favor of a family member or a larger raise was given to a family member than an unrelated employee, these practices are not considered discriminatory.

195. Answer: (E). All of the answers raise questions and could result in wrongful termination if the circumstances are not properly documented.

196. Answer: (A). It is okay to ask on a job application about criminal convictions in a yes or no form. However, details of the criminal record are largely confidential, and the law regarding them varies from state to state. If the business calls for a confidential security clearance, a clean criminal record would be considered a bona fide occupational qualification (BFOQ), and an employer could ask about it.

197. Answer: (C). Employers may conduct a security investigation on an applicant after the applicant has signed a form allowing the investigation to take place as a condition of employment. Employers may not conduct security clearances without the signed permission of the applicant or employee. Employers can make an informed job offer, not make

one, or make employment decisions based on this information.

198. Answer: (A). This question asks for an exception. In this scenario, employers have the right to ask questions about criminal records if a past criminal history relates to the job. Answer (A) is the exception, because it seeks to find out about convictions only, which would be considered discriminatory without a reason to ask or as a condition of employment.

199. Answer: (E). The question asks for an exception, and there is none. The answers (A) through (D) describe many of the elements found in a learning organization.

200. Answer: (A). All of the answers could be useful; however, answer (A) most fully describes the legal process of using a criminal record to exclude a job applicant from the pool.

201. Answer: (E). All of the answers would be considered a form of discrimination if employees were terminated or applicants were excluded from hiring on the basis of financial hardship.

202. Answer: (A). Title VII of the Civil Rights Act does not include provisions for gay and lesbian employees; however, employers are still responsible for providing a workplace that is free from harassment. Harassment policies include all employees, whether or not they are gay or openly lead an alternative lifestyle.

203. Answer: (A). This is the first bill that addresses discrimination in the workplace on the basis of sexual orientation, as given in answer (A), but it does not explicitly cover the answers given in (B) and (C). If approved, the bill will be officially enacted and titled the Employment Non-Discrimination Act of 2007.

204. Answer: (B). This question can be confusing because of similar terms and conditions, which is why it was included as part of this exam. Terms to pay attention to are *discrimination* and *nondiscrimination,* the Civil Rights Act and all of the revisions to it, as well as Title VII and Executive Order HR 3685, which will become the Employment Non-Discrimination Act of 2007. While all deal with issues of discrimination in the workplace, all are explicitly different.

205. Answer: (A). In this case, if the act was not put into place at the federal level, then the law must be followed at the level it was introduced and in the state where the business operates.

206. Answer: (B). All of the answers given are involved in employment discrimination legislation in one way or another, but employers, (B), are ultimately responsible for carrying out the law.

207. Answer: (A). This question may be considered a trick question; however, upon scrutiny, only Title VII of the Civil Rights Act addresses gender discrimination and prohibits sexual harassment. Answers (B), (C), and (D) concern nondiscrimination in the workplace but address different issues.

208. Answer: (E). All of the answers given in this question describe possible sexual harassment allegations. Answer (D), various behaviors that may create a hostile work environment, is recognized as a potentially serious sexual harassment allegation.

209. Answer: (C). This question calls for the exception, which is answer (C). Both coworkers consent to become intimate together even though company policy discourages it. Company policy does not explicitly state that a condition of employment is not to become involved with coworkers; therefore, sexual harass-

ment has not been demonstrated in this scenario. The other answers demonstrate situations where sexual harassment has taken place.

210. Answer: (B). In this scenario, it is assumed that married coworkers may not formally bring charges of sexual harassment against each other. All the other examples, these can be named as perpetrators in a sexual harassment allegation.

211. Answer: (B). The answer asks for the exception, which is answer (B). Title VII does not recognize gay relationships for purposes either of sexual harassment or discrimination. The other answers describe scenarios that could be considered harassment under the provisions of Title VII.

212. Answer: (A). Only answer (A) relates to the actual statistics collected for sexual harassment claims.

213. Answer: (B). Answer (B) is the correct answer, even though it might seem imprudent to pursue an investigation if the victim feels threatened or unsafe. To reduce the risk of sexual harassment in the workplace, investigations of harassment allegations are needed. If a victim feels threatened by the harasser, steps must be taken to protect the victim. The other answers are all part of an effective sexual harassment policy.

214. Answer: (A). The correct answer is (A); 50 is the minimum number of employees required for a company to be mandated to provide supervisors with at least two hours of harassment training every two years. While answer (D) is desirable, and many employers already require sexual harassment training for all employees, it is not yet required by law.

215. Answer: (C). The question asks for the agency that enforces sexual harassment laws. Answer (C) is the correct answer.

The EEOC is the Equal Employment Opportunity Commission, and it is the agency responsible for making sure that employers comply with the law.

216. Answer: (A). Answer (A), the Equal Pay Act, includes all employers regardless of the size of the business.

217. Answer: (C). The answer addresses the question of which law to follow: federal, state, or local law. It is not generally assumed that federal law is to be followed any more than state or local laws. The higher standard, in most states, is the standard that serves most to protect employees.

218. Answer: (A). Answer (A) is correct. Nonwork time, breaks, vacation time, and leaves of absence are at the discretion of the employer. Discretion takes into account workplace hardship—will the work be adequately and safely covered if an employee takes a break or goes on vacation or a leave of absence? If an employee is singled out and denied nonwork time but other employees are not denied, this becomes a discrimination issue. *Discretionary* refers to the best allocation of nonwork time that will not present a hardship to the business or to others.

219. Answer: (C). This is a question that presents very subtle differences among the answers. However, in this scenario, much is at stake when an employee has been placed on probation for a violation of company rules or policy. Until the violation has been mediated or resolved, it is best to treat the employee the same as all other employees regarding benefits. Answers (A), (B), and (D) address the same issue: withholding benefits from one employee is considered discriminatory if all employees receive the same benefits.

220. Answer: (E). While many might argue for the family dog, it is not recognized in most company policy manuals. Immediate family members generally include those named in answers (A) through (D).

221. Answer: (D). The question asks about qualified workers. According to the law, a qualified worker is entitled under FMLA to take time off when sick or to care for family members who are sick. Depending upon the employment situation, the leave can be unpaid or paid time off.

222. Answer: (E). Answers (A) and (B) are the typical reasons for granting or denying a request for a leave of absence. Whether or not it is paid or unpaid is determined by the employee's employment status with the company and if the company benefit program provides benefits for a leave of absence.

223. Answer: (C). Answer (C) describes PTO as the aggregate time allowed for an employee to take time off from the job. Its calculation depends on employment status, benefits, holidays, and other company perks determined by the employer. Answer (A) includes vacation time but does not address other time-off categories. Answer (B) may be included in a PTO policy but does not address the entire policy. Answer (D) is incorrect, and answer (E) is true but does not define PTO.

224. Answer: (A). Answer (A) is the correct answer and provides an explanation for the ongoing controversy about sick leave pay. This is a reason to develop the concept of PTO. More companies are rewarding employees for not taking sick leave time by providing incentives and/or rewards in exchange for time not taken. All of the other answers address the issue to some degree; however, answer (A) addresses the controversy most directly.

225. Answer: (C). Answer (C) is the correct answer and addresses the well-being issue found in most workplaces today. All of the other answers are plausible; however, they address case-by-case scenarios and are not typically addressed by vacation policies.

Practice Test: SPHR Exam 2

1. All of the following resources are considered appropriate to inform of a discrimination or harassment claim against the employer, except:

   A. HR
   B. A government agency
   C. An in-house representative
   D. The harasser
   E. None of the above

2. An employee informs Human Resources that his boss has been spending time on the internet at work viewing child pornography and sharing its contents with fellow workers. The boss has potentially violated one or more work policies according to:

   A. The Employee Handbook
   B. Sexual harassment guidelines
   C. Creating a hostile work environment
   D. All of the above
   E. None of the above

3. The employee informs Human Resources about sexual harassment allegations confidentially shares the information with a trusted representative in the workplace, who serves as the investigator for harassment claims. The representative is known as the:

   A. Informant
   B. Whistle blower
   C. Co-worker
   D. Hostile witness
   E. All of the above

4. Shortly after the company is made aware of harassment allegations leading to an investigation, the informant is laid off and the harasser is placed on temporary leave. The informant files a complaint against the employer claiming:

   A. Retaliation
   B. Back pay
   C. Severance pay
   D. Employee benefits
   E. All of the above

5. In the case identified above, the law may interpret actions by the employer toward the informant as:

   A. Illegal

   B. Punishment against the informant

   C. A covert measure to get rid of the problem

   D. Retaliation due to the timing of event(s)

   E. All of the above

6. According to the law, an adverse action that someone takes against an employee because s/he filed a complaint is called:

   A. Discrimination

   B. Quid pro quo

   C. Retaliation

   D. Harassment

   E. Demotion

7. Employees who participate in an investigation are:

   A. Protected by law.

   B. Unprotected by law.

   C. Protected by the collective bargaining agreement, if the employee is a member of a union shop.

   D. Protected for one year, according to the statute of limitations.

   E. Protected by the EEOC.

8. If the original complaint of harassment turns out to be judged false, the informant may be able to demonstrate retaliation because:

   A. The employee was laid off.

   B. The informant was transferred to another department.

   C. Negative consequences resulted from the investigation.

   D. The informant and the harasser can no longer work together.

   E. All of the above

9. Adverse action may include:

   A. Demotion.

   B. Discipline.

   C. Firing.

   D. Salary reduction.

   E. All of the above

10. When taking steps toward corrective action, it is important to consider that:

   A. Change should include the informant and everyone involved in the allegation(s).

   B. Change should only include the informant.

   C. Change should only include the harasser.

   D. Change should include the entire organization.

   E. Discipline is the only change that should be taken.

11. The difference between retaliation and employee discipline is:

    A. Adverse action is retaliatory because the employee complained

    B. Employee discipline is not retaliatory

    C. A negative performance evaluation is given as a result of past performance problems

    D. Action can be taken against an employee for other reasons, even if that employee has complained about discrimination or harassment

    E. None of the above

12. If forced to take adverse action against an employee who complained about discrimination, the best course of action is to be prepared to show:

    A. That you had valid reasons for discipline unrelated to the complaint.

    B. Reasons for the action taken should be supported by those who know the complainant.

    C. Prior documentation and/or warnings to the employee should be carefully stated.

    D. The employee to the door.

    E. All of the above

13. It is illegal to ask interview questions that appear to discriminate candidates according to EEOC guidelines and Title VII of the Civil Rights Act. The following question(s) are illegal to ask in an interview except:

    A. Are you a U.S. citizen?

    B. Can you legally work in the United States?

    C. Are you authorized to work in the United States?

    D. May I see your Driver's License?

    E. none of the above

14. Questions about spoken language are illegal to ask in an interview except:

    A. What is your native language?

    B. I love your accent; what is your native tongue?

    C. Where did you grow up?

    D. What languages do you speak or write fluently?

    E. Where were you born?

15. Inquiring about religion or religious holidays is illegal in a job interview. Which of the following question(s) is legal?

    A. For the purpose of work planning, what religion do you practice that may require time off from work?

    B. Which holidays do you observe?

    C. Are you available to work according to our established work schedule that includes nights, weekends, and holidays?

    D. Do you observe Christmas and Easter?

    E. Will you be needing time off for holidays, excluding Christmas and Easter?

16. Seeking information about a candidate's age is discriminatory according to EEOC, ADEA, and Title VII of the Civil Rights Act. The correct way to inquire about one's age in an interview is to ask:

    A. Is it okay to ask how old you are?
    B. For the purpose of job reporting, what is your age?
    C. May I see your driver'slicense?
    D. Are you legally old enough to work in this job?
    E. All of the above

17. According to the ADA, asking job candidates about their disabilities is discriminatory. All of the following questions are illegal except:

    A. Tell me about your disability.
    B. Do you have a disability that would interfere with this job?
    C. Are you able to perform the essential functions of this job with or without a reasonable accommodation?
    D. How can we reasonably accommodate your disability?
    E. Asking any question that can be interpreted as discriminatory is illegal.

18. It is okay to ask a job candidate about a conviction when:

    A. The job requires a high level of security.
    B. When they have been arrested or convicted of a crime.
    C. The job requires a BFOQ.
    D. Both (a) and (c)
    E. None of the above

19. Constructive discharge can be thought of as:

    A. Discharge as though the employer wrongfully terminated the employee.
    B. Termination.
    C. Setting up a constructive plan of actionable goals to encourage an employee to improve performance.
    D. Covert pressure to get an employee to quit.
    E. All of the above

20. Due to the complexity of employment relationships and situations, the best management practices are those that impact:

    A. Legal issues that may result in discrimination
    B. Wrongful termination due to uninformed management practices
    C. Workplace safety that may result in employee deaths
    D. Its human resources
    E. The strategic goals of the organization

21. Many employment issues are governed by applicable federal and state law. Where the employment relationship is based on a valid contract entered into by the employer and the employee:

    A. State contract law will usually dictate the rights and duties of the parties,
    B. Federal law prevails.
    C. It depends whether state law addresses the issue or not.
    D. The higher standard more often applies.
    E. All of the above

22. All employees have basic rights in the workplace, including all of the following except:

    A. The right to privacy
    B. Fair compensation
    C. Freedom from discrimination
    D. Freedom of speech
    E. All of the above

23. A job applicant has legal rights prior to being hired as an employee. Those rights include all of the following except:

    A. the right to be free from discrimination
    B. Age discrimination
    C. Gender preference
    D. Disability
    E. All of the above

24. In most states, employees have the right to privacy in the workplace. This includes all of the following except:

    A. Right to privacy
    B. Personal possessions
    C. Handbags or briefcases
    D. Storage lockers accessible only by the employee
    E. Private email addressed only to employee

25. An employer may not conduct a credit or background check about an employee or prospective employee unless the employer:

    A. Notifies the individual in writing
    B. Receives permission to do so
    C. Notifies the individual in writing and receives permission
    D. Has already decided to hire the applicant, then permission is not needed
    E. None of the above

26. The reason most employees consider joining a union is:

    A. leadership is important to job security.
    B. Employees want to belong to a group.
    C. Job security.
    D. It provides a safe and secure working environment.
    E. Unions give people a collective voice at work.

27. Which statement accurately defines the Taft-Hartley Act?

    A. It prohibits paycheck deduction for union dues.
    B. It allows employers to file unfair labor practice allegations against unions.
    C. It established the growth of the union movement.
    D. Employers are able to negotiate collective bargaining agreements.
    E. None of the above

28. The NLRA serves to:

    A. Open the door to collective bargaining agreements by union members

    B. Prohibit arbitrary injunctions

    C. Balance interests of management and labor

    D. Prohibit employers from unfair labor practices

    E. All of the above

29. Right to work laws were established by:

    A. Some states

    B. All states

    C. The federal government

    D. Unions

    E. The EEOC

30. The primary purpose of right to work laws was to:

    A. Cap the federal minimum wage rate

    B. Pay less than the minimum wage rate

    C. Forbid forced membership in unions

    D. Allow forced membership in unions

    E. None of the above

31. Common law is derived from a body of law known as:

    A. Legislation

    B. Employment law

    C. Decisions by the courts

    D. Federal law applicable to all of the states

    E. Supreme Court rulings

32. Statutory law is governed by legislation and enforced by:

    A. The courts

    B. The EEOC

    C. Federal law

    D. Employment law

    E. All of the above

33. Employment at-will is a concept that allows three exceptions. Which exception deviates from the concept that an employee or employer may sever the employment relationship at any time for any reason?

    A. An employee is terminated who does not have an employment contract

    B. Both employee and employer agree to end the employment relationship

    C. An employee is terminated for filing workers' compensation benefits

    D. An employee is terminated for causing a riot

    E. An employee steals from the company

34. When is it possible to begin mediation between two parties prior to an investigation?

    A. When it is requested by the EEOC

    B. When a claim is filed within one year of the incident

    C. When an employee has filed a lawsuit

    D. When the employer wants to mediate

    E. All of the above

35. To improve relations with its employees, a trucking company sets up an employee feedback system. In order to motivate employees to become involved, which incentive may be viewed as an NLRA violation?

    A. A committee votes to stop shipping products that don't meet company standards.

    B. A management committee proposes an increase in vacation time for its truckers.

    C. Safety violations are identified and corrections are put into place.

    D. Union members and other employees become eligible for a pay increase after completing a training program.

    E. All of the above

36. When employers hire employees to work for the company, employers have a duty to:

    A. Protect employees from other workers who pose a risk

    B. Protect employees from negligent applicants

    C. Protect employees from misconduct taking place after hours

    D. Protect business interests after hours

    E. Get applicants to sign the application as proof that the interview took place

37. Learning organizations are those that:

    A. Conceptualize and operate from a systems thinking perspective

    B. Learn how to combine systems thinking with strategic plans and MBOs

    C. Work together in teams

    D. Define a shared vision

    E. Are trained by HRD

38. Which of the following is an indicator of employee satisfaction?

    A. Absentee rate

    B. Grievances

    C. Turnover

    D. All of the above

    E. None of the above

39. HRM activities:

    A. Are concerned with quality control and organizational output

    B. Are viewed as the "soft" side' of management

    C. Serve as the ombudsman for performance appraisals

    D. Are driven by HR objectives

    E. Drive the organization

40. Today, more than ever, it is assumed that:

    A. HRM is responsible for contributing to the organization's efficiency and equity

    B. HR effectively matches employees and their appropriate job functions

    C. HRM is directly responsible for linking the organization's profitability, market share, and growth

    D. HRM is the key driver to attract and hire talent management in a competitive environment

    E. All of the above

41. HR activities should be derived from:

    A. Organizational goals and objectives

    B. Evaluation strategies

    C. Compliance and labor costs

    D. The organization's strategic plan for growth through its talent management

    E. HR activities and planning

42. HRM's strategic management is best conceptualized as:

    A. Affecting revenue goals of the organization through development of its talent management and human resources

    B. Integrating systems development through its employees

    C. Training and development of its human resources

    D. Affecting senior management's view of its talent management in order to meet the needs of the organization

    E. None of the above

43. The Senior Vice President of HR reports to senior management on the progress of an HRM initiative affecting the organization at large. The SVP leads the project and assumes the role of project _____:

    A. Leader

    B. Director

    C. Manager

    D. Front-runner

    E. Sponsor

44. The VP of HR is informed by senior management that a new employee initiative will be implemented during the first quarter of the new year. HRD is given the task of training managers who will announce it to employees. In this scenario, the change agent is:

    A. Senior management

    B. VP HR

    C. HRD

    D. Department managers

    E. Employees

45. Which interview question would not be considered discriminatory?

    A. Do you plan to have children?

    B. How many children do you have?

    C. Do you care for children?

    D. What experience do you have working with children?

    E. All of the above

46. Which interview question below is discriminatory?

    A. Can you travel on short notice?

    B. Is there anything to prevent you from traveling on short notice?

    C. Are you prevented from traveling on short notice?

    D. What would prevent you from traveling on short notice?

    E. If you have childcare can you travel on short notice?

47. Which question(s) below would be the best way to ask a non- discriminatory question about extracurricular activities in an applicant interview?

    A. Which organizations do you belong to?

    B. Tell me about organizational work you do.

    C. Tell me about organizations that may affect the ability to do this job.

    D. What kinds of non-work groups are you a member of?

    E. Are you involved in other work that contributes to or may affect your ability to perform the job?

48. It is difficult to implement organizational strategic planning without knowing its:

    A. Goals and objectives

    B. Organizational chart

    C. Mission statement

    D. Value proposition

    E. None of the above

49. Implementing organizational change is most effective when:

    A. Planning takes place in advance of the intended change

    B. Senior managers are responsible for inputs and outcomes

    C. Employees are part of the change process

    D. HRM conducts a needs analysis to determine whether a change is feasible

    E. All of the above

50. Outsourcing is a process determined by:

    A. Stakeholders

    B. Its product or service

    C. Goals and expectations

    D. A realistic budget

    E. A needs analysis

51. Short-terms objectives include all of the following except:

    A. Long-range goals

    B. Identifying milestones

    C. MBOs

    D. Allocating resources

    E. Establishing priorities

52. HRM is concerned with an organizational balance sheet because it:

    A. Defines organizational assets, liabilities, and revenue goals

    B. Outlines goals and objectives

    C. Allocates budgets for salaries and raises

    D. Projects hiring costs

    E. Determines cost per hire

53. Centralization is concerned with:

    A. Operating units that need to collaborate

    B. Combining departments into one central location

    C. Centralizing operating units where decisions are carried out

    D. Decision making authority at the highest levels in the organization such as the company's headquarters, executive or corporate office(s).

    E. Reporting relationships

54. A decentralized organization works best in environments where:

    A. Organizational decision making takes place in all operating units

    B. Decision making authority is given to department managers and supervisors

    C. Authority to make decisions is given to lower levels in an organizational hierarchy when there are multiple locations

    D. Quick decisions impact the organization's success

    E. None of the above

55. An organization willing to exceed the standard pay range is in which stage of the organizational cycle to attract key talent management?

    A. Growth stage

    B. Introductory stage

    C. Outgrowth stage

    D. Maturity

    E. Eecline

56. Controlling labor costs while an organization is still in a growth cycle is characterized by its:

    A. Maturity

    B. Growth

    C. Margin

    D. Stakeholders

    E. All of the above

57. An organization in decline due to the economy, competition, or poor marketing strategy is likely to be characterized by:

    A. downsizing

    B. Rightsizing

    C. Layoffs

    D. Attrition

    E. All of the above

58. Organizational resistance to policies, rules, lack of incentive, and resistance to change are likely to be found in which stage of the organizational cycle?

    A. Decline

    B. Growth

    C. Transition

    D. Acquisition

    E. Chaos

59. An organization which requires training and development of its talent, and is able to target the knowledge, skills, and abilities (KSAs) necessary to effectively train its human resources, is characterized by its:

    A. Maturity level

    B. Growth stage

    C. Competition

    D. Incentive

    E. Motivation

60. And HR unit that reports directly to corporate headquarters is described as a:

    A. Functional unit

    B. Matrix managed unit

    C. Field unit

    D. Decentralized unit

    E. None of the above

61. In an organizational chart, multiple reporting relationships are demonstrated by:

    A. Its divisional structure

    B. Its functional structure

    C. A dotted line to corporate headquarters

    D. A dotted line to the functional unit

    E. Matrix managed authority

62. A narrow span of control is implemented in all of the following situations except:

    A. When employees are properly trained

    B. When workers are inexperienced

    C. When employees are improperly trained

    D. When tasks are complex

    E. When units operate under tight deadlines

63. Span of control refers to:

    A. Poorly trained employees who need close supervision

    B. The number of employees under a supervisor's control

    C. The number of supervisors needed to operate a business

    D. The number of departments that report to a single supervisor or manager

    E. Employees learning new KSAs until transfer of training has been achieved

64. HR audits are conducted primarily in order to determine:

    A. Span of control

    B. Compliance with EEOC guidelines

    C. The overall effectiveness of the HRM function

    D. Whether employee training programs meet the needs of the organization

    E. Discriminatory hiring practices

65. An architectural engineer works for a firm as a paid intern and freelances as an independent contractor. The engineer has been asked by a client to design plans for his home. Ethically, this creates a situation that would be considered:

    A. Illegal

    B. Insider information

    C. A conflict of interest

    D. A kickback

    E. Moonlighting

66. In the above example, who is creating potential liability?

    A. The engineer
    B. The client
    C. Both the engineer and the client
    D. The contracting organization
    E. All parties involved in the situation

67. In the above example, who is creating a conflict of interest?

    A. The employer
    B. The intern/freelancer
    C. The contracting organization
    D. The HR department
    E. None of the above

68. Under the ADA, the law pertains to employers with:

    A. 15 or more employees
    B. 20 employees
    C. 50 or more employees
    D. All employers
    E. Government contracts

69. Under the ADA, all of the following statements are false except:

    A. managers over 40 years of age have no mandatory retirement requirements
    B. Employees over 40 years of age are protected by law and may not be fired
    C. Employees over 40 years of age may be fired under the at-will provision
    D. Employees over 40 years of age may be fired for cause
    E. Employers are not required to offer insurance to employees covered by Medicare

70. An applicant who worked as a marketing manager in the past is refused employment at another company because of a mental health diagnosis. According to Title I of the ADA, the applicant is:

    A. Qualified under the law
    B. Qualified, and may be granted a BFOQ for a mental health condition
    C. Unqualified, depending on the mental health diagnosis
    D. Protected by law since the mental health diagnosis is confidential
    E. Protected by law unless certain requirements of the job require disclosure of the mental illness

71. Under the ADA, all of the following conditions are protected by law except:

    A. Epilepsy
    B. AIDS
    C. Illegal drug use
    D. Stealing pens as a symptom of obsessive compulsive disorder
    E. Bipolar disorder

72. Reasonable accommodations need not be met under the following conditions if the accommodation:

    A. Is a hardship for the employee
    B. Results in undue hardship for the employer
    C. Is a need for medical marijuana during working hours for the employee
    D. Complies with the employer's affirmative action plan
    E. All of the above

73. Both identity and the right to work in the U.S. is verified by an applicant's:

    A. U.S. passport
    B. Driver's license
    C. Green card
    D. Visa
    E. Social security card

74. The burden of proof when hiring an applicant who is eligible to work in the U.S. lies with the:

    A. Employee
    B. Employer
    C. Applicant
    D. Immigration and Naturalization Service
    E. Form I-9

75. All of the following statements about the Privacy Act are true except:

    A. it allows federal employees the right to know of information collected about them
    B. It allows federal employees the right to review their files
    C. It does not allow federal employees access to their files
    D. It restricts the law to federal employees
    E. None of the above

76. Employers may require polygraph tests for employees when:

    A. It is suspected that a theft has taken place
    B. An employee is suspected of selling information to a competitor
    C. An employee is suspected of drug abuse
    D. An employee has access to distribution of controlled substances
    E. Never; polygraph tests are never required

77. If an employer denies a promotion based on a credit report, according to the FCRA, an employee is entitled to:

    A. Deny the accuracy of the report
    B. Receive a "pre-adverse action disclosure" prepared by the FTC
    C. Sue the company
    D. Take legal action against the FTC
    E. All of the above

78. A qualified white male is denied an opportunity for a job because preference is given to a member of a protected group. Under the law, this is known as:

    A. Reverse discrimination
    B. Affirmative action
    C. Title VII
    D. Discrimination based on gender and race
    E. Meeting a hiring quota system

79. The legal doctrine that holds employers and organizations responsible for discriminatory acts by supervisors is known as:

   A. Hostile work environment

   B. Sexual harassment

   C. Four-fifths rule

   D. Vicarious liability

   E. Quid pro quo

80. Employing fewer members of a protected class than availability indicates is called:

   A. Underutilization

   B. Discrimination of a protected class

   C. Violation of the 4/5ths rule

   D. Confirmation bias

   E. None of the above

81. Which court case established the ruling of disparate impact and lack of discriminatory intent?

   A. Albermarle Paper v. Moody

   B. McDonnell Douglas Corp v. Green

   C. Griggs v. Duke Power

   D. Smith v. Barnes & Noble

   E. AT&T v. Brown

82. Federal contractors are routinely investigated by compliance officers to conduct accuracy audits of:

   A. EEO postings

   B. Compliance checks

   C. Offsite review

   D. Human resource practices

   E. None of the above

83. When evaluating data, the ability of a study to measure what it is intended to measure is called:

   A. Internal consistency

   B. Validity

   C. Reliability

   D. Quantitative analysis

   E. All of the above

84. Which research design allows respondents to add additional information to questionnaires?

   A. Quasi-experimental designs

   B. Rating scales

   C. Surveys

   D. Essay questions

   E. Multiple-choice

85. Experimental designs:

   A. Are the most rigorous research design

   B. Are the least rigorous design

   C. Do not require control groups

   D. Do not require randomly assigned groups

   E. Can be quantitative, qualitative or anecdotal as long as there is a control group

86. All of the following are measures of central tendency except:

   A. Mode

   B. Median

   C. Range

   D. Mean

   E. Average tendency

87. The measure of central tendency that appears as the midpoint in a distribution is called its:

A. Mean

B. Mode

C. Median

D. Range

E. Central tendency

88. The difference between the highest and lowest scores in a selection or distribution is called its

A. Range

B. Central tendency

C. Average score

D. Mode

E. None of the above

89. Trend analysis is the ability to accurately project future trends based on:

A. Length of time

B. Trends of competitors

C. The relationship between two variables

D. Correlating two predictor variables and determining differences that exist between the two

E. Needs analysis conducted by the organization

90. The difference between a job description and a job specification is:

A. One describes the job and the other describes its requirements

B. One describes duties and the other describes qualifications

C. One describes job requirements and the other describes tasks

D. They are essentially the same

E. None of the above

91. An effectve training program must rely upon a job analysis and the tasks needed to perform the job. This is called:

A. Job training

B. Transfer of training

C. KSAs

D. Duties, tasks, and skills

E. Competencies, requirements, and structure

92. Employees are informed about internal company job opportunities through a:

A. Job posting system

B. Internet job board

C. Human Resource Department

D. Word of mouth

E. All of the above

93. The best referral source of qualified job candidates is through:

A. Employee referrals

B. Internet postings via an internet job source

C. College placement programs

D. Friends and relatives

E. Position postings

94. Attrition is to retention as:

A. Turnover is to stability

B. Layoff is to termination

C. Hiring is to firing

D. Promotion is to stagnation

E. None of the above

95. An essential job function requires:

    A. Reasonable accommodations determined by ADA

    B. BFOQs determined by the essential features of a job

    C. Highly specialized skills

    D. The work to be done at least 50% of the time

    E. A college degree

96. Yield data is factual information that can be used to determine:

    A. Recruitment effectiveness

    B. New hires vs. turnover

    C. Retention vs. attrition

    D. Affirmative action efforts

    E. All of the above

97. Employee selection is a process best determined by:

    A. Comparing the most desirable candidate qualifications to the least desirable

    B. Hiring the best candidate for the position

    C. Hiring the most preferred candidate for the position

    D. Identifying the most suitable candidate

    E. Affirmative action guidelines

98. The key difference between submitting a resume or CV and completing an application is:

    A. The resume displays a personal and professional "picture" of the individual applying for the job, even though you can't see him or her

    B. The application allows for uniform information to be categorized according to EEOC guidelines

    C. An application asks applicants to verify that the content in the application is correct by signing the form with their signature

    D. A CV more often discloses information that an application may not be allowed to ask

    E. All of the above

99. The biggest advantage to employers for hiring temp-to-hire employees is:

    A. The employer gets to try out a potential employee

    B. The employer may not need a permanent employee

    C. The temp more often displays their best skills in temporary situations

    D. A temp position is temporary and requires no benefits

    E. You don't have to fire a temp employee, you simply ask for a new temp from the staffing agency

100. What is the best kind of interview to seek information about how an applicant handles a previous situation to an actual workplace situation:

    A. Behavioral

    B. Structured

    C. Stress

    D. Directive

    E. Truthfulness

101. Which is the best type of interview seeking information to compare the top three candidates for a high-level position?

    A. Behavioral

    B. Structured

    C. Stress

    D. Directive

    E. Truthfulness

102. Which is the best type of assessment method for feedback from superiors, colleagues, and subordinates?

    A. Rating scale

    B. Forced ranking

    C. MBTI

    D. 360 evaluation

    E. MBO

103. Interview bias may take place in situations when one applicant overshadows all of the rest. When an interviewer prefers the answer to a question or personality style compared to other candidates, the outcome may be a consequence of the:

    A. Halo effect

    B. Contrast effect

    C. Cultural preference

    D. Personality effect

    E. Visual overshadowing

104. When an interviewer is turned off by something an applicant says and disregards everything else from the same interview, the interview has committed the overshadowing interview effect called:

    A. Negative outcome

    B. Contrast effect

    C. Halo effect

    D. Horn effect

    E. Information bias

105. If an assessment is needed to measure an applicant's ability to acquire new skills, the best type of assessment is:

    A. An achievement test

    B. A personality profile

    C. An in-basket exercise

    D. An aptitude test

    E. All of the above

106. A managerial-level applicant is asked to take several assessment instruments to determine best fit. The applicant is asked to complete an exercise where simulated work situations (all requiring decisive decision making) are presented in a 20-minute time frame. This type of assessment is frequently called:

    A. An in-basket exercise

    B. A stress interview

    C. A multiple-choice test

    D. A structured interview

    E. A case study

107. In a position where there is high turnover, what is the most reliable measure of job success during the interview stage?

    A. A personality assessment comparing successful candidates to unsuccessful ones

    B. An in-basket exercise presenting typical day-to-day situations

    C. A realistic job preview

    D. A stress test

    E. A company tour

108. The difference between construct validity and content validity is:

    A. Construct validity measures specific job traits corresponding to statistical outcomes that establish its validity

    B. Content validity measures knowledge, skills, and abilities needed to perform the job

    C. Construct validity measures outcomes and content validity measures job tasks.

    D. All of the above

    E. None of the above

109. A learning organization may best be described as one that:

    A. Houses an HRD department

    B. Embraces training for its employees

    C. Combines the efforts of HRD to develop its employees to manage change in conjunction with the organization at large

    D. Adapts to its environment

    E. Functions as matrix managed entity

110. The key difference between an organization's HRD department and HRM is:

    A. HRD focuses on training and development

    B. HRM focuses on hiring qualified employees for the organization

    C. HRD focuses on organization development

    D. HRM focuses on operations and planning of its human resources

    E. None of the above

111. From an organization development viewpoint, adult learners are:

    A. Motivated by intrinsic rewards vs. extrinsic rewards

    B. Motivated by benefits more than the job itself

    C. Motivated by career growth vs. job titles

    D. Valued for their previous experience and ability to share alternative solutions

    E. Not valued

112. The key difference between an organization's training and development programs and organization development programs is:

    A. Training and development is focused on teaching new KSAs to perform essential tasks of a job

    B. OD is focused on an organization's ability to manage change

    C. Training and development is focused on teaching new policies that are mandated by legislation

    D. OD is focused on an organization's ability to adapt to its environment

    E. All of the above

113. A freelance writer is offered an opportunity to write the company's employee handbook. The copyright for the published handbook is owned by:

    A. The company
    B. The freelance writer
    C. Both
    D. Neither
    E. It all depends what's in the contract

114. A PhD-level adjunct faculty member is hired to write a course for a university. The faculty member has published several articles independent of writing the course.The articles are published online as part of the course called "supplemental materials". In this scenario, who owns intellectual property rights to the course?

    A. The university
    B. The faculty member
    C. The university owns the course but not the articles
    D. Neither
    E. It depends what's in the contract

115. As KSAs are learned and acquired to perform a complex task, a worker's learning curve will appear:

    A. Less curved at the beginning, more curved at the end
    B. More curved at the beginning, less curved at the end
    C. To decrease as familiarity increases
    D. S-shaped
    E. As a bell curve

116. Employees are more likely to quit their job:

    A. If their physical and social needs are not met on the job
    B. If their opinions are not valued
    C. If they perceive that they are not treated fairly
    D. If they do not agree with organizational objectives
    E. If they have no opportunities for growth

117. Gaps between actual performance and desired performance in a training program can be measured by:

    A. The ADDIE model
    B. A 360 performance evaluation
    C. Forced ranking
    D. OJT
    E. Group performance

118. The best method to determine if desired performance has been achieved on the job is:

    A. OJT
    B. MBO
    C. 360 gap analysis
    D. Transfer of training
    E. Training evaluations

119. Variable ratio reinforcement on the job would most likely occur:

    A. Rarely
    B. Occasionally
    C. At fixed intervals
    D. Unexpectedly
    E. Randomly

120. An example of fixed interval reinforcement on the job is:

    A. The mid-performance review

    B. Quarterly incentives

    C. Bi-weekly paychecks

    D. Holiday pay

    E. Bonuses

121. All of the following goals should be included in a company's new hire orientation program except:

    A. Understand company policies and procedures

    B. Familiarize employees with the Employee Handbook

    C. Sexual harassment training

    D. Establish cooperative relationships with on board employees

    E. None of the above

122. The primary purpose of a new hire orientation program is to:

    A. Familiarize employees with organizational culture

    B. Discuss the employee benefits package and options

    C. Become familiar with company paid holidays and time off

    D. Understand policies and procedures written in the Employee Handbook

    E. Establish a working relationship with the company and co-workers

123. Transfer of training is a key goal in all of the following situations except:

    A. New hire orientation

    B. Sexual harassment training

    C. Supervisory training

    D. OJT

    E. Computer training

124. Transfer of training would be most critical in:

    A. Essential job tasks requiring complex skills

    B. OJT

    C. Specific training skills that could pose a danger to self or others if not properly trained

    D. Situations where temp employees are hired

    E. All of the above

125. Transfer of training refers to a participant's ability to:

    A. Train others to do the same job

    B. Successfully complete a post-test at the end of the training session

    C. Perform skills learned in a training program to the actual job

    D. Evaluate whether or not the training program was successful

    E. All of the above

126. HRD is able to demonstrate that implementing realistic job previews during the applicant phase of the interview process reduced turnover by 10% compared to the same time one year ago. This evaluation was determined as a result of:

    A. Management by objectives

    B. Goal setting

    C. Forecast planning

    D. Measurable outcomes

    E. Revenue sharing

127. The primary difference between internal career management and career planning is:

   A. Career management considers all of the employees in the organization

   B. Career planning considers all of the high potentials in an organization

   C. Career management considers the goals and objectives of the organization compared to its available internal talent management

   D. Career planning considers employees who work for the organization compared to the needs of the organization

   E. All of the above

128. Succession planning is based on an organization's ability to identify:

   A. Key management in the event of a disaster

   B. Executive management in advance of a sudden event

   C. Candidates who can be developed to take over key role in the organization

   D. A replacement strategy for short term and long range planning

   E. All of the above

129. Increasing the variety of job tasks and responsibilities but not increasing a job's skill level is called:

   A. Job enrichment

   B. Job enlargement

   C. Job design

   D. Job motivation

   E. Job redesign

130. Increasing the skill level of a job requiring increased responsibility for planning, organizing, and evaluation is known as:

   A. Job redesign

   B. Job enrichment

   C. Job motivation

   D. Job enlargement

   E. Job specialization

131. Which job redesign below is intended to improve motivation and attitude but may not improve productivity?

   A. Job simplification

   B. Job enlargement

   C. Job enrichment

   D. Job motivation

   E. Job specialization

132. The management theory that says the most effective leaders are equally concerned about employees and production is:

   A. Blake-Mouton

   B. Bass

   C. Hersey-Blanchard

   D. Tennar-Pogso

   E. Fletcher-Olwyler

133. Identifying leadership characteristics of individuals with a high need for achievement is the work of:

   A. Bennis

   B. Harkins

   C. Senge

   D. McClelland

   E. Kouzes

134. Performance that depends upon the interaction taking place between how favorable a group situation is compared to one's leadership style is known as:

    A. Trait theory
    B. Situational theory
    C. Contingency theory
    D. CBT
    E. TA

135. A transformational leader is one who:

    A. Inspires workers to develop to their potential according to their unique ability
    B. Provides vision to the organization
    C. Intervenes when standards are not met
    D. Delivers rewards through incentives
    E. Motivates workers through personal attention

136. The difference between a multicultural workforce and an organization with a strong corporate culture is:

    A. A multicultural workforce refers to the mix of cultural backgrounds, race, and religion of its workers
    Б. A strong corporate culture refers to organizational identity based on its values and public image
    C. One is concerned with ethics and the other is concerned with values
    D. Both a and b
    E. None of the above

137. As an organization grows, the need for more HR managers and possible multiple locations arise. In a matrix managed organization, HR managers are more than likely to:

    A. Report to one individual
    B. Report to several individuals
    C. Report to at least two individuals
    D. Report to several departments
    E. Report to the division head where the employee works

138. Referring to #137, as the organization continues to grow and more employees are hired, conflicts begin to arise that impact reporting relationships, worker efficiency, and impacting performance goals. OD conducted a needs analysis and determined that this is due to:

    A. Organizational conflicts
    B. Organizational structure
    C. Outdated organizational charts
    D. Technological interference
    E. A PIP issue

139. The HR Director is asked to address the organization's Board of Directors about turnover, attrition, and retention of its employees over the past five years. The best way to diagram and chart this summary is to use a:

    A. Bell curve
    B. Pareto chart
    C. Histogram
    D. Check sheet
    E. Flow chart

140. A forced distribution rating scale is an appraisal method used to compare the performance:

    A.   Of employees by random selection

    B.   Of employees by forced choice

    C.   Of each employee to all others

    D.   Of employees using a checklist

    E.   None of the above

141. A performance appraisal is used to rate all workers in the fast food industry. Only the results of the performance appraisals in the northeast region determined that older workers make more mistakes than younger workers. It appears that:

    A.   The interviewer for the northeast region was biased

    B.   Older workers in the northeast make more mistakes than all other workers in the company

    C.   The interviewer prefers younger workers

    D.   Younger workers are more efficient in the northeast region

    E.   The management style in the northeast region is different than in all other regions

142. When an employee's performance in one area causes the appraiser to give high or low ratings in all other areas in a performance appraisal, it is likely that:

    A.   The recency affect impacted the appraisal

    B.   A halo effect has occurred

    C.   Bias in one area is more likely to result in bias in all areas

    D.   Employees are rated either all good or all bad

    E.   All of the above

143. In order for a pension plan to qualify under ERISA:

    A.   It must include a vesting schedule

    B.   It may be communicated to employees

    C.   It must offer it to all employees

    D.   It must allow participants to opt

    E.   All of the above

144. The primary difference between exempt status and non-exempt status is:

    A.   Exempt status employees are usually managerial and paid on an annual salary

    B.   Non-exempt status employees are usually union members

    C.   Exempt status employees are paid a salary without over-time benefits

    D.   Non-exempt status employees are paid a salary with over time benefits

    E.   Exempt status employees have hiring and firing authority

145. The Equal Pay Act attempts to prohibit wage discrimination between males and females who hold the same qualifications to perform the same job. Under this ruling, employers:

    A.   Must pay equal wages to males and females for the same work

    B.   Must pay all employees regardless or age or gender the same salary for the same work

    C.   Do not have to pay equal wages if there is a bona fide occupational exception

    D.   Still pay wages that are unequal when comparing national averages

    E.   Must pay a similar wage based on comparable work

146. If the state's minimum wage is higher than the federal minimum wage, employers must follow:

    A. Federal guidelines

    B. State guidelines

    C. Whichever rate benefits the employee

    D. Whichever rate benefits the employer

    E. The higher standard

147. Of the following, which one is not regulated by FLSA?

    A. Minimum wage

    B. Overtime

    C. Exempt status

    D. Non-exempt status

    E. Fringe benefits

148. Under revised DOL ERISA regulations, employers are required to:

    A. Report all unfavorable rulings to the federal government

    B. Vest employees in a defined benefit plan

    C. Modify all health claim procedures stating claimant's rights including access to information about claims at no charge

    D. Offer a retirement plan to all employees

    E. All of the above

149. An employee who was on FMLA for 12 weeks for a serious health condition decides not to return to work. Under FMLA guidelines:

    A. The employee is entitled to continue coverage under COBRA

    B. The employee's dependents are entitled to benefits under COBRA

    C. The employee must return to work before COBRA can be offered

    D. The employee must give notice to resign before COBRA can begin running

    E. FMLA is unrelated to COBRA specific conditions

150. An employee's daughter who graduates from college is no longer a dependent on the family's medical insurance program. According to COBRA,

    A. The employee's daughter is ineligible

    B. The employee's daughter is eligible up to age 24

    C. The employee's daughter may continue benefits for 36 months

    D. The employee's daughter may continue benefits for 18 months

    E. None of the above

151. The FASB is the authoritative arm of the SEC that:

A. Communicates financial rulings to shareholders

B. Determines how financial information is to be reported to shareholders

C. Decides how a company will announce its public status

D. Interprets IRS revenue rulings regarding independent contractors and other employee status rules

E. None of the above

152. Benchmarking includes none of the following except:

A. The position appears in the middle of the pay range

B. The job changes frequently and is unique in its classification

C. It is the position frequently used outside of the organization to compare with other labor market wages

D. A key position in the organization not well understood

E. None of the above

153. Of the following benefits which is considered to be direct compensation?

A. Company car

B. Company laptop computer

C. Paid life insurance

D. Cash achievement award

E. All of the above

154. All of the following statistical methods are quantitative assessments except:

A. Point scales

B. Weighting

C. Bell curve

D. Job classifications

E. Job ranking

155. Typically, compensable factors determine how work is done as it is described in a position description. Factors considered compensable include all of the following except:

A. KSAs

B. Seniority

C. Education

D. MBOs

E. Job skills

156. Job evaluations classified into a classification system with a determined number of grades is commonly used in government and:

A. Public sector jobs

B. Military rankings

C. DOD contracts

D. Non-exempt positions

E. Exempt positions

157. The best known classification system that groups jobs into predetermined grades and descriptions used for job comparisons is the:

A. General Schedule system used by the federal government

B. GS System that include rankings from 1-15

C. Hay system

d. Performance based

158. Establishing a hierarchy of jobs in an organization and comparing it to other job evaluation resources helps to determine its:

    A. Job evaluation
    B. Relative worth
    C. Internal pay equity
    D. Job enrichment
    E. Job enlargement

159. Adjusting salary data to remain current in the marketplace, it is necessary to calculate salary to recent trends. This process is known as:

    A. Data analysis
    B. Benchmarking
    C. Aging
    D. Trend analysis
    E. Value proposition

160. In order to calculate a weighted average of salaries within an organization, it is necessary to:

    A. Consider each salary and divide it by the number of salaries given
    B. Consider how many individuals receive an annual salary × the number of the actual salaries given ($30,000 × 2 = $60,000)
    C. Add each individual salary × the number of actual salaries ÷ (divided) by the number of persons receiving each salary
    D. Calculate the mean score to determine a weighted average
    E. None of the above

161. Job grades are impacted by all of the following variables except:

    A. Internal worth
    B. How the organization pays compared to marketplace averages
    C. Internal pay policies
    D. Organizational size
    E. Promotions

162. Broadbanding allows organizations to:

    A. Pay lower salaries
    B. Group large amounts of employees who earn similar base rates
    C. Reduce the number of reporting levels in an organization
    D. Combine several salary grades with similar pay ranges into one band for flatter organizations
    E. Reduce the number differentiated salaries into bands or groupings

163. In single or flat rate pay systems, employees:

    A. Are paid the same rate
    B. With higher performance evaluations are minimally compensated
    C. Who qualify for seniority status are based on longevity
    D. Qualify under exempt status
    E. Are motivated to earn more through incentives

164. Pay increases that occur on a predetermined schedule are considered to be:

    A. Annually based
    B. Performance based
    C. Productivity based
    D. Time based
    E. Seniority based

165. A discretionary bonus versus a performance-based bonus occurs as the result of:

   A. End of a time period considered discretionary
   B. Previously determined MBO's
   C. The discretion of management judgment
   D. An objective compared to a percentage of profits
   E. Exceeding goals and objectives

166. A direct pay plan that is immediately taxable and subject to IRS rulings is:

   A. A 401K plan
   B. An IRA
   C. Cash profit sharing plan
   D. IPO announcement
   E. Deferred compensation

167. All of the following statements about long-term disability protection is false except:

   A. It expires after 26 weeks
   B. It begins once sick leave benefits have been exhausted
   C. It is integrated with Social Security benefits
   D. It covers non-work-related illnesses
   E. It covers work related injuries

168. Which managed care plan integrates a PPO and PPA plan and allows access to specialists?

   A. POS
   B. PPO
   C. HMO
   D. PPA
   E. EPO

169. Which managed care plan does not allow or cover participants' medical costs for providers outside of the network?

   A. POS
   B. PPO
   C. HMO
   D. PPA
   E. EPO

170. All of the following company benefits are considered indirect taxable compensation except:

   A. Employee discounts
   B. Tuition reimbursement
   C. Tips
   D. Business company vehicle
   E. All of the above

171. Recently Starbucks was fined $106 M for:

   A. Allowing employees to share tips
   B. Not sharing tips with employees
   C. Not paying tax on shared tips
   D. Not filing tax returns that included tips to employees
   E. Not reporting income to the IRS

172. OSHA's General Duty clause covers:

   A. The employee's right to work in a hazard free environment
   B. The employer's duty to provide a work environment free from hazards
   C. Employee's right to stay home from work if they believe it is a hazardous place to work
   D. Employer's duty to develop workplace safety standards
   E. Employee's duty to report unsafe working conditions

173. OSHA gives employees the right to:

    A. File a claim for unsafe working conditions

    B. Request a workplace investigation for unsafe working conditions

    C. Decide whether or not they will wear safety goggles

    D. Ignore safety claims; if injured on the job, compensation is waived

    E. File a complaint for unfair labor practices

174. By contrast, OSHA allows employers the right to:

    A. Refuse an OSHA inspection unless they are required to comply with a search warrant

    B. Disregard OSHA standards if they believe that safety standards have been met and considered sufficient

    C. Apply for a temporary variance for violation(s) of safety standards

    D. Bargain in front of a court

    E. Sue OSHA if they are improperly fined

175. Which OSHA standard requires that employees be informed of hazardous substances in the workplace?

    A. Control of Hazardous Energy

    B. Personal Protective Equipment

    C. Occupational Noise Exposure

    D. Hazard Communication

    E. Poison Control Exposure

176. An MSDS report contains:

    A. A list of inspection reports for mines and suspicious damage

    B. An inventory listing of hazardous chemicals

    C. A summary of mine safety and death resulting from accidents

    D. A listing of all known chemicals, hazardous and non-hazardous, at a worksite

    E. A report following a hazardous chemical spill

177. Which one of the following occupation-related injuries must be recorded?

    A. All disabilities

    B. All injuries, even those requiring a simple bandaid

    C. Injuries that result in a job transfer

    D. Injuries by workers whether or not anyone was witness to the accident

    E. All of the above

178. Employers calculate job injury and illness rates for injuries and illnesses to determine:

    A. The company's accident rating in the industry

    B. 100 full time employees and number of lost work days per 100 employees

    C. Frequency of OSHA inspections

    D. Employer compliance

    E. Safety training needs

179. The OSHA Form 200 Log and Summary must be completed in organizations:

    A. With more than 11 employees

    B. By all employers

    C. Within one week of a work related death or injury

    D. Within one day of a work-related death

    E. By all witnesses to the accident

180. Which one of the following situations is considered to be the highest priority?

    A. All high hazard industries

    B. Known non-reporting of workplace chemicals

    C. Catastrophes and fatal accidents

    D. Imminent danger

    E. Anonymous phone calls reporting a potentially dangerous situation

181. By contrast, which OSHA violation is considered to be the least serious?

    A. Small infractions or violations

    B. Other than serious

    C. De minimis

    D. Repeat

    E. Teasing penalty

182. Ideally, which one of the following measures fosters a strong safety culture in the workplace?

    A. Creating incentives for reporting workplace safety violations

    B. Having employees participate in the creation of a safety culture program

    C. Awarding employees for compliance of safety regulations

    D. Ensuring confidentiality when reporting a safety violation

    E. Having a clear workplace policy about safety

183. Which injury or symptom is associated with the repetitive nature of work?

    A. Skin rash

    B. Nausea

    C. Carpal tunnel

    D. Migraine headache

    E. Allergies

184. The highest priority at the scene of an accident is:

    A. call 911

    B. Notify management asap

    C. Protect others from injury and move them to a safe place

    D. Move the injured person to a safe place

    E. Take photos of the evidence

185. All of the following statements regarding workplace EAPs are false except:

    A. Reporting an employee's progress to his or her supervisor

    B. Counselors may report information about an employee's progress to HR

    C. Employees who do not show up for appointments are dropped from the program

    D. Employees are encouraged to contact their EAP directly

    E. None of the above

186. The best workplace substance abuse prevention is through:

    A. Unannounced drug testing for all employees

    B. Random drug testing for employees showing symptoms of abuse

    C. Drug searches through lockers, desks and company owned vehicles

    D. Written policies, training, and enforcement

    E. An open door policy

187. The degree of probability that a loss will occur which an organization may become exposed is referred to as:

    A. Hazardous waste

    B. Vulnerability analysis

    C. Hazardous containment

    D. Prevention planning

    E. Investigative research

188. Protecting proprietary information will be most effective when:

    A. Installation of a security system and indoor/outdoor surveillance cameras are installed

    B. Workplace safety measures that include confidential information includes multiple passwords and security clearances

    C. Confidentiality and non-compete agreements

    D. Not allowing employee owned software to be downloaded on company computers

    E. Having access to employee email and internet browsing

189. Workplace incidents that lead to workplace violence can be controlled by which of the following measures?

    A. Domestic counseling

    B. Self-esteem programs

    C. A stable economy

    D. Productivity goals and objectives

    E. Lowering gas prices

190. What kind of organizational structure requires a multiple chain of command?

    A. Military

    B. Private sector

    C. Matrix management

    D. Divisional

    E. Line and staff

191. An AAP is required to include data for:

    A. Reporting the number of workers past age 40

    B. Hiring employees in protected groups

    C. Analyzing current employees in protected groups

    D. Reporting current employees in protected groups by department

    E. The number of requests for reasonable accommodations for people in protected groups with disabilities

192. When two parties are in conflict about an issue and the solution benefits one but not the other, it in fact represents a gain for the other party, this is called:

    A. Union circumvention

    B. Win/lose

    C. Lose/win

    D. Lose/lose

    E. Distributive bargaining

193. Performance appraisals that rate employees on the highest performing worker in a group is committing what kind of rating error?

    A. Bias

    B. Halo effect

    C. Oneness

    D. Contrast

    E. Inflexibility

194. Under the ADA, which of the following provisions is false?

    A. A medical examination requested prior to a job offer is legal in order to determine reasonable accommodations.

    B. A job offer may be conditional pending the results of a medical examination.

    C. Buildings must be accessible to the disabled.

    D. Ramps must be put into place whether or not a disabled person works there.

    E. Employers must consider reasonable accommodations that do not present a hardship to the business's viability.

195. The most effective method for training senior managers to be critical decision makers is:

    A. Textbook

    B. Online courses

    C. Self study

    D. Case study

    E. OJT

196. Three factors that define a relevant labor market for pay purposes are:

    A. unions, inflation, compensation

    B. Real estate, economy, gas prices

    C. Stock market, world economy, wartime

    D. Occupation, geography, industry

    E. Product demand, bull market, interest rates

197. The best way to avoid a defamation lawsuit or charge is:

    A. Making truthful statements about employees

    B. Keeping a record of all written or spoken statements

    C. Keeping consistent employee records

    D. Communicating only positive attributes about employees

    E. Writing general statements in performance appraisals

198. Of the exceptions to the Employment At Will Doctrine, which one protects employees from being fired for disclosing illegal, immoral, or illegitimate practices?

    A. Implied contract

    B. Covenant of good faith and fair dealing

    C. Public policy

    D. All of the above

    E. None of the above

199. An organization in the maturity phase of its lifecycle must increase productivity in order to remain competitive in the workplace. Which strategy is most likely to increase worker productivity?

    A. Creating a new vision

    B. Providing incentives

    C. Introducing a training program focused on productivity

    D. Emphasizing productivity goals

    E. Diversifying

200. To determine exempt or non-exempt status, which one of the following positions does not require any criteria to determine employment status related to salary criteria?

    A. Managers

    B. Supervisors

    C. Secretaries

    D. Sales people

    E. Teachers

201. A new-hire orientation program may include all of the following topics except:

    A. Company history

    B. Creative problem solving

    C. Policies and procedures

    D. Benefits

    E. Employee/employer introductions

202. HR originally began as a/an:

    A. Administrative function

    B. Managerial function

    C. An office where people applied for jobs

    D. Operational function

    E. All of the above

203. All of the following statements about employment law are false except:

   A. An offer of employment must be made before a contract can be forwarded.

   B. For a contract to be legally enforceable, one individual must give and receive something of value.

   C. Once a contract is signed, no revisions can be made to it.

   D. A contract is subject to legal provisions only (vs. provisions that may be illegal).

   E. None of the above

204. All of the following employees are eligible to vote in a union election except those:

   A. Taking sick leave

   B. On temporary layoff

   C. On a leave of absence

   D. Taking vacation days

   E. All of the above

205. Prior to extending an offer of employment in a biotech company, the interviewer should verify:

   A. Permission to call the candidate's employer for verification of employment

   B. A medical exam to rule out drugs or contagious illnesses

   C. A credit report

   D. Written pre-authorization to call a list of work references

   E. All of the above

206. While a union organizing campaign was taking place, employer representatives filter throughout the organization seeking information from employees about union activities. This illegal practice is known as:

   A. Threat of reprisal

   B. Bargaining

   C. Hostile work environment

   D. Quid pro quo

   E. Implied promise

207. The best way to assess a job candidate's ability to perform the job is best facilitated by:

   A. A skills test

   B. An aptitude test

   C. A work sample test

   D. An achievement test

   E. A KSA

208. The Privacy Act of 1974:

   A. Allows federal employees access to their employee file

   B. Restricts distribution of confidential information

   C. Allows the right to have incorrect information removed

   D. Allows employees to know the kind of information the file contains

   E. All of the above

209. An individual's occupational choice is influenced by all of the following except:

   A. Educational preparation

   B. Professional experience

   C. Salary

   D. Motivation

   E. Opportunity

KAPLAN

210. Statistics show that recruitment strategies are most successful when:

    A. Referrals come from employees

    B. Recruiters are accountable for filling positions

    C. Internal candidates are promoted

    D. Job postings include incentives

    E. The company has a good reputation in the community

211. External resources that influence the design of recruitment programs include all of the following except:

    A. EEO laws

    B. Labor market forces

    C. The economy

    D. Competition

    E. Job analysis

212. A one time payment to employees who have been separated include all of the following except:

    A. Severance pay

    B. PTO balances

    C. Termination pay

    D. Holiday pay

    E. Separation pay

213. When an employer has been charged with negligent hiring, its best defense is:

    A. Documentation

    B. Proof of reference checking

    C. Proof of a signed application form

    D. Proof of a completed application form

    E. Evidence that a duty to protect other employees is written into a policy manual

214. A systematic study of a job analysis or a classification of jobs includes the activities of the job, its relationships to other jobs in the classification ranking, and when and where the job will be performed. Its outcomes will include:

    A. How to identify qualified candidates for the job

    B. Job specifications and job descriptions

    C. Identifying conditions under which the job will be implemented

    D. Identifying a job description

    E. None of the above

215. Of the following performance appraisal methods, which one compares employees from lowest to highest?

    A. Forced choice

    B. Graphic scale

    C. Bell curve

    D. Ranking

    E. 360 assessment

216. Who carries the duty to compile a list containing the names and addresses of all eligible bargaining unit employees within seven days following consent to an election?

    A. Excelsior

    B. Union shop

    C. Human Resources

    D. The employer

    E. A union representative

217. Net income is the difference between:

   A. Assets and liabilities

   B. Salary minus deductions

   C. Revenues and expenses

   D. Manufacturing costs and sales

   E. Balance sheet and bottom line

218. The value of human capital lies in:

   A. Hiring knowledgeable, well trained employees

   B. Developing resources

   C. Creating a vision where employees understand its mission

   D. Using superior products attract talented human capital

   E. Finding cheap labor in third world countries

219. In an organizational security program, the first factor to analyze is:

   A. A feasibility study

   B. A risk analysis

   C. The degree to which the loss will occur

   D. Calculate the risk that the loss may occur

   E. The loss to the community

220. In a base pay system, which one links pay to the knowledge, skills, and competencies of the job?

   A. Time based system

   B. Performance based system

   C. Productivity based system

   D. Person based system

   E. Hourly based system

221. An organization has doubled in size every year since it first began operating. To determine whether or not jobs and classification systems need to be redesigned, HR needs to:

   A. Engage a highly trained compensation consultant

   B. Determine hiring expectations guided by the company's AAP

   C. Conduct a needs analysis to determine current and future projections

   D. Meet with company supervisors and managers to gather data around required KSA's and time utilization

   E. Capitalize on its talent management

222. An organization's training and development of its human capital:

   A. is a dynamic, often complex mix of variables successfully achieved through careful planning and development.

   B. Includes careful planning and a construct known as an employee value proposition, a term used to describe the characteristics of a job and the experiences that attract and retain motivated, high-potential employees

   C. Is a key initiative for the organization at large.

   D. Is shared by the team members who must continue to develop and mentor its new team member(s).

   E. None of the above

223. A controversial dynamic between HRD, its training department, and the department where the employee performs the job is called:

    A. KSAs.

    B. KM.

    C. Transfer of training.

    D. TQM.

    E. Synchronous learning.

224. Training methods run the gamut from classroom or seminar training to e-learning and experiential training. Training methods and program materials used to deliver training programs include all of the following EXCEPT:

    A. active training methods such as case study, facilitation, simulation, Socratic seminar (Q&A), and vestibulE.

    B. passive training methods such as conference, lecture, and/or presentation style formats.

    C. email methods such as synchronous, asynchronous, or live e-instruction.

    D. experiential such as demonstration, one-on-one, and performance.

    E. All of the above

225. Program delivery methods for training and development programs do NOT include:

    A. training taking place at a nearby location, on-site or off-site.

    B. blended learning.

    C. distance learning.

    D. self-instruction.

    E. EPSS.

Answers to Questions and Explanations

1. Answer: (D). Answers (A), (B), and (C) are appropriate resources to inform and file a discrimination claim. Contacting the harasser is not considered appropriate since the harasser may respond inappropriately through such means as retaliation or violence. Confidentiality is the rule of thumb in harassment and discrimination claims.

2. Answer: (D). (A), (B), and (C) describe workplace policies and law that refers to a worker who is violating harassment policies found in an Employee Handbook that discusses sexual harassment guidelines and creating a hostile work environment. Additionally, federal and state legislation prohibit sexual harassment in the workplace. In this scenario, viewing child pornography on company property in the workplace is violates a through (C) above.

3. Answer: (B). The whistle blower, is the person who informs the organization of illegal matters taking place that. The contact person would most likely be a representative from HR.

4. Answer: (A). In this scenario, the informant claims retaliation because s/he was laid off following the harassment allegation made by the informant. Answers (B), (C), and (D) refer to other employee/employer benefits that could be claimed as a result of a layoff but not in response to the harassment allegation.

5. Answer: (E). If the allegations reached the level of a court hearing, actions taken against the informant could be seen as anyone or all of the answers given in (A), (B), (C), or (D) above.

6. Answer: (C). Retaliation is the legal term when an adverse action is taken against an employee because s/he filed a complaint against an employee or the employer, or served as a whistleblower or informant. Answer (A) refers to any type of discrimination but would not be considered an adverse action in this case; answer (B) refers to "this for that" or a favor in return for a favorable employment agreement (e.g., sexual favors in response to a reward, promotion, or some type of employment perk); answer (D) could result in harassment but does not describe the kind of harassment in this scenario; and answer (E) could result in response to the complaint but does not refer to the law in this case.

7. Answer: (A). Employees are protected by the employer through any legal action that may ensue, and they are protected by the confidentiality of the investigation. The right to confidentiality may be revoked if an investigation reaches a court of law and records are seized, subpoenaed, depositions taken, or employees are ordered to testify in a court of law. More typically, employees are protected by their employer so that an investigation will be possible and lead to a resolution.

8. Answer: (C). The question describes a decision that is reached following an investigation. Answer (C) describes negative consequences that may result following an informant's action even though the decision proves false. If negative consequences

result from an investigation, such as a lay off or demotion, the informant may prove retaliation as a result of the investigation.

9. Answer: (E). Answers (A) through (D) describe actions that could be taken as a result of an adverse action taken against an employee. The same actions could be taken against an employee for other reasons; however, adverse action relates to those conditions that result in negative consequences to employees in response to an event that could possibly place an employee in disfavor with the employer or another employee.

10. Answer: (A). In this question, "change" refers to steps taken to resolve a situation. Answer a describes the most appropriate action since it does not point the finger at anyone. Answers (B) and (C) could be discriminatory, depending on the change action; answer d is not appropriate since corrective action typically involves a small number of individuals; and answer (E) is inadequate because it does not consider the entire situation, only the person who committed the violation.

11. Answer: (E). Differences are not described in any of the answers given; therefore, (E) is the correct response.

12. Answer: (A). A court of law would determine whether or not there were valid reasons unrelated to the complaint that would justify the action taken against an employee. Answers (B) and (C) are important in terms of documenting the events leading up to a disciplinary action or discharge.

13. Answer: (C). According to EEOC guidelines regarding legal and illegal interview questions to ask job candidates, answer c is the most appropriate way to phrase a question about U.S. citizenship and eligibility to work in the U.S.

14. Answer: (D). All of the answers described in this question are considered illegal, therefore discriminatory, according to EEOC guidelines except answer (D), which does not presume ethnic, religious origin, or cultural background.

15. Answer: (C). Similar to question 14 above, all of the answers except answer c presume answers that would be considered discriminatory according to EEOC guidelines for ethnic, religious, origin, or cultural background.

16. Answer: (D). Although it is not the best way to phrase the question, only answer would be considered legal according to the law and EEOC guidelines. After a job offer is made, question (C) is okay to ask, and question (B) may be asked on a written form; however, the applicant has discretion not to answer nor complete the form.

17. Answer: (C). The Americans with Disabilities Act (ADA) prohibits employers from asking about disabilities and asking questions that seek information about a disability. Questions need to be limited to whether the applicant can perform the essential functions of the job with or without reasonable accommodations. Answer (C) is the correct way to phrase the question in this scenario.

18. Answer: (D). This question asks under what circumstances it is okay to ask about a prior conviction. Typically it is illegal to ask about arrests but it is okay to ask about convictions. If the reason for the conviction justifies a business necessity, then rejecting the applicant is also justified. However, a conviction does not necessarily prevent an applicant from being a viable candidate for a job if the conviction is unrelated to the job itself.

19. Answer: (A). Answer a is the only plausible answer in this question. Constructive discharge leads to the discharge of an

employee given a set of planned circumstances. Answer (B) does not give enough information; answer (C) relates to goals to improve performance; answer (D) is incorrect since constructive discharge would typically be a documented overt plan, not a covert plan.

20. Answer: (D). It is believed that the best management practices impact its human capital, or human resources.

21. Answer: (D). Stated many times regarding the law, when federal and state law conflict, the higher standard applies. The higher standard will be found in the more detailed law and often favors the employee. In this scenario, when the employment relationship is based on a valid contract, a similar standard will apply.

22. Answer: (D). It can be argued that employees may no have the right to privacy yet it depends on the situation. In most circumstances, employees have a right to privacy. Employees have the right to fair compensation, freedom from discrimination, and other basic rights according to the law. Answer d, freedom of speech, is not a guaranteed right in the workplace.

23. Answer: (D). Answer (D), disability, does not guarantee legal rights prior to being hired as an employee. If the organization cannot reasonably accommodate a person with a disability because it presents an economic hardship to the organization, or places others in danger, then a job applicant does not have a legal right to employment prior to being hired as an employee because the disability cannot be reasonably accommodated.

24. Answer: (E). While this represents a controversial topic, answer (E), private e-mail addressed only to the employee, does not guarantee the right to privacy in the workplace. Answers (A), (B), (C), and (D) are workplace examples of privacy issues but not the exception which the ques-

tion asks. Employees may have a right to privacy regarding telephone conversations or voicemail messages; however, employees have very limited rights to privacy in e-mail messages and internet usage while using the employer's computer system and company computer

25. Answer: (C). Interestingly, a prospective employee may decline a credit or background check but usually concludes the applicant process. The prospective employer must receive permission in writing before a background check can be implemented. In this scenario, answer (C) is the best response.

26. Answer: (D). Employees will join a union for a variety of reasons; however, in the majority of cases, answer (D), it provides a safe and secure working environment, is the reason why most workers join a union.

27. Answer: (B). The Taft Hartley Act includes the LMRA and the LMRDA, which served to prohibit closed shops and allow union shops with the consent of a majority rule. Further, it prevented union abuse and allowed the states to outlaw closed union shops with the right to work laws. An important feature of the Taft-Hartley Act is the power of the President to order union workers back to work during a union strike for an 80-day period. Answer (B) most accurately reflects the intent of the Taft Hartley Act and the acts that followed to support it.

28. Answer: (E). Also known as the Wagner Act, the National Labor Relations Act was passed during President Franklin Roosevelt's New Deal. The NLRA allowed employees to organize and bargain collectively. Answers (A) through (D) describe the major tenets of the NLRA.

29. Answer: (A). Right to work laws were passed in 21 states that prohibited the use of union shop security clauses in labor

agreements. Answer (A) reflects the most correct answer of the answers given in this question.

30. Answer: (C). The primary purpose of Right to Work laws prohibited the use of security clauses in labor agreements that allowed forced membership in unions. Answer (C), forbid forced membership in unions, is the correct response.

31. Answer: (C). Common law is a body of law, or decisions by the Courts, dating back to the 18th century. It is regarded as decisions by the courts covering employment legislation. Answer (C), decision by the courts, is the correct response, because it accurately reflects a collection of decisions that established employment legislation.

32. Answer: (B). The EEOC - Equal Employment Opportunity Commission, is the federal administrative agency that enforces laws prohibiting discrimination in the workplace. The EEOC acts to ensure that non-discrimination in employment is enforced.

33. Answer: (C). An employee may not be terminated for filing worker's compensation benefits in this scenario. Answers (A), (B), (D), and (E) are examples when the at will employment relationship may terminate at any time for any reason.

34. Answer: (A). The EEOC has jurisdiction to intervene and begin mediation between two parties prior to an investigation taking place.

35. Answer: (B). Answer b, management proposes an increase in vacation time for its truckers, would be seen by the NLRA as a violation of its labor agreement— even though it was intended to motivate employees. Answers (A), c, d, and e are inappropriate responses to the question.

36. Answer: (A). Employers are obligated by law to provide safe working conditions for its employees. Safe working conditions also include other workers who may pose a risk to other employees.

37. Answer: (A). Learning organizations seek to understand every aspect of the business and combine an integrative system for planning all work groups as a shared vision through team learning, utilizing mental models, and defining what personal mastery means to the organization. A learning organization "learns" from its processes, errors, success, and implements change when a system or process needs to be realigned. A learning organization also learns from its competition and stakeholders. From this viewpoint, answer (A), learning organizations are able to conceptualize and operate from a systems thinking perspective, is the best choice.

38. Answer: (B). Employee satisfaction can be measured in by attitude, motivation, and employee satisfaction surveys. In this question, answer (B), grievances, are believed to hold answers to what makes employees satisfied at work. Answers (A) and (C) identify employee dissatisfaction.

39. Answer: (D). All of the answers given in this scenario are plausible; however, HRM's activities are driven by HR objectives. HR objectives are driven by the goals and objectives of the organizational strategic plan.

40. Answer: (A). HRM is responsible for attracting talent to the organization in order to ensure that the organization's efficiency and equity needs will be met through its efforts

41. Answer: (A). Organizational goals and objectives, drive HRM activities and the best choice for this question. Answer c, compliance and labor costs follow answer (A) in terms of HRM priorities and ensuring proper compliance of labor and

employment laws. Answers (B), (D), and e fall under HRM's departmental strategic plan.

42. Answer: (A). Affecting revenue goals, answer (A), compares HRM's strategic alliance with the organization compared to costs associated with training and development of its human resources. By comparing costs of training employees to organizational revenue goals, HRM's impact can be measured to determine how much training is needed or if HRD programs are effective. Answer (C), training and development of its human resources, does not include revenue goals associated with the value that HRM brings to the organization.

43. Answer: (E). Answers (A) through (E) are plausible as the SVP could be seen as any of those titles; however, sponsor refers to the highest level of authority for the project.

44. Answer: (D). A change agent is an OD term that describes the person who is responsible for implementing the change. HRD will create the training program to train department managers, and the managers will implement the change to its employees. Answer (D), department managers, is the correct answer to this question.

45. Answer: (D). Questions associated with children can be discriminatory since historical data demonstrates that applicants with children, or those who have responsibility for their care, have been discriminated against and more often eliminated from a job pool of applicants. It is discriminatory to reject applicants based on this assumption. Answers (A) through c seek information that would be considered discriminatory. Answer (D), the correct response, does not assume that the applicant has direct responsibility to care for children.

46. Answer: (E). This question presents many similar questions to elicit information about childcare; however, answer e would be considered discriminatory in this scenario. Answers (A) through (D) would be considered non-discriminatory in its intent. Note that answers a through d do not mention the word childcare. Another way to get around the childcare issue is to describe the travel requirement associated with the job. Simply asking, "Can you meet these requirements?" would be non-discriminatory in its intent.

47. This question poses many risks to the interview. Any or all could be considered discriminatory if it leads to a discussion of affiliations that suggest religion, race, or ethnic affiliations. Answer e, is the best way to phrase this question, since it simply asks for a yes or no response. If the applicant wants to describe them, it is the applicant's choice to disclose this information. All of the other questions create risk and might be considered discriminatory in intent.

48. Answer: (C). Answer (C), mission statement, is the correct response and describes the reason why the organization is in business. Answer (A), goals and objectives, should support the mission statement; answer (B), organizational chart, describes roles and authority in the organization; answer (D), value proposition, describes how the organization impacts its stakeholders.

49. Answer: (C). This question relates to TQM—total quality management, or quality programs, that seek to motivate employees by empowering them with larger responsibility by taking ownership in the goals and mission of the organization. Organizational studies demonstrate that, answer (C), employees are more open to the organizational change when they feel part of the change process, is most effec-

tive and the correct response to this question.

50. Answer: (E). Outsourcing is determined by many variables. In order to determine if outsourcing is needed, a needs analysis is required to determine first, if outsourcing is needed, and second, what kind of outsourcing will remedy the current situation.

51. Answer: (C). In all of the answers given, answer (C) is the best response. MBO's—management by objectives, describes a set of pre-determined goals and objectives to be met over a period of time, usually scheduled over the course of a year, and established in an employee's performance review. Short term objectives are usually determined over a brief period of time that can range from immediate, weekly, monthly, to a few months.

52. Answer: (A). Answer (A), describes assets, liabilities, and goals in terms of cost, debt, and revenue to the organization. HRM affects an organization's balance sheet through its cost per hire, training and development programs, terminations, and future planning to meet the demands of organizational growth and training. All of these activities impact organizational revenue goals. Answer (B) does not give enough information; answers (C), (D), and (E) cannot be determined without knowing the organization's balance sheet;

53. Answer: (D). Centralization refers to decision making authority in an organization. If centralized, decisions are made at the highest level in the organization or at its corporate headquarters. As opposed to decentralized where decision making authority is dispersed throughout the organization. Answer (D) is the correct answer to this question since it refers to decision making authority.

54. Answer: (C). Decentralization is more effective when there are multiple locations and decisions need to be made in a timely manner. Answer (C) is the best response to this question. Answers (A) and (B) are plausible but not the best response; and answer (D) is a true statement not knowing whether a quick decision will be right or wrong, and does not answer the question.

55. Answer: (B). This question presents an interesting dilemma since answer b is the correct response to this question. Organizations willing to pay the standard pay range may need to attract individuals with specific backgrounds not easily found in a particular industry. If qualifications are plentiful, an organization in its introductory stage may pay less so more dollars can be spent toward organizational growth strategies rather than salaries. One way to make up for this shortfall is to build in a bonus structure to attract qualified individuals and motivate them through pay incentives.

56. Answer: (A). Typically more dollars are spent toward an organization's growth in its early stages. As an organization matures, controlling labor costs becomes more efficient as key personnel are hired to analyze finances and where dollars are spent. Answer (A), maturity, is the correct response to this question. Answers (B) through (E) are factors associated with an organization's growth cycle but indirectly linked to labor costs.

57. Answer: (E). Answers (A), (B), and (C) are essentially the same term to shrink the organization's human capital; answer (D) speaks to competition or poor marketing strategies; and answer (E) is the correct response, since all of the responses characterize an organization in decline described in the question.

58. Answer: (A). Answer (A) is the best response to this question even though it

could be argued that answer e is also plausible; however, an organization in chaos also characterized by its status quo is more often associated with decline. An organization in chaos is motivated to change rather than resisting it since employees are dissatisfied with the current status quo. Answers (B), (C), and (D) are not typically characterized by a lack of incentives.

59. Answer: (A). When organizations are able to define the necessary skills and abilities needed to train and develop it talent management, its maturity level has reached a state of knowing what KSA's are needed to get the job done effectively. Answer (A) is the correct response to this question. Answer (B), growth stage, KSA's are not easily known but projected based on past growth; answer c is knowledge that is known apart from the organization; and answers (D) and (E) do not describe what KSA's are needed for effective training but may speak to how well an employee performs after training has been completed.

60. Answer: (A). A functional unit is refers to an organization's structure and the grouping of jobs that perform similar work. In this scenario, an HR unit is a grouping of jobs that perform similar work so the correct response is answer (A) The key words in this question are "HR units" which defines this work group as a functional entity that reports to corporate headquarter. In this case, it would not be answer (D), decentralized unit, since it does not have independent decision making authority; answer b, matrix managed, would not be typically found reporting directly to corporate headquarters; and answer (C), field unit, may not report directly to corporate headquarters but to a regional manager.

61. Answer: (C). More than one HR regional unit will have many reports. When there are multiple locations and units, reporting relationships are usually identified with a

dotted line to corporate headquarters and a solid line to the functional unit it reports to.

62. Answer: (A). Narrow span of control is defined by implementing less control rather than more control. All of the answers given except answer a describe situations where more control is needed. When employees are properly trained, answer (A), less control is needed; therefore, a narrow span of control will be implemented.

63. Answer: (B). Span of control refers to a range of control over employees that a manager or supervisor controls. Answer (B), number of employees under a supervisor's control, is the best response to this question. Answer (D) appears to say the same thing; however, it does not describe a span of control over employees, only departmental relationship.

64. Answer: (C). HRM comprises more than compliance and training programs. HR audits are conducted to ensure the smooth running of all functions that make up an HR Department. All other functions in HR are secondary to its effectiveness. The organization counts on HR to ensure that all programs meet the needs of each department for compliance, training, OD, recruitment, ADA, ADEA, if the organization has a union shop, HRIS, EEOC, and numerous other functions that operate through the HRM function. The correct response is (C); all other responses are items that HR is concerned about.

65. Answer: (C). Ethically, this presents a conflict of interest, answer (C), because the intern was introduced to the client as a paid intern at the company where he works. The idea that he freelances is not unethical; he has been asked to design plans in the same line of work as an independent contractor for a company client is the problem. Answers (A), (B), (D), and

(E) do not meet the criteria for a conflict of interest in this scenario.

66.   Answer: (E). All parties involved in the situation are liable.

67.   Answer: (B). This is a tricky question since it appears that the client is creating a conflict of interest. He is no doubt creating a conflict for the intern, but if the intern accepts his offer, the intern has committed the conflict of interest because of his association as an intern where the client also engages in business transactions. Answer (B) is the best response in this scenario.

68.   Answer: (A). Employers with 15 or more employees must consider reasonable accommodations in the workplace for disabled employees. Answer (A) is the correct response.

69.   Answer: (D). Employees over 40 years of age can be fired for cause such as poor performance. Answers a is incorrect; high level managers may be required to retire if they have company sponsored retirement benefits; answer b and c are false; and answer e is incorrect as all employees must be offered the same insurance benefits.

70.   Answer: (A). In this scenario, the applicant is qualified under law since discrimination for a mental health condition is unlawful. While the applicant may be qualified based on work history, the applicant may be required to undergo a psychiatric evaluation if the job is considered high stress, or if the diagnosis will place other workers in a dangerous situation. Under those circumstance, the employer may refuse employment.

71.   Answer: (C). Answers (A), (B), and (E) are protected by ADA and anti-discrimination laws due to medical conditions; answer d is protected as OCD is a mental health diagnosis and covered under law; answer (C), the correct answer, is not covered under ADA.

72.   Answer: (B). The correct answer, (B), providing a reasonable accommodation for an employee or applicant that presents undue hardship for the employer, would be justified under ADA and the accommodation need not be met. Answer (A) is incorrect since providing a reasonable accommodation is to redesign a work space or working conditions as to allow the employee to continue working; answer (C) would need to be approved by a third party such as a physician who has the authority to prescribe medical marijuana to the employee; and answer (D) may or may not be in compliance, depending upon the outcome of the situation.

73.   Answer: (A). Answer (A) is the only document listed that demonstrates an individual's identity and right to work in the U.S. All other responses demonstrate one factor in the question, not both.

74.   Answer: (B). The correct response, (B), is the best answer to this question as employers must be able to verify applicant and employee identify and right to work in the U.S. Employers typically require an applicant to complete Form I-9 which asks for two forms of identification. The burden placed on the employer to make sure that the applicant has completed it and the employer verifies the information before an official offer of employment is made.

75.   Answer: (C). All of the answers are true except answer (C), the Act protects federal sector employees who have the right to know what kind of information has been collected about them.

76.   Answer: (D). In this scenario, answer d is the correct response. It is legal to require a polygraph test to employees who will be working with controlled substances. Answers (A), (B), and (C) may result in a request for a polygraph test but the employee may refuse under the law and may stop the test at any time if taken. Answer e is incorrect.

77. Answer: (B). report is required to disclose to the employee and a copy must be provided. All of the other responses are possible actions that an employee may take to defend him or herself if the promotion is denied due to a negative credit report.

78. Answer: (A). By law, white males fall under a non-protected group. When preference is given to a minority who is considered part of a protected group but who may be less qualified, answer (A), reverse discrimination, resulted for the white male who was discriminated against in favor of a less qualified minority. This can happen when a quota system has not been filled to fulfill the 15% requirement by law; however, the U.S. Supreme Court has ruled in the past against strict quota systems in favor of non-protected groups when higher level qualifications are met.

79. Answer: (D). By law, answer (D), vicarious liability, is the legal doctrine holding organizations responsible for the actions of their supervisors and managers. It requires employers to take measures to end harassment through appropriate intervention strategies.

80. Answer: (A). Underutilization exists when it can be demonstrated that a greater number of protected class individuals are available for hire than actual hiring statistics demonstrate.

81. Answer: (C). Griggs v Duke Power demonstrated that it is not enough to simply show lack of discriminatory intent, but that members of a protected class are somehow treated differently than others of the same class.

82. Answer: (B). Compliance checks are conducted by compliance officers of the federal government to ensure compliance of policies and procedures taking place at a worksite. Answer (B) is the correct answer.

83. Answer: (B). Validity is the criteria used to demonstrate that a study measures what it is intended to measure.

84. Answer: (D). Answer (D) is the best response to this question. Occasionally, answer a, quasi-experimental designs allow for additional information to be added if it is asked for on the questionnaire. Answers (B), (C), and (E) are information specific and do not require additional input from respondents.

85. Answer: (A). Experimental designs typically use a control group and each group is randomly assigned. Experimental designs are considered to be the most rigorous research design.

86. Answer: (E). Average tendency does not measure central tendency, but measures the number of times something could happen.

87. Answer: (C). Answer (C), median, is the correct response and measures the middle tendency or midpoint on a scale or distribution.

88. Answer: (A). Range is the difference between scores on a distribution. It demonstrates the difference between the high and low scores.

89. Answer: (C). Trend analysis, also known as ration analysis, is accurately forecasting past figures or performance with future demands. In this sense, it analyzes two variables and determines whether or not they will change based on past figures and current conditions. Answer (C) is the correct response to this question.

90. Answer: (B). A job description lists duties and responsibilities of the job and a job specification lists qualifications needed to perform the job and apply for consideration as an applicant. A job specification summary is information described in published ads, recruitment strategies,

and used as a qualification checklist for determining candidate selection. A job description is an internal document.

91. Answer: (C). KSA's is a familiar term and acronym used to describe knowledge, skills, and abilities needed to perform a job. It is known that if transfer of training did not take place following a training program, it is assumed that the training program was ineffective. An effective job analysis begins with interviews, inquiries, analysis about the job and feedback from direct reports and others who perform the job. Answer (B) follows KSA's and used to determine if transfer of training in fact occurred. Answers d and e look similar to (C); however, KSA's is the standard term used in training.

92. Answer: (E). Employees may find out about job postings through a variety of internal job postings listed in answers (A) through (D).

93. Answer: (A). It is known that employee referrals are the best source of finding qualified job applicants. Answers (B) through (E) are additional ways to support the referral source effort; however, answer (A) is the best referral source.

94. Answer: (A). Attrition refers to the number of employees who leave a company; retention refers to those who stay over a period of time. Turnover is a similar term for attrition and stability is a similar term for retention. Answers (B) through e are incorrect.

95. Answer: (C). Answer (C) is correct and describes job specifications needed to perform the job. Essential job function(s) describe the main components of the job to be performed and the KSA's needed to perform a job effectively.

96. Answer: (A). Yield data is a combination of variables that can be used to analyze recruitment outcomes. It is based on objec-tive criteria that can be measured through resources used to recruit job candidates. By comparing resources, the greatest yield, or outcome, can be determined.

97. Answer: (D). This is a tricky question but answer (D) is the correct response. Identifying the most suitable candidate does not assume best, least, most desirable, or preferred. Suitable refers to criteria given in the job specification summary compared to the job description, environment where work is to be performed, candidate selection availability, and the culture of the organization.

98. Answer: (C). The key difference between a resume/CV and an employment application is verification of the facts completed by the candidate applying for the job. The candidate signature is used as proof that the candidate completed the job and answered all of the questions truthfully. If any information is false, the application can be used as verification of proof that the applicant lied their way into the job. It is also used as a document for EEOC reporting but not the main criteria for using an application.

99. Answer: (B). All of the answers given in this scenario are plausible and may be used as a basis for many temporary situations; however, answer (B) is the correct response. A temp employee is hired for a brief period of time and typically not needed on a permanent basis.

100. Answer: (A). A behavioral question seeks to observe how a candidate acted in a previous role or how the candidate might solve a future situation. A behavioral question could be addressed as: "How did you react when you were told that your department would be downsized by six people but that you would remain in your position?"

101. Answer: (B). A structured interview allows the interviewer to compare responses to

the same questions in a structured interview. Structured interviews prepare questions in advance and all questions are the same for all candidates. This prevents bias from occurring when every candidate is expected to respond to the same set of questions.

102. Answer: (D). A 360 evaluation allows feedback from a circle of workers that an employee interacts with in the workplace in the course of his job. It is called a 360 evaluation because it is a performance assessment based on feedback from coworkers that include superiors, colleagues and subordinates.

103. Answer: (A). A halo effect occurs when the interviewer likes the style or personality of the interviewee and preference is given to this candidate versus viewing the information shared in the interview. Answer (A) is the correct response when preference is given due to likeness personality style,

104. Answer: (D). A horn effect is committed when the interviewer is turned off by something an applicant says or does, and disregards all of the other information or qualifications that an applicant brings to the interview. This error overshadows the interview and all other information may be determined from a negative viewpoint. Answers (A) and (E) suggest other negative outcomes, but this scenario describes a horn effect.

105. Answer: (D). Otherwise known as an ability test, the best type of assessment to measure one's ability to learn or acquire new skills is answer d, an aptitude test. Answer (A), achievement test, measures what an applicant already knows but now whether s/he has the ability to acquire new skills. Answers (B) and (C) will give additional information about an applicant but not about acquiring new skills.

106. Answer: (A). Answer (A), in-basket exercise, allows the applicant to demonstrate

her decision making skill set in simulated work situations. A set of situations requiring quick decision making over a 20-minute time frame requires the applicant to act quickly and make decisions by answering questions and responding quickly about what is needed for each task. This is particularly known to be an effective assessment tool when hiring managerial level applicants.

107. Answer: (C). Answer (C), a realistic job preview, allows the applicant to experience the job as it is by introducing the applicant to the workspace, employees who work in the department, and observing the actual job prior to acceptance. Answers (A), (B), (D), and (E), are plausible, but not the best answer for this question.

108. Answer: (D). An internal job description lists job traits (construct validity) and job skills (content validity). Another way to analyze a job is by task (construct) and desirable outcome (content).

109. Answer: (C). A learning organization combines the efforts of HRD to train its employees how to manage change from a systems perspective. It takes into account the entire organization. Answer (A) is incorrect; (B) embraces training needed to establish a learning organization; (D) also needed to establish a learning organization; and e may or may not be a part of a learning organization. Answer (C) is the best response to this question.

110. Answer: (E). The key difference between HRD and HRM is HRD is the human resources development arm (training and development) under a human resources department. All of the separate entities under HRM report to HRM. In this question, HRD reports to HRM.

111. Answer: (D). Adult learners are valued for their experience and ability to generate alternative solutions to organizational problems, answer (D). Answers (A), (B),

and (C) are true but this is from the view point of the adult learner not from OD; and answers (D) is false.

112. Answer: (E). Answers (A) through (D) are all true, and summarize the key attributes of each area.

113. Answer: (A). This is a work for hire agreement between a free-lance writer and the company. The freelance writer has been hired by the company to write the employee handbook; therefore, the property (employee handbook) belongs to the company. The fee will be paid by the company and used as the employee handbook by the company. The author of the employee handbook will be asked to sign a form that states s/he does not hold a copyright to the employee handbook.

114. Answer: (A). The university holds the copyright to articles published online even though they were written and published by the author prior to the course. In this scenario, the articles are considered part of the course materials. The university commissioned the faculty member to write the course so the course is owned by the university, including the supplemental materials. The faculty member will be asked to sign a waiver that the intellectual property in this scenario belongs to the university.

115. Answer: (A). Otherwise known as "increasing returns," the more an employee practices new skills learned on the job, the more accurate and faster s/he will become to perform the job. In linear language, the curve will be less curved at the beginning and more curved at the end; or new knowledge versus experienced knowledge.

116. Answer: (C). This is based on Equity Theory; employees expect to be treated fairly. If they perceive that they are not treated fairly, they are more likely to quit their job than all of the other answers given in this question. All are plausible;

however, answer c is the most likely reason why an employee will quit their job first.

117. Answer: (A). The ADDIE model is the standard training model used to develop a training program. ADDIE is the acronym for the training and instructional design process - analysis, design, development, implementation, and evaluation.

118. Answer: (D). Answer (D), transfer of training, is the term recognized and used to determine whether or not successful training was transferred to the job. Answer (A), OJT, stands for on the job training; answers (B) and c are two types of performance appraisals; and answer (E) is incorrect even though participants are asked to complete evaluations at the completion of a training program.

119. Answer: (B). Answer (B) occasionally describes variable ratio reinforcement or responses that occur every so often—more than rarely, but not at fixed intervals, unexpectedly, or randomly. An example could be praise, an incentive, or a reward that occurs on the job.

120. Answer: (C). Biweekly paychecks are expected on a fixed schedule or interval. Answers (A) and (B) may occur at occasional intervals but not fixed; answer (D) is unknown depending upon work classification; and answer (E) could be unexpected, expected, random, or unknown.

121. Answer: (C). Sexual harassment training is not part of a new hire orientation program. While the topic may be covered as part of a new hire orientation, harassment training usually occurs shortly after a new hire orientation and considered a separate training program.

122. Answer: (E). Aswer e is the correct response, regarding its primary purpose in a new hire orientation: establishing working relationships with the company and other co-workers. Answers (A), (B), (C),

and (D) are topics covered in a new hire orientation but not the primary purpose.

123. Answer: (A). A new hire orientation does not prepare an employee for the job they were hired to perform and not considered a training program. Answers (B), (C), (D), and (E) are considered training programs and can be evaluated in terms of knowing whether or not transfer of training occurred.

124. Answer: (C). All of the answers are plausible; however, answer (C) is the best response in terms of critical need for dangerous jobs that could jeopardize the health and safety of the employee and others.

125. Answer: (C). Evaluation considers all of the responses given in this question; however, answer (C), perform skills learned in a training program to the actual job, refers to the participant's ability to transfer skills, or KSA's, learned in the training program and the correct response.

126. Answer: (D). Answer (D), measurable outcomes, is the result of comparing turnover rates from the year before and implementing realistic job previews the following year. If nothing else was done to improve turnover for the following year, it might be assumed that comparing this variable to turnover from the year before significantly impacted turnover rates the following year at a 10% improvement rate.

127. Answer: (C). The terms may be used interchangeably in an organization; however, an HRD department understands that an internal career management program considers the goals and objectives of the organization first in order to determine its available internal talent management. Career planning for the organization's talent management takes place as a result of organizational needs and objectives.

128. Answer: (B). Answers (A) and (B) are similar, and (C) and (D) are considered in a succession plan program. However, answer (B) is the primary reason why a succession plan is developed. The key phrase is "executive management." After executive management replacement strategies are identified, answer (A) would be the next priority in an organizational hierarchy.

129. Answer: (B). Job enlargement increases the amount of job tasks or responsibilities but skill level is not considered. Answer (A), job enrichment, requires skill development; answer (C) is incorrect; answer (D) could impact job motivation in either direction; and answer e is incorrect.

130. Answer: (B). Answer b, job enrichment, is the correct response, but it should not be assumed that this brings added motivation or productivity. Answer (A) requires a new skill level; and answers (C), (D), and e are incorrect.

131. Answer: (C). Not to be confused with job enlargement, it increases the depth and possible motivation in a job but may not impact productivity. Job enlargement, answer (B), is intended to decrease boredom associated with job familiarity or over simplification.

132. Answer: (A). Mouton's theory proposes that management is equally concerned about employees and production.

133. Answer: (D). McClelland's Achievement Motivation Theory, proposes that leaders have a high need for achievement, and demonstrate trait characteristics of individuals associated with leadership ability. Answer (D), McClelland, is the correct response.

134. Answer: (C). Contingency Theory is the correct response. Performance is contingent upon the leader's style, interaction taking place among group members, how

favorable group members respond to its leader style, the situation at hand, tasks to be performed, and the position power of the leader directing the group.

135. Answer: (B) above and beyond (A) Answers (A) and (B) are characteristics associated with a transformational leader; however, answer b, provides vision to the organization, is the primary goal of the transformational leader and the correct response. Answer (A) follows answer (B). The leader's vision must be accepted among workers in order to be inspired by the leader to develop their own unique potential.

136. Answer: (D). Corporate culture refers to its identity based on its values and public image. A multi-cultural workforce refers to the mix of cultural backgrounds of its workforce. Answer (D) is the correct response.

137. Answer: (C). In a matrix-managed organization, an HR manager will report to at least two individuals; one at a single location and another at corporate headquarters.

138. Answer: (B). An organization that continues to grow needs to stay current with its organizational structure. Structural intervention strategies analyze how efficient an organization is managed by its organizational structure. In this scenario, answer (B) is the correct response.

139. Answer: (C). Answer (C), a histogram, is the correct response. A histogram utilizes a bar-graph chart to summarize data and is best used for analyzing how change occurs over time. It can also be used to analyze data by year so that trends can be detected. All of the responses in this question refer to quality programs that use data to improve performance of products and services introduced in the quality movement.

140. Answer: (C). A forced distribution scale aligns all employees on a rating scale and compares the performance of each employee to all others on the scale. It is a quantitative performance appraisal measure that can be seen as a distribution on a rating scale.

141. Answer: (A). All of the answers are plausible in this scenario; however, bias must be considered when all other possibilities seem implausible. Answer a, the interviewer was biased, is the correct response. Bias occurs when an interviewer's beliefs or possible prejudice distorts ratings. When compared company wide, it appears that the interviewer's ratings are out of sync with the rest of the organization. In this case, bias occurred.

142. Answer: (B). A halo effect occurs when an appraiser rates an employee high or low in all areas due to one issue that stands out among the rest. Answer b is the correct response. For example, if the employee is known to be excellent in producing technical reports, all areas on the performance appraisal may be biased toward an excellent rating whether or not the employee deserved it.

143. Answer: (A). Under ERISA, a pension plan must be communicated in writing and include a vesting schedule. It also includes eligibility for accrued benefits. Answer a is the correct response.

144. Answer: (A). Exempt status employees are generally paid on salary, and non-exempt status employees are paid hourly with overtime benefits. Answer (A) is the correct response to this question.

145. Answer: (A). While answer e is true, answer (A) is nonetheless the correct response. The question asks about the Equal Pay Act, not national averages.

146. Answer: (C). As is true in most employment rulings, whichever benefits the employee

more is the rule of thumb between federal and state law. In this question, answer (C), whichever rate benefits the employee, is the correct response.

147. Answer: (E). The Fair Labor Standards Act (FLSA) also known as Wage and Hour laws, governs child labor, employee status, minimum wages, overtime, and record keeping. Fringe benefits are not covered by FLSA.

148. Answer: (C). Under revised Department of Labor ERISA regulations state that answer (C), employers are required to modify claim procedures for all plans under ERISA.

149. Answer: (A). Under COBRA, the employee is entitled to maintain their health benefit coverage for 18 months from the date the leave began. Answer (A) is the correct response. Answer (B) is also correct but does not answer the question about the employee's coverage. Answer (C) is incorrect; answer (D) is conditional; and answer (E) is incorrect.

150. Answer: (C). Interestingly, eligible dependents may continue COBRA coverage for an additional 36 months. A dependent who loses dependent status may continue coverage during this time period. In this scenario, answer (C) is the correct response.

151. Answer: (B). The Financial Accounting Standards Board (FASB) is a privately held organization that decides how, answer (B), financial information is reported to shareholders. It works with the SEC and financial executives about financial reporting.

152. Answer: (C). Benchmark jobs are key positions that are recognizable in the marketplace and used for comparing and assigning wages throughout industry.

153. Answer: (D). A cash achievement award is direct compensation. Indirect compensation refers to benefit programs and perks such as a company car, laptop computer, other types of insurance. Answers (A), (B), and (B) refer to indirect compensation.

154. Answer: (E). Job ranking is a listing of jobs that are placed in a hierarchal way to assign importance but not how much more important; therefore, no numeric value is attached to it. All other responses in this question are quantitative measurements.

155. Answer: (C). While it may be assumed otherwise (e.g., years of education are worth so much in the marketplace), compensable factors flow from the job itself not from the person performing the job nor his education. Answer (C), education, is the correct response.

156. Answer: (A). Job classification systems are used to group jobs into similar groupings and assigned a number of grades or classifications. In government, the best known classification system is the GS or General Schedule system. Answer (A) is the correct response since public sector jobs also use a classification system to group jobs in terms of grade and pay levels, and used for compensation rankings.

157. Answer: (A). As mentioned in the previous questionthe GS system used by the federal government, is the best known classification system.

158. Answer: (B). Answer (B), relative worth, is the correct response. Relative worth compares a hierarchy of jobs to other job evaluations used to determine its worth in the hierarchy.

159. Answer: (C). Answer (C), aging, is the correct response. Aging takes older salary data and compares it to recent trends. It then calculates salary to meet current figures.

160. Answer: (C). The weighted average includes the number of employees actually receiving the salary, versus answer (B), which combines the total number of individuals who receive an annual salary but is not divided.

161. Answer: (B). Job grades are based on internal worth not external influences such as marketplace averages.

162. Answer: (C). Broadbanding is a process of combining job classifications and salary grades with narrow pay ranges into one band (vs several) that will allow a wider salary spread. This helps to reduce the number of reporting levels in an organization given in answer (C).

163. Answer: (A). Generally used for hourly or non-exempt levels in pay classification systems, single or flat rate pay is paid at the same rate regardless of seniority or performance. Fast food chains are an example of a flat rate system. Unions also use a flat rate system established during the collective bargaining process.

164. Answer: (D). A time based system is a set schedule over time that determines pay increases. It presumes that worker skills will increase over time and as their value to the company also increases.

165. Answer: (A). A discretionary bonus is considered to be an award at the end of a time period versus a performance based bonus which considers a percentage of profits.

166. Answer: (C). Answer (C), cash profit sharing plan, is the correct response. It is based on profitability and compensated to employees in addition to the employee's normal rate of pay.

167. Answer: (C). It is believed this avoids any duplication of disability coverage which may begin at an early age up to age 65.

168. Answer: (B). Answer (B) is the correct response. A Point of Service (POS) man-aged care organization combines the Preferred Provider Organization (PPO) and the Preferred Provider Arrangement (PPA). It also allows access to medical specialists. Answer (C) is a Health Maintenance Organization (HMO); and answer (E) is an Exclusive Provider Organization. Answers (C) and (E) require participants to use providers in the network for payments to be made.

169. Answer: (E). Exclusive Provider Organization or EPO. An EPO does not allow outside specialists nor payment to be made if providers go outside of the network.

170. Answer: (C). As in the case of Starbucks, which was ordered to pay $106M dollars in unreported tips to its employees (not filing tax returns that included tips), tips are considered direct taxable compensation or income.

171. Answer: (D). Answer (D) is the correct response. Starbucks was fined for not filing tax returns that included tips to employees.

172. Answer: (B). The employer has a duty to provide a work environment free from hazard or danger. Where there are hazardous conditions, the employer's duty is to develop workplace safety standards and train employees on proper reporting and procedures.

173. Answer: (B). Employees have the right to report unsafe working conditions and request a workplace investigation for what they believe to be unsafe working conditions.

174. Answer: (A). Employers may refuse an OSHA inspection until a search warrant is delivered, then the employer is required to comply with the search warrant. However, this gives the employer time to review the situation or problem prior to an inspection taking place.

175. Answer: (D). Answer (D) is the correct response. A Hazard Communication includes labeling, communication, and training programs for its employees.

176. Answer: (B). A Material Safety Data Sheet (MSDS) report contains an inventory and listing of hazardous chemicals used at the worksite.

177. Answer: (C). Any injury that results in a job transfer due to the injury must be recorded. This includes injuries that also result in death, disability, lost workdays of one or more days, medical treatment, and temporary or permanent restriction of work or motion.

178. Answer: (A). Answer (A) is the correct response. Employers calculate incidence statistics rates to determine where a company stands in the industry compared to the Standardized Industrial Classification (SIC).

179. Answer: (A). The OSHA Form 200 Log is used to record all incidents of injury or occupational illness within 6 working days from the day/time the employer is notified of the incident. Work-related deaths or hospitalization of three or more employees must be recorded and reported to OSHA within 8 hours of the incident.

180. Answer: (D). Answer (D) is the correct response. Imminent danger is defined as reasonable certainty that danger exists and the situation can be corrected through normal enforcement procedures. Answer (C) is given 2nd priority; answer (E) is given 3rd priority; answer (A) is given 4th priority; and answer (B) is known but not reported.

181. Answer: (C). Answer (C), de minimis, is the correct response. De minimis is a bona fide violation that has no immediate relationship to job place safety.

182. Answer: (B). Having employees participate in the creation of safety culture programs encourage employees to be involved in safety awareness and compliance of safety regulations.

183. Answer: (C). Carpal tunnel is also known as a cumulative trauma disorder due to its repetitive nature, motion, assembling products, computer operators, and repetitive use of the wrist, hand, or neck.

184. Answer: (C). Protecting others from injury or harm, and moving them and others to a safe place is the highest priority at the scene of an accident.

185. Answer: (D). Confidentiality is the rule when dealing with employees who need assistance or help through an employer provided Employee Assistance Program (EAP). Employees are encouraged to contact their EAP directly to preserve confidentiality.

186. Answer: (D). Substance abuse in the workplace is best dealt with through written policies, training, and employer enforcement. Substance abuse prevention programs are usually available through the employer provided EAP and sometimes through the employer's medical insurance program.

187. Answer: (B). Vulnerability analysis measures the degree of probability that a loss will occur by assigning levels of probability for losses that a company may be exposed.

188. Answer: (C). Having employees sign confidentiality and non-compete agreements is the best measure for protecting proprietary information. Answer (A) has minimal impact regarding proprietary information; answer (B) regards safety measures; and answer (D), preventing employees from downloading software on company owned computers is the best measure of protecting computer networks.

189. Answer: (D). Conditions that cause employees to become frustrated include rigid rules, management inflexibility, and constant pressure to perform at a certain level. By having employees commit to productivity goals and feel part of the process has been shown to reduce workplace violence.

190. Answer: (C). Answer (C) is the correct response. In a matrix managed organization, an employee will have two (possibly more) direct reports. Neither report assumes higher authority over the other.

191. Answer: (D). An Affirmative Action Plan (AAP) is required for reporting current employees classified in protected groups by department.

192. Answer: (E). Distributive bargaining occurs when parties in a conflict over an issue result in a loss for one party but a gain for another

193. Answer: (D). Contrast error occurs when employees are compared to each other rather than on individual performance goals and objectives.

194. Answer: (B). Medical examinations are prohibited until after an employment offer has been made but the offer may be conditional pending the results of the examination.

195. Answer: (D). Case studies allow for situations that require careful analysis of people, behavior, and outcomes; this is often conducted with a group of managers who enter into a discussion about consequences and outcomes.

196. Answer: (D). A relevant labor market considers job skills and demand, the distance that employees are willing to travel or commute, and competition with other employers for services or products.

197. Answer: (A). Truthful statements about employees cannot be disputed in a defamation lawsuit nor charges brought against an employee or employer. Documentation of employee records and statements made would be the next best insurance in a defamation action.

198. Answer (C). Public policy allows the employee to take action as a "whistle blower" to disclose illegal, immoral, or illegitimate practices taking place in the organization and be protected under the law.

199. Answer: (C). Introducing training that can increase KSA's is necessary to increase and improve the skills of its workforce. In order to remain competitive in the workplace, updated training is always needed.

200. Answer: (D). Sales people often work on commission; and it is not necessary to determine employment status relative to salary guidelines. Usually sales people earn a % of sales. However, many employees in sales also earn a salary. When they do, a compensation and classification system will exist just like any other position in the organization.

201. Answer: (B). New hire orientation programs include all of the answers given in (A), (C), (D), and (E).

202. Answer: (A). Historically, HR, originally known as Personnel, began as an administrative function that included hiring and payroll.

203. Answer: (B). The key word is "enforceable;" and one person must give and receive something of value for a contract to be valid between two parties.

204. Answer: (C). Only employees who are on active payroll during pay periods immediately before and after the date of the election are eligible to vote in a union election. Those on a leave of absence may not vote.

205. Answer: (D). Interviewers should always receive a pre-authorization to call a list of

work references in any organization where the applicant has previously worked, not only bio-tech organizations.

206. Answer: (A). Filtering throughout the organization can be treated as a threat of any kind, including bribes, that are intended to keep employees from joining unions is considered a threat of reprisal. This practice is illegal.

207. Answer: (C). Asking a job candidate to complete an actual job task or work sample test is most often the best way to determine success performing the actual job.

208. Answer: (E). Answer e is the correct response and includes all of the answers given in (A) through (D).

209. Answer: (C). Contrary to popular opinion, an individual's occupational choice is influenced by education, opportunity, motivation, and experience. It is not influenced by pay, answer (C), which is the correct answer to this question.

210. Answer: (A). Statistics show that the most successful recruitment strategies come from referrals from other employees.

211. Answer: (E). Job analysis does not influence the design of recruitment programs but labor market influence, the economy, competition, and legislation does. Answer (E) is the exception and the correct answer in this question.

212. Answer: (D). employees are entitled to other payment as required and through benefits; however, they are not entitled to holiday pay.

213. Answer: (C). One of the most important reasons for completing an employment application is to have the applicant sign the document as proof that the information they gave on the application was true and correct. In the case of negligent hiring, the company may use the signed application form as evidence about the

applicant's qualifications verified by the applicant signature.

214. Answer: (B). Job specifications and job descriptions will be used in recruitment strategies, career planning, and compensation decisions.

215. Answer: (D). Ranking compares employees from lowest to highest but it does not take into account differences in employee positions.

216. Answer: (A). The Excelsior List contains the names and addresses of all eligible bargaining unit employees within 7 days following the consent to an election. The List is given to the union and failure to provide the list may be evidence of unfair labor practices.

217. Answer: (C). Answer (C) is the correct response and refers to the company's balance sheet to determine how well the organization is performing.

218. Answer: (B). Human capital is a term to describe the company's employees and how much training and dollars are invested in their continuing development. HRD is responsible for employee development programs and designing training programs around the goals and objectives of the organization's strategic plan.

219. Answer: (C). This question relates to organizational insurance coverage and risk associated with loss. In an organizational system, the first factor to analyze is the degree to which loss will occur.

220. Answer: (D). In a person based system, the number of skills performed is proportional to the level of competency to determine its evaluation.

221. Answer: (D). Gathering data around required KSA's is conducted for the purpose of deciding whether jobs need to be redesigned. It is believed that company supervisors and managers are the best

source of information gathering about job specifications and categorizing them into a classification system.

222. Answer: (A). As organizations are constantly in motion and change is constant, an important task of an HRD department is to understand the ebb and flow of the organization at large so that the right mix of individuals' talents and backgrounds complement and fit into the organizational climate culture. A well-run training and development department takes into account all of these variables and includes them in the training effort.

223. Answer: (C). Transfer of training is one of the best measures of training evaluation. The key questions are "Did transfer of training successfully take place at the end of the training program?" and "If not, why not?" This tension between HRD and the organization is a constantly changing dynamic due to a variety of variables not found in the training program itself, such as KSAs, candidate selection, management style, leadership, KM, and worker motivation.

224. Answer: (C). While online training programs may be synchronous, asychronous, or delivered via live e-instruction, they are not typically part of an email format. E-learning is the correct term, and it is usually accomplished by logging into a website with a password where class participants have been enrolled in advance and where online units or modules are sequentially published as part of a course or seminar.

225. Answer: (D). Self-study should not be confused with self-instruction. Self-instruction is not a recognized program delivery method, but self-study is. Self-study is intended to be directed and controlled by the learner, but the learner needs to communicate with a trainer or mentor to complete the training program.

Appendix A: Exam Codes and Test Specifications

The following list of human resource work functions will help determine which human resource job function(s) you report on the exam application. You will select a job function from the list below to qualify your eligibility to take the PHR or SPHR exam. This important information will be completed on the application.

WORK FUNCTION CODES

50 HR Generalist

51 Employment/Recruitment

52 Benefits

53 Compensation

54 Labor/Industrial Relations

55 Training/Development

56 Organizational Development

57 Legal

58 Health/Safety/Security

59 Employee Assistance Programs

60 Employee Relations

61 Communications

62 EEO/Affirmative Action

63 HRIS

64 Research

65 Consultant

66 Administrative

67 International HRM

68 Diversity

Note: The PHR and SPHR examinations are geared to the HR generalist in content and application. Selecting another job function does not disqualify you from taking the exam; however, if you are a specialist and unfamiliar with the content covered in a generalist role, you may want to consider if this is the exam you want to prepare for and take.

POSITION CODES

Position codes are job titles with corresponding numbers that you will select and complete on the HRCI exam application.

The information below describes position codes for your situation. This information will help determine qualification and eligibility to take the PHR or SPHR exam. If you do not see your job title below, review the information on how to select a proper position code and visit HRCI's website at www.hrci.org.

Note: Students or recent graduates and recertification-by-examination candidates will not complete this portion of the application. A Student/Recent Graduate Verification form will be completed in place of this section. Thus, it is still a good idea to review the list of position codes that may be found in an HR department!

Approved Position Codes

001   AA/EEO Specialist

002   AA/Policy & Procedure Administrator

003   AA/EEO Analyst

004   AA/EEO Manager

005   AA/EEO Director

006   Assistant HR Manager

007   Assistant HR Director

008   Assistant VP Human Resources

010   Benefits Specialist

011   Benefits Director

012   Benefits Supervisor

013   Change Management Manager

014   Classification/Compensation Administrator

015   Classification/Compensation Analyst

016   Compensation & Benefits Specialist

017   Compensation & Benefits Administrator

018   Compensation & Benefits Analyst

019   Compensation & Benefits Manager

020   Compensation & Benefits Director

021   Compensation & Benefits Supervisor

022   Compensation & Benefits Vice President

023   Compensation & Benefits Consultant

024   Compliance Specialist

025   Education & Development Manager

026   Employee Benefits Manager

027   Employee Benefits Supervisor

028   Employee Relations Administrator

029   Employee Relations Analyst

030   Employee Relations Manager

031   Employee Relations Director

032   Employee Relations Specialist

033   HR Professor (full-time)

034   Employee Relations Vice President

035   Employment Specialist

036   Employment Administrator

037   Employment Analyst

038   Employment Manager

039   Employment Director

040   Employment Vice President

041   Employment Law Attorney

042   Employment Practices Specialist

043   Employment Practices Administrator

044   Employment Practices Analyst

045   Employment Practices Manager

046   Employment Practices Director

047   Employment Practices Vice President

048   Health & Safety Specialist

049   Health & Safety Administrator

050   Health & Safety Analyst

051   Health & Safety Manager

052   Health & Safety Director

053   Health & Safety Vice President

054   HR Administrator

055   HR Analyst

056   HR Specialist

057   HR Manager

058   HR Director

059   HR Vice President

060   HR Consultant

061   HR Generalist

062   HR Research Analyst

063   HR Supervisor

064   HRD/Training & Development Specialist

065   HRD/Training & Development Administrator

066   HRD/Training & Development Analyst

067   HRD/Training & Development Manager

068   HRD/Training & Development Director

069   HRD/Training & Development Supervisor

070   HRD/Training & Development Vice President

071   HRIS Specialist

072   HRIS Administrator

073   HRIS Analyst

074   HRIS Manager

075   HRIS Director

076   HRIS Supervisor

077   HRIS Vice President

078   Industrial Relations Specialist

079   Industrial Relations Administrator

080   Industrial Relations Analyst

081   Industrial Relations Manager

082   Industrial Relations Director

083   Industrial Relations Supervisor

084   Industrial Relations Vice President

085   Job Developer/Specialist

086   Job Placement Specialist

087   Labor Relations Specialist

088   Labor Relations Administrator

089   Labor Relations Analyst

090   Labor Relations Manager

091   Labor Relations Director

092   Labor Relations Supervisor

093   Labor Relations Vice President

094   Military Personnel Officer

095   Organizational Development Specialist

096   Organizational Development Administrator

097   Organizational Development Analyst

098   Organizational Development Manager

099   Organizational Development Director

100   Organizational Development Vice President

101   Payroll/Benefits Specialist

102   Recruiter

103   Recruitment Manager

104   Recruitment Director

105   Safety Manager

106   Staffing Administrator

107   Staffing Manager

108   Staffing Director

109   Staffing Supervisor

110   Staffing Vice President

111   Trainer

112   Vice President of People

113   Workers' Compensation Specialist

114   Workers' Compensation Analyst

115   Workers' Compensation Manager

116   Workers' Compensation Director

117   Workforce Planning Manager

TEST SPECIFICATIONS

Test specifications—also called the Body of Knowledge (BOK)—are reflected below and will continue to be represented on the exams beginning with the May–June 2007 testing window. Exam questions are updated every five years to reflect the most current HR practices with the most recent updates having occurred in 2005.

Following is the breakdown of the types of questions and BOK to expect on the PHR and the SPHR exams (as of the testing year 2008):

	PHR	SPHR
Strategic Management	12%	29%
Workforce Planning and Employment	26	17
Human Resource Development	17	17
Total Rewards	16	12
Employee and Labor Relations	22	18
Risk Management	7	7

The percentages that follow each functional area heading are considered to be the PHR and SPHR best practices BOK, respectively. On the examination itself, you can expect to find these percentages of test questions that will appear for each content area. Test questions will appear in random order and not by content area.

This information can be found in the HRCI's handbook at www.hrci.org. For the most up-to-the-minute information, please visit the website.

Appendix B:
PHR/SPHR Case Study

As you prepare for the exam, use this case study as a guide. This case study focuses on an HRM strategic planning topic geared to the senior-level SPHR practitioner. The PHR practitioner should focus on how to support the director as a key staff member.

A company is comprised of high-level, high-functioning research scientists, MDs, PhDs, and other doctoral-level practitioners. The organization is a biotech division of a major drug manufacturing company with offices situated worldwide. The division that houses the research arm is located in California, but scientists and other practitioners were hired from all over the world. Six different languages and nine different cultures are represented and integrated into the research division of this biotech organization. Senior scientists, who field separate teams for different projects, are committed to preparing doctors for academic and scientific research and to publishing their findings in research journals.

The division is currently led by a German scientist who insists that everyone speak and write in the English language *only*. This division director has been in his post for 15 years and has no intention of leaving the organization or taking another position. Senior scientists who field different teams come from a variety of backgrounds, languages, and countries, including China, Spain, Germany, Italy, Russia, and France. In all, there are 50 scientists. Support staff includes interns, technical staff, and secretaries. Five senior staff members are eligible for retirement, two staff members have been in the group for seven years, and six new scientists were brought to the United States from China, but they feel disconnected, overworked, and frustrated with the German director because of communication challenges. The division is short-staffed by ten support staff. As a result, scientists and support staff must divide responsibilities among them. Recently, there have been concerns with the quality of scientific data in terms of accuracy and reporting. These concerns have been expressed at meetings, but the director is motivated to publish results as quickly as possible and largely dismisses their complaints.

The HR and Training and Development Departments have been asked to do the following:

1. Help improve communications internally and externally.
2. Orient new scientists to the division, its culture, work ethic, expectations, and need for quality improvement.

3. Conduct a needs analysis to identify internal and external threats and stakeholders and to find out what is really going on behind the scenes.

4. Improve the division's meeting effectiveness and morale by being present and facilitating key division meetings and team meetings.

5. Support the division director in his role to review and refine key functional leadership roles and responsibilities and to create a collaborative team environment.

6. Address language difficulties with the new scientists from China who insist that they write and communicate much more effectively in their native language. They feel ineffective trying to learn and conduct research in the English language only.

7. Identify assessments that will benefit the organization and teams toward working together in a collaborative team environment.

As the director of HR, you are aware of the following:

- The division director will stay in his position and historically has shown little interest in working with the organization to fix its problems.

- This director has some managerial and leadership potential, but would rather work independently with all of the team leaders reporting to him separately in his office. The director does not encourage scientists to collaborate outside of their immediate task group; therefore, when all of the scientists attend meetings, no one is really certain what is going on.

- This is a matrix managed organization, in theory, but no one speaks to each other either at the office or away from the office. There is a company cafeteria, but team members stick together and do not mingle with other scientists. Several different languages can be heard at meal times until the division director walks in, then the cafeteria atmosphere becomes very quiet.

- The division is presently understaffed, but talk about the need for growth and change is at a standstill.

For the SPHR Practitioner

As an HR director, discuss what strategies you would use from an HR strategic position to change this situation over the short term (next six months) and long term (three years). You have eight HR staff members who assist you in running the department. You report to this division director and a vice president of HR who is housed in New Jersey.

For the PHR Practitioner

Discuss how you would support the HR director as a key HR staff member. Rather than focus on a strategic direction, your role is to assist the HR director as an HR operations specialist. Address numbers 1 to 7 in the HR Training and Development section above. What role(s) will you take to support HR, HRD, and the in-house Training and Development Department?

Appendix C: Resources for Human Resource Professionals

For additional information about the human resource field, certification, or job opportunities, there are many resources that can be found online:

American Society for Healthcare Human Resources Administration
www.hrleader.org

Department of Academic Human Resources at University of Illinois—Urbana-Champaign
www.ahr.uiuc.edu

Gay & Lesbian Human Resources Network
www.gayhr.org

HR Jobs
www.jobs4hr.com

Human Resource Certification Institute
www.hrci.org

Human Resource Professionals of Minnesota
www.hrpmn.org

Human Resources Department at University of California—Irvine
www.hr.uci.edu

Human Resources Professionals Association of Ontario
www.hrpao.org/hrpao

Job-Hunt.org: Resources for HR Professionals
www.job-hunt.org/HR.shtml

National Human Resources Association
www.humanresources.org

Northeast Human Resources Association
www.nehra.com

Northwest Human Resources Council
www.mynhrc.org

Ohio Department of Administrative Services (DAS)/HRD Office of Training &
Development—Human Resources Academy
www.das.ohio.gov/hrd/hra

Professional Outplacement Assistance Center (POAC)
www.dllr.state.md.us/poac

Professionals in Human Resources Association (PIHRA)
pihra.org

Profiles International Human Resources Management & Employment
Assessment Tools
www.profilesinternational.com/syc_intro.aspx

Society for Human Resource Management
www.shrm.org

Index

C